Peace-Maintenance

Peace-Maintenance explores the controversial concept that has evolved from diplomatic peacekeeping and military peace-enforcement. Jarat Chopra, the architect
of peace-maintenance, outlines the limitations of traditional peacekeeping principles reliant on the increasingly questionable consent of belligerents. He traces
the evolution of the political, administrative, legal and judicial ingredients of international authority. He draws on his extensive experience of peace operations
with the United Nations, using many examples to illustrate the context and
evolution of peace-maintenance, including in-depth studies of Somalia and
Western Sahara.

This book is invaluable in identifying the necessary ingredients for long-term,
legitimate and effective peace-maintenance at a time when it is needed most.
Chopra's study explores a course of action that is logically indicated by the long
evolution of peacekeeping in the twentieth century and, importantly, he argues
that we can no longer fail to respond to violent crises because we do not know
how to.

Jarat Chopra is Director of the International Relations Program at Brown
University, Lecturer in International Law and Research Associate at the Thomas
J. Watson Jr Institute for International Studies. He has observed a number of
peace operations including those in Sri Lanka, Namibia, Nicaragua, Western
Sahara, Cambodia, Tajikistan, Moldova, El Salvador, Somalia, Georgia and
Macedonia.

Routledge Advances in International Relations and Politics

Peace-Maintenance

The evolution of international
political authority

Jarat Chopra

London and New York

First published 1999
by Routledge
11 New Fetter Lane, London EC4P 4EE

Simultaneously published in the USA and Canada
by Routledge
29 West 35th Street, New York, NY 10001

Typeset in Baskerville by Routledge
Printed and bound in Great Britain by
T.J. International Ltd, Padstow, Cornwall

British Library Cataloguing in Publication Data
A catalogue record for this book is available from the British Library

Library of Congress Cataloguing in Publication Data
Chopra, Jarat.
Peace-maintenance: the evolution of international political authority/
Jarat Chopra.
Includes bibliographical references and index.
1. International police. 2. United Nations – Armed Forces.
I. Title.
JZ6374.C48 1999
341.5'84 – dc21 98–27103

ISBN 0–415–19483–0

This book is dedicated to my mother and my father, to whom I owe all things

Contents

Preface

The concept of peace-maintenance has proved controversial. If, to some, the idea of international political authority is necessary for human survival – and, perhaps, at last possible – to others it is a frightening prospect. Still others take refuge in believing that a global rule of law and order is unrealistic, or, put more kindly, that peace-maintenance is a 'bold' proposal. Any conclusion considered out of context is sure to evoke such doubt. Yet, I would argue that peace-maintenance is only an incremental step, a logical corollary to the multifunctional peace experiments conducted in and around the violent events of the 1990s.

The aim of this book is to outline the scope of tests in the international laboratory – invariably those pitiful wastelands of internal conflict – and the extent of longer-term institutional developments that have already provided the necessary ingredients for legitimate and effective peace-maintenance. Tracing the trajectory in the evolution of disparate diplomatic, military, administrative and judicial components leads logically to the need for a unifying political concept like peace-maintenance, as a kind of civilian joint doctrine. Responding to broken societies with only one of these elements, or with all of them entirely independently of each other, is patently dysfunctional. The chapters that follow indicate how bits and pieces have been tried in different locations: in judicial terms, for instance, where a jail was established there may not have been a means of prosecution; and where there was a means of prosecution there may not have been a capacity for apprehension. In turn, the result of organizing a police force outside a rule of law can only be collapse of the effort. If it is accepted in national governance that an executive, legislature and judiciary are mutually reliant institutions, it follows that international interventions cannot focus on only one or two structural fronts; each must be buttressed by all the others.

Consequently, practitioners have yearned for unity of command and action in the field, but the rhetoric in international organizations has been drenched by calls for better 'coordination' between separate functional kingdoms. Peace-maintenance is a means of centralizing political control in the field and genuinely combining specializations so that they serve a common operational purpose. Such a need flows naturally from past and recent experiences on the ground, even if in isolation the idea seems 'bold'. It is true, however, that the implication of an incremental doctrinal development may be significant for the current stage of international relations. The collective exercise of national polit-ical authority – so much needed in so many failed peace missions; and not as the luxurious result of a great peace plan or abstract theory of world order consti-tutes a real step towards a kind of transnational governance that is beyond the periodic intervention symptomatic of a community of sovereign states.

As obvious as some of the logic of peace-maintenance may appear to be in retrospect, my own conclusions regarding the concept were reached only gradu-ally and in response to many profound experiences in the field and a good deal of writing and debates on the subject of peace operations generally. In 1989 – a watershed year for the ending of the Cold War and the caesarian birth of a destructive peace – I saw, in Sri Lanka, Indian peacekeepers, who had expected and were prepared only to referee the terms of a diplomatic agreement, become a fighting force in what turned out to be a brutally challenging environment. Some of us knew then, if not for some time before, that factional conditions foreshadowed the limitations of traditional peacekeeping principles reliant on the increasingly questionable consent of belligerents. And indeed, it is what I subsequently witnessed on the ground, in some senses in Namibia, Nicaragua and El Salvador, but particularly in Cambodia and Western Sahara throughout the next decade.

Change was apparent and acknowledged at a meeting of the peacekeeping cognoscenti that colleagues and I convened at Airlie House, Virginia, in November–December 1989. During my time at the International Institute for Strategic Studies, London, I edited the conference papers for a special issue of *Survival* (May/June 1990) and as a result of my contact with Chester A. Crocker, architect of the Namibia agreements, the notion of a joint monitoring mecha-nism to govern peace processes lodged in my mind. But my thoughts were by far preoccupied with calling for a new concept of international military operations functioning without the consent of parties in conflict.

And in 1991, with the decisive support of Sir Brian Urquhart, the Ford Foundation provided a grant to us at Brown University to develop a limited use of force doctrine for peace missions. On one occasion, in the conference room at the Thomas J. Watson Jr Institute for International Studies, I suggested as a project title 'second generation operations'. I was thinking, by comparison, of the multiple generations of computers and human rights, but not necessarily of weapons systems (the association with which General Indar Jit Rikhye was concerned). Objecting to the duplication of the '-tion' sound, John Mackinlay wanted to include 'multinational forces'; so Tom Weiss combined the two. 'Second generation multinational forces' became the call-signal for our work over the next few years and variations were widely adopted by the UN Secretary-General and other researchers and analysts to refer to the overall experience of peace operations at the time.

As important as a new military doctrine was, it was also becoming clear that soldiers were in no position to dominate multifunctional exercises that necessi-tated a considerable variety of civilian expertise. By the time I was in Somalia, my thinking had already taken this next turn, and what I saw there crystallized the operational distinctions between diplomatic peacekeeping, military peace-enforcement and the requirement for an overall political response. I was also able to compare these findings with my experiences in the former Soviet Union, where the dominance of the Russian military in Tajikistan could be contrasted with Moscow's more politically sensitive and sophisticated approaches taken in Moldova, South Ossetia and Abkhazia.

I connected these conclusions with the results of one of a number of trips to Western Sahara. In July 1993, I had been a member of a bi-partisan American visiting mission to the region and was given access to the positions of each of the interested parties. That August, I secreted myself away to draft the mission report and laid out the conflicting perspectives. In attempting to solve the puzzle of how to render a dysfunctional and unaccountable peace process more effective and legitimate, the Namibian joint monitoring commission was retrieved in my mind. I applied a form of the mechanism to the case and designed a peace proposal which I argued for over successive years. Out of this, as one by-product, began to emerge another element of peace-maintenance.

By the summer of 1994, poor results in places like Somalia led to the Security Council's approval of great power missions in Haiti, Abkhazia and Rwanda. Another step had to be taken, beyond the original 'second generation' concept of military force, to improve the chances of success. In early 1995, in a special issue of *The Bulletin of the Atomic Scientists* (March–April) commemorating the fiftieth anniversary of the UN, I first published the idea of political peace-maintenance. The following year, a more detailed article appeared in *Political Geography* (March–April). A brief exchange took place in *Security Dialogue* (June 1997), and in early 1998, the fiftieth anniversary of UN peacekeeping, a special issue of *Global Governance* (January–March, and subsequently republished as *The Politics of Peace-Maintenance*) was devoted to debating peace-maintenance as an operational concept.

Throughout these four years, I presented my ideas before scholars, practitioners and policy-makers and planners at a number of fora in Europe, Africa, Asia and North and Central America. The peace-maintenance concept was gradually refined and increasingly took shape with each public discussion. It also benefited from the publication of a number of sketches: in *International Peacekeeping* (Autumn 1994); as a chapter in Thomas G. Weiss's *The United Nations and Civil Wars* (1995); in the *Texas International Law Journal* (Summer 1996); *Global Society* (May 1997); and *Survival* (Autumn 1997). The peace-maintenance dialogue was also extended in translation, in Italian (*Europa/Europe*, October–December 1995); Spanish (*Naciones Unidas*, March 1996; *Cuadernos Jurídicos*, April 1996); Japanese (*NIRA Policy Research*, September 1997); and German (*der überblick*, December 1997).

Drawn from these and many other fragments, the current volume combines as part of a single conception the extensive developments in each of the specialized components of peace-maintenance. In a first introductory chapter, political *peace-maintenance* is distinguished from diplomatic *peacekeeping* and military *peace-*

enforcement. The joint mechanisms for exercising political authority in the field are described and the operational categories of peace-maintenance are outlined, varying in their descending degree of local engagement between *governorship, control, partnership* and *assistance*. These categories are the result of differentiating between the kinds of operations deployed in the past, but they are separated particularly to better appreciate the flexible scale of potential political responses to social conflicts. In implementation, though, there may be some fluidity between such neat distinctions.

The second part of the book traces the evolution of the political, administrative, legal and judicial ingredients of international authority. Chapter 2 focuses on the nature of political development, nationally and internationally. By discerning generic stages in the historical process of national development – namely, *constitution, construction, consolidation* and *chaos* – a spectrum of operational environments and their range of functional requirements can be identified. Acknowledging the demands on the ground according to the specifics of each stage of political development can help determine the type of peace-maintenance needed. Because of the essential nature of the task in each case, which calls for the collective exercise of or participation in national executive authority, successful peace-maintenance will indicate a shift between stages in the development of international political authority.

Relying on the terminology so far defined, Chapter 3 delineates the historical experiments in international civil administration. It covers examples from the time of the League of Nations and before, as well as from the Cold War period of the United Nations, and includes the extensive tests of the 1990s. The results of this twentieth-century laboratory illuminate some general principles and considerations for peace-maintenance administration.

The fourth and fifth chapters concern the current standing of international laws and means of order applicable to the justice dimensions of peace-maintenance. Chapter 4 articulates the scope of international criminal law, which after decades of definition entered an era of implementation in the wake of the Cold War. The non-derogable nature of such laws provides a substantial constitutional basis for the exercise of law and order functions in peace-maintenance operations. Chapter 5 describes the many international attempts to exercise judicial powers and enforce criminal law. If peace-maintenance is going to function according to international law and is to help establish a local rule of law, then missions require independent means of policing and prosecution, including the capacity to apprehend, detain and punish responsible individuals.

While many of the relevant peace operations deployed to date are described in varying depth throughout the text, the third part of this book considers in greater detail the cases of Somalia and Western Sahara. Chapter 6 addresses the political requirements in Somalia's dynamic anarchical setting, where a myriad of factions vied for central control of power. Chapter 7 assesses the type of political mechanism necessary in Western Sahara, where the parties are well-defined and the conditions static. The comparison between the two environments highlights the quite different challenges possible for peace-maintenance and the interactions in practice between its operational categories, from governorship to assistance.

Finally, in a concluding chapter, some of the puzzles of peace-maintenance are tackled, including its feasibility, sustainability, selectivity, capability and morality. This book ends with the point that we can no longer justify failing to respond to violent crises because we do not know what to do; we fail to do so only because of the callousness of our collective consciences. Essentially, this book is about identifying a course of action that is logically indicated by the long evolution of peace experiments throughout the twentieth century. If there is to be failure, it cannot be regarded as a failure of knowledge; it can be only a conscious choice.

This book could not have come to be without the dogged insistence of Thomas J. Biersteker, Director of the Watson Institute, and Thomas Weiss, Director of the Institute's Global Security Program. I am grateful for their persistent encouragement – and considerably more. I am also thankful to Chris Wing and the Ford Foundation for providing funding to my research project on Peace-Maintenance Operations, that helped finalize this manuscript. I wish to acknowledge, too, Patrick Proctor and Routledge for accepting the book for publication and their subsequent editorial efforts. The text has benefited from the comments of many individuals over time, from Anthony McDermott to more recent anonymous reviewers, and I duly recognize their help in improving the quality of my arguments. Ultimately, I am indebted to my mother, father and brother, Nicholas, to whom I owe so much. And here I express my appreciation for Sarah's years of support, and applaud her acts of courage under fire.

Jarat Chopra
Brown University
April 1998

Acronyms

ARENA	Nationalist Republican Alliance (El Salvador)
CAT	(UN) Committee against Torture
CEDAW	(UN) Committee on the Elimination of All Forms of Discrimination against Women
CERD	(UN) Committee on the Elimination of Racial Discrimination
CIVPOL	(UN) Civilian Police
CODESA	Convention for a Democratic South Africa
CPP	Cambodian People's Party
CSW	(ECOSOC) Commission on the Status of Women
DC	(UNOSOM II) District Councils
DK	Democratic Kampuchea (Khmer Rouge)
DPKO	(UN) Department of Peace-Keeping Operations
ECOSOC	(UN) Economic and Social Council
FAR	(Moroccan) Royal Armed Forces
FMLN	Frente Farabundo Martí para la Liberación Nacional
FUNCINPEC	National United Front for an Independent, Neutral, Peaceful and Cooperative Cambodia
IAEA	International Atomic Energy Agency
ICC	International Criminal Court
ICCPR	International Covenant on Civil and Political Rights
ICJ	International Court of Justice
ICRC	International Committee of the Red Cross
ICTY	International Criminal Tribunal for the Former Yugoslavia
IFOR	Implementation Force (former Yugoslavia)
ILC	International Law Commission
ILO	International Labour Organisation
IMT	International Military Tribunal (Nuremberg)
INTERPOL	International Criminal Police Organization
IPTF	International Police Task Force (former Yugoslavia)
JCC	Joint Control Commissions (former Soviet Union)
JMC	Joint Monitoring Commission (Namibia)
JMMC	Joint Military Monitoring Commission (Namibia)
LAS	League of Arab States

MINURSO	United Nations Mission for the Referendum in the Western Sahara
MSC	(UN) Military Staff Committee
NATO	North Atlantic Treaty Organization
NGO	Non-governmental organization
NSC	(US) National Security Council
OAU	Organization of African Unity
O(C)SCE	Organization for (formerly Conference on) Security and Cooperation in Europe
OIC	Organization of the Islamic Conference
ONUC	United Nations Operation in the Congo
ONUSAL	United Nations Observer Mission in El Salvador
OPCON	(US/UNOSOM II) Operational Control
OPLAN 1	(UNOSOM II) First Operational Plan
PDD	(US) Presidential Decision Directive
PN	National Police (El Salvador)
PNC	National Civilian Police (El Salvador)
POLISARIO	Frente Popular para la Liberación de Saguia el-Hamra y de Rio de Oro
POW	Prisoner of war
QRF	(US/UNOSOM II) Quick Reaction Force
RC	(UNOSOM II) Regional Councils
SADR	Sahrawi Arab Democratic Republic
SDM	Somali Democratic Movement
SFOR	Stabilization Force (former Yugoslavia)
SNA	Somali National Alliance
SNC	Supreme National Council (Cambodia)
SNF	Somali National Front
SNL	Somali National League
SNM	Somali National Movement
SOC	State of Cambodia
SPM	Somali Patriotic Movement
SR	(UN) Special Rapporteur on Torture
SRC	Somali Revolutionary Council
SRSG	Special Representative of the (UN) Secretary-General
SSDF	Somali Salvation Democratic Front
SSNM	Southern Somali National Movement
SWAPO	South West Africa People's Organization
SYL	Somali Youth League
TACON	(US/UNOSOM II) Tactical Control
TNC	(UNOSOM II) Transitional National Council
UN	United Nations
UNFICYP	United Nations Peace-keeping Force in Cyprus
UNGA	United Nations General Assembly

UNGOMAP	United Nations Good Offices Mission in Afghanistan and Pakistan
UNIFIL	United Nations Interim Force in Lebanon
UNIKOM	United Nations Iraq–Kuwait Observation Mission
UNITA	National Union for the Total Independence of Angola
UNITAF	Unified Task Force (Somalia)
UNOSOM I	First United Nations Operation in Somalia
UNOSOM II	Second United Nations Operation in Somalia
UNPREDEP	United Nations Preventive Deployment Force (Macedonia)
UNPROFOR	United Nations Protection Force (former Yugoslavia)
UNSF	United Nations Security Force (West Irian)
UNTAC	United Nations Transitional Authority in Cambodia
UNTAG	United Nations Transition Assistance Group (Namibia)
UNTEA	United Nations Temporary Executive Authority (West Irian)
US	United States
USC	United Somali Congress

Part I

Introduction

1 Peace-maintenance

We have been at war. We now understand this to have been true, statistically. The five years between 1990 and 1995 proved to be twice as lethal as any half-decade since the end of the Second World War. According to avowedly conservative estimates, there were ninety-three wars involving seventy countries. Of the 22 million people who perished in armed conflict since 1945, 5.5 million of them, some one-quarter, died in the early 1990s. Furthermore, war has ceased to be primarily a profession of arms: if at the beginning of the twentieth century 85 to 90 per cent of war deaths were military, by the end, on average, about three-quarters are civilians – and in some cases the figure is considerably higher.[1] The current character of inter-state relations, conditioned by the grand diplomacy of the Cold War, could not avert the internecine killing by peoples redefining themselves and their positions globally.

It is as if the organizational pattern established by the political competition of the last great war fifty years ago is now being challenged, perhaps almost unconsciously – more as the natural result of social imperatives not accommodated by that pattern than by virtue of some new and compelling ideology. And the even limited response of the Security Council is no less profound. The year 1992 should have been a kind of '1917' or '1789' for the United Nations (UN). At that time were conducted perhaps the greatest experiments in international organization since the drafting and signing of the Charter. That is, the largest and most complex operations in UN history were deployed simultaneously to the former Yugoslavia, Cambodia and Somalia, to stop wars and secure a degree of well-being for local populations.

While significant, the diplomatic and military limitations of these and other vast efforts to resolve internal conflicts indicated that social competition necessitated political management. Already, the static diplomatic character of traditional, inter-state peacekeeping had burst its bounds in a hot peace after a cold war, and the use of military force was called on to fill the gap in what became the so-called 'second generation' of UN peace operations.[2] This period witnessed the re-emergence of the term *peace-enforcement*. In the years immediately before and after the signing of the UN Charter, peace-enforcement was virtually synonymous with the idea of collective security, in which military force was authorized jointly and employed by powerful states to prevent and halt acts of aggression. It referred to what has come to be known simply as 'enforcement', of the kind envisioned in Article 42 of Chapter VII.

However, after four decades of *peacekeeping* – a word that neither appears in the Charter nor was uttered during the period of its formulation – other 'peace' terms gained currency which fitted more in the context of distinguishing lower-level operational categories and doctrine than referred explicitly to the existing model of international organization. On 31 January 1992, the first summit meeting of the UN Security Council requested the new Secretary-General, Boutros Boutros-Ghali, to develop proposals for a strengthened security system.[3] His response in June, *An Agenda for Peace*, became the focus of the 47th session of the General Assembly that autumn. It referred to 'peace-enforcement', which described what had been already identified as a middle ground in the use of force, between defensive peacekeeping and high intensity enforcement. This 'third option' was not synonymous with the kinds of total war that might be necessitated in the suppression of aggression.

During the genesis of Article 1(1) of the UN Charter, concerning collective measures for the maintenance of international peace and security,[4] the term *peace-maintenance* is referred to intermittently between the time of the Atlantic Charter in 1942 and the 1945 drafters' conference in San Francisco. The principal planners, including particularly Franklin D. Roosevelt, attempted to express the scope and purpose of a novel form of permanent organization. The passive preservation of a diplomatic status quo was not envisioned; rather, it was the active determination of law and order internationally in the manner of a domestic political community. Peace was not to be elusive and only occasionally kept, but convincingly and perpetually 'maintained'. Indeed, there had been 'a gathering consensus among senior officials in favour of a central global authority to maintain peace in the postwar period'.[5] The extent of earlier proposals was narrowed, first by the wartime agreements of the United States, Britain and the Soviet Union; second, by the opinions of smaller powers; and finally, by the subsequent paralysis of the superpowers' geopolitical competition. But the remaining political kernel defined the unprecedented character of the UN.

Now, after the Cold War, in the midst of new conflagrations, and after its conditioning by decades of peacekeeping and years of second generation experiments with the use of force, *peace-maintenance* is reborn as a 'unified concept' for peace operations. This introduction distinguishes diplomatic peacekeeping and military peace-enforcement from political peace-maintenance. Recognizing the need for an internationally effective political capability reflects that the evolution of peace operations doctrine has entered a third, and perhaps final, phase.

DIPLOMATIC PEACEKEEPING AND MILITARY PEACE-ENFORCEMENT

The first phase, the era of traditional 'peacekeeping', lasted from 1948 to 1989, during which some fifteen operations were deployed.[6] This Cold War period was characterized by diplomatic frameworks, the result of what conventional UN parlance referred to as 'peace-making'. As a consequence of diplomacy, limited military forces and civilian personnel were deployed symbolically as third parties to guarantee negotiated settlements, invariably between two sovereign states that could no longer envision victory on the battlefield. Peacekeepers were referees and only had the physical means to observe conditions in the no-man's-land they occupied. This narrowly constrained practice developed certain basic assumptions known as the 'UNEF II Rules':[7]

1   a Force had to operate with the full confidence and backing of the Security Council;
2   a Force operated only with the full consent and cooperation of the parties in conflict;
3   command and control of the Force would be vested in the Secretary-General and Force Commander, under the authority of the Security Council;
4   the composition of the Force would represent a wide geographic spectrum, although conventionally excluding the permanent members of the Security Council, and contingents were supplied voluntarily by member states upon the Secretary-General's request;
5   armed force would be used only in self-defence, although self-defence included defence of the mandate as well as the peacekeeper; and
6   the Force would operate with complete impartiality.

Observers in blue berets or peacekeepers in blue helmets supervised clear lines separating belligerents in places as diverse as the Golan Heights between Israel and Syria, Kashmir between India and Pakistan, and between Greek and Turkish communities in Cyprus. The UN's deployment to Lebanon in 1978, the last peacekeeping operation for nearly a decade, in the midst of factional militia manipulated by neighbouring governments in Syria and Israel, warned of the future landscape of the UN's Dien Bien Phus. A turning point occurred in 1989 when a decolonization mission arrived in Namibia, with a wider range of tasks than mandated for previous verification observers or interposition forces.[8]

Traditional peacekeeping principles were necessarily challenged. In particular, consent of the parties in conflict was not always forthcoming or sometimes withdrawn once given.[9] In response, UN operations would have to consider using force. This would require sufficient assets to do so and the inclusion in operations of armed forces from Security Council permanent members. In turn, the issue of command and control of assets would become more acute. Impartiality would be defined as the objectivity with which the mandate was executed rather than the degree of submission to the will of the parties in conflict.[10] The Security Council, therefore, would have an even more crucial role in developing clear instructions, continually supporting the force in the field with the solidarity of its will and expanding mandates as changes in ground conditions required. These new requirements reflected that a second generation of operations had come into being, beyond symbolic peacekeeping but short of Gulf War-style enforcement.

In this next phase, specifically between 1989 and 1994, some eighteen operations were deployed, more than had been dispatched in the UN's first forty-five years. There had been a mood swing from Cold War cynicism to a euphoric, unrealistic optimism with nostalgia for the system envisioned in 1945. But it was a brave new world.[11]

The challenging environment of internal conflicts necessitated the development of a concept for the limited and gradually escalating use of armed force in multinational missions 'fighting for peace'. UN military operations could be divided into nine categories, arranged in three levels of varying degrees of force. At one extreme were Level One operations, the familiar tasks of Observer Missions and Peacekeeping forces. At the other end of the spectrum were the Level Three tasks of Sanctions and High Intensity Operations, which are characteristic of Articles 41 and 42, respectively, of the UN Charter. The five Level Two tasks in between represented the latest doctrinal developments:[12]

1   Preventive deployment: A UN force may be deployed to an area where tension is rising between two parties to avoid the outbreak of hostilities or the maturing of an existing conflict. This area may be between two states or two factions within a state. Examples have included the UN Preventive Deployment Force (UNPREDEP) in Macedonia and the trigger mechanism between Gulf War adversaries, the UN Iraq–Kuwait Observation Mission (UNIKOM).

2   Internal conflict resolution measures: A UN force may be required to underwrite a multiparty cease-fire within a state. It may have to demobilize and canton warring factions, secure their weapons and stabilize the theatre of conflict. UN operations in Cambodia and Mozambique illustrated this type of activity.

3   Assistance to interim civil authorities: A UN force may be required to underwrite a transition process and transfer of power in a country re-establishing its civil society from the ashes of conflict. It may have to provide security during the repatriation of refugees, the organization and conduct of elections, and the early stages of infrastructure rehabilitation. This series of tasks was essential in transitional operations in Namibia, Cambodia and El Salvador.

4   Protection of humanitarian relief operations: A UN force may be deployed to establish a mounting base, a delivery site and a corridor between the two to protect the provision and distribution of humanitarian relief by UN and non-governmental civilian agencies. There were varying degrees of success with this activity in northern Iraq, Somalia, Bosnia and Rwanda.

5   Guarantee and denial of movement: A UN force may be called on to secure the rights of passage in international waterways and airspace, or across national territory. It may be required also to restrict movement of parties

designated as delinquent by the international community. Examples include the efforts in Bosnia and northern and southern Iraq.

It was in reference to this middle ground in the use of force that Boutros-Ghali, on the advice of James Sutterlin of Yale University, included the term 'peace-enforcement' in *An Agenda for Peace*. The idea reflected a discussion among scholars and practitioners that had crystallized earlier in the year calling for a new operational concept,[13] which unfortunately was not adequately developed before large US forces deployed to Somalia, eventually claiming the 'peace-enforcement' label as their mandate. After the UN was militarily routed in Mogadishu, Boutros-Ghali reverted to the black-and-white options of defensive peacekeeping and high intensity enforcement, relegating peace-enforcement back to the latter and equating it again with Article 42-type action.[14] This reaction was impractical to sustain, and at a press conference only two days after issuing the 'Supplement to An Agenda for Peace', the Secretary-General had to distinguish between peace-enforcement and 'huge peace enforcement operations'.[15] Meanwhile, in national departments and ministries of defence, such as in the United Kingdom, the term 'peace-support' has been used to refer to the variety of military tasks undertaken in multifunctional missions. While the underlying doctrine indicates support of a framework, it does not identify the nature of that framework.[16]

The term 'peacekeeping' was expanded, but it was unclear how far. The Secretary-General had affirmed the classic principles of peacekeeping in *An Agenda for Peace*, but welcomed broadening the tasks of operations, without any further indication of what this meant. Traditional peacekeeping nations, such as Canada and Austria, preferred to keep the term and apply it to nearly all UN peace activities – either to ensure the place of their historical experience or due to constitutional restrictions prohibiting them from engaging in enforcement actions. A misnomer emerged, 'second generation peacekeeping'.[17] This confused the narrowly defined practice of peacekeeping and second generation operations, which were not exclusively reliant on consent of belligerents and did not use force only in self-defence. Precisely the application of a diplomatic peacekeeping approach in challenging environments proved fatal in the former Yugoslavia, Cambodia, Angola, and in most other operations as well.

Furthermore, the artificiality of a 'third generation' of peace operations has exacerbated the confusion. When the UN Secretary-General first acknowledged the emergence of a second generation, he added that this suggested the existence – simultaneously, and rather illogically, therefore – of a third, defined by institutional 'peace-building'.[18] These concepts have since become more distorted by a reversal of their meanings: second generation operations have been defined as consensual peace-building and third generation operations as peace-enforcement equated with high intensity enforcement.[19]

Boutros-Ghali also replicated contradictory meanings of the term 'peace-making'. He included under this broad rubric not only the diplomatic settlement of disputes, but also coercive economic sanctions and military enforcement. One activity was entirely reliant on consent of disputants, the other not. 'Peace-making' became confused, and no more than a shorthand for referring to Chapter VI and VII of the Charter. Seasoned UN officials accustomed to peace-making as diplomacy continued to refer to it as such; those who had understood peace-making as the employment of bombs and bullets, in the North Atlantic Treaty Organization (NATO), for instance, continued to interpret it accordingly.

An Agenda for Peace further conceived of action before the outbreak and after the conclusion of hostilities. It referred to 'preventive diplomacy', which included early identification of crises and troop deployments to avoid their esca-lation. However, there has tended not to be international political will mobilized until a pitch of violence manages to shock public opinion, invariably through press imagery – which is not available prior to the outbreak of hostilities.

The complex, multifunctional operations of the second phase, designed to supervise transitions from conditions of social conflict to minimal political order, had limited impact because of reliance on either diplomatic peacekeeping or military peace-enforcement. Consequently, transitional arrangements required but did not achieve better coordination between military forces, humanitarian assistance and civilian components organizing elections, protecting human rights or conducting administrative and executive tasks of government. In *An Agenda for Peace*, 'post-conflict peace-building' was equated with longer-term development, strengthening institutions and fostering conditions that could vitiate violence as a means of political competition. But this kind of 'assistance' is incapable of either ensuring accountability of an oppressive regime or reconstituting fragmented authority.[20] Another concept has been needed.

POLITICAL PEACE-MAINTENANCE

On the ground, the UN has had to contend with the contradictory phenomena of too much order and authority by a powerful government, such as in El Salvador or Namibia, and varying degrees of anarchy, as in Cambodia and Somalia. In the incoherent malaise of factionalism, a kind of 'warlord syndrome' emerged in which the local appetites of power were stronger than the diluted responses of the international community. Factional leaders proliferated and inherited the areas of ineffective UN deployments. Inter-state diplomacy conducted by institution-reliant bureaucrats between warlords in internal conflicts served to fragment further conditions of anarchy. Military force without always clear political objectives led inevitably to confrontation. Commanders reacted to the imperatives of combat and defeat of an enemy, rather than proac-tively securing conditions that could be supported and sustained in the long term.

The current third phase of peace operations doctrine needs to elaborate func-tional dimensions of a political framework.[21] Another mood swing is beginning to revive pessimism as the world community retreats not just from places like Somalia, but also from internationalism.[22] However, there is an opportunity to balance idealism and realism rather than lurch back and forth between hope and despair. Despite the danger of adding yet another debased 'peace' term to a prevalent kind of 'blue-speak' – and not as the result of the desire to coin a new phrase, but as a natural reconsideration of the essential basis of the UN Charter – the goal of 'peace-maintenance' can be associated with this phase. The term must be used in its intended sense.[23] *Peace-maintenance* means here specifically the overall political framework, as part of which the objectives of diplomatic activities, humanitarian assistance, military forces and civilian components are not only coordinated but harmonized. The concept provides a link between the strategic and operational levels of command and control, and constitutes the exercise by the international community as a whole of political authority within nations.

The United Nations tends to confuse the words 'diplomatic' and 'political'. In Clausewitzian fashion, former US Secretary of State James A. Baker III argued that 'diplomacy *is* the continuation of politics'.[24] This would imply that the two are related but not synonymous. Yet the UN refers to a 'political process' as the attempt to reach a degree of reconciliation between factions or states. This is considered 'political' not just because the process addresses the conclusion of a long-term settlement between states, or the establishment of a unified executive authority internally. But 'political' is also distinguished from the other components of an operation – military security, humanitarian assistance or electoral organization, for instance. However, in such 'political processes' the UN behaves as a diplomat and interlocutor, a representative of an authority far away, but fails to exercise executive powers itself.

Diplomacy may be logical between two states, since in each there is a government with political authority. In the no-man's-land in between, it is not imperative for the UN to come to terms with its jurisdiction over an area, and with its relationship to the territory, the local population or executive powers. It need be concerned only with the limited locations of its deployments and the placement of troops and armaments of the belligerents, since the government of each state is still juridically responsible for a portion of the buffer zone up to the international boundary, even if the exact position of that boundary is in dispute.

Within a state, however, such a diplomatic approach is not tenable. The UN cannot remain aloof of its relationship to territory and the local population, over which it may have claimed jurisdiction, and therefore must recognize its role in the exercise of executive political authority. It may have to fulfil this role independently in anarchical conditions, or jointly with an existing regime. Even in the latter case, if the UN is to effectively ensure accountability, it needs an independent political decision-making capability, as well as law and order institutions available at its disposal in the field. In both cases, it is self-defeating to rely on local authority structures, either coherent and oppressive or fragmented and probably non-existent, and at the same time attempt to reconstitute a new authority.

In fact, doing so draws the mission into the existing conditions of local authority, as the UN gravitates towards what it is permitted to do by a regime or warlords. The mission either becomes beholden to the will of a powerful government or is undermined by factionalism in anarchical conditions. In Western Sahara and El Salvador, the UN strengthened the hand of the stronger, of Rabat and the government in San Salvador, respectively. In Cambodia, the UN joined the factional competition for control of Phnom Penh, which for centuries never implied control of the rest of the country. In Somalia, the irresistible forces of anarchy fragmented a loosely arranged coalition when the UN proved incapable of replacing United States leadership.

To ensure its independence, the UN must establish a centre of gravity, following a decisive deployment, around which local individuals and institutions can coalesce until a new authority structure is established and transferred to a legitimately determined, indigenous leadership. In the interim period, the UN needs to counterbalance or even displace the oppressor or warlords. This implies that the UN claims jurisdiction over the entire territory, and ought to deploy throughout if it can. It establishes a direct relationship with the local population that will eventually participate in the reconstitution of authority and inherit the newly established institutions.

This is the meaning of a political framework, an overall blue umbrella, under which law and order are maintained once a UN centre and periphery are delineated. It is distinct from the notion of intervention as part of inter-state relations, in which entry into an area is only partial and territory is incidental to limited objectives. Authority cannot be exercised based on a perceptual axis of inside, outside and between, as is the essence of diplomacy. A political framework is all-pervasive and connected to the total social process locally. It links that domestic population with an international mandate as the basis of authority, in defiance of malevolent institutions of belligerents. Like the purpose of a rule of law, peace-maintenance must be a means of transforming the position of the weak as against the strong; it is an outside guarantor of a kind of internal self-determination.

Could the UN possibly do this? In the manner that it commands and controls fully integrated operations, the answer is probably no. During the second phase, at times the UN had to assume executive political powers on paper; but in the field, with a peacekeeping mandate, it exercised its authority diplomatically, through negotiation rather than independently. Consequently, the UN did not control political institutions in Cambodia, was manipulated by Morocco in Western Sahara, and broke apart into the separate agendas of contributing contingents in Somalia.

In the 1990s, the UN as an essentially diplomatic organization failed generally to meet a historic moment of change that required a political and not diplomatic mindset. The consequences highlight the need for an international political organization, for which peace-maintenance operations can provide the germ. Peace-maintenance is a kind of test: if the United Nations cannot or if member states are unwilling to meet this challenge, where it counts most, in a rather phoenix-like manner to stay crippling pessimism, then the range of peace operations will continue to dysfunction.

The limitations of the organization as a whole in this regard may mean that the moment calls for a different system altogether, however seemingly unlikely.[25] It has been the case that peace plans in at least the last five centuries have been proposed or implemented in the wake of widespread war.[26] Is the end of the Cold War insufficient, or does humanity need a hot and bloody war to provoke not reform of the old but the revolutionary establishment of entirely new organizations, as has been the tendency in the past?[27] Is the idea of reforming the UN tantamount to rearranging the deckchairs on the *Titanic*?[28]

In the meantime, on the ground, the shortcomings of the UN and the need to address social conditions politically may be bridged by the notion of an interim executive body as a 'joint authority', combining legitimacy and effectiveness. Not only would the entire effort be mandated collectively, but the active role of the UN, as a representative of the will of the international community as a whole, would ensure that the authority behaved accountably on behalf of the organization and in accordance with international legal standards, particularly with regard to human rights. While this accountability may be enhanced by the participation of representatives of regional organizations, giving effect to decisions made will rest with individual states participating with military, policing and other civilian assets. Headquarters of specialized agencies of the UN and non-governmental organizations concerned with humanitarian assistance will have to begin to accept harmonization of objectives if they are to have an optimum impact on victim populations.[29]

Through this unification of international efforts the kind of resources already deployed to the field in the past can be rearranged for effective peace-maintenance.[30] By far the greater difficulty is shifting away from a diplomatic mindset and fostering the willingness to exercise effectively the political powers already assumed by the international community. There is the capability and the need, but is there a genuine depth of sincerity among 'good samaritan' organizations, agencies and nations to respond successfully?

Ultimately, the critical factor for success or failure of peace-maintenance rests with the role of the local community, whom the effort is intended to help.[31] Reliance on prejudicial local structures has proved mistaken, since the UN serves to affirm and not challenge the status quo. At the same time, warlords and factions are well-armed facts and the power of existing regimes is self-evident. Therefore, they must be part of any equation, but they cannot be permitted to dominate an international authority. No authority, malevolent or benign, can survive without the balance of popular consent in its favour. Successful peace-maintenance is premised on this fact. Therefore the role local representatives play in a joint authority will have to be determined according to the specifics of the case.

Peace-maintenance is not some colonial enterprise.[32] While there are generic principles that can be learnt regarding the administration of territory and population from any model of governance, the purpose and behaviour of peace-maintenance is opposite to colonialism and, in fact, it can be a means of decolonization, as in Western Sahara. Colonial domination is a unilateral enterprise; a joint interim authority is a collectively accountable body. In the past, the difference between a colony and a trust territory may have been limited, with a variation, perhaps, in the manner of policing the two. The peace-maintenance project, however, is rooted in another context, tackles another set of tasks and is motivated by another dimension of imperatives. While a colonial power draws resources from a colony, an international authority directs resources into a nation. A colonial power plays the role of master and the colonized, the servant. But in peace-maintenance, the international authority is the servant of both an international and locally supported rule of law and order.

The goal of peace-maintenance is not imposition of an alien system or preconceived style of operation functioning in a social vacuum. The require-ment for a local international authority is precisely to create a flexible decision-making capability that can respond to indigenous needs with political, anthropological and sociological sensitivity. While generic facets of peace-maintenance can be identified, their implementation has to be locally responsive and directed on an ongoing basis.

The question arises as to the plain meaning of 'maintenance' if operations are deployed as a catalytic transition to secure and construct peace. In other words, the maintenance of what peace in the midst of conflict? This is not comparable to 'keeping' peace, when pacific conditions have naturally prevailed after war fatigue has led to diplomatic settlement. It reflects the goals of the UN Charter in the historical context of peace plans. Peace strategists attempted to design perpetual systems that could regularly prevent conflicts or respond to aggression, since there did not exist internationally the institutions that main-tained law and order nationally. A political framework underwrites any perpetual system and so peace-maintenance becomes the actions and framework that buttress the primary objective of the UN system.

The first purpose and opening line of the UN Charter after its preamble is, 'To maintain international peace and security, and to that end: to take effective collective measures.' Legal scholars and the International Court of Justice (ICJ) have affirmed the implied powers of Article 1(1) as a constitutional premise for the range of operations between the pacific settlement of disputes described in Chapter VI and the acts to counter aggression outlined in Chapter VII.[33] Unfortunately, Chapters VI and VII have been artificially interpreted recently and applied to peacekeeping and peacekeeping-plus operations conceived in a linear fashion to sit between these provisions. Insufficient regard has been given to other parts of the UN Charter which have remained dormant since its drafting.

In the same manner that the second generation of UN operations required an expansion of traditional peacekeeping principles into a wider doctrine, so too the current phase requires a doctrine for a political framework and the variety of civilian tasks associated with it.

OPERATIONAL PEACE-MAINTENANCE

There is a fracture between the political legitimacy of decisions made by the international community as a whole and the effectiveness of operations implementing these decisions. On the one hand, this has led to the questionable accountability of states implementing UN decisions, such as the widely criticized, disproportionate response of the US to Iraqi aggression in Kuwait.[34] On the other, it has led to legitimate but ineffective UN operations, as in Angola and the former Yugoslavia. Peace agreements brokered by UN diplomats could not be translated into action because operational considerations had not been adequately assessed, and either the Secretariat did not have the means or the capability to implement increasingly challenging mandates issued by the Security Council, or it was practically not possible to fulfil the military and civilian tasks in the field assumed diplomatically in New York.

Political authority

With diminished consent of parties in the field and eroded support of a tired international community for the level of commitment required by UN operations, there is a need to fill the void of the missing link. A cell composed of the parties, the UN and key member states is one way to generate political will on a continuous basis not only to conclude peace agreements initially, but to interpret these on an agreed basis, and perhaps even to implement them through a joint presence in the field. This should reduce reliance on peace-enforcement, which can be reserved for specific tasks as part of a well-integrated political strategy. It would also enable states limiting their participation at the UN to remain engaged in a cost-effective or politically sustainable manner and could in fact lead as a catalyst to greater commitment to success in the field.

Something of an indirect analogy may be drawn from the Joint Monitoring Commission (JMC) that supervised the decolonization of Namibia. It was composed of Angola, Cuba and South Africa, with the United States and Soviet Union as 'active observers'. The JMC helped develop consensus and a peace agreement initially and it played a significant role when the process nearly derailed on 1 April 1989, and subsequently.[35]

True of the unique conditions of most UN operations, the variable factors in Namibia and other missions are not directly comparable. Nevertheless, the JMC was of general significance as a kind of 'court of appeal' that met regularly and could call emergency sessions to discuss all political and military aspects of implementation of agreements made. There was also a Joint Military Monitoring Commission (JMMC) composed of the same military powers and responsible to the political JMC. As a link between the diplomatic, military and political aspects of the operation, the JMC could fill gaps in negotiated agreements and ensure common interpretation of provisions.

It provided *confidence* and *leverage* in the process. The parties could not be relied on exclusively to keep the process on track; at the same time, it was their process and only they could ensure success. The UN as a court of appeal was not adequate, and one goal of the JMC was to keep the United States and Soviet Union continuously engaged. The UN Special Representative and Force Commander, Martti Ahtisaari and Lieutenant-General Prem Chand, participated as 'expert observers'. The JMC could have become a proto-regional organization, but it did not; and its impact should not be overestimated since a large number of factors contributed to overall success in the field, including the historical role of Namibia on the international agenda, the years of preparation before implementation, and the Special Representative's diplomatic acumen.

Russia has employed a similar mechanism in its 'peace-creation' operations in the 'Near Abroad' conflicts of the former Soviet Union.[36] The end of the Cold War meant a redefinition of mission and restructuring of forces for both Moscow's Ministry of Defence and the US Pentagon. This included the need: to respond to a different scope of low-intensity operations; to experiment with peacekeeping, in which both conventionally had not participated; and to shift from preparing for mass-scale war. But by virtue of necessity, Russian forces have had to develop more radically new instruments than has the United States for the challenges they face not far away but close to home. They have resorted to a species of peace-enforcement and applied a unique variation of this in the newly independent republics, which in turn has developed a sophisticated mechanism for peace-maintenance.

Russian operations in the Near Abroad are securing specifically Moscow's interests, whether of the Ministry of Defence, of President Boris Yeltsin, or in some cases of the general in the field. However, delete Russian interests and insert genuinely international interests and the result is a valuable model and set of lessons for UN operations. Developing limited use of force strategies and tactics, much as European powers did during their colonial run-down, is not the reason for the effectiveness of Russian operations. It is, rather, the sensitivity with which military forces and political goals are orchestrated among both high- and low-ranking officers in the field, perhaps partly as a result of the historically political culture of the Soviet military.[37] Also, Russians are well acquainted with the areas and players where they operate, unlike the UN; and unlike the tendency of the UN, the Russians take full advantage of this fact.

The mechanism that coordinates political goals and military forces is a Joint Control Commission (JCC). It has developed gradually, and where it was not used, as in Tajikistan, the imperatives of combat proceeded uncontrollably. In Moldova, the JCC was composed of the two parties, Moldova and the puppet regime of the Dniester Republic, with Russia as a big brother and first among equals. The Conference, now Organization, on Security and Cooperation in Europe (OSCE) was supposed to be an observer to ensure its impartiality, but only recently was permitted access to the body. Responsible to the JCC was a separation of forces 'peacekeeping' mission, with checkpoints in a buffer zone manned by Russia and the belligerents themselves. Russia provided heavy armaments and therefore the 'peace-enforcement' element of the mission. There were also 'observers' responsible to the JCC that monitored the checkpoints. The nearby 14th Army, formerly commanded by the formidable General Aleksandr Lebed, provided a deterrent capability and ensured a cease-fire that has held since its inception.

However, the JCC in Moldova was not impartial and it proved to be an effective means by which Russia could manipulate the parties to suit its interests. Nevertheless, an accountable form of this could be a means of controlling recalcitrant warlords, whose participation is necessary in a peace process, and who have managed successfully to challenge the international law and authority of the United Nations. A similar mechanism is pending in South Ossetia with the full participation of the OSCE, but it is yet to be realized. Most significantly, in the proposal for the first genuinely joint international–Russian mission to Nagorno-Karabakh, OSCE observers were to be deployed throughout key posts of the Russian forces, which were to be responsible to a JCC-like framework under OSCE chairmanship. This provided an example of a realistic and flexible mechanism worth considering given limited international resources, overall fatigue and the need to provide accountability for great power action. A similar experiment to note was the deployment of US 'liaison' personnel with Russian units participating in the Implementation Force (IFOR) in Bosnia.

These designs can be distinguished from the situation in Abkhazia. UN military observers deployed in a separate mission, but loosely cooperating with Russian forces, did not gain adequate access to Russian decision-making. The overall diplomatic framework for negotiations in Geneva under UN chairmanship, furthermore, could not provide the kind of confidence and leverage that was required for accountability in the field.

The Nagorno-Karabakh proposal also was unlike the model in Cambodia, in which a Supreme National Council (SNC) composed of the warring factions did not include the UN in an integrated manner and led to confrontation rather than combined action. The absence of a joint mechanism between the factions and the UN at the operational level meant that each administrative issue that arose assumed political proportions at the highest echelons and led to the UN negotiating with factional representatives. The cost of the UN not exercising its wide powers was the fracturing of the SNC at the political level and the overall dysfunction of the operation.

Operational categories

A UN political directorate may be deployed in one of several transitional scenarios. The UN might assume exclusive responsibility in an area and administer as a governor-in-trust, or it may participate in some joint arrangement in which it assumes responsibilities of a transition phase but does not physically conduct all the tasks of governance. In the latter case, it would exercise varying degrees of authority and either control local bureaucracy, enter into a partnership with it or render it assistance.

Governorship

The UN assumes full responsibilities for conducting the affairs of government. This may occur when there is a total collapse of local state structures or where the state structures were imposed by a colonial or occupying power that has withdrawn. The UN may assume the tasks of governance itself and deploy a specific operation for the purpose or it may, in the manner of the trust territories, assume these responsibilities in name and appoint a single power or group of powers as agents to perform tasks on its behalf. This would require some mechanism of effective accountability that was not characteristic of the trusteeship system and that would ensure continued direction by the UN of the powers conducting the operation.

Control

An operation deployed to the area in question may have been authorized under a mandate to exercise the powers of 'direct control'. In this event, the UN authority in the field would deploy throughout the instruments of the state or administering authority – including ministries, the judicial system and police and armed forces. Once deployed, UN observers would monitor the local authority conducting the affairs of state. In the event that local officials commit an infraction according to the terms of the overall mandate of the transition process, the UN has the overriding authority to 'take corrective action' by dismissing personnel or redirecting a local policy decision.

Partnership

The local authority may be powerful and may have adequate resources, because it is a colonial power repatriating, another kind of occupation force withdrawing or a totalitarian regime submitting itself to a democratizing process. In this case, the UN authority-in-trust may behave more as a partner of the local authority, given the coherent structures of governance in place. Being at least an equal in the joint authority, the UN would have a veto power in decision-making and a final say in the transition period. With the robust support of the Security Council or committed engagement of outside powers, the UN may achieve a status of 'first among equals'.

Assistance

The local administration may not be in complete disarray and the trust authority provides some overall coherence and an international standard for the development of government structures. Local institutions may have been mishandled or abused, spawned an opposition and constituted a source of conflict. The trust authority behaves as an independent adviser, identifying flaws in the local system and suggesting corrections.

A UNIFIED CONCEPT

Peace-maintenance as a 'unified concept' for multifunctional UN operations needs to integrate diplomatic, military and humanitarian activities as part of an overall political strategy. The umbrella framework that coordinates these elements will need to be the UN administrator as politician if complex transitional arrangements in internal conflicts are to be successful. The tasks of political authority and civil administration are ultimately the glue that maintains the coherence of a comprehensive strategy. If any of the diplomatic, military or humanitarian aspects of operations dominates the others, an imbalance results from the vacuum of subordinated elements. It will be the challenge of the UN authority-in-trust, of whatever kind and magnitude, to orchestrate this essentially political framework.

The UN to date has not adequately developed political strategies commensurate with diplomatic, military and humanitarian activities. This has led to limited success in the field and, at times, failure. The specifics of military operations and humanitarian assistance are being identified, but while civilian administration in the first four decades of UN practice was linked to the evolution of military forces within diplomatic frameworks, now there is a greater imperative to develop a political capability if multifunctional operations are to function at all. A coherent and effective politico-military strategy is needed as much for settling disputes as winning wars; and a joint politico-humanitarian strategy is needed in winning and sustaining peace.

The assumption by the UN of enormous administrative tasks seems unlikely given the results of this decade. At the same time, the evolution of civil administration and the UN's political role in internal conflicts build on the organization's experience and in joint form they will be more cost-effective than reliance on military peace-enforcement. Furthermore, political administration provides a vehicle for the development of military capabilities in a palatable manner and for humanitarian activities in a better-coordinated manner.

If peace-maintenance is to become effective and accepted as legitimate then it should be collectively underwritten by the international community as a whole. Sovereignty and the barriers that the concept has raised cannot resist UN concern for issues that are deemed international, and the scope of 'international' is widening to the point that collective political authority becomes a necessity rather than an infringement.[38] However, the psychological shift among populations in the area of peace operations or on home fronts of nations contributing personnel has not kept pace with these global developments. The costs in the long term of not intervening will have to be understood as greater than those of intervening in the short term. As national fragmentation proliferates in the former second and third worlds, that point may be upon us.

The warlord grows in the fertile ground of anarchy. Global fragmentation has been a proliferating feature of recent years, and this in turn leads to popular acceptance of the strongest warlord with the greatest promises. Unfortunately, in the past people have feared anarchy more than they have disliked tyranny. This partly accounts for the consent that underwrites malevolent orders. Permitting the success of the warlord out of failure to develop a countering mechanism is to prepare the ground for the super-warlord, the messianic leader, the Hitler. Fifty years after the century's greatest tragedy, the behaviour of nations today resembles more and more the impotence of supporters of appeasement in the 1930s. With the impotence of the 1990s, are we moving towards a similar or even greater tragedy, in which nations will be forced to band together in the grip of a traumatic crisis, and from which a new international order may emerge from more ashes? Or will power first pay tribute to reason?

Part II

The evolution of international political authority

2 International political development

Peace operations and the practice of development are currently shifting between archetypal stages of organization. The complexity of political systems evolves in stages distinguished by their arrangement of four universal elements of social organization, corresponding in the modern state to population, territory, government and sovereignty. After the Cold War, the international community is occupied with internal consolidation of nations as the objective of development. Yet development through diplomatic assistance is unlikely to lead to sustainable results locally. The current political proportions of social environments, internationally and locally, alter the points of reference of conventional, inter-governmental development. The goal of political peace-maintenance is the establishment of a flexible mechanism for administrative control that can extend transitional phases. It aims to enable a local population to choose its future development between conditions of violence and calm. In turn, the ability of the international and local communities to exercise control authority jointly in the interim would indicate a shift in the complexity of the international system as a whole.

Peace-maintenance is a concept that acknowledges the prevailing need for a transnational capability to exercise political authority as a means of internal conflict resolution, establishing order and fostering justice. 'Assistance', however, has been the limited response of a diplomatic community of states to social scourges locally. 'Development' has tiptoed around the sovereignty of executive bureaucracies, while 'progress' relies on liberal-style, capitalist democracies as a global standard of measurement. The pace of demand for resources in Africa, Asia, the Middle East, Latin America and the Caribbean has surpassed the growth in supply from major Western donors.[1] 'Transitions' in the former second world have exacerbated this gap. Boutros Boutros-Ghali declared development to be 'the most important task facing humanity today'.[2] Yet his *Agenda for Development* was set in the constricted context of diplomatic assistance. Development cannot be a diplomatic process; it requires means of interim political control.

Inter-governmental assistance reflects the crystallization, and perhaps ossification, of development during the Cold War. But the field has entered a new stage that corresponds to the dominant imperatives internationally of intra-state consolidation of economic, social and political institutions within contested societies. Individual human rights, a nation's financial welfare and other internal conditions were formally linked with external spheres of international jurisdiction, particularly peace and security, when the Security Council took account of the non-military sources of conflict.[3] Boutros-Ghali's term 'peace-building', though, was in the cast of consent-reliant assistance, unlike the expanded notion of peace-enforcement.

Both were vague 'peace' ideas, not operational concepts that could guide the planning and conduct of increasingly multifunctional deployments. Missions in complex environments revealed the limitations of development assistance within local communities. In Cambodia, for instance, the powers of 'direct control' and a distinct rehabilitation component were not underwritten with sufficiently independent means of implementation. The UN exercised its control powers through assistance with minimal impact.[4] In Somalia, by comparison, as described in Chapter 6, the UN's enforcement powers contradicted its assistance mandate and a combat phase interrupted its development effort. When the UN did focus on reconstruction, in the absence of a local authority, it could not rely on development through assistance and resorted to powers of control, although by then it was too little too late.[5]

The idea of assistance pales in comparison to the scope of development imperatives in peace operations: disarmament, demobilization and reintegration into civil society of combatants; dissolution of security forces and establishment of politically neutral police and armed forces; demining habitable land; electoral reform; formation of political parties; organization and conduct of elections; reconstitution of civil authority; judicial reform; human rights protection; determining financial policies; repatriation of refugees and relocation of the internally displaced; political and social reconciliation; restoration or creation of public services; physical, material and psychological attention to vulnerable groups, such as children or the handicapped; and the growth of community action and non-governmental organizations. The expanding literature on the subject does not confine such tasks to the context of assistance.[6]

Nevertheless, when Boutros-Ghali decided the UN could not achieve the kinds of non-consensual missions that characterized its second generation, he reverted to development assistance as one among more attainable goals.[7] However, the inability of the UN to do more than peacekeeping successfully does not mean that more was not needed. Similarly, development approached exclusively through assistance is sure to founder.

Whether or not there will be adequate international or local commitment to tackle the political question in peace-maintenance is not known.[8] The indications to date have been dim. However, it is significant as a historical marker and functional standard to recognize that the requirements in the field are political. Defining the problem on the ground according to what is acceptable in New York or in national capitals led to dysfunction in Cambodia, Somalia, the former Yugoslavia and elsewhere. To bridge the gap between available resources and diplomatic will on the one hand and the genuine proportions of crises on the other, the varying operational scope of peace-maintenance – ranging from *governorship* and *control* to *partnership* and *assistance* – can provide multiple options.

A political system may be at a particular historical juncture which is perceived to circumscribe the internal role of an external third party. Consequently, there has been a tension between fears of involvement and regrets of abandonment. Did the belligerents in the former Yugoslavia have to finish fighting before the international community could begin to engage? Was an abrupt departure from Somalia unavoidable? Was failure to stop slaughter in Rwanda inevitable, and is it ever justifiable to permit a sovereign government's mistreatment of its population? Affirmative answers to these questions would be tantamount to a general retreat to 'assistance-at-best'.

In determining effective and legitimate responses to social conditions, stages in the evolution of political systems need to be identified. In this manner, categories of peace-maintenance environments can be distinguished and mandates drafted accordingly. There is a stage of *constitution* in which the elements of a system – such as state territory, population, government and sovereignty – are in formation. This is followed by the *construction* of an external identity as well as internal *consolidation*. Finally, there is a *chaotic* stage in which a system fragments and its elements are transformed into ingredients for a new constitutive stage of a similar, more or less complex kind of organization. These four stages are a common pattern in: complex systems generally; the establishment of the modern state; the conceptual foundations of 'development'; the history of international organization and peace operations doctrine; and each deployment in the field.

Development is situated between the short-term impact of peace operations and longer-term social conditions. Consideration of the so-called 'relief continuum'[9] between humanitarian assistance and development tends to disregard the political context of assistance and the overall stages of historical development. In this larger dynamic, the nexus between peace operations and development can be defined. Since both are currently concerned with social and political consolidation within states, a flexible peace-maintenance mechanism, for joint international and local administrative control, can be designed. If this can be accomplished, however, then the direct connection between the international diplomatic and local social communities would indicate a new stage in the formation of an international political system, of a means of transnational governance for civil society.[10] The concept and standard of measurement of inter-governmental 'development' would have fundamentally altered.

COMPLEXITY

Political systems tend towards 'complexity'. In their evolution, complex systems display coherence in space over time as they undergo transitions between degrees of order and kinds of organization. Such systems are consistently identifiable as the nature of their constituent elements transforms. They are also conditioned by their external environments, which may be larger systems.[11]

There are four generic stages discernible in the evolution of complexity: *constitution, construction, consolidation* and *chaos*. These stages vary in the hierarchy, type of linkage and level of balance existing between their component elements. They are evident in anthropological and sociological concepts of political development, such as: stabilization, consistency and closure;[12] integration;[13] adaptation and stability;[14] institutionalization;[15] and centralization and continuity.[16] Robert Axelrod describes the emergence, growth and maintenance of cooperation.[17] Similar patterns have been discovered in scientific theories of complex systems.[18]

In a first *constitutive* stage, the ingredients of a system are formed. Some elements cohere and begin to exert minimal forces of attraction and repulsion. They can be discerned in a loose relationship with one another.

During a second *constructive* stage the system is established within a coherent framework. Combined elements are transformed into something more than the sum of the parts. The perimeter and parameters of the system are determined. The definite link between elements distinguishes an initial order and the logic of the whole as a whole. The structure is organized to secure external identification and delimits the capacity for growth.

The third *consolidative* stage concerns a rearrangement of ingredients within the system. The ordering of the parts shifts, even if a realignment in hierarchy does not necessarily occur. The linkage between elements is ensured by an organic equilibrium that results, additional to a formal infrastructure.

Finally, the fourth *chaotic* stage is characterized by the dual forces of destruction and reconstitution, of deconstruction and reconstruction. This stage is the link between one system and the next, at a level of comparable, lesser or greater complexity. Stagnation at the end of a consolidative stage leads to disequilibrium. The existing link between elements weakens and snaps, and the system fragments into separate components. The elements are reformed, redefined and reconceptualized as the primary ingredients of a new constitutive stage. In this manner, particularization can be the other face of universalization, and diversification of unification.

These functional categories are also theological and philosophical archetypes in conceptions of time, change and history.[19] George Steiner, for instance, has described how, in the political and philosophic history of the West, 'scientific' and 'social scientific' fields of inquiry and explanation have replaced the mythological properties of Old and New Testament biblical theology. He considers Karl Marx and social history, Claude Lévi-Strauss and anthropology, and Sigmund Freud and psychology – all of whom he regards as 'secular messiahs'. Inherent in their teachings are conceptions of: a Creation and ultimate source of the world and its truths; a Fall and original sin in which humanity must find its own bearings; at the end, hope for a Promised Land, for ultimate redemption; and in between, the unfortunate present conditions of life. Each doctrine is a bridge from the wilderness to utopia; its only cost: faith.[20] The tetrahedral scheme is not only Judaeo-Christian. The Hindu *Laws of Manu* and Buddhist

Dhammapada share cosmological origins, perceive humanity in suffering, conceive of enlightenment as liberation, and in between define the Path from pain to bliss.

This kind of 'progressive' logic and the tendency towards complexity in four stages have characterized the history of the sovereign state as a political system. Modern statehood is positively defined as consisting of four ingredients: a permanent population, a defined territory, government and the capacity to enter into relations with other states, or sovereignty.[21] Like their four stages of evolution, these elements are archetypes of social organization. As constants, they are repeatedly combined in one form or another.[22]

In the *constitutive* stage of state formation, elements are gradually shaped. A population begins to conceive of itself as a group, in which individuals associate with others they do not know personally. Successive generations of occupation obscure any geographic location of origin and inhabitants begin to identify, mythically, with the place of settlement. Social hierarchy stratifies as a division of labour necessitated by organizing a community's survival. Political ordering by the force of the strongest accelerates an organic, compelling centre of gravity. Kinship becomes kingship. It is supported by common ideas, a way of life and by the belief in one or many supreme beings – transcendent and more powerful than the politically strong.[23]

The distinguishing feature of this stage is the tentative, unstable connection between the elements. Significantly, the logic of unity is defined when the political kingdom is identified with a religious or metaphysical realm. In his classic study of kingship in the ancient Near East, Henri Frankfort asserted that the king in Mesopotamia was only the foremost citizen, but the Egyptian ruler was descended from the gods.[24] As the polity and the deity bond, the psychological and therefore physical ties between political power, social community and territorial location are tightened, in a kind of intensifying centripetal momentum.

By the second *constructive* stage, a critical mass point is surpassed. This is achieved by the expropriation altogether of the metaphysical by the political. The unique connection that results between elements transforms the logic of the whole. Sovereignty is precisely the consequence of the subordination of the gods in heaven to the king on earth.[25] The prevention of this in medieval Europe, by the separation between the head of the king and the crown, ensured metaphorical unity and physical division.[26] The principle of such political supremacy was enunciated for the first time in the first century AD, when extra-legal authority was bestowed on the Roman emperor.[27] This was made possible not least by the deification of the imperial person. Sovereignty is not less than the deification of the political element. Added to the fact of power is the quality of absolute legitimacy, which together constitutes supreme authority. The connection of legitimacy and power enables a rule of law to emerge, not because rules from a collective source of law can be enforced by the centralized use of violence, rendering them effective and more than theological proposition, but because local law can be more than the naked will of the enforcer.

The metaphysical combination of elements becomes a single system. It is a construct with internal coherence and external identity. The elements condition each other and further strengthen the system: individuals become 'citizens' and the population is more a definition than a fact; territorial 'place' becomes the 'space' of the state and its boundaries represent not just physical occupation but the extent of the system. There is stringent organization, centralization, conformity and the mental assurance of unity.

To flourish, however, the state passes through a third *consolidative* stage. A structural skeleton turns into a living organism. Without social fluidity, instability destroys the unity achieved. Philip of Macedon was succeeded by an Alexander, and expansion followed expansion; so the life of that Greek empire may have been splendorous, but it was short. Julius Caesar, in comparison, was replaced by an Augustus, and expansion was matched by consolidation; so the Roman empire was massively durable. To quantitative, 'objective' criteria of statehood are added qualitative, 'subjective' standards, such as self-determination and non-discrimination.[28] Power passes from the monarch to the legislature; the Republic can become the Democracy; the security of the whole can tolerate distinctions between the parts; and the demands for duty give way to protection of rights, as order can afford justice. Bodin's sovereignty for the prince is limited by Rousseau's popular sovereignty. The relationship between ruler and ruled is altered.[29]

Eventually, states reach a final *chaotic* stage in which disequilibrium between the population and its government renders the idea of their linkage hollow, without social energy and eventually without political authority. The loss of integrity of 'state-space' leads to division of territorial place as a consequence of a people redefining itself, splintering and reclaiming authority. The transformation of the elements, as the compound of statehood dissolves and the former identity of the system decomposes, provides new ingredients for the next constitutive stage.[30]

Extreme nationalism can lead to either parochialism or internationalism. Following their chaotic stages, political systems may shatter into independent components, or they may be integrated into larger systems.[31] In the latter case, they have tended to merge with neighbours or some other aggregate, such as a confederation. But it is the nature of confederations, as the result of a unifying centripetal force, to become a federation; or to break apart as the result of a centrifugal force stronger than the intermediary ties that may have been forged. Whether or not modern states are generally approaching a chaotic stage, to be followed by a universalizing constitution of international society, remains to be seen.[32]

In an imperial configuration, indigenous elements are disassembled and reassembled to fit the logic of empire. If a local system has managed in a constructive stage to subordinate the metaphysical to the political, then imperial incorporation is more difficult diplomatically, militarily and politically. But, once conquered, the logic imposed can be less destabilizing in the long term than if a local system, at the time of capitulation, was either in a constitutive stage or had proceeded according to a logic other than sovereignty in its political history.

Japan's conquest and occupation of Formosa (1895–1945), Korea (1905–45) and Manchuria (1932–45) can be contrasted with European empires. As a result of the Meiji Restoration in 1868, the secular power of the *shogun* was surrendered to the heavenly lineage of the emperor. A rigorous constructive regeneration of Japan followed, in which it adopted from Western governments highly centralized and authoritarian versions of their institutions, and in which a fragmented feudal order was unified. Similarly, the Chinese emperor ruled with the Mandate of Heaven. After Sun Yat-sen's revolution in 1911, the Mandate was not so much revoked as transferred to the government of a republic in the form of nationalism. Historically, Korea was subjected to the nature of authority in both countries, ruled as it was by each in turn.

By the time of Japanese expansion at the end of the nineteenth century, there was not only a degree of cultural compatibility, if enmity, between conqueror and conquered, but a measure of consistency in the logic of governance. Therefore, after emancipation in 1945 there was rapid evolution of one kind or another. Powerful constructive forces led to war in Korea and revolution in China. After all, destruction can be one feature of the competition for authority in the process of centralization. Subsequently, Taiwan, North and South Korea and China shifted to their own versions of consolidation.

In medieval India, by contrast, a common spiritual consciousness was never matched by, let alone subordinated to, a single secular authority.[33] Even the authority of Moghul administration, which may have achieved some physical unity by force, operated according to a logic in which an Islamic god was forever supreme in heaven. In the wake of Moghul fragmentation, princely states re-emerged with absolutist rulers, Hindu, Sikh and Muslim, but all divided between earthly body and heavenly head.[34] Under British rule, the doctrine of 'paramountcy' was a kind of supreme sovereignty in which political agents and military units selectively controlled the Indian princes, but which did not fundamentally alter the elements in or replace entirely the logic of their states. Nevertheless, the loose supremacy of one logic over another had its impact: 'In terms of resources of coal and iron and land for cotton-growing as well as in the supply of skilled weavers India should have been the seat of the first industrial revolution.'[35]

Eventually, the forging of an Indian Republic in 1947 spread a European, Christian logic of sovereign statehood from the subcontinental territory fully administered by British bureaucracy to the remainder of areas under princely rule. For them, the sovereignty of Delhi was more of a rearrangement than had been alien dominance. Knitting together indigenously centralized points of authority around an inherited imperial core facilitated national construction. However, shifting to a consolidative stage has proved a gradual and monumental task for governors of India as a result of this historical cocktail of political systems.

In further contrast, British 'indirect rule', in Nigeria for instance, relied on so-called 'tribes' to 'divide and conquer' and as a tool of administration.[36] But at independence the elements coalesced irresistibly around the colonial structure of centralization and ultimate sovereignty. A foreign logic and the local abuse of unchecked power arrested the transition from a sudden constructive to a longer-term consolidative stage of evolution, despite the wealth of the country. Frantz Fanon warned in his *Wretched of the Earth* of the final triumph of colonialism through adoption of Western institutions at independence. More recently, Basil Davidson declared the failure of the nation-state project in Africa.[37]

Are such nations to return to a constitutive stage and develop more indigenous systems? Is it possible to shift in both directions between the four stages of complexity, like a scale, or is their evolution linear, one-directional, as a feature of time? Is it possible to jump stages, from a constitutive to a consolidative? Is it possible to revert from a consolidative to a constructive stage in order to reconsolidate in an alternative manner? And what are the non-linear links between systems at either comparable or different stages? Is it possible to pass from consolidation at one level of complexity to the constitutive stage of a more complex system?

Placed in this historical dynamic, the concept of 'development' can be reconceived. It is understood neutrally as movement of a social and political system between generic stages of evolution, ascending levels of complexity and as the result of links with other systems. Notions of 'backwards' and 'forwards', of 'developed' and 'undeveloped', lose their meaning. Development as a means of choosing the future becomes the dynamic response to linearity.

STAGES OF POLITICAL DEVELOPMENT

The idea of 'development' itself, as a field of inquiry and practice, can be divided into four stages: before the Second World War, during the Cold War, the current era and a potential future.

These correspond perceptually to the stages of sovereign-state formation as a standard of measurement for the North's treatment of local systems. Before 1945, European powers regarded polities in the South as being in a *constitutive* stage. During the waves of decolonization between the 1950s and 1970s, East and West conducted their relations with newly independent nations as if they had achieved a *constructive* stage in their evolution. After 1989, focus has shifted to a *consolidative* stage, not just in terms of the West's policies regarding internal transitions in the South and the former second world; it too is perpetually in this phase, balancing between central order and social justice.

Constitution

A characteristic feature of the first stage of development was the notion of 'progress'. Its logic relied on the kind of scheme outlined by Steiner: a starting point, a reason for movement and a perfect end, towards which movement was aimed. Change meant betterment, from the inferior to the superior, from the primitive to the civilized, and from undeveloped to developed. The agents of change, the chosen standard-bearers, were the European peoples; their nations, the standard; and the vehicle for the noble effort, the imperial project or regional dominance. The idea was rendered palatable: for the French it was *une mission civilisatrice*; for the British, the White Man's Burden; and for the United States, Manifest Destiny.

The age of greatest faith in 'progress' lasted from 1750 to 1900.[38] The French historian F.P.G. Guizot lectured in the 1820s on progress as the defining criterion of 'civilization'. He followed in the late eighteenth-century tradition of the French evolutionary sociologists. Anne Robert Jacques Turgot was considered to have discovered the 'law of progress' by his biographer and successor, the Marquis de Condorcet, who believed in the inevitability of human progress and the power of science and technology to transform life and society.

Progress was subsequently affirmed in the natural world. With the publication of Charles Darwin's *The Origin of Species* in 1859, biological evolution proceeded through higher and higher orders of life. In 1871, the anthropologist E.B. Tyler in his study of the evolution of human implements, *Primitive Culture*, concluded that history was an 'upward development'. An engineer, philosopher and sociologist, Herbert Spencer, had considered progress a law of the universe.

Within a generation, and not least as a consequence of the shocking impact of the First World War, the idea of decay was resuscitated. In 1908, Georges Sorel wrote *Les illusions du progrès*. Oswald Spengler published in 1920 *The Decline of the West*, which considered the organic nature of 'cultures' subject to generation, growth and decay. Arnold Toynbee's research culminated in 1946 in *A Study of History*, which described the genesis, growth, breakdown and disintegration, as well as eventual universalization, of civilizations.

The environmental limits to growth gained notoriety in another generation at the end of the Cold War, with the publication in 1987 of the Brundtland Report of the World Economic Commission entitled *Our Common Future*, and the introduction of the concept of 'sustainable development'.

Construction

Despite these pessimistic trends before its beginning and at its end, the second stage of development reflected earlier perceptions of 'civilization'. In fact, the word 'development' seemed to have become a twentieth-century version of nineteenth-century 'progress'. It spawned theories of 'modernization' as 'Westernization' – which amounted to rapid state construction out of third world elements. In economics, W.W. Rostow contended that self-sustained economic growth is the result of industrialization.[39] Dichotomies in classical sociology were applied.[40] In *Economy and Society*, Max Weber had distinguished between traditional and rational bureaucratic authority and Emile Durkheim between mechanical and organic solidarity in *The Division of Labour in Society*. Political development was understood as structural evolution.[41]

The challenge to 'modernization' as 'progress' appeared in the form of left-wing disagreements with classical Marxism. Marx had presumed, for instance in *Das Kapital*, that the spread of capitalism to less-developed societies would lead to their industrialization and development. Similarly, V. I. Lenin, in *Imperialism, the Highest Stage of Capitalism*, maintained that the export of capital to overseas colonies would lead not only to their development, but to decay in the imperial centres. By the 1950s, however, it was being asserted that capitalism did not lead to, and in fact prevented, development.[42] The theory of 'underdevelopment' or 'dependency' was enunciated, particularly in the context of Latin America.[43] It was argued, contrary to Lenin, that the movement of capital from a periphery group of countries to a core group of developed states increasingly impoverished the former.[44]

In its turn, dependency theory was challenged in the 1970s, when Bill Warren proclaimed that universal economic development was an inevitable fact of capitalism.[45] This was accompanied by Keynsian calls for redistribution to bridge the gap between rich and poor in North and South.[46] Within the decade, the victory of capitalism was celebrated.[47] According to the Development Assistance Committee of the Organization for Economic Cooperation and Development, by the 1990s 'privatization' had become the preferred means to economic development.[48]

In reality, there had been a kind of 'uneven development', in which capitalism led to industrialization in some areas, such as East Asia, and not others, like Africa.[49] This should not have been enough to vindicate it as the only means to development. The displacement of one promise by another is hardly a success story if conditions of violence and poverty do not improve. Nevertheless, capitalism, like democracy, has become an 'autonomic' force, a hidden hand beyond the control of human consciousness.[50]

If a future is to be chosen – which is essential to the effectiveness or legitimacy of any concept of development – then the critical issue is one of control within and between political systems. Throughout the Cold War era of development, third world nations achieved nominal political freedom, or external sovereignty as a kind of diplomatic independence. The defining feature of this period, as a consequence of the logic of relations between constructs, was the idea of development through 'assistance'.

However, in a local social process there were limits to diplomatic engagement in the form of asocial governmental relations. External political emancipation and internal economic advance were to be the corollaries of juridical independence. Bureaucratic elites had to transform an alien logic and skeletal structure into an organism with social life. But this constructive period had not been the result of a naturally compelling constitutive period; its timing and character had been forced. The overwhelming imperatives of centralization and order led to disequilibrium among the elements and to social upheaval. Metaphysically absolute political authority rendered possible diplomatic independence, but without corresponding internal checks and balances the abuse of power was not illogical and the lack of consolidation a natural consequence.

If diplomatic-style economic assistance was ineffective and political and social imbalance a barrier to consolidation, then the geopolitical imperatives of the superpowers contributed another set of distortions. Development was charged with the terms of confrontation between East and West. On the one hand, the filter of assistance reflected not only indigenous aims of obtaining external independence, but a time of grand diplomacy of Cold War deterrence and brinkmanship. On the other, the pursuit of US–Soviet interests did not remain in the realm of diplomacy but extended by proxy, and at times directly, into factional competition within developing states. To the idea of development as modernization was added a redefinition of progress: alliance with the defender of the faith of capitalism or communism as a means to the promised land of ideological victory.

Consolidation

Only now, in a third, post Cold War stage, can joint control of development be considered. There are prevailing dangers that a new standard will be employed to measure the old formula of development as progress. 'Autonomic' capitalism and democracy appear the test of advancement. These are today's equivalent to 'civilization' and 'modernization'. They are alien, arbitrary and narrower conditions applied in a broader context: if both East and West were 'modern' models for the South, then capitalism and democracy are criteria of the West for consolidation in both the former second and third worlds. Paternalistic development has yet to be applied to first world nations, but they too are subject to further evolution. Still, this perceptual 'development gap' divides the earth in two – not so much between East and West or North and South, but between contested and contented societies. Disequilibrium and violence distinguish one from the other, in an era dominated by international imperatives of internal consolidation.

Most of the three worlds are in between a constructive and consolidative stage, or in varying degrees of one or the other. Some individual states are in the midst of chaotic stages. The axis that is connecting action by the international community as a whole and local communities in transition between stages of complexity seems to be a new centre of gravity. This would alter fundamentally the logic of a diplomatic community of states. In an international political system, the standards of measurement for development would be of a different kind, certainly other than the institutions and forms of elements that characterized the stages of sovereign-state evolution. As such, worldwide efforts to consolidate internally would indicate the constitutive stage of a more complex form of international authority.

CONTROLLING POLITICAL DEVELOPMENT

Peace-maintenance is a concept for joint political control of internal consolidation. It is a means of manoeuvring, for both a local population and the international community, between systems and stages of complexity. It is the ability, as part of an international social process, to determine the means and goals of development and to choose a future locally.

International organization and peace operations

Peace-maintenance is the result of the historical evolution of international organization and peace operations in four stages comparable to the stages of development. In a first *constitutive* stage before the Second World War, elements of international organization were in formation. Limited bodies emerged, particularly in the period between the establishment of the International Telegraphic Union (1865) in the nineteenth century and the League of Nations (1920) in the twentieth. As a 'cooperative' organization, the League was not a construct greater than the sum of its parts, and Article 1 of the Covenant referred only to the 'Members'. A variety of disparate experiments were conducted in peace operations, which are further described in Chapter 3. In 1920–1, military forces and civilian commissions supervised plebiscites in Schleswig, Allenstein and Marienwerder, the Klagenfurt Basin, Upper Silesia and Sopron. Territory was administered-in-transition in Danzig (1920), Memel (1920–4), the Saar Basin (1920–35) and Leticia (1933–4). A truce was supervised between Greece and Bulgaria (1925) and troops accompanying the administrative commission in Leticia acted as an interpositionary force between Columbia and Peru.

A second *constructive* stage of international organization and peace operations lasted from 1945 to 1989, and like its corresponding stage of development, this era of traditional peacekeeping was dominated by a diplomatic habit. Unlike the League, the United Nations was a 'collective' arrangement and something more than the sum of its parts. Article 2 of the Charter distinguished between 'the Organization' and 'the Members'. Its legal personality was affirmed by the International Court of Justice (ICJ).[51] With external independence, it functioned between states in an assistance manner.

After 1989, peace operations entered a *consolidative* stage as they were dispatched to conflicts inside states. However, the continued diplomatic behaviour of the UN either caused further fragmentation, as in Somalia,[52] or failed to redirect significantly the indigenous balance of power, as in Cambodia.[53] The use of military force was grafted on to the diplomatic framework of a constructive era to fill the gap created by the imperatives of internal consolidation. Unless military force can be focused and directed politically, it can cause considerable disequilibrium in a system.

As important as are diplomacy and military force, they have proved entirely unsuitable as exclusive responses to the social and political demands of a consolidative stage. This requires peace-maintenance and the capacity to administer-in-transition local elements. However, as a diplomatic institution, the UN is inherently limited in its ability to shift from a constructive to a consolidative stage of international organization. Consequently, the evolution of peace operations has outstripped the logic of 'united nations'. In the same manner as development, if peace-maintenance can bridge the gap between constructivist tools and consolidation, then it will have linked peace operations to a constitutive stage of international law and order maintenance, beyond inter-state organization. Alternatively, the UN may be on the verge of a chaotic stage.

Operational environments

While the objective is internal consolidation, a peace-maintenance operation may have to deploy in any of a state's constitutive, constructive, consolidative or chaotic stages. In a constitutive environment, a peace-maintenance operation provides, in the absence of centralized authority, a link-in-transition between elements as they organically coalesce and indigenously unify. The UN trustee-ship system at times operated in such a context, but it was dominated by the imperial interests of the colonial power charged with governance, including the British in Tanganyika, the Belgians in Rwanda and, to a lesser extent, the Italians in Somalia. Administering authorities tended not to be genuinely concerned with successful self-rule after independence. At the other extreme, explained in Chapter 7, a diplomatic approach by the UN to a constitutive process in Western Sahara, which included defining elements such as the popula-tion belonging to the territory, proved fatal.

A contested society can be the result of too much power at the centre, and conflict is a consequence of disequilibrium in the system at the cost of the many. As such, it may be, like El Salvador, at an arrested stage of construction.[54] A peace-maintenance operation focuses on correcting the imbalance between excessive powers of government and inadequate political participation of the population.

There may be political violence or threatening instability during a nation's consolidative process, as in Argentina[55] or the former Soviet Union.[56] A peace-maintenance operation would be able to conduct or supervise an election, verify a transfer of power or ensure compliance with human rights standards.

A state may have descended into the fragmentation of a chaotic stage, comparable to Cambodia[57] or Somalia.[58] There are likely to be several factions vying for central authority. A peace-maintenance operation circumventing this competition might be tantamount to: returning to a constitutive stage if complete deconstruction of elements is likely before reconstruction can begin; shifting to a constructive stage if a core can be re-established; or, in the best-case scenario, reverting immediately to a consolidative stage if institutions are suffi-ciently intact in spite of claims for their control. Therefore, successful missions need the capacity to maintain a presence through several stages.

Similarly, a peace-maintenance operation may have to contend with more than one stage at once. In the case of Namibia, supervising the withdrawal of South African forces at the same time as a new authority inherited power, was shifting away from both a constructive stage at one level and a constitutive stage at another. This was intended to result in a new constructive stage better able to consolidate in time.[59]

Furthermore, once a contested society has passed from one stage to another through a peace-maintenance operation, there is no guarantee that it will not revert to its previous condition, or, as the result of new and separate causes, shift to another stage of disequilibrium. The lesson of recent events has been that comparatively consolidated nations like the former Yugoslavia can quickly descend into chaos.[60]

This regressive tendency raises the question of a link between internal conditions and external concerns in the form of a permanent international presence or arrangement in commonly contested societies. It could expand or contract according to requirements on the ground. Or it could act as a kind of early warning of civil disturbance and trigger mechanism for an international response, in the manner that the UN Iraq–Kuwait Observation Mission is a kind of trip-wire between Iraqi movements and US military force. Boutros-Ghali has proposed a similar concept, but it is yet to be accepted. This, like 'peace-building', is a species of conflict prevention.[61]

Peace-maintenance operations

Peace-maintenance operations range in their suitability for each stage of state complexity. *Assistance* is ideally suited to an existing, if marginal, consolidative stage. It may be unavoidable in a constructive stage as a result of the strength of the existing authority. In such cases, the mission has few independent means to ensure a sustainable impact, unless it symbolically represents external influence. *Partnership* is suited to a constructive stage, but is also applicable in consolidation. *Control* is the most flexible type of operation and can be applied at any stage, in principle. Control is the functional constant in each category, while the juridical context determines the measure in which that control is conducted by the local community or the peace-maintenance authority. Control is the instrument that determines political development. This is clearest in the context of constructive and, to a lesser extent, consolidative stages. Also, it may be unavoidable in a chaotic stage if divided factions have some coherent structure. *Governorship* is most applicable at the extremes of state disorder, during constitution and in chaos.

As a system, itself, a peace-maintenance operation that intends to control conditions in any environment is conducted in four stages. This is regardless of whether the authority-in-transition is in one measure or another international or local. In a first *constitutive* stage, the challenges in the field and the elements of the operation are identified. Deployment is a second *constructive* stage, in which the mission arrives decisively and establishes itself as an international authority with local jurisdiction. The third *consolidative* stage is formally a transitional phase in which the international authority and local population function together to achieve a sustainable result. In a fourth stage, peace-maintainers either withdraw altogether or a longer-term presence is accepted locally.

Peace operations to date have expected too much too quickly. Internal, national consolidation has been anticipated as a result of a single, relatively short, transitional phase. It has amounted to a 'quick fix' world view. Capitalism, democracy and the institutions of Western, liberal-style states have been the measurements of instant-development. For successful peace-maintenance, these cannot be the standards of first instance. The transitional phase needs to be divided into two parts, a first dominated by an international authority and a second by the local community.

The goal of peace-maintenance operations is to establish a flexible administrative mechanism for control in longer-term transitions. It is the establishment of an interim social process between contested and contented societies. A population should be able to control its environment, regardless of the stage of complexity. As an effective and legitimate form of transitional administration, it would be a kind of temporary system, until such time as questions concerning construction and consolidation can be decided. Development could be genuinely chosen, not 'autonomically' accepted.

PEACE-MAINTENANCE TRANSITIONS

The requirements of a society-in-transition include a flexible mechanism for control, the generation of social momentum and direct linkages between internal strata and other systems.[62]

Peace-maintenance is not 'development' or 'peace-building' as state-building. It cannot be bound by state conceptions of the elements: sovereignty, government, citizens and territorial boundaries dividing inside and out. Instead, it may be based on archetypal equivalents. A genuine form of self-determination is a kind of interim sovereignty. The control mechanism replaces the role of government in the transitional period. Direct participation in governance corresponds to 'representational' citizenry. Rather than territorial place, there is administrative space.

A control mechanism maintains political coherence and social equilibrium. If it becomes too exclusive, the system collapses, for the reasons that construction without consolidation equals extinction. The perennial balance between central direction and decentralized administration is critical. Individuals can identify with a series of associations ascending in size: the district or town, the region or province, the state and, in principle, the international community.[63] Local inhabitants will depend on an administrative structure that can link them to each level simultaneously and perpetually.[64]

To balance centralization, decentralization and internationalization, peace-maintenance rests more on the support of the many than on the power of the few. The key to social momentum is a basic unit of administration that generates individual participation at each level of association. Its size is limited to ensure social relevance through personal familiarity among members. This avoids the supremacy of anonymous bureaucracy, and can therefore limit abuses of power. Like the control of surplus production in capitalism, bureaucracy for government is control of surplus social energy. Direct participation reduces excess social surplus, and its accumulation is restricted by the separation of powers between each level of administration. A national centre retains control primacy, but not exclusivity.

Economic development accelerates social momentum. The welfare of local communities will increasingly rely on a network of direct connections internationally. The means to global economic domination has meant incrementally replacing ownership of the means of production with control of an impersonal, and virtual, market. Through technology, production steadily has become decentralized. By shifting their focus of activity, powerful inter-continental corporations vie for primacy in a world trading space that has expanded beyond the capacity of many nations to be competitive. The market has extended, in an unprecedented manner, the distance between producer and consumer to the benefit of the trader.[65]

In the same manner that Europe wished to circumvent traders by discovering a direct sea route to Asia, the economic survival of fragile societies will be the result of their ability to avoid dependence on the market-space. As direct trade relies more and more on transnational social and administrative links, short-term financial benefits will strengthen inter-communal ties in the long term. As a rule of momentum, it is the nature of wealth to beget wealth, for there is 'a ferocious law which states: "to he that has, will be given; from he that has not, will be taken away"'.[66]

The task of a peace-maintenance operation is to generate this kind of momentum for eventual self-perpetuation. It establishes a political control mechanism and constructs an administrative apparatus as part of a transitional social process. It approaches political development through assistance, partnership, control or governorship, depending on the stage of complexity of the local community, whether constitutive, constructive, consolidative or chaotic. The international objective is universal internal consolidation. Yet the ability to achieve this would indicate the advent of a constitutive stage of an international political system. Consequently, extreme particularism will have led to universalism.

3 International civil administration

In the 1990s, the United Nations was called on to: organize elections; protect human rights; arrest, detain, prosecute and punish individuals; control government ministries or administer conflict areas in their absence; and transfer power from one authority to another. All of this was done, whether successfully or unsuccessfully, in the name of the international community as a whole and in trust on behalf of the local community victimized by war. It marked a shift from a period of definition to an opportunity for implementation: three generations of civil and political, economic and social, and peoples' rights; individual responsibility under international criminal law; and the responsibility of states regardless of their sovereignty, for five decades had all been progressively identified and clarified. But the pace of implementation in the last decade outstripped the scope of definition and the agenda of fifty years.

Vast peace exercises have raised a number of questions. What is the extent of civilian powers mandated on paper to UN officials in the field and the degree of authority they effectively exercise? Is this a legitimate activity or East River imperialism? Is the role of a third party in local governance effective, and can it alter social and political conditions and establish for the first time or reconstruct traumatized civil society? Or are nations at fundamentally different stages of historical development in which the international community can play a minimal role at best? Should the UN become an international administrator or can it be only an observer and perhaps the occasional participant? Can the gap be bridged between, on the one hand, the demand for abuses of power and excesses of violence to be stopped, and the desire to do so; and on the other, the resources to be able to respond? Can the basis of legitimacy and suspicion of motivation for intervening be reconciled? And if the UN is to do the job, how can it?

CONSTITUTIVE EXPERIMENTS

The notion of administration is tied to the development of the centralized exercise of authority, and is the link between this authority and the territory and peoples it claims as part of its jurisdiction. The area of territory and number of population tends to increase between the authority of the family head, the tribal king, state sovereign and hegemonic emperor. As more and more territory and population come under central authority, the more powerful that authority is said to be; but the further its power is extended from the centre, the weaker it becomes and the greater the need for bureaucracy, as a rule of organization generally, to ensure effective control of the area. The authority is institutionalized by maintaining order through a military, upholding law through courts, managing an economy through finance structures, and implementing its will through executive mechanisms.

Authority by definition is delegated power. Therefore, it is exercised by a minority that exists by virtue of exerting influence over a majority. Regardless of the political system in place or its underlying ideology, whether it is abusive and exploitative or protective and distributive, tyrannical or popularly legitimate, this fact of authority and the fact of administration it necessitates remain constant. As such, paradoxically, the opposing forces of colonization and decolonization were both concerned with centralized control of territory, one in the name of a foreign sovereign and the other on behalf of the local population. Whether or not there was popular participation in government subsequently depended on the nature of the new political system or the individuals who inherited the powers of government.[1] In either case, there was not a dispute about authority meaning control by the few over the many, only about whether the few were democratically representative or autocratically not. Consequently, at one time it seemed reasonable to entrust colonial powers with the administration of League of Nations mandates or UN trust territories in their transition to independence.[2]

As international organizations assumed some functions of local administration in different parts of the world, they could not be immune from this fact of authority, not only because they were composed of states based on this logic, but because of the nature of authority they tried to institute or underwrite. This was in spite of the fact that they were considerably less centralized as organizations than their component parts or the institutions they supported in the field. Curiously, it would be precisely because of the decline of state authority generally that international organizations would be able to play a greater role in strengthening government institutions of specific national administrations. The logic of an international organization underwriting state structures at a time when their general influence was declining would be one of the limitations of international administration altogether.

International administration by international organizations is principally a twentieth-century development.[3] This is not only because international organizations themselves formally emerged in the nineteenth and twentieth centuries. It is also because for the first time administrative tasks would be carried out not in the name of a single sovereign or emperor, but by a number of nations not in the name of any one. Ad hoc arrangements had existed before, when groups of states, usually victors after a war, jointly acted in a particular venture in their individual interests and not even in the interests of the limited group. Multinational administration of territory, of whatever kind, posed its own practical challenges and was distinct from condominiums in history, when more than one sovereign shared jurisdiction over a particular area. International organizations did not represent themselves as sovereigns but as the international community as a whole, and administered territory, therefore, not according to exploitative motives but in a purposefully temporary manner.

Prior to the United Nations, the distinction between separate arrangements of a group of states administering an area in their own interests and more formal arrangements of international organizations with limited or nominally universal membership, as in the case of the League, was blurred.[4] In 1897, for instance, the European powers, including Britain, France, Italy and Russia, invaded Crete to prevent its union with Greece. They established an effective governmental organ, a 'Commission of the Consuls' of the powers that were nominally responsible to the 'Board of European Ambassadors' at Istanbul. The administration of Crete, which lasted until 1909, was underwritten by an international police force that replaced the military contingents on their withdrawal. A similar model was used in Peking after the 1900 Boxer rebellion threatened the safety of the European community. International troops from seven states under joint direction of a council of war marched from Tientsin to relieve the city. Thereafter, a German Commander-in-Chief was appointed, the main force was evacuated and a police force was left behind to support an international body with administrative powers.

The administration of the international concessions of Shanghai and the international zone of Tangier in the inter-war period represented a wider but by no means universal set of interests. The International Settlement of Shanghai resembled 'an international city state, governed by a Municipal Council of international composition and subject only to the somewhat tenuous jurisdiction of the Consular Body consisting of the consuls of the fourteen foreign powers with extraterritorial rights'.[5] The Municipal Council was underwritten by a municipal police force and the Shanghai Volunteer Corps, a small army with British, American, Chinese, Portuguese, Russian, Filipino and Jewish companies. Similarly, the international administration of Tangiers was backed by a multinational police force.

To implement the peace treaties that had concluded the First World War, the victorious Principal Allied and Associated Powers, namely Great Britain, France, Italy, Japan and the United States, established commissions to delimit the frontiers of the new political map and hold plebiscites in disputed areas. The commissions were responsible to a Conference of Ambassadors established in Paris, composed of the signatories of the peace treaties from whom the commissions derived their authority. Following the withdrawal of troops of contending parties, commissions were to administer the disputed territory, delimit it or supervise a plebiscite. The civilian administration of the area was to be underwritten by a police or military force that could maintain order and enforce the decision of the civilian authority. Germany, Austria and Hungary at the Paris Conference demanded that the commissions be composed of nationals of neutral states; that is, neither Allies nor defeated states.

Most commissions, however, were composed of members from Allied powers and largely separate from the League. Nevertheless, the Allied administrators were a departure from the past: their presence was intended to be temporary and their goal was to settle a dispute or act in some way on behalf of the local community. While the context in which they operated, under the architecture designed by the peace agreements, served the strategic interests of the victors, the specific administrative tasks, though imposed, were not meant to be exploitative and required minimal pressure beyond the enforced consent that had initiated the process.

For instance, the disputed port of Danzig between East Prussia and Poland was placed under the League's 'guarantee' and established as an autonomous Free City. Before this could be finalized, Danzig and its surrounding area were placed under the interim administration of the Allied Powers. A British diplomat was appointed its Administrator and two battalions of British and French troops were deployed to maintain law and order during the transition between February and November 1920. After 1920, there remained an international administrative body, the Danzig Port and Waterways Board, which could rely on the Danzig police and in 1934 established its own Harbour and River Guard.

Similarly, from 1920 to 1924, the disputed territory around the port of Memel, between Lithuania and East Prussia, was placed under Allied administration. A French High Commissioner was appointed and three companies of French troops were deployed to maintain law and order. After the settlement of the dispute in 1924, an international Harbour Board remained with its own police force.

Varying degrees of administrative authority were exercised by the Plebiscite Commissions. In Schleswig, between Denmark and Germany, the Commission supported by 3,000 British and French troops divided the territory after the plebiscite in May 1920, with the approval of the Conference of Ambassadors. Two Plebiscite Commissions in Allenstein and Marienwerder, between East Prussia and Poland, transferred the territory to Germany as the plebiscite results of July 1920 dictated, with the assistance of 2,000 British, Italian and French troops. In Upper Silesia, between Poland, Germany and Czechoslovakia, a French, British and Italian Commission with some 20,000 troops failed to resolve the issue following the 1921 plebiscite, which favoured Germany's claim. The Commission split, with France, which had fielded three-quarters of the troops, favouring Poland. The matter went to the League of Nations Council, which produced a partition plan implemented successfully by the Allied Commission and forces in 1922. While the administration in each of these cases was under civilian authority, the military contingents carried out many of the conventionally civilian tasks, not just of policing, but of registering voters, supervising polls and checking intimidation.

The League of Nations played a limited role in assisting resolution of disputes the Allied Powers had been unable to settle, such as in Upper Silesia and in the city of Vilna between Lithuania and Poland from 1920 to 1922. However, it assumed administrative responsibilities independently in the coal and iron-ore rich Saar, between Germany and France. This would be the first instance, given the universality – if not separate legal personality – of the League as an international organization, in which it could be said administration was carried out by the international community as a whole in the interest and on behalf of the local population. In other words, it was not merely a *cooperative* but a *collective* action.

As a victor, France hoped to annex the Saar, but British and other fears that this would provide Germany with a *cause célèbre* led to a compromise in 1920 in which the territory was placed under the League's administration for fifteen years. A five-man Governing Commission exercised full governmental powers and had 2,000 French troops to maintain law and order. As the date for a plebiscite approached, this was later replaced by a larger multinational force of 3,300 from Britain, Italy, the Netherlands and Sweden. There was high visibility of the international presence, which did not have to resort to armed force at any time. After a 90 per cent vote in favour of joining what had become Nazi Germany, the League relinquished control and transferred power to Adolf Hitler on 1 March 1935.

In contrast to this fully integrated model, a League Commission assumed control for one year, from 1933 to 1934, of the disputed district of Leticia between Colombia and Peru. Instead of a multinational force, the Commission maintained order through 150 Colombian troops seconded to the League. The Colombians, however, functioned no less as an international or collective force than did the French or other troops in the Saar, since their authority lay exclusively with the League. As such, they wore blue armbands and flew the League's blue and white flag.

In the meantime, another form of administration had developed as part of the system of the League: colonies of defeated powers were distributed among the victorious Allies. But these were not to be the booty of conquest, which they would have been quite legitimately earlier in the previous century. Nor were they to be possessions in the manner of the other colonies. They were to be administered in trust and in transition, in preparation for the peoples in the territory to exercise eventual self-rule. These mandated territories continued to be internationally administered under the United Nations in somewhat different form as trusteeships. The League and the UN could not have had the resources or capability to adapt the Saar arrangement to vast tracts of land worldwide. They required the colonial powers to adopt the task. But there was a cost attached: colonial administrators meant colonial administration. Despite the philosophy of the trust system, the mandates and trusteeships achieved independence no more quickly than the other colonial possessions and had to wait until the waves of decolonization in the 1950s and 1960s.

In principle, the idea of a state with the resources and capability to do so fulfilling a task on behalf of the international community as a whole and in the interest of the local community was sound and was not less collective than if an international organization physically administered the area itself. But this was provided that the authority of the international community, of the League or of the UN, was being exercised regularly through the individual state as an instrument of that international authority. But this integration was not the case. In most instances, mandatory powers had specific interests in the areas they administered, although mandatory administration tended to be more restrictive than the same colonial power's rule in its own colonies, such as the difference between British rule in Kenya and Tanganyika next door. Still, even when they accepted control of areas somewhat disinterestedly, colonial administrative policies were dictated by economic or other factors. As a fundamentally 'cooperative' organization, the League could demand little accountability from its own members.

The United Nations, however, as genuinely 'collective', was something more. After the Second World War, with the ascendant roles of the United States and the Soviet Union, both critical of colonial policies, and ultimately due to the willingness of colonial powers themselves to gradually surrender their empires, the UN was able to remind the territorial authorities that trusteeships were to be administered in such a manner as to prepare the local population for self-rule.[6] While the decolonizing powers left behind many structures that would form the basis of authority and political culture in the newly independent states, they nevertheless tended not to adequately train for government service the peoples they administered.

However unpalatable the experience of colonial administration, its origins and motivations, including the experience of the mandates and trusteeships, it nevertheless developed many mechanisms for administering large populations and geographic areas. If genuinely international administration is to be effective, then UN planners may have to revisit the lessons of this experience. British colonial administration, for instance, had a well-developed system of provincial and district officials, to whom military and police units were responsible and who could therefore exercise effectively the executive powers they had in their local area. They would be responsible to the Governor, who worked with Legislative and Executive Councils which tended to be appointed, not elected, but which eventually included individuals from the local population.

If what the UN has assumed on paper is to function, a sincerely motivated combination of these models will have to be examined. The issue here is to appreciate the lessons of organization and to ensure that the administration is conducted on the part of the international community as a whole, in the interests of the local population and not in the interests of the authority at the cost of the population, and in spite of the international community.

CONSTRUCTIVE EXPERIMENTS

Much of the experience of early experiments was swept away by the currents of the Second World War and the need to create a stronger international organization. Attempts to resuscitate international cities as transitional arrangements failed in the early days of the UN system, partly due to the Cold War and the absence of any international policing mechanism to underwrite ad hoc administrative authority, in the manner that Allied Powers had done after the First World War. But it was also partly due to the fact that the international community and the UN could be challenged militarily by small factions and new, weak states.

The UN Security Council devised a plan to establish the disputed city of Trieste between Italy and Yugoslavia as a Free Territory. It was to be administered by the Security Council initially through local police, and armed forces were to be restricted in the area according to the Council's instructions. However, the United States and the Soviet Union disagreed on the appointment of a Governor of the Territory. In reaction, the Western powers engineered a new resolution that awarded the area to Italy and an interim measure was turned into the status quo as a fait accompli.

A similar plan had been drawn up for Jerusalem. The UN General Assembly proposed that Jerusalem and its surrounding areas should have a separate status after the partition of Palestine. It would have a UN Governor, be demilitarized, and a special police force would be responsible to the Governor to maintain law and order. Instead, fighting broke out between the new Israeli state and its Arab neighbours, and the city was divided between Israeli and Jordanian forces.

In the meantime, there gradually developed the UN practice in observation of cease-fire lines and armistice agreements, and eventually the deployment of armed forces for the purpose as international referees. The restrictive political atmosphere of the Cold War meant these activities were limited in scope, had few military, policing or other resources and could be deployed in only rare instances – where the strategic imperatives of the superpower rivalry could accept their presence. In this context, UN administrative practices in the field had their debut. Unlike the constitutive period, when civilian administration designated and subordinated to it troops or policing units, now UN administration developed as part of the evolution of military forces in observation and peacekeeping tasks, which themselves had been subordinated to the diplomatic culture of the UN system.

Throughout the Cold War, civilians carried out administrative tasks in observation and peacekeeping missions. It was typical for a headquarters staff in the field to include: Political Officers, Legal Affairs Officers, Public Affairs Officers and Chief Administrative Officers. However, these positions tended to focus on the administration of the UN mission and much less on the area that the mission was responsible for. In the cases of interposition forces, it is true that UN forces were responsible for maintaining the status quo in the areas they occupied. But these areas tended to be thin strips of no-man's-land, which, albeit strategic, sat between two opposing armies and did not include in themselves divided communities and the administrative complexities this implied.

Furthermore, the authority of the mission was limited since it could not enforce its will or maintain law and order independently, in defiance of local authorities. UN forces were present in their areas of operation by the grace of a status-of-forces agreement with the parties, a larger peace agreement between belligerents and a UN resolution, usually from the Security Council. Although it represented the will of the international community, it relied on local consent to function.

These limitations were some of the growing pains of the shift from powerful states independently administering areas extraterritorially; through limited international control of areas underwritten by the assets as well as the interests of powerful armies; to, finally, genuinely international or collective administration by the international community as a whole and in the local interest. The next phase of this shift was to enable the UN to administer as effectively as was required of an interim authority governing-in-trust on the one hand, and as legitimately acceptable internationally and locally on the other.

The first operation deployed for the purpose of transition administration was the United Nations Temporary Executive Authority (UNTEA), which supervised the decolonization of Dutch West New Guinea and transferred the territory to Indonesia between 1962 and 1963.[7] For seven months a UN Administrator had exclusive and full authority, under the direction of the Secretary-General, to administer the territory. The Administrator had the power: to appoint governmental officials and members of the representative councils; to legislate for the territory; to issue travel documents to Papuans for travel abroad; and to fulfil UNTEA's commitments and guarantees regarding civil liberties and property rights. UNTEA was to adapt the Dutch institutions in the territory to an Indonesian pattern. Above all, having secured the reins of power, it was to transfer this to a new authority.

It was also envisioned that the UN would conduct a plebiscite in 1969 as a genuine exercise of self-determination to establish whether or not the inhabitants wished to be part of Indonesia. A Representative of the Secretary-General with a staff would advise, assist and participate in the arrangements, which were primarily the responsibility of Indonesia. However, once the territory had been transferred, the matter was effectively closed.

To underwrite UNTEA's authority, a United Nations Security Force (UNSF) was deployed. It was composed of 1,500 Pakistani troops and 110 naval personnel to man Dutch patrol vessels transferred to the UN. Its primary task was the maintenance of law and order, and to do this it would cooperate with local Papuan police, the Papuan Volunteer Corps whose links to the Dutch army would be severed, and at the discretion of the Administrator Indonesian armed forces could be used. The UNSF also had an observation role to implement cease-fire terms and supervise the repatriation of prisoners. The Force was exclusively responsible to the civilian Administrator.

Despite these extensive powers, UNTEA turned out to be an anomaly. The UN experience in the Congo, occurring simultaneously between 1960 and 1964, effectively halted the development of multifunctional operations and returned the international community to the conventional tasks of peacekeeping.[8] The Opération des Nations Unies au Congo (ONUC) was considerably larger than UNTEA, with 20,000 troops at its height, but it was juridically less authoritative: while UNTEA was an exclusive authority that secured power before transferring it, ONUC assisted an authority once power had already been transferred. ONUC's most difficult task was assistance to the central government in the restoration and maintenance of law and order as the local authority fragmented and resulted ultimately in its collapse and the emergence of a secession. This left ONUC at one point in the position of being the effective authority in the area, which necessitated the Security Council's expansion of its powers to use force.

ONUC did not deploy under the terms of a comprehensive agreement and a mandate addressing the overall problems in the Congo. It operated under limited but vague Security Council resolutions which had to be updated several times. The operation formed its character through trial and error and by reacting to ground conditions as they developed. By the end of the operation, ONUC would have carried out a number of complex tasks. To maintain the territorial integrity and political independence of the Congo, ONUC contemplated using force to compel a Belgian withdrawal and had to prevent the secession of Katanga. To assist the central government in the restoration of law and order, ONUC was to protect life and property from unlawful violence, disarm elements threatening internal law and order, and help reorganize the national security forces. To prevent the occurrence of civil war in the territory and to secure the withdrawal of foreign military forces and mercenaries, ONUC used force to apprehend and deport.

ONUC, therefore, exercised extensive policing powers, but it did so often in the absence of a local central authority, and the UN was not in a position to behave as a replacement. The effective exercise of authority outside a coherent framework, without a comprehensive strategy, meant ONUC could only react to events and could not bridge the gap between the vacuum of authority in the capital, surrounded by rival competitors, on the one hand and the UN's capabilities and mandate on the other. The UN would have to begin considering its ability or willingness to provide some continuity as a third party, including its own role as a comprehensive, centralized authority, when local authority fragmented, factions formed and breakaway tendencies threatened the territorial integrity of the area and its neighbours.

It is difficult to exercise executive powers during an operation if they were not intended from the outset. Furthermore, the UN would have to be prepared not just to assist local police forces in the maintenance of law and order, but to develop an independent means of maintaining and restoring law and order when local systems collapsed altogether. Finally, the 'Congo shuffle', the withdrawal of the UN in a face-saving manner with an inflated perception of success, meant that although such efforts could have a life-saving impact in the short term, UN governance tasks would have to leave behind genuinely coherent and sustainable structures of authority after the operation's withdrawal.

Many of these issues, however, would not be addressed for nearly three decades. The international community was psychologically unprepared for the UN to assume such extensive powers; Cold War interests confronted third party impartiality and possibly undesirable outcomes of the UN's role in internal conflicts; and the public perception that ONUC in particular, but also the use of force and the exercise of UN authority generally, had been failed experiments led to the view that they should not be tried again. Instead, the conventional tasks and practice of peacekeeping crystallized in the Sinai, Cyprus, the

Lebanon and elsewhere. Civilian functions reverted from exercising authority to administering peacekeeping operations.

The role of the Special Representative of the Secretary-General (SRSG) developed as a negotiator or at most as a supervisor of settlements, rather than as an instrument of UN authority or a governor. Diplomatic-style civilian authority, typical of conventional peacekeeping missions, reached its apex in 1988 with, for instance, the UN Good Offices Mission in Afghanistan and Pakistan (UNGOMAP), which did not address the Afghan conflict as such, but verified the Soviet withdrawal from the area. This occurred as the end of the Cold War began to alter the whole landscape of UN operations.

CONSOLIDATIVE EXPERIMENTS

During the second generation of UN peace missions, the development of civilian administrative capabilities increasingly shifted in focus from internal organization of operations to governance over territory. The first steps were taken in 1989 by the United Nations Transition Assistance Group (UNTAG) in Namibia. As a decolonization operation, UNTAG was effectively a joint administration of Namibia by the UN and South Africa, as a powerful occupying force about to withdraw.[9] The original plan in the 1970s envisioned the UN assuming executive powers and exclusive control over the territory. But agreement could not be reached on what particularly South Africa rejected; and given the capabilities of the UN secretariat and available resources, it would have been unsuccessful operationally.

Nevertheless, this partnership model enabled the UN to develop its own multifunctional approach to problems. The civilian–military interface became an acute issue for the first time given the unprecedented scope of civilian activities. Although the military Force Commander was subordinated to the civilian Special Representative, this relationship was not well integrated and military assistance to civilian tasks was not as forthcoming as was needed. In the end, due to inertia from previous operations and an inability to predict the results of the Namibia experiment, it turned out that the size of the military component was overestimated and the civilian resources underestimated.

The SRSG exercised a kind of veto authority in the process and began to behave as a quasi joint-governor-in-trust. While he could not control the South African Administrator-General or his civilian administration or military forces, the Special Representative nevertheless acted as a restraint on decisions made or executed that did not agree with the spirit of the process. At his disposal were forty-two political offices around the country, which did not have local executive powers but which could verify the integrity of the process and report to the SRSG if this was violated; ultimately the issue could be passed to the Secretary-General, Security Council and superpower brokers of the process to pressure South Africa to comply. This was an unwieldy mechanism, but a conventional peacekeeping chain of influence, and quite different from the colonial provincial administrator.

Other innovations included information dissemination, public education and political conscious-raising efforts among an almost entirely illiterate population. But the main feature of the Namibian operation was the experience the UN gained holding elections in a more open global strategic climate and verifying them as 'free and fair'. While the SRSG did not have exclusive responsibility to organize and conduct the election, UNTAG nevertheless was instrumental in drafting an electoral law and ensuring the South African administration's compliance with it. Electoral components would become one of the best-developed arms of civilian administration in the future as the UN came to rely more and more on elections as a final point of transitional arrangements and as a means of justifying withdrawal.

However, although not an acute problem in the relatively benign environment of Namibia, a fragmented model of UN administration was developing. UN military units in the countryside were responsible not to the local political officer but to the Force Commander in Windhoek. Similarly, UN civilian police (CIVPOL) units were responsible to their Commissioner in the capital. The police were not responsible for conducting law and order tasks independently. Of conventional policing powers to report incidents, investigate violations, search premises, seize evidence and arrest and detain suspects, UNTAG CIVPOL had only the first of these, posing problems in at least three cases which required UN investigation.[10] A quasi-judicial body was appointed, but it did not have independent prosecutory powers of any kind and was responsible only to the South African Administrator-General. While the O'Linn Commission was established to hear cases of electoral intimidation and malpractice, it did not convict anyone. The essential features of administration would have to be consolidated, integrated and less reliant on local structures if the UN was to exercise effective political authority.

The Namibian process proved to be mostly calm and the occupying power was essentially amenable. Conditions in Cambodia, by contrast, were considerably more hostile. Yet the UN relied too heavily on the Namibia 'success', lulled as it was into a kind of false sense of security. The UN Transitional Authority in Cambodia (UNTAC) in 1992 and 1993 was the most extensive administrative operation to date.[11] It tested the ability of the UN to exercise authority, not just independently but in spite of four intransigent and well-defined factions. Each had controlled Phnom Penh at one time or another and so had a historical reference point as a basis of unity and for determining membership. Their identity was further consolidated by the fact that all four had fought one another for at least a decade. Despite the traditional fragmentation of Cambodian authority and its disconnection between the capital and the provinces in the countryside, the UN model of administration was itself fragmented and unable to fulfil the mandate of direct control of local power.

The SRSG could no longer afford to be a diplomat, whose sub-culture was to maintain a status quo as smoothly as possible or only ever to mediate any change. Now it was a political job and executive powers had to be exercised and not merely negotiated.[12] But the man in the position, Yasushi Akashi, was a diplomat and refused to be what the mandate effectively required, a 'MacArthur of Cambodia' as he put it.[13] Powers that existed on paper, but that were negotiated rather than exercised, meant that UN authority would be necessarily weak and UNTAC would be unable to transfer power since it had not secured it in the first place.

Even if the SRSG had exercised more of his powers, the operation was limited in its ability to implement executive decisions. UNTAC's terms of reference to 'control' Cambodia's administration included the power to politically neutralize ministries through the removal of personnel, but there were no means to independently enforce this and local opposition meant it could not be done. The concept of UNTAC's CIVPOL was very much a traditional one of assistance in the maintenance of law and order by local forces, and so its powers were restricted. But rather like the reactive experience in the Congo, these had to be expanded. Arrests were made, but detention required a UN jail. For the first time one was established, but it was never used because CIVPOL refused to guard it and prisoners had to be detained by military contingents. The powers of arrest had been necessitated partly by the establishment of a Special Prosecutor as a means for the UN to be seen to be responding to growing political violence as the elections approached. However, the executive core of UNTAC effectively prevented prosecutions for political purposes, contradicting UNTAC's human rights education in the legal system regarding independence of the judiciary.

Similarly, the military, while more integrated into the operation as a whole and providing more assistance to civilian activities than in Namibia – partly because it had the time and resources to do so given the failure of the demilitarization phase of the operation – still relied on the conventional 'peacekeeping' formula. But non-peacekeeping conditions undermined the independence of UN forces, which never managed to create a secure environment for the conduct of elections.

On paper, the human rights component had many of the powers human rights bodies had always wanted to hold local authorities accountable. The sub-culture of human rights workers to challenge authority was a valuable asset in Cambodia, but the component's ability to transform the legal system and educate the population about their rights was hampered by the limitations of the operation generally, as further described in Chapter 5.

In the meantime, operations dispatched to the Western Sahara and El Salvador provided lessons of their own. A mission deployed to hold a referendum in the exercise of Western Sahara's self-determination failed to reach its goal. It was, perhaps, the operation with the widest powers mandated and the least means available to underwrite these powers, as illustrated in Chapter 7. The UN claimed the authority to be an exclusive administrative governor of the area, with powers of repealing local legislation and with military and security units able to exercise independently full law and order functions. Instead, for the longest time, it failed to deploy more than a few hundred observers due to the occupying power's intransigence.

In El Salvador, the first human rights operation outside a larger framework with military and police units was deployed in 1991.[14] While the process was underwritten by an extensive negotiating capability, linked with the direct involvement of the Secretary-General, the ability of the UN to investigate, report on and sometimes protect human rights rested with the support of the Farabundo Martí National Liberation Front (FMLN). This acted almost as an enforcement mechanism for the UN by challenging government forces, and its eventual neutralization meant also that the authority of the UN was curtailed as well.

Finally, the Somalia experience did not represent the culmination of all these experiments, although it proved to be the largest UN operation to date due to the role of the United States. Instead, it evolved almost by itself through four phases: conventional cease-fire observation between July and November 1992; forcible delivery of humanitarian assistance between December 1992 and March 1993; combat operations between June and October 1993; and nation-building proper after October 1993. Although the UN had a mandate to assist Somalis, in the absence of a centralized authority it was forced to behave as a *de facto* replacement when restructuring government institutions. In effect, as described in Chapter 6, the UN did in Somalia what it said it would do in Cambodia, namely 'control'; and it did in Cambodia what it said it would do in Somalia, namely 'assist'.

Even considering the special role of the US, it can be said that international authority was exercised more forcefully and independently than before, albeit at times to excess and unaccountably. The Security Council issued its first arrest warrant. Detention facilities were established and held overall some 1,000 arrested prisoners. More significant was the UN's attempt to establish a Somali police force, judiciary and transitional government. Somalia was the first place since Dutch West New Guinea where the UN could have secured power and been in a position to transfer it to a legitimate authority. But the UN proved incapable of doing so. How could it successfully administer territory in the future? And should it?

PEACE-MAINTENANCE ADMINISTRATION

In each of the four categories of peace-maintenance, the UN may intend to organize and conduct or supervise an election in order to transfer power from one authority to another. In the interim period, the UN may have assumed juridical authority over the area on paper, even if in the past it has not managed to do this physically. To be an authority in the area, a mission must accept the juridical implications of being in possession of power if it is to be in a position to transfer that power to a new authority. To do so, it must manage to physically wrest authority from an unaccountable regime, or assume it and establish a centre of gravity in the midst of anarchical conditions.

Mandate

The mandate is a critical feature of peace-maintenance, for it is this that ensures the operation is conducted 'in trust', in the interests of the territory and population in question, and by the international community as a whole. A charge against UN mandates is that they imply the imposition of the UN Charter and international law, essentially instruments developed by Western, Christian values, on different cultures. However, it is an unfortunate aspect of the international system that it first evolved in a single region and that nations from other traditions have had to accept much from it. As the biases of the international system itself erode, so too will mandates have to keep pace.

If trust authorities are to be successful, however, they must take full sociological account of the nature of authority in the areas of their new jurisdiction. How UN authority will be exercised in this context will be the challenge of a Special Representative or governor-in-trust. It is not that the UN must exercise authority in the local style, nor exercise authority in a manner so alien to the local population that it fails to be regarded as authority. The supremacy of the mandate must be assured, and it is easier to do so if during the drafting of the mandate account is taken of the nature of local authority.

For instance, a joint authority may have to decide whether, anthropologically, an election is the correct means of establishing or transferring authority. In Cambodia and Somalia, the UN perception was not shared by factions that election results implied some finality, with a winner, a loser and a transfer of power; in both countries they were perceived as just one bargaining chip in a self-developing balance of power, which the UN was unable to control. Either elections may not have been the best means to identify a new authority or, if they were to be carried out, then attention needed to be focused on how to ensure that the local factions would comply with the results. Instead, the UN has treated elections more as an exit strategy for itself than have elections resulted in sustainable results. As such, they have been short-term responses to conditions requiring longer-term attention. Therefore, joint authority cannot be exclusively reliant on elections as an end by themselves; they can be only one of a number of institutions, all of which require each other as part of a single framework if order is to be sustainable.

Transition

The question arises as to the meaning of a transition period. Essentially this is the period during which the UN is exercising its authority within a particular territory. Further questions concern when this period should begin and end. Under what circumstances should the UN decide to assume the powers of governance-in-trust? Is this entirely at the discretion of the Security Council or the invitation of whichever local factions or officials exercise effective administration? What conditions should prevail in the territory and at which stage should the UN act: In the midst of conflict? When a cease-fire has been declared after a conflict? Or before a conflict during an economic crisis, or when central authority has fragmented into factionalism and outbreaks of violence threaten larger-scale hostilities? When exactly should the transition period end? What standard of law and order should be achieved before the trust authority can justify its withdrawal? How different from the period before the UN's involvement must the new era be to be justified as a success?[15]

Perpetual international presence

The concerted exercise of UN authority in a particular location requires significant commitment. Can the need for it resulting from breakdowns of national administration be averted? Like the notion of a constant police presence on the streets in national society to avoid incidents or the escalation of incidents, perhaps the international community needs to reach the stage of deploying trigger units in areas with the potential for crisis. Some notion of 'the potential for crisis' will need to be determined. But once deployed, these units could be increased and decreased in number as crises intensify or settle. Sometimes a significant massive presence may stabilize an area without the need for exercising much authority and may avoid the costs of even larger operations when the situation escalates out of control. The current proposals for rapid reaction forces still fall short of such permanent vigilance.[16]

Effectiveness

In peace-maintenance, if the UN is to exercise the powers of administration, it will need the resources to do so; it will have to ensure the accountability of the mission, as well as its independence in the field.

Resources

Will the UN Secretariat or appointed state or group of states be able to muster the extensive resources and political commitment to conduct the more complex and long-term tasks of peace-maintenance? This raises the issue of whether or not an operation should be funded entirely from external sources, or whether local resources, if in abundance, can be harnessed to finance some of the activities of administration as part of the overall rehabilitation of the country. The answer to this question may depend on whether local resources are readily available or whether, in the case of a poor country wealthy in untapped natural resources, they can be developed.[17]

Accountability

If the UN appoints agents with the will to commit resources to a peace-maintenance project, will they be acting impartially in the best interests of the territory concerned, or will they have ulterior motives? Will the UN as the ultimate mandating authority have the means to exercise control over its agents to ensure impartial commitment to its mandate? After all, the administering authority may be a major power, regionally or internationally. The problem is particularly acute since the most willing and least desirable candidates will have specific interests, such as a geographical, economic or historical link to the conflict area, and therefore be driven by a separate agenda. While such countries may not want to aggressively occupy an area in flagrant violation of the UN Charter and international law, they may desire a fig-leaf arrangement in which peace-maintenance on the paper of a Security Council resolution can amount to illegitimate occupation. In this manner, peace-maintenance must be distinguished from colonial or imperial acts by its mechanisms of accountability to the international community as a whole acting on behalf of a local population.

Independence

The powers of direct control or corrective action will have to be underwritten by an independent capacity to exercise the UN's will. While this may be selectively applied in instances where a flaw exists or an infraction has been committed, the operation will nevertheless need to have available effective means of governance at its disposal. Addressed in the next two chapters, these include: a criminal law developed for UN operations generally, that takes account of human rights issues; an independent means of criminal prosecution; and UN civilian police forces. Such activities may be possible only in the context of a secure environment provided by multinational military forces, and they need to be combined with material and humanitarian assistance – not only so that order guarantees justice, but for a real change to be felt by the population.

Instruments of authority

Criminal law

In addition to the overall mandate of the transition process, a specific criminal law that is applicable to both local and UN offenders is needed. This should be a simplified document that takes account of various legal systems and will probably be limited in the first instance to blatant violations. Practice and application will create the larger body of law for this activity.

Human rights

While the criminal law may focus on basic crimes, such as murder and monetary corruption, special account should be taken of the unique dimensions of human rights law. Integration between domestically conceived criminal activity and human rights violations will have to be achieved.

Criminal prosecution

The peace-maintenance authority will need an independent ability to prosecute. It will require a panel of judges, which may include local appointments, but the UN cannot rely on the inconsistencies of domestic systems of prosecution, which may be dependent on an executive authority that is corrupt or ineffective. The transitional judicial mechanism should be available for trying both local offenders and members of the UN operation guilty of criminal activity. It must be also independent of the executive officers of the UN mission.

Civilian police forces

Unlike civilian police units in peacekeeping operations in Cyprus, Namibia and even Cambodia, a police force capable of effectively enforcing law and order decisions of the UN political authority will require a clear mandate with full policing powers of reporting, investigation, search, seizure, arrest and detention. While local police forces should bear the brunt of law and order duties, with which CIVPOL may cooperate, the UN force must be able to conduct its tasks independently of the local police, particularly in the event of the local forces refusing to enforce a decision of the peace-maintenance authority or if the local police themselves are guilty of violating the UN mandate in place. CIVPOL should be prepared not to underwrite but to challenge local law or act in its absence according to the UN law regulating the transition process.

4 International rules of law

If a peace-maintenance authority is to continue to be accepted as legitimate by the local population, and is to sustain, therefore, a long-term presence while it devolves responsibility to the developing local authority, it will need to contend with the re-establishment of law and order. A peace-maintenance rule of law will have to be sufficiently effective to make a difference in people's daily lives, particularly if it is to be popularly supported as an alternative to the abusive status quo. This means genuinely protecting the individual from the bully and generally transforming the position of the weak as against the strong, automatically according to a common standard rather than as the result of an executive whim. Two ingredients are critical for achieving such a transitional order.

First, the peace-maintenance law and order mechanisms must be sufficiently independent of local authority structures if the mission is not to be subordinated to the divided will of factional leaders. Without this independence in principle and functionally, the international political authority cannot protect the victim population from the perpetrators of human rights and other violations. A peace-maintenance authority will have to exercise its own free will if it is to fulfil its purpose with an ability to help redirect or openly identify flaws in a transitional process. The degree of independence will vary depending on whether the mandate is *assistance, partnership, control* or *governorship*. It will be greater in the latter two categories, but in assistance and partnership an operation may need to be more cautious if it is to avoid the kind of bureaucratic capitulation that flows from following the line of least resistance. Only in this manner can a peace-maintenance authority either consolidate its displacement of a warlord competition or help create accountability in a standing local government.

Second, the peace-maintenance authority must be accountable itself, and not in some way above the law. This has implications for both its legitimacy and its effectiveness. A peace-maintenance authority does not need to and cannot be configured in a sovereign manner, as an ultimate source of law – as the authority of statehood is considered to be. Rather, it functions within the framework of existing international laws, including UN Charter provisions and customary practice accepted as law. In addition to the content of these laws, the procedural rules applicable to the legal status of its mandate also conditions the context in which peace-maintenance is established – whether it is by virtue of a Security

Council or General Assembly resolution, or in some other multinational or regional arrangement, such as under Chapter VIII. Therefore, while peace-maintenance has the political authority to assume tasks of governance, and acts as a source of law and order locally – with a kind of quasi-legislative capacity-in-transition – it derives this authority from elsewhere, internationally. 'It is fair to say,' after all, 'that international law has always considered its fundamental purpose to be the maintenance of peace.'[1]

Consequently, civil officials and military contingents participating in peace-maintenance operations are subject to an interim rule of law, no less than is the local population. Again, the control of this rule of law may vary between the local and international authority, depending upon the stage and category of the operation – as outlined in Chapter 2 – and particularly whether it is in a consti-tutive or consolidative scenario. But a mission without judicial means, independent not just of the local but also of its own executive, will be charged as illegitimate and decrease in effectiveness as it loses the trust and confidence of the local population. Furthermore, its ability to re-establish local law and order will have diminished since its hypocrisy will prevent the emergence of the very institutions it cannot accept for itself.

The problems with achieving such a commonly applicable rule of law are, on the one hand, left over from diplomatic-style peacekeeping and UN principles of immunity, and on the other, due to the reluctance of nations to submit their armed forces to a collective disciplinary procedure. Solving these will require a reconceiving of status-of-forces agreements for peace operations, sometimes in the absence of local consent and to contend with UN violations of international law. Independence from local authority does not mean immunity from lawful prosecution. And legal accountability is not tantamount to submission to local, non-neutral means of prosecution. One of the very reasons for peace-maintenance political authority in the field is the need for local and international legal accountability.

Furthermore, it is difficult to re-establish local law and order by reviving only one part of what is an integrated whole. In Somalia, for instance, redeploying a local police force required a court system, which in turn needed some law to interpret as the basis of its judgements. None of this could survive without a political authority and some body with a legislative capacity. The UN established its second jail in Somalia, but without a means of prosecution, no charges were laid against the arrested, no defence therefore could be provided, and ultimately long-term detention of some was affirmed as a UN human rights violation. In contrast, for the former Yugoslavia there is a means of prosecution at The Hague and a Dutch prison for incarceration, but no means of arrest. In a peace-maintenance mission, all the instruments of law and order need to be integrated; without any one of them, the logic of the whole collapses. Such issues are considered at greater length in the next chapter.

But none of these means of order are possible without rules of law. Most significantly, peace-maintenance law and order requires a criminal code. This is already taking shape at the functional level. Amnesty International, for instance, has listed a number of non-treaty UN documents to be incorporated into peace agreements that outline generally accepted human rights standards in codes, principles and procedures for law and order.[2] An attempt has been made to collate some of these into a single handbook.[3] Human rights field manuals are appearing.[4] Also, Mark Plunkett, the former Special Prosecutor in Cambodia, has worked extensively on creating 'justice packages' for peace operations that include critical ingredients for re-establishing law and order in peace-maintenance.[5]

In spite of the considerable number of guidelines, widely regarded as authoritative by human rights organizations and experts, there is still the perception in national ministries of defence and foreign affairs that such a generally applicable rule of law and order in peace operations is far-fetched. However, in the overall evolution of international political authority, there is already the existence of a criminal code that is one of the most sacrosanct parts of international order. These 'international criminal laws' are obligations without permissible exceptions between all states and individuals, and the international community as a whole. Their collective nature is regarded as comprehensively applicable, and cannot be qualified by claims of jurisdictional immunity. As such, they constitute a code of behaviour for any individual or institution, whether they belong to a local population, a UN civilian component or military contingent, or the highest levels of sovereign government. In this manner, the universality of international criminal law provides an overarching framework for the rules of peace-maintenance law and order, and indicates that a basis exists for a collective disciplinary system.

There tend to be two parts to international criminal law: the content of the prohibition and some provisions for countering violations. During the unmanaged changes that have occurred in the 1990s, the full complement of international crimes seem to have burst forth in their fullest form since the end of the Second World War. Crimes against peace, crimes against humanity and war crimes are as virulent now as the instances were that helped define the scope of the law in the first place – leading also to another category of crimes against the United Nations.

The Gulf War was precipitated by an act of aggression. Rabat's unlawful occupation by the use of force continues in Western Sahara, as does Jakarta's in East Timor and Beijing's in Tibet. And force has been used by newly independent republics or break-away 'principalities' in the former Yugoslavia and Russia's Near Abroad to alter or create territorial boundaries.

Genocide has stocked new killing fields in Bosnia and Rwanda. The principles of apartheid have been applied in various ways by Belgrade, Zagreb and Sarajevo, and appeared to be the logic of the 1995 Dayton Accords. And Srpska was a kind of self-manufactured Bantustan. The practice of torture is widespread, as a government policy or the habit of corner bullies, in Moroccan-controlled Western Sahara, the former Yugoslavia and in the Middle East, for instance. Slavery is once again identifiable, not least in the form of forced prostitution in Bosnia. The pulse and tempo of all of these crimes are dictated by ideologies of discrimination.

Grave breaches of humanitarian laws of war have been committed by local forces in the former Yugoslavia and by the UN in Somalia. And for their part, UN troops have been taken hostage in Cambodia and Bosnia, and massacred in Mogadishu.

The means of countering international crimes have not kept pace with their identification and clarification. Certainly, peace-maintenance can provide an opportunity to help enforce such laws and prevent the worst excesses of human beings. But the mandate to do so, in a transitional rule of law and order, can be found in the international rules of criminal law themselves. By holding individuals criminally responsible, separate from the corporate entities with which they are associated – whether it be a sovereign state, an armed faction or unrecognized civilian organization – international criminal law binds local and internationally deployed officials and private persons equally, according to a single standard. This erases the divide between the indigenous population and a peace-maintenance authority, and subordinates both to common rules of law.

INDIVIDUAL CRIMINALITY

An 'international crime' is a violation of an obligation to the 'international community as a whole'. Article 19(2) of the International Law Commission (ILC) Draft Articles on State Responsibility (1996) defines an international crime as, 'An internationally wrongful act which results from the breach by a State of an international obligation so essential for the protection of fundamental interests of the international community that its breach is recognized as a crime by the community as a whole'. However, this would not render a state criminal in the manner that an individual would be criminal under municipal law. It only identifies a category of delicts, separate from other wrongs, which 'are serious enough as to warrant *collective* sanctions'.[6] The injuries suffered as a consequence of an international crime are suffered by the international community as a whole.

International crimes are linked to the concepts of *jus cogens* and international obligations *erga omnes*. Article 53 of the Vienna Convention on the Law of Treaties (1969) refers to a norm of *jus cogens* as

> a peremptory norm of general international law…accepted and recognized by the international community of States as a whole as a norm from which no derogation is permitted and which can be modified only by a subsequent norm of general international law having the same character.

Article 53 does not specify the content of the norms, but distinguishes them from others as no derogation is permitted. While the scope of the content of international crimes and norms of *jus cogens* may overlap and it may be difficult to distinguish between them precisely, the two are not equivalent. They are both, however, categories of obligations *erga omnes*, or obligations of states towards all other states and the international community as a whole.[7]

An 'international crime' can be distinguished from a 'crime under international law', which, while possibly similar in content, is committed by individuals and not states and is comparable to the sense of 'crime' as it is understood in municipal law. The ILC Draft Code of Crimes Against the Peace and Security of Mankind (hereafter referred to as the 'Draft Code') is an attempt to codify this area of law.[8] In 1947 the UN General Assembly (UNGA) requested the ILC to prepare a Draft Code based on the Nuremberg Principles.[9] The ILC submitted this to the Assembly in 1954, but its consideration was postponed until a definition of aggression could be formulated. A resolution was finally accepted in 1974.[10] And in 1982, the ILC resuscitated its development of the Draft Code. This was completed at the Commission's 43rd session (29 April–19 July 1991) and was presented to governments of UN member states for comments, which were due on 1 January 1993. It began a second reading during its productive 46th session (2 May–22 July 1994) and delivered its thirteenth report on the Draft Code the following year (2 May–21 July 1995). In 1996, the ILC adopted a finalized Draft Code of 20 Articles, which it presented to the 51st General Assembly.[11] Disagreement between states focused on the definition and scope of the crimes to be listed. The future of the Draft Code now may be linked to the conclusion of a convention for an International Criminal Court (ICC).[12]

While the concept of 'international peace and security' embodied in the UN Charter tended to be interpreted as pertaining to peaceful relations between states, 'peace and security of mankind' as envisioned in the Draft Code is applicable to individuals and private groups. Article 2 imputes responsibility, and Article 3 liability to punishment, to individuals who commit the crimes defined in the Code. Does this mean *any* individual? It had been argued that the Draft Code should apply only to individuals acting as organs or agents on behalf of states, because such crimes as genocide and apartheid can be committed only by states.[13] Unofficial perpetrators of 'ethnic cleansing' in the former Yugoslavia and Rwanda proved this view fallacious. In fact, personal motive is one characteristic of criminality in Article II of the Convention on the Prevention and Punishment of the Crime of Genocide (1948). The inapplicability of the Draft Code to private individuals, and the preservation of a distinction between public and private acts, would have weakened obligations arising from the nature of the act. It would have led to the absurdity that individuals could argue in their defence that they acted in their personal capacity and were therefore not liable under the Code. The ILC now distinguishes only aggression from the other crimes enumerated as peculiarly committed by state officials. This affirms, therefore, private responsibility for all other criminal categories in the Draft Code.

As such, determining guilt can be problematic. Identifying responsibility for acts and those liable to prosecution at Nuremberg raised several questions which have yet to be adequately answered according to some kind of reliable international criminology. How comprehensive can the list of guilty individuals be? In a place like Cambodia, where the structure and administration of auto-genocide were so pervasive throughout the country, how many of the civilian population can be regarded as having participated in the process and be held liable for prosecution? The Nuremberg Tribunal charged criminal organizations, including the Gestapo, the SS (*Schutzstaffel*), and the SA (*Sturmabteilung*). Under Article 10 of the Charter of the International Military Tribunal (IMT), membership alone was basis for prosecution. But was this distinction viable, for in the end not all members were or could be prosecuted? Can the doctrine of collective guilt be extended to an entire population in the event that civilians provide encouragement and material support for the crimes in question? One of the US prosecutors at Nuremberg, Telford Taylor, concluded that 'the task of selecting the defendants was hastily and negligently discharged, mainly because no guiding principle of selection had been agreed on'.[14]

The Draft Code provides significant guidance but is not entirely conclusive with regards to the extent of liability. Article 2(3) considers an individual responsible for a crime against the peace and security of mankind who:

a   intentionally commits such a crime;
b   orders the commission of such a crime which in fact occurs or is attempted;
c   fails to prevent or repress the commission of such a crime in the circumstances set out in Article 6 [on responsibility of the superior];
d   knowingly aids, abets or otherwise assists, directly and substantially, in the commission of such a crime, including providing the means for its commission;
e   directly participates in planning or conspiring to commit such a crime which in fact occurs;
f   directly and publicly incites another individual to commit such a crime which in fact occurs; or
g   attempts to commit such a crime by taking action commencing the execution of a crime which does not in fact occur because of circumstances independent of his intentions.

However, these categories may be difficult to distinguish. It may not be clear in an organization who is making decisions.[15] And how 'direct' does the incitement to commit the crime have to be for the act to be considered participation and the individual liable to prosecution?[16] In particular, while the acts of commission are set out, the extent of individual responsibility for acts of omission seems to be a matter of judgement.[17] Certainly, the current Draft Code has widened the scope of individual responsibility in comparison to its earlier versions, but acts of omission are still easier to ascertain in the context of bureaucratic hierarchies than with regard to private individuals or organizations.

The question turns critically on the coverage of subparagraph (c), which clearly pertains to acts of omission on the part of a superior. In the ILC's commentary on Article 6, a 'superior' is understood to be a military commander or civilian authority in a position of responsibility and able to exercise control over subordinates. The provision is not drafted to apply exclusively to a state bureaucracy, and therefore could apply to a non-state, armed organization, such as the military arm of a national liberation movement, or the kinds of groups functioning in the former Yugoslavia and Rwanda. Similarly, it ought to be applicable to a civilian responsible for a non-governmental organization or the operations of a private corporation, in the manner that it covers an official of a non-recognized state, such as Srpska. There is also the militarized non-governmental organization, like Executive Outcomes, that would fall into this category. The distinguishing feature of Article 6 is its applicability to an organized structure, and not necessarily to a public as opposed to private organization.

The Draft Code mitigates somewhat the lack of clarity by restricting defensible arguments: a crime committed 'pursuant to an order of a Government or a superior' does not relieve the individual of criminal responsibility (Article 5); 'The fact that a crime...was committed by a subordinate does not relieve his superiors of criminal responsibility...if they did not take all necessary measures within their power to prevent or repress the crime' (Article 6); and 'The official position of an individual...even if he acted as head of State or Government, does not relieve him of criminal responsibility' (Article 7).[18] It also enumerates the acts which constitute each crime (Articles 16–20). Furthermore, the ILC considered admissible defences under Article 14, such as self-defence, duress or coercion, and military necessity. While accepting some and rejecting others, a clear line is not drawn, leaving the final decision to a competent court – whether eventually the ICC, an ad hoc Tribunal, as for the former Yugoslavia or Rwanda, or a judicial body established within a peace-maintenance framework.

Article 6 of the Nuremberg Charter, which established the scope of jurisdiction for the IMT, distinguished between three categories of crimes for which there is individual responsibility: crimes against peace, crimes against humanity and war crimes. The ILC further listed the individual crimes that could fit under these broad categories: aggression; threats of aggression; intervention; colonial domination and other forms of alien domination; genocide; apartheid; systematic or mass violations of human rights; exceptionally serious war crimes; recruitment, use, financing and training of mercenaries; international terrorism; illicit traffic in narcotic drugs; and wilful and severe damage to the environment.[19] At the end of its 47th session in 1995, the ILC reduced the list to six 'core crimes': aggression; genocide; crimes against humanity; war crimes; international terrorism; and illicit traffic in narcotic drugs. The final text further narrowed this to include only: aggression; genocide; crimes against humanity; crimes against United Nations and associated personnel; and war crimes.

However, the more general Nuremberg categories – as modified by the addition of crimes against the UN – are used in this chapter for the sake of convenience and are intended to be illustrative, not exhaustive, because they each share similar characteristics. Also, they correspond generally to the changes over time in the Draft Code and to the related conventions that evolved between 1945 and 1996. The conventions applicable in each context vary in their consideration of individual responsibility and in the national and collective means they call for to counter international criminal behaviour. Together, these constitute the jurisdictional scope of peace-maintenance rules of law.

CRIMES AGAINST PEACE

Article 6(a) of the Nuremberg Charter referred to 'crimes against peace' as the 'planning, preparation, initiation or waging of a war of aggression, or a war in violation of international treaties, agreements or assurances, or participation in a common plan or conspiracy for the accomplishment of any of the foregoing'. This was a departure from the past as the first articulation of individual responsibility for 'crimes against peace'. Broadly stated as it was, 'if it had been given maximum possible effect, the Charter could have been used to indict a large portion of the entire German population since it participated, however slightly, in a common plan or conspiracy for the accomplishment' of such crimes.[20]

While the laws were applied retroactively – perhaps on questionable grounds[21] – they nevertheless found support in later sources. In 1946, the General Assembly affirmed 'the principles of international law as recognized by the Charter of the Nuremberg Tribunal and the judgement of the Tribunal'.[22] Article 2(4) of the UN Charter prohibits 'the threat or use of force against the territorial integrity or political independence of any state, or in any other manner inconsistent with the Purposes of the United Nations'. Chapter VII of the UN Charter provides for the identification of and responses to threats to the peace and acts of aggression, including in Article 51 the customary right of individual or collective self-defence if an armed attack occurs. UNGA Resolution 2131 (XX) of 21 December 1965, the Declaration on the Inadmissibility of the Intervention in the Domestic Affairs of States and the Protection of their Independence and Sovereignty, regards as inadmissible foreign state intervention in the affairs of other states. UNGA Resolution 2625 (XXV) of 24 October 1970, the Declaration on Principles of International Law Concerning Friendly Relations and Cooperation among States in Accordance with the Charter of the United Nations, considers that: 'A war of aggression constitutes a crime against the peace for which there is responsibility under international law.' Article 5(2) of the UNGA Definition of Aggression affirms that: 'A war of aggression is a crime against international peace. Aggression gives rise to international responsibility.'

The Draft Code identifies the crime of aggression in the inter-state context. Article 16 states that: 'An individual who, as leader or organizer, actively participates in or orders the planning, preparation, initiation or waging of aggression committed by a State shall be responsible for a crime of aggression.' In earlier versions, the Draft Code also listed the threat of aggression and intervention, and enumerated the same acts which constitute aggression in Article 3 of the UNGA Definition:

a   the invasion or attack by the armed forces of a State of the territory of another State, or any military occupation, however temporary, resulting from such invasion or attack, or any annexation by the use of force of the territory of another State or part thereof;

b   bombardment by the armed forces of a State against the territory of another State or the use of any weapons by a State against the territory of another State;

c   the blockade of the ports or coasts of a State by the armed forces of another State;

d   an attack by the armed forces of a State on the land, sea or air forces, or marine and air fleets of another State;

e   the use of armed forces of one State which are within the territory of another State with the agreement of the receiving State, in contravention of the conditions provided for in the agreement, or any extension of their presence in such territory beyond the termination of the agreement;

f   the action of a State in allowing its territory, which it has placed at the disposal of another State, to be used by that other State for perpetrating an act of aggression against a third State;

g   the sending by or on behalf of a State of armed bandits, groups, irregulars or mercenaries, which carry out acts of armed force against another State of such gravity as to amount to the acts listed above, or its substantial involvement therein;

h   any other acts determined by the Security Council as constituting acts of aggression under the provisions of the Charter.

Given the powers of determination by the Security Council of other acts and according to Article 4 of the UNGA Definition, this list is not intended to be exhaustive.

Countering aggression

The United Nations Charter contains in Chapter VII the principal provisions for countering aggression, but it focuses on the act, not the actor. It is concerned with mitigating the effects of aggression and restoring the *status quo ante*, not with punishing the aggressor. This is inherited from the theory of collective security, which aims at maintaining and restoring peace and order and suppressing the crime, not the criminal. The use of force to punish a state, or reprisals, is impermissible under international law. D.W. Bowett states: 'Few propositions about international law have enjoyed more support than the proposition that, under the Charter of the United Nations, the use of force by way of reprisals is illegal.'[23] The prohibition against reprisals is intended to avoid unilateral enforcement of international law, which can blur the distinction between prosecution of the law and persecution of another state, politically justified on legal bases. However, it does not exclude any state from its domestic prosecution and punishment of individuals under international criminal law. Although limited to state officials, the ILC, in its commentary on individual responsibility under Article 2, explicitly distinguished between acts of commission and omission, and found culpability for the personal failure to prevent the act of aggression. The broad provisions of the UN Charter do not make such a distinction, designed as they were for whole state actions.

Chapter VII envisages an escalating response to aggression. The power of the Security Council under Article 39 to 'determine the existence of any threat to the peace, breach of the peace, or act of aggression' may, by identifying an aggressor, act as a condemnation. It may be used as a sanction in this manner, as an end in and of itself. But the context surrounding Article 39 renders it principally a means to an end: identifying an act of aggression warrants further action. This may mean making 'recommendations' for further action, deciding 'what measures shall be taken in accordance' with other Articles of the Chapter, or moving to action based on other Articles. Given the importance of determining aggression as a starting point for action, legal instruments concerning aggression since the signing of the Charter have focused on definition. Article 40 'provisional measures' aim at preserving the altered status quo 'In order to prevent an aggravation of the situation'. Article 41 'measures not involving the use of armed force' and Article 42 'action by air, sea, or land forces as may be necessary' aim to restore the *status quo ante*. Retribution is not one of the functions of these provisions.

The context of internal conflicts may have qualified somewhat the conceptions of inter-state aggression, but its character is little different from crimes against peace and their threat to the international community. Consequently, the UN Charter has provided a legal basis for collective action against individuals responsible for aggression, including the securing of their custody, their detention, and prosecution and punishment. This interpretation poses a series of legal and practical problems, including uses of force and the circumstances when action can be viable, which are considered in the next chapter. Above all, such action requires no less than a court of law, a standard by which to judge the extent of individual culpability.

CRIMES AGAINST HUMANITY

Article 6(c) of the Nuremberg Charter referred to 'crimes against humanity' as 'murder, extermination, enslavement, deportation, and other inhuman acts committed against any civilian population before or during the war;[24] or persecutions on political, racial or religious grounds in execution of or in connection with any crime within the jurisdiction of the Tribunal, whether or not in violation of the domestic law of the country where perpetrated'.

The concept of crimes against humanity predates the Nuremberg trials. The Hague Conventions of 1899 and 1907, No. II and No. IV respectively, refer to the 'laws of humanity' but do not elaborate on their content. They were understood to refer to war crimes, perpetrated by states against soldiers who were foreign nationals. The crimes perpetrated by Germany against its own civilian population led to the argument that a category of crimes separate from war crimes, for which individual responsibility could be attributed, was required. However, the Nuremberg Tribunal did not interpret 'crimes against humanity' to be perpetrated during peacetime. They were confined to acts committed during wartime.

Crimes against humanity have since been expanded. The so-called 'International Bill of Rights' provided a foundation for this. It is comprised of the Universal Declaration of Human Rights (1948), the International Covenant on Economic, Social and Cultural Rights (1966), the International Covenant on Civil and Political Rights (1966) and its Optional Protocol (1966). These led to the elaboration through multilateral treaties of such crimes as genocide, apartheid, torture, slavery and discrimination.

Genocide

Genocide is defined by Article II of the Genocide Convention[25] and Article 17 of the Draft Code as 'any of the following acts committed with intent to destroy, in whole or in part, a national, ethnic, racial or religious group, as such':

a   killing members of the group;
b   causing serious bodily or mental harm to members of the group;
c   deliberately inflicting on the group conditions of life calculated to bring about its physical destruction in whole or in part;
d   imposing measures intended to prevent births within the group; or
e   forcibly transferring children of the group to another group.

This list is meant to be exhaustive. While it includes physical or biological destruction, it does not include altering the identity of a group linguistically, religiously or culturally – so-called 'cultural genocide'. The defining feature of genocide is not successful destruction of a group but the *intent* to destroy a group as such. Article III of the Convention regards as punishable acts, in addition to genocide, conspiracy to commit genocide, direct and public incitement to commit genocide, attempt to commit genocide and complicity to commit genocide. A problem arises with regard to defining a national, ethnic, racial or religious group, as their meanings are not clear under international law.[26]

Unlike the Nuremberg interpretation, Article I of the Convention affirms that genocide is a crime under international law 'whether committed in time of peace or in time of war', and Article IV imputes responsibility to individuals. The ICJ has observed that the Convention is not an ordinary treaty; it imports special kinds of obligations. States Parties to treaties are usually permitted reservations to the terms that they have accepted. While still permissible, even in the absence of a reservation clause explicitly stating so, the right is severely restricted under the Genocide Convention. According to the Court[27] this is because the principles enshrined in the Convention are binding regardless of the Convention and because of the universal character of the condemnation of genocide and the cooperation required to counter it. The Convention has been widely accepted and genocide is considered an obligation *erga omnes*[28] and as part of *jus cogens* it is a peremptory norm of international law.

Countering genocide

The Genocide Convention envisages both domestic and collective implementation. Article VI states that

> Persons charged with genocide...shall be tried by a competent tribunal of the State in the territory of which the act was committed, or by such international penal tribunal as may have jurisdiction with respect to those Contracting Parties which shall have accepted its jurisdiction.

In the absence of a standing or existing ad hoc tribunal, reliance is placed on the state whose territory was the location of the crime. This may not be practical if the violator still wields governmental authority or leads an opposing faction with effective control of parts of the country. In the first instance there would be an unwillingness to prosecute, and in the second a ruling regime in conflict with the faction may not be able to apprehend the well-protected offender. Also, if the offender flees to another country, there is no obligation to extradite under the Convention, except that under Article VII extradition cannot be refused on the basis that the offence was a political crime and therefore non-justiciable.

Nevertheless, the Convention obliges states to punish guilty persons. Article IV states that: 'Persons committing genocide...shall be punished, whether they are constitutionally responsible rulers, public officials, or private individuals.' The word 'shall' reflects the obligatory character of this provision. Similarly, under Article V, Contracting Parties 'undertake to enact...necessary legislation to give effect to the provisions of the present Convention and, in particular, to provide effective penalties for persons guilty of genocide'.

The preamble to the Convention emphasizes the need for 'international cooperation' to 'liberate mankind from such an odious scourge'. Article VIII provides for collective action authorizing Contracting Parties to 'call upon the competent organs of the United Nations to take such action under the Charter of the United Nations as they consider appropriate for the prevention and suppression of acts of genocide'. Given the general terms of this provision and the wide latitude afforded the UN, it is not clear whether Article VIII obliges the UN to act. Given the nature of the obligation arising under the law concerning genocide generally, however, it is unlikely that the UN would not be bound to act. Furthermore, Article IX authorizes Contracting Parties to submit to the ICJ disputes 'relating to the interpretation, application, or fulfilment' of the Convention.[29] Unfortunately, despite attempts,[30] the Convention has rarely been used to prevent, suppress or prosecute the crime of genocide – such as the current case before the ICJ of *Bosnia and Herzegovina v. Yugoslavia (Serbia and Montenegro)* that is pending an outcome.[31]

Apartheid

Apartheid is defined by Article II of the International Convention of the Suppression and Punishment of the Crime of *Apartheid* (1973)[32] as

> any of the following acts based on policies and practices of racial segregation and discrimination committed for the purpose of establishing or maintaining domination by one racial group over any other racial group and systematically oppressing it:

a   denial to a member or members of a racial group of the right to life and liberty of person;

b   deliberate imposition on a racial group of living conditions calculated to cause its physical destruction in whole or in part;

c   any legislative measures and other measures calculated to prevent a racial group from participating in the political, social, economic and cultural life of the country and the deliberate creation of conditions preventing the full development of such a group;

d   any measures, including legislative measures, designed to divide the population along racial lines, in particular by the creation of separate reserves and ghettos for the members of a racial group, the prohibition of marriages among members of various racial groups or the expropriation of landed property belonging to a racial group or to members thereof;

e   exploitation of the labour of the members of a racial group, in particular by submitting them to forced labour; or

f   persecution of organizations and persons, by depriving them of fundamental rights and freedoms, because they oppose *apartheid*.

While the Convention criminalizes the former policies of South Africa, it is not meant to be restricted to that case. Its general terms are applicable to situations other than apartheid but that fall within the scope of its provisions. The Convention has been accepted by the majority of UN members, although excluding many Western states of Europe and North America, and the crime is considered serious enough to warrant special condemnation.

An earlier version of the Draft Code referred to leaders or organizers who commit or order the commission of the crime of apartheid, and one theory argued that only state authorities by virtue of their position could be guilty. Explicit reference to apartheid has since been removed, and a broad provision included as subparagraph (f) under the general rubric of crimes against humanity in Article 18, which holds not only governments, but any organization or group, responsible. The Convention, on the other hand, imposes individual responsibility perhaps too broadly, in the manner of the Nuremberg Charter. Article III imputes international criminal responsibility to individuals, members of organizations, institutions and state representatives whenever they commit, participate in, directly incite, abet, encourage or cooperate in the commission of the crime of apartheid. This would imply that there is an individual duty to explicitly object to such a regime to avoid responsibility, silence being tacit complicity in the crime. Given the pervasive nature of such a form of social organization in every sphere of activity, it would be difficult to determine who is 'participating' in the crime, who is acquiescing and who is passively resisting. Nevertheless, Article X empowers the UN Commission on Human Rights to prepare an international wanted list of liable individuals, organizations, institutions and state representatives. Also, Article 19(3)(c) of the ILC Draft Articles on State Responsibility holds states criminally responsible for the commission of apartheid.

Countering apartheid

Provisions of the Apartheid Convention are similar to the Genocide Convention with regard to obligations on the part of States Parties, but collective implementation has developed further. Article IV obliges States Parties to undertake to adopt:

> any legislative or other measures necessary to suppress as well as to prevent any encouragement of the crime of *apartheid* and similar segregationist policies or their manifestations and to punish persons guilty of that crime [and] any legislative, judicial and administrative measures to prosecute, bring to trial and punish in accordance with their jurisdiction persons responsible for, or accused of, the acts defined in Article II of the present Convention, whether or not such persons reside in the territory of the State in which the acts are committed or are nationals of that State or of some other State or are stateless persons.

Article V states that accused persons may be tried by a competent tribunal of any State Party which may acquire jurisdiction over the accused or by an international tribunal as may have jurisdiction. Article XI invalidates political offence exceptions contained in extradition agreements.

While jurisdiction in the Genocide Convention is based on the territory where the crime was committed, Article VI of the *Apartheid* Convention envisages universal jurisdiction based on the custody of the offender. Also, there was an attempt by the UN in 1980 to establish the international tribunal referred to in the Convention. A Statute for the court was opened for signature on 19 January 1981, but has received limited support and not come into force.[33] Consequently, states are left as the principal enforcers of the Convention.

Nevertheless, States Parties are obliged by Article VI 'to cooperate in the implementation of decisions adopted by other competent organs of the United Nations with a view to achieving the purposes of the Convention'. Additionally, Article VIII authorizes States Parties 'to call upon any competent organ of the UN to take such action under the UN Charter as it considers appropriate for the prevention and suppression of *apartheid*'. Articles IX and X authorize the UN

Commission on Human Rights to consider periodic reports submitted by States Parties on legislative, judicial, administrative or other measures adopted to give effect to provisions of the Convention. The 46th General Assembly called upon the Commission to intensify its efforts to identify lists of individuals, organizations and representatives of states who are responsible for crimes under the Convention, as well as those against whom legal proceedings have been undertaken.[34] Article XII authorizes states to submit disputes regarding the interpretation, application or implementation of the Convention to the ICJ, but unlike the Genocide Convention requires all, not 'any', parties to do so.

In southern Africa, prosecution of violations of the crime of apartheid has been overshadowed by other events. In South Africa, an all-white referendum on 18 March 1992 voted, with an 85 per cent turnout, two to one in favour of dismantling apartheid. Apartheid laws have been repealed, but a troubled and violent transition to democratic rule and the fragile Convention for a Democratic South Africa (CODESA)[35] arrangement eclipsed notions of apartheid trials. Instead, a Truth and Reconciliation Commission was established as a means of social, if not judicial, redress.[36] In Namibia, apartheid laws were repealed in the early 1980s, although the practice of apartheid was not prohibited until independence in March 1990. Since then, the struggles of a new nation coupled with the departure to South Africa of many individuals responsible for the dictation or enforcement of apartheid have not led to trials there either.

Torture

Torture is prohibited by a number of human rights instruments.[37] It is referred to in Article 18(c) of the Draft Code and defined in Article 1 of the UN Convention against Torture and Other Cruel, Inhuman or Degrading Treatment or Punishment (1984)[38] as:

> any act by which severe pain and suffering, whether physical or mental, is intentionally inflicted on a person for such purposes as obtaining from him or a third person information or a confession, punishing him for an act he or a third person has committed or is suspected of having committed, or intimidating or coercing him or a third person, or for any reason based on discrimination of any kind, when such pain or suffering is inflicted by or at the instigation of or with the consent or acquiescence of a public official or other person acting in an official capacity. It does not include pain or suffering arising only from, inherent in or incidental to lawful sanctions.

Unlike other human rights instruments, Article 2(3) of the UN Torture Convention binds individuals and not only states. The Draft Code now extends this individual responsibility beyond an official governmental capacity to members of private organizations or groups.

Despite its continued wide practice,[39] the rule against torture is considered non-derogable. The legislation and constitutions of most countries include guarantees against torture. The ICJ considers basic human rights as obligations *erga omnes*[40] and the prohibition against torture is becoming a part of *jus cogens*.

Countering torture

Under the Torture Convention, obligations of States Parties are more extensive and collective implementation mechanisms better developed than in both the Genocide and *Apartheid* Conventions. Article 2 obliges States Parties to take 'effective legislative, administrative, judicial or other measures to prevent acts of torture in any territory under its jurisdiction'. Torture must be punishable under domestic criminal law with appropriate penalties which consider the seriousness of the crime. Unlike many human rights instruments, according to Article 2(2) exceptional circumstances, such as a state of emergency, cannot be used to justify torture.[41] Article 7 obliges States Parties to prosecute torturers and Article 5 obliges a state to establish jurisdiction over acts when: committed on its territory; on board a ship or aircraft registered in that state; or when the offender is present within its territory. Article 8 categorizes torture as an extraditable offence – obligatory if a state does not prosecute – and Article 8(2) provides that in the absence of an extradition treaty in force between States Parties, the Torture Convention may be considered a legal basis for extradition.

Unlike the Genocide and *Apartheid* Conventions, and similar to the principal human rights treaties,[42] the Torture Convention has an independent supervisory committee composed of expert members who monitor compliance with its provisions, the Committee against Torture (CAT).[43] States Parties to the Convention may recognize the competence of the Committee on an optional basis to receive inter-state complaints in cases where both states are parties to the Convention. Article 21 empowers the Committee to consider the complaint. Under Article 22, States Parties may recognize the competence of the Committee to receive communications from, or on behalf of, individuals subject to its jurisdiction claiming to be victims of violations of obligations specified in the Convention. Reports on compliance with the Convention are reviewed by the Committee in public session. The Torture Committee is considered a useful model for supervising international criminal prosecution and ensuring compliance with the Convention because of the standing it gives to individuals in an international forum and the strength of its optional procedures.

Another supervisory mechanism is the Special Rapporteur (SR) on Torture, a 'special procedure' of the Commission on Human Rights. The SR takes action on emergency reports of torture cases and examines the current situation and prevention of torture in countries, visiting some by request. The SR intervenes in an attempt to stop instances of torture and asks governments to respond to allegations. Visits are considered by the SR to be 'consultative' and 'preventative', not 'accusatory' or 'investigative'. The Rapporteur's annual report publishes details of individual cases, correspondence with responsible countries and recommendations made to specific governments or generally to diminish the practice of torture.

When renewal of the SR's mandate was reviewed at the 1991 session of the UN Economic and Social Council (ECOSOC), it came under attack. In response, Japan's Deputy Ambassador to the UN stated: 'Of all the means at the disposal of the Commission, the Special Rapporteur approach was one of the most effective, and his [the Special Rapporteur's Torture] report showed that he could display creativity and imagination in his recommendations without going to extremes.'[44]

The European Convention for the Prevention of Torture and Inhuman or Degrading Treatment or Punishment (1987) has its own, more far-reaching, supervisory mechanism. Article 1 establishes a European Committee for the Prevention of Torture and Inhuman or Degrading Treatment or Punishment, which is authorized by States Parties under Article 2 to visit any place of detention. Article 8 obliges states to provide a visiting Committee access to places of detention or other places where persons are deprived of their liberty, and any other information required by the Committee. Under Article 9 parties may make representations to the Committee against a visit on such grounds as national defence or public safety. The Committee may take follow-up action including reporting and making public statements on the case.

Slavery

Slavery has been outlawed since 1815 when the Congress of Vienna sought means to suppress it.[45] Article 1(1) of the International Slavery Convention (1926)[46] defines slavery as 'the status or condition of a person over whom any or all of the powers attaching to the right of ownership are exercised'. This was extended by the Supplementary Convention on the Abolition of Slavery, the Slave Trade, and Institutions and Practices Similar to Slavery (1956)[47] which abolished institutions and practices similar to slavery, including debt bondage, serfdom, the promise or gift of a woman in marriage without her consent in exchange for payment, liability of a woman to be inherited upon the death of her husband to another person, and various types of exploitation of child labour.

The International Labour Organization (ILO) has adopted two comparable conventions. The 1930 Forced Labour Convention (No. 29) defined 'forced labour' as all work or service 'exacted from any person under the menace of any penalty and for which the said person has not offered himself voluntarily'. The ILO's Abolition of Forced Labour Convention (No. 105) adopted in 1957 obliged members to suppress and not to make use of any forms of forced or compulsory labour as a means of political coercion, discipline or punishment for having participated in strikes, or to mobilize labour for purposes of economic development, or as a means of racial, social, national or religious discrimination. Both conventions now have been ratified by the majority of states.

The prohibition on slavery has a non-derogable status. The ICJ considers it a part of *jus cogens* and stated that it is among the rights of such importance that

'all states can be held to have a legal interest in their protection; they are obligations *erga omnes*'.[48] Slavery is regarded as criminal and its prohibition has been
reiterated in a number of international human rights instruments.[49] Individuals
are punishable under Article 6(1) of the 1956 Supplementary Convention.

Countering slavery

The practice of slavery is set apart from the other crimes of international law
with regard to the scene of the crime and the nature of the offender. Slave-
trading was and continues to be perpetrated on the high seas and on aircraft in
neutral airspace. Also, even after states were committed not to undertake slavery,
private individuals continued the practice of capturing, transporting and
supplying persons for the purpose of slavery. Therefore, there was special need
for cooperation to detect and punish slave-traders operating outside the jurisdiction of any state. Originally, universal jurisdiction was applicable to piracy and
slavery, because of the gravity of the crimes and the non-location of the acts,
and this gave states wide powers to suppress and punish offenders. Article 2 of
the Slavery Convention obliges states to 'prevent and suppress the slave trade
and to bring about…the complete abolition of slavery in all its forms'. Article 3
obliges parties 'to undertake to adopt all appropriate measures with a view to
preventing and suppressing the embarkation, disembarkation and transport of
slaves in their territorial waters and upon all vessels flying their respective flags'.
Under the Supplementary Convention, slavery must be a criminal offence under
the laws of a State Party, and there is an obligation to take effective measures to
prevent and punish persons guilty of the practice.

Cooperative approaches are emphasized by the Supplementary Convention
and the ILO Forced Labour Conventions. Article V of the former obliges states
to cooperate with each other and the UN to implement the Convention, and
imposes a duty on parties to communicate to the UN Secretary-General copies
of laws, regulations and administrative measures enacted to do so. Article 8(3)
authorizes the Secretary-General to disclose information from communications
received to other parties and ECOSOC for the purposes of documentation,
discussion or recommendation. Similarly the ILO generally requires states which
have ratified a convention to report on its law and practice in implementing
international labour standards. Under Article 19(5)(e) of its Constitution, the
ILO has requested member states which have ratified the Forced Labour
Conventions to report on their law and practice.

Discrimination

Non-discrimination is logically part of the content of other prohibitions
regarding crimes against humanity, including genocide, apartheid and slavery,
since these are themselves conducted on a discriminatory basis. The Draft
Code once distinguished discrimination separately, although now it is listed as
one among other crimes against humanity in Article 18(e), which refers to

'persecution on political, racial, religious or ethnic grounds' committed 'in a systematic manner or on a mass scale'. Article 1(3) of the UN Charter states one of the purposes of the organization to be the achievement of 'international co-operation in solving international problems of an economic, social, cultural, or humanitarian character, and in promoting and encouraging respect for human rights and fundamental freedoms for all without distinction as to race, sex, language, or religion'.[50]

One of the central principles of the application of human rights is non-discrimination.[51] For instance, Article 2(1) of the UN Declaration on the Elimination of All Forms of Racial Discrimination[52] provides that: 'No state, institution, group or individual shall make any discrimination whatsoever in matters of human rights and fundamental freedoms in the treatment of persons, groups of persons or institutions on the ground of race, colour or ethnic origin.' Under the International Convention on the Elimination of All Forms of Racial Discrimination (1965),[53] Article 5(b) obliges states to

> undertake to prohibit and to eliminate racial discrimination in all its forms and to guarantee the right of everyone, without distinction as to race, colour, or national origin, to equality before the law, notably in the enjoyment of...[t]he right to security of person and protection by the State against violence or bodily harm, whether inflicted by government officials, or by any individual, group or institution.

The centrality of non-discrimination in the UN Charter and the essential role of discrimination in crimes against humanity led the ICJ to categorize non-discrimination as an obligation *erga omnes*.[54]

Countering discrimination

Because of the applicability of the principle of non-discrimination to most crimes and human rights abuses, implementation mechanisms vary between specific types of discrimination. Characteristically, many of the UN bodies focus on acts of governments rather than private individuals. The Racial Discrimination Convention aims to eliminate racial discrimination rather than to prosecute and punish offenders. To prohibit and eliminate racial discrimination, Article 6 obliges States Parties to provide effective protection, remedies and competent enforcement through national tribunals and other state institutions. Article 8 establishes a supervisory mechanism like the CAT, the Committee on the Elimination of Racial Discrimination (CERD). It may receive communications alleging violations against a State Party which has recognized the competence of the Committee to do so.

Similarly, the Committee on the Elimination of Discrimination against Women (CEDAW) receives reports from States Parties and monitors the implementation of the UN Convention on the Elimination of All Forms of Discrimination against Women (1979). The Convention, adopted three years into the UN Decade for Women (1976–85), obliges states to meet the standards it sets for conditions under which women live and work. CEDAW focused on violence against women, a matter not explicitly addressed in the Convention, following a recommendation in 1991 of the ECOSOC Commission on the Status of Women (CSW) to draft an international legal instrument on the subject. The use of mass rape as a weapon of war in the Yugoslav crisis highlights the dimensions of the problem and separates it from other categories of abuse.[55]

The Special Rapporteur on Religious Intolerance is another 'special procedure', like the SR on Torture, of the Commission on Human Rights. The Rapporteur monitors implementation of the Declaration on the Elimination of All Forms of Intolerance and Discrimination based on Religious Beliefs (1981) and reports on particular country situations. A systematic inquiry is sent to governments in the form of a questionnaire regarding: distinctions in national legislation concerning religious groups, treatment of believers and non-believers, and measures that might protect religious minorities; reciprocity for foreigners, conscientious objection, clashes between religious groups; and action against expression of 'extremist or fanatical' opinion relating to religious groups, as well as remedies and conciliation mechanisms. Although many governments respond at a higher rate than to enquiries by other Special Rapporteurs, their replies are too brief to be illuminating. The SR does not generally comment on replies nor offer country-specific recommendations for alleviating infringements, though he manages to focus attention on problem areas.

The Subcommission on the Prevention of Discrimination and Protection of Minorities operates with its own working groups and rapporteurs on a wide variety of topics. Working groups have covered complaints of gross violations of human rights, contemporary forms of slavery, indigenous populations and detentions. Special studies are conducted by members of the Subcommission, sometimes referred to as 'special rapporteurs' though their function is different to the Commission's SRs. These have focused on discrimination of minorities and peaceful solutions to minority problems. The Subcommission reported annually on banks engaged in business with South Africa as well as on: countries claiming states of emergency; impunity of human rights violators and victims' rights to restitution; freedom of expression; rights to a fair trial; independence of the judiciary; the detention of UN staff members; and various other social and human rights issues.

The work of the Subcommission was strengthened by the adoption of the Declaration on the Rights of Persons Belonging to National or Ethnic, Religious or Linguistic Minorities by the UN General Assembly in December 1992. This calls on states to protect the existence and identity of minorities. It also gives persons belonging to minorities the explicit right to participate effectively in decisions on the national and regional level that concern them.

WAR CRIMES

Article 6(b) of the Nuremberg Charter referred to 'war crimes' as

> violations of the laws or customs of war. Such violations shall include, but
> not be limited to, murder, ill-treatment or deportation to slave labour or for
> any other purpose of civilian population of or in occupied territory, murder
> or ill-treatment of prisoners of war or persons on the seas, killing of
> hostages, plunder of public or private property, wanton destruction of cities,
> towns or villages, or devastation not justified by military necessity.

Humanitarian laws of war date back to ancient times[56] and vary in
approach.[57] Prior to the Nuremberg Charter, only states were considered to be
liable under international law for war crimes, which were understood to be
perpetrated against military personnel, although the Hague Regulations afforded
some indirect protection to civilians under Section III. The Charter expanded
the application and content of the crimes, holding individuals responsible and
including civilians in their scope.

Much of the extensive codification completed at The Hague in 1899 and
1907[58] and Geneva in 1929[59] was incorporated in the four Geneva Conventions
for the Protection of War Victims of 1949.[60] The first three Conventions
substantially expanded the humanitarian law applicable to the sick, wounded,
shipwrecked and captured members of armed forces, and included improved
devices for their implementation and enforcement. The Fourth Convention was
a departure from the past and provided for protection of the civilian population
in the domestic territory of the enemy and occupied territory. Another significant innovation was Article 3 common to all four Conventions, which regulated
the actions of parties to armed conflicts 'not of an international character occurring in the territory of a State Party'. Unfortunately this proved largely
ineffective, not only in the absence of a monitoring device but also because of
the strategic, ideological confrontation during the Cold War in internal conflicts
and the frustration of these provisions by state disagreements over recognition of
non-state belligerents. Nevertheless, the 317 Articles of the four Conventions
comprise the core of the contemporary humanitarian law of war in force and
nearly all states in the international community have accepted them.

The Geneva Conventions have since been reiterated and expanded in other
instruments.[61] In particular, two Protocols additional to the Geneva Conventions
of 1949 were established in 1977. These were necessitated by shifts in the conditions of warfare: technology produced conventional weapons capable of massive
destruction; weapons proliferated as they became more available; inter-state
conflicts were eclipsed by the increased number of internal conflicts and the use
of guerrilla, rather than conventional, warfare; and percentages of civilian casualties increased dramatically. Protocol I imposed the most severe limitations upon
the conduct of hostilities by belligerents and focused extensively on the protection of civilians. Articles 48–60 attempted to limit collateral damage to civilians.

Articles 43–5 extend belligerent and prisoner of war (POW) status to national liberation movements. Protocol II was the first international instrument exclusively concerned with regulating internal conflicts. It retained Article 3 of the 1949 Conventions with all its ambiguities but emphasized protection of civilians in the manner of Protocol I.

While breaches of any of these provisions are considered 'war crimes', the Geneva Conventions identified a more serious category of crimes for which individuals could be held responsible. These so-called 'grave breaches'[62] are probably a part of *jus cogens* given the virtual universal recognition of the Conventions. The Draft Code once chose for its exhaustive list only the most serious 'grave breaches', which it referred to as 'Exceptionally serious war crimes' and enumerated as:

a   acts of inhumanity, cruelty or barbarity directed against the life, dignity or physical or mental integrity of persons [in particular wilful killing, torture, mutilation, biological experiments, taking of hostages, compelling a protected person to serve in the forces of a hostile power, unjustifiable delay in the repatriation of prisoners of war after the cessation of active hostilities, deportation or transfer of the civilian population and collective punishment];

b   establishment of settlers in an occupied territory and changes to the demographic composition of an occupied territory;

c   use of unlawful weapons;

d   employing methods or means of warfare which are intended or may be expected to cause widespread, long-term and severe damage to the natural environment;

e   large-scale destruction of civilian property; and

f   wilful attacks on property of exceptional religious, historical or cultural value.

'Seriousness' in this list was determined by the seriousness of the effects of the violation. It represented a compromise between members of the ILC who favoured a general definition and those who preferred to list all possible war crimes covered by the Article. It was therefore vague in areas – such as the meaning of 'unlawful weapons' – to allow for progressive application. The absence of other war crimes from this list was not to prejudice their applicability under international law outside the Draft Code. In the current text, Article 20 expanded and significantly clarified serious war crimes. It now enumerates a number of acts under such broad headings as: violations of humanitarian law; violations causing death or serious injury to body or health; outrages upon personal dignity; violations of the laws or customs of war; humanitarian violations in non-international armed conflicts; and warfare not justified by military necessity.

Countering war crimes

The Geneva Conventions and Additional Protocols seek to prevent, control or repress violations of humanitarian law.[63] Means of *prevention* take several forms. Basic respect by states in good faith of the provisions of the Convention provide the essential guarantee of compliance. This basic obligation under customary international law and Article 26 of the Vienna Convention on the Law of Treaties (1969), *pacta sunt servanda*, is explicitly stated in Article 1 common to the four Conventions. Parties not only undertake to 'respect' but to 'ensure respect', that is respect by others, for the Convention. Article 80 of Protocol I obliges parties to 'take all necessary measures for the execution' of the Convention. Another motivation for voluntary compliance is reciprocity, the knowledge that the enemy can act in an equally abominable manner.

Other forms of prevention rely on awareness of the provisions of the Convention and training. Each of the four Conventions, in Articles 47–48–127–144 respectively, obliges parties to disseminate the texts of their provisions as widely as possible prior to the outbreak of hostilities. Article 83(1) of Protocol I states:

> The High Contracting Parties undertake, in time of peace as in time of armed conflict, to disseminate the Conventions and the Protocol as widely as possible in their respective countries and, in particular, to include the study thereof in their programmes of military instruction and to encourage the study thereof by the civilian population, so that these instruments may become known to the armed forces and to the civilian population.

Furthermore, Articles 127(2) and 144(2) of the third and fourth Conventions respectively require that the civilian or military authorities who will be responsible for application of the Conventions 'must possess the text of the Convention and be specifically instructed as to its provisions'. This is reiterated in Article 83(2) of Protocol I. Also, military commanders are obliged by Article 87(2) of Protocol I to ensure that members of the armed forces are aware of their obligations.

Contracting Parties are obliged by Article 6(1) of Protocol I 'to train qualified personnel to facilitate the application' of the Convention and Protocols, and Article 82 requires that legal advisers are available to military commanders. To avoid differences of interpretation during wartime, Articles 48, 49, 128 and 145 respectively of the four Conventions and Article 84 of Protocol I require that states translate the instruments if their language is other than one of the official languages of the available texts.[64]

Means of *control* rely either on state implementation or supervisory mechanisms. As mentioned above, Article 1 common to the four Conventions obliges parties not only to 'respect' but to 'ensure respect' for the instruments. Therefore, in the event of breaches by a party's own armed forces, it is obliged, by Articles 49(3), 50(3), 129(3) and 146(3) of the Conventions and Article 85(1) of Protocol

I, to put an end to such violations. This places special obligations on military commanders under Article 87(1 and 3) of Protocol I to suppress, punish and report to competent authorities on breaches of the Conventions and Protocols.

The system of supervision envisioned is the 'Protecting Powers'. A 'Protecting Power' is a 'State instructed by another State (known as the Power of origin) to safeguard its interests and those of its nationals in relation to a third state (known as State of residence)'.[65] The system is supposed to be obligatory under common Article 8–8–8–9 of the Conventions. States are obliged to appoint a Protecting Power, facilitate the tasks of visiting representatives of delegates of Protecting Powers and restrict their activities only in exceptional and temporary circumstances, such as military necessity. However, delegates chosen by the Protecting Power are 'subject to the approval of the Power with which they are to carry out their duties'. Also, Protecting Powers 'shall not in any case exceed their mission', which is only vaguely outlined. States are responsible for designating a substitute, such as the International Committee of the Red Cross (ICRC), in the event that it is not possible to appoint a Protecting Power. Article 5 of Protocol I, which strengthens and expands the obligation to facilitate supervision, also refers to 'any other impartial humanitarian organization'.

In practice, the system of Protecting Powers has not worked as expected. Reliance on states to appoint or accept Protecting Powers has rendered the system inoperative. Appointment of a Power would recognize that a conflict exists or would recognize the other party if it had not been recognized. Open diplomatic channels might render the mechanism unnecessary, or there may not be a party acceptable to both sides. Only the ICRC has acted as a substitute and then only in a quiet and confidential manner. Proposals for an independent, collective monitoring body have not succeeded.

Other supervisory mechanisms are also envisioned. Common Article 52–53–132–145 of the Conventions provides for an enquiry procedure. However, parties must agree on the umpire who will be responsible for determining breaches. This has failed since states, even if they are willing to desist from violations, are unwilling to accept public condemnation of their activities. Article 90 of Protocol I instituted a Fact-Finding Commission which may enquire into any allegation of a grave breach or other serious violation with or without the agreement of the accused party. However, this requires that the party make an express declaration recognizing the competence of the Commission to do so. Also, the conclusions of the Commission cannot be made public without the agreement of the parties concerned, and it may report and recommend to the parties concerned. This procedure has never been tried. It should be noted that the media plays a significant role in the supervision of violations, although it is not included in any provision.

The *repression* of violations by State Parties is obligatory under the system of 'grave breaches'. Under Articles 49, 50, 129 and 146 of the Conventions, states are obliged to try or surrender to another party authors of such breaches. This obligation is absolute and under common Article 51–52–131–148 cannot be altered by agreement between the interested parties. Article 86 of Protocol I considers an act of omission a grave breach. Contracting Parties must incorporate these provisions in their national legislation. Also, states must afford under Article 88(1) of Protocol I mutual assistance in any proceedings relating to such breaches and cooperate under Article 88(2) 'when circumstances permit' in matters of extradition.

In addition to these obligations, Protocol I emphasizes the means of repression. Military commanders are given special responsibility to repress violations of subordinates under Article 87(1–3) and if they fail to do so can be implicated themselves under Article 86(2). Unfortunately, these provisions have not proved effective, perhaps for three reasons:

1   the psychological difficulty, in a wartime atmosphere leading generally to hatred of the enemy, of condemning 'excessive zeal' used against the enemy;
2   the fact that in many cases the authorities themselves are responsible for breaches, of which they are guilty either intentionally or more often because their instruction in international humanitarian law has been neglected, and that the separation of legal and political powers is often seriously compromised in such situations; and,
3   the lack of compulsory jurisdiction and supranational means of coercion whereby States can be forced to respect their engagements.[66]

However, Article 89 of Protocol I states that: 'In situations of serious violations of the Conventions or of this Protocol, the High Contracting Parties undertake to act, jointly or individually, in co-operation with the United Nations and in conformity with the United Nations Charter.' While the terms of this provision are vague, it may provide a starting point for a more effective peace-maintenance mechanism for implementation of humanitarian law.

CRIMES AGAINST THE UNITED NATIONS

A late addition to the Draft Code, only in 1996, was separate Article 19 concerning 'Crimes against United Nations and associated personnel'. This followed the 1994 adoption by the General Assembly of the Convention on the Safety of United Nations and Associated Personnel.[67] According to Article 9 of the Convention, crimes against UN and associated personnel, for which an individual can be punished and which 'shall be made by each State Party a crime under its national law', include 'the international commission of':

a   a murder, kidnapping or other attack upon the person or liberty of any United Nations or associated personnel;
b   a violent attack upon the official premises, the private accommodation or the means of transportation of any United Nations or associated personnel likely to endanger his or her person or liberty;

c   a threat to commit any such attack with the objective of compelling a physical or juridical person to do or to refrain from doing any act;

d   an attempt to commit any such attack; and

e   an act constituting participation as an accomplice in any such attack, or in
an attempt to commit such attack, or in organizing or ordering others to
commit such attack.

The Draft Code defines these crimes more narrowly than the Convention, but
does not prejudice the wider application of Article 9.

The Convention is not understood to codify existing customary law, but
creates a new category of crimes. This has occurred particularly rapidly, in reaction to the widespread violence against UN missions, most dramatically on 5
June 1993, when twenty-four Pakistani troops were dismembered by a local mob
in Mogadishu, for which the international community was poorly equipped to
respond, psychologically, juridically, and functionally. Between 1993 and 1995,
some 450 UN personnel were killed in the line of duty. In 1994, the average rate
of loss was one life every two days. The seriousness of these assaults was considered by the ILC in its commentary on Article 19 when it stated that:

> Attacks against such personnel are in effect directed against the interna-
> tional community and strike at the very heart of the international legal
> system established for the purpose of maintaining international peace and
> security by means of collective security measures taken to prevent and
> remove threats to the peace.

Predictably, when it came time to codify aspects of peace operations, the
legislative process would confront doctrinal disagreements, which had by no
means been settled by 1993 or 1994. On the contrary, the timing of the
Convention coincided with the period in which contention over the expansion of
Security Council activities beyond traditional peacekeeping was at its height. So,
the scope of application of the Convention was the most difficult part on which
to reach agreement. What types of operations and kinds of personnel did it
cover?

Inadvertently, the Convention contributed to that doctrinal debate. The
preamble refers to 'preventive diplomacy, peacemaking, peace-keeping, peace-
building and humanitarian and other operations'. Conspicuously, it excluded
reference to 'peace-enforcement', reflecting disagreement among states about
the use of force in peace operations. However, this middle level, as described
earlier in Chapter 1, was effectively affirmed in the definitional section of the
Convention. Article 1(c), outlining the meaning of 'United Nations operation',
includes in subparagraph (i) an operation with 'the purpose of maintaining or
restoring international peace and security'. These were code words for mandates
with Chapter VI or VII powers.[68] Furthermore, Article 2(2) excludes the application of the Convention to 'enforcement action under Chapter VII of the
Charter of the United Nations in which any of the personnel are engaged as

combatants against organized armed forces and to which the law of international conflict applies'. Therefore, a distinction is made between lower-level non-consensual operations under Chapter VII and high-intensity enforcement of the kind envisioned in Article 42 and that characterized the Gulf War. It had been argued

> that there would be no need for a convention on the protection of UN personnel if the UN was involved only in consent operations or if the convention were to limit itself to such operations. It was precisely because operations were taking place in States where there was no viable government (e.g., Somalia) or where there was such turmoil and tragedy that consent was not an option (e.g., Rwanda), that UN personnel was coming under attack.[69]

Clearly, therefore, the Convention is not restricted to traditional peacekeeping – as its non-specific title suggests – and would extend to policing missions within peace-maintenance.

The exclusion in Article 2(2), however, confuses the relative applicability of 'the law of international conflict' in middle level 'peace-enforcement' and high-intensity 'enforcement'. At one point in the deliberations regarding the Convention it was argued that when the United Nations deploys in an internal conflict, it automatically internationalizes that conflict, which then ceases to be exclusively internal. This would trigger, therefore, the application of international laws of war in internal peace-enforcement operations. Unfortunately, the wording of Article 2(2) might seem to refute this, but such an interpretation would contradict other parts of the Convention, described below, regarding the general applicability of international humanitarian law to UN operations.

Furthermore, Article 1(c) defines a UN operation as being 'established by the competent organ of the United Nations in accordance with the Charter of the United Nations and conducted under United Nations authority and control'. This compromise language extends coverage of the Convention to include not just operations under the command and control of the UN, but also those conducted by member states and only authorized by the UN – again, provided they are not 'Desert Storm' category enforcement actions. There is a contradiction in the language, though, between an operation 'conducted' under UN authority and the meaning of 'United Nations operation' as being 'established' by a UN organ. An operation only authorized by the UN would be established by member states.

Disagreement also focused on the meaning of 'United Nations personnel' and 'associated personnel'. Article 1(a) defines the former as 'members of the military, police or civilian components of a United Nations operation', as well as officials and experts on a mission of the UN, its specialized agencies or the International Atomic Energy Agency (IAEA). Article 1(b) includes as 'associated personnel': (i) individuals seconded from governments or inter-governmental organizations; (ii) contractors engaged by the UN; and (iii) a humanitarian

NGO or agency under an agreement with the UN 'to carry out activities in support of the fulfilment of the mandate of a United Nations operation'. Subparagraph (i) is understood to include members of a non-UN multinational force supporting a UN mandate. Subparagraph (iii), interestingly, extends to certain NGOs rights and duties that are usually the preserve of officials of governments or international organizations. The meaning of 'support' as the basis of 'association' and the link to coverage by the Convention is an obvious area to be defined by practice.

The problem with this Convention for the purposes of a peace-maintenance criminal code, and the reasons why it needs to be considered in combination with the remainder of international criminal law, is that it does not sufficiently cover crimes committed by UN personnel. According to its title and preamble, the aim is to protect international personnel from local actors, and not the reverse. Nor does it cover acts by other individuals against those not associated with the UN – whether the local population, independent NGOs, or members of a separate multinational force. Its historical context of 1993 and 1994 betrays a time of greater attention focused on attacks against the UN rather than on crimes committed by international forces or agents – ranging from internal fiscal corruption to local violations of human rights and humanitarian law.[70] Indeed, the reference point for early drafts of the Convention was existing anti-terrorist conventions.[71]

Nevertheless, there are seemingly subordinate provisions that bind United Nations and associated personnel to accountable norms of behaviour, tying this Convention to the remainder of international criminal law. Article 20(a) states that the Convention shall not affect 'the applicability of international humanitarian law and universally recognized standards of human rights as contained in international instruments in relation to...the responsibility of...[United Nations and associated personnel] to respect such law and standards'. This provision would seem to place both international and local individuals under common rules of law. Furthermore, Article 20(c) obliges the relevant personnel to act in accordance with the terms of the UN mandate, which in turn has to adhere to the humanitarian and human rights purposes of the UN under Article 1 of the Charter. In Article 6(1) of the Convention, UN and associated personnel must: (a) respect local laws and regulations – if they exist; and (b) 'Refrain from any action or activity incompatible with the impartial and international nature of their duties'.

Within these provisions, overall, not only are international personnel bound by humanitarian and human rights standards, but the issue of corruption by UN or associated personnel could be included in the understanding of the nature of their duties under Article 6(1)(b). Under Article 6(2), the UN Secretary-General is supposed to 'take all appropriate measures to ensure the observance of these obligations'. However, the UN tends not to exercise any disciplinary authority over soldiers participating in peace operations, nor would it be able to over 'associated personnel'. The centralization of discipline would require a new kind of understanding between the UN, host states and participating troop-contributors.

Indeed, this would be a critical step in establishing genuinely accountable UN operations. The problem will be mitigated somewhat by the conclusion of a code of ethical conduct for peace operations currently being developed at the UN in cooperation with the ICRC.[72] The harmonization of such standards through national law might be another approach, but unwieldy and unreliable.

Countering crimes against the United Nations

The ILC in its commentary on Article 19 of the Draft Code emphasized that the international community had to assume the responsibility for ensuring effective prosecution and punishment of guilty individuals, since such acts 'often occur in situations in which the national law-enforcement or criminal justice system is not fully functional or capable of responding to the crimes'. In effect, states are now required to fulfil law and order tasks within collapsed states. This is explicitly affirmed in Article 7(3) of the Convention, which requires States Parties to cooperate with the UN in the implementation of the Convention 'particularly in any case where the host State is unable itself to take the required measures'. Therefore, there is a duty under Article 7(1) not to commit one of the enumerated crimes, as well as responsibility under Article 7(2) for acts of omission, by which States Parties are to protect United Nations and associated personnel, and under Article 11 they are to take preventive action. And under Article 7(3) there is a duty to enforce against the acts of commission of others. This indicates an extra-territorial capacity to arrest and prosecute offenders. While the universality of international criminal law suggests such powers, this clarification, for law enforcement by the international community as a whole within nations, is a critical ingredient for peace-maintenance operations.

Most of the provisions in the Convention concerning prosecution of offenders are consistent with other parts of international criminal law, and cast largely in the context of individual state action. Article 10 outlines the conventional bases for a state's establishment of jurisdiction in international criminal cases. Article 13 reiterates the general duty to try or extradite, and expands on this in Articles 14 and 15, respectively. However, unlike other conventions, which oblige states to try or extradite within their own territorial jurisdiction if an offender is arrested there, the context of this Convention, and the explicit reference in Article 7(3), extend the obligation to prosecute to areas where states are participating in a 'United Nations operation' as defined by Article 1(c). Therefore, there would be multiple jurisdiction for individual states to prosecute in the field regardless of an overall UN mandate to do so. Conceivably, this could cause conflict within an operation, most likely between those states that wished to prosecute and those that did not.

Alternatively, in an effective peace-maintenance mission, such prosecution should be conducted by the operation as a whole. Whatever the obligation on the part of individual states, the Security Council is able to include prosecutory functions in its mandates and establish specific mechanisms for the purpose, in the manner that it created the Yugoslav and Rwandan Tribunals. But unlike these, the prosecutory body should be functionally linked to the civilian policing and military security capability under a common authority. The rules of law need to be connected to the means of order. This is the defining feature of a peace-maintenance rule of law and order in transition.

A PEACE-MAINTENANCE CRIMINAL CODE

Despite the special obligations placed by conventions upon individuals and states not to violate international criminal law, and the general responsibility to counter on-going criminal activities and prosecute and punish or extradite offenders, the international community has been grossly delinquent in its failure to respond effectively to breaches of law. An international criminal code has preceded comparable means of law enforcement. While one of the characteristics of international crime is that it warrants collective action, there were no collective prosecutions and punishments between the Nuremberg and Tokyo Trials in the 1940s and the establishment of the Tribunals for the former Yugoslavia and Rwanda in the 1990s. Even the German and Japanese prosecutions may be regarded as cooperative but not collective, since: (1) although the intention of the Nuremberg Charter was to establish universally applicable law, it was not applied equally to victor and vanquished – for no Allied airman, for instance, was tried for indiscriminate bombing over Germany, and in any case the jurisdiction of Article 6 of the Nuremberg Charter was limited to the Axis powers;[73] (2) the composition of the Tribunal was limited to the victors and did not include judges from the vanquished or neutral nations; and (3) consequently, the trials could not be considered as actions of the international community as a whole.[74]

Article 9 of the Draft Code reflects this gap between the collective nature of obligations and the absence of a collective response mechanism. It obliges a state with custody of offenders to either try or extradite them, giving special consideration to the state in whose territory the crime was committed. It also envisions the establishment of an international criminal court, but does not refer to any other implementation procedure. Similarly, other conventions – including those prohibiting aggression, genocide, apartheid, torture, slavery, discrimination, war crimes and even crimes against the UN – affirm that cooperation between states is required to implement their provisions but tend to marginalize collective or joint mechanisms. Instead, domestic enforcement with some jurisdictional link is relied on primarily, although there is a tendency, supported by the practice of the Yugoslav and Rwandan Tribunals, to give primacy to an existing collective body over the concurrent jurisdiction existing for custodians of an offender.

Domestic enforcement has the practical advantage of available, developed police forces and court systems, but suffers from a number of shortcomings. States tend to be reluctant to prosecute individuals unless they or the crime committed have some direct link to the state.[75] On the other hand, states may find tenuous jurisdictional links to individuals they have some interest in trying.[76] Some states may offer safe haven to offenders for political reasons,[77] or they may refuse extradition on technical grounds.[78] A state with custody may not have an extradition treaty with a state wishing to prosecute. A state may be unwilling to try or surrender its state officials or former officials either on principle, for fear of implicating the corporate state in the crime, or for fear that the trial of one indi vidual may implicate others in the country, including members of the ruling regime. This can lead to the anomaly of requiring consent to prosecution from the guilty party. Given the disparity in legal systems worldwide, reliance on unilateral state prosecution of individuals based on international law is unlikely to lead to a coherent system of enforcement.[79] Facing these barriers to prosecu- tion, a state may choose extraordinary unilateral means to apprehend and try an individual.[80]

Collective implementation, on the other hand, has been limited in scope for practical reasons, in the absence of an international policing force or authority to ensure compliance with international law. This inadequacy has led to concrete plans for an international criminal court, but for now collective implementation has meant not much more than supervision of and reporting on conditions surrounding a particular crime. Reliance is placed on voluntary compliance based on the desire for reciprocity, fear of embarrassment or condemnation and isolation. Exceptionally there may be economic sanctions – invariably for polit- ical reasons rather than out of objective judicial necessity.[81]

The obligations arising under international criminal law on the part of the international community as a whole highlight the need to enhance collective enforcement mechanisms. That is to say that while there is a right of a state indi- vidually and the international community collectively to try individuals, there is also an obligation to do so. States may base their claims to prosecute an offender on any of five grounds: (1) if the crime was committed on its territory, or the territorial principle; (2) if the criminal is one of its nationals, or the nationality principle; (3) if a national interest is injured by the offence, or the protective principle; (4) if the offender is in its custody, or the universality principle; and, of dubious validity, (5) if one of its nationals is injured by the offence, or the passive personality principle.[82]

The universality principle is the most relevant, but not exclusive, basis for peace-maintenance jurisdiction. It is applicable, *inter alia*, to individuals whose offences are so egregious that they injure the international community as a whole and therefore 'have no particular geographical location'.[83] The principle has been rarely applied – in the *Eichmann* case, for instance – and inconsistently inter- preted. Originally it was linked to the location of the crime and in the nineteenth century was applied to slavery and piracy on the high seas, or *res communis* beyond sovereign jurisdiction. At Nuremberg it was applied to the nature of the crime, specifically to grave breaches of law, regardless of loca- tion.[84] While the universality principle provides a basis for jurisdiction, it does not by itself oblige prosecution. Nevertheless, the repeated obligation on the part of states in relevant conventions to try or extradite criminals and the ILC's attempt to codify this in the Draft Articles on State Responsibility and the Draft Code indicate prima facie that there is an obligation to prosecute offenders. In any case, non-prosecution could be considered a derogation from *jus cogens* and therefore impermissible, or a non-fulfilment of obligations *erga omnes*. To argue the obverse would deny the obligatory character of the prohibitions against international criminal activity. Unfortunately, existing mechanisms have not proved adequate to enforce international criminal law, generally and in peace operations. But the existing law does constitute the basis of a peace-maintenance criminal code.

5　International means of order

Implementation of a peace-maintenance criminal code has tended to be a matter beyond the scope of judicial reasoning and poses a number of practical hurdles in the apprehension, detention, prosecution and punishment of offenders. Throughout the Cold War, the conventional view held that the existing mechanisms for enforcing international criminal laws were unlikely to develop further; they reflected the status quo of international order. Even some of the means envisioned in the provisions of conventions in force, it was argued, could be employed only under extraordinary circumstances, in the wake of a general war or the disintegration of a state. Codification dramatically outstripped the capacity of the international community to enforce its criminal laws. Regardless of special obligations arising under crimes against peace, crimes against humanity, war crimes (and now crimes against the United Nations), there was little recourse to collective means of enforcement. Non-derogable obligations were left to the interests of individual states to police. Too much reliance was placed on implementation by consent, in some cases even consent of the violator. The resulting travesty was that the worst crimes were responded to least.

Events in the 1990s illustrated the increasingly acute requirement for an independent, joint mechanism to enforce international criminal laws, and as a means of guaranteeing order in peace-maintenance operations. The practical basis for universal jurisdiction and collective action is custody of the offender. Meaningful prosecution and punishment rest on a capacity to apprehend, detain and imprison. These tasks were not adequately addressed in the preparations for an International Criminal Court (ICC), the establishment of a war crimes tribunal for the former Yugoslavia, and in UN peace operations in Cambodia and El Salvador. Any form of international prosecution suffers without integrated means of order.

While these experiments have revealed the problems of collective enforcement, they are also indicative of a transition and an opportunity to establish a law and order capacity for peace-maintenance. It is more needed because it is more possible. The presence of UN and other multinational forces on the territory where violations have taken place can constitute the means for enforcement of criminal law, although this capacity has not been comprehensively developed or adequately considered in the context of reform of peace operations. Or worse, justice – and probably long-term peace – have been sacrificed in favour of reaching short-term and unreliable agreements between belligerents. Many of the doctrinal requirements of UN missions today parallel the tasks of international law enforcement, including problems of consent and uses of force. As these puzzles are resolved for UN forces generally, it may be possible to apply the resulting mechanisms to policing international criminal law.

UNIVERSAL PROSECUTION BY AN INTERNATIONAL CRIMINAL COURT

In November 1992, the UN General Assembly issued a mandate to the International Law Commission to draft a Statute for an International Criminal Court 'as a matter of priority'.[1] This was a response to the detailed examination by the ILC of the issues concerning the desirability and possibility of establishing an ICC. The 'Report of the International Law Commission on the work of its forty-fourth session, 4 May–24 July 1992',[2] and in particular the 'Report of the Working Group on the question of an international criminal jurisdiction' annexed to it, concluded that the previous mandate from the General Assembly[3] regarding analysis of the question was completed and that further action to draft a Statute required a new mandate.

The ILC completed a Draft Statute for an International Criminal Court in 1993, and following considerable comments by governments managed to complete a redraft the following year.[4] The text was finalized following the direct participation of states in an Ad Hoc Committee established for the purpose by the 49th session of the General Assembly and a Preparatory Committee established in November 1995. The final report of the Preparatory Committee, with the consolidated text of the Statute, was submitted to the 51st General Assembly and it was decided to convene a diplomatic conference of plenipotentiaries in 1998 to finalize and adopt a convention on the establishment of an ICC.[5]

Calls for establishing such a criminal court have had a considerable history in the twentieth century. The idea was debated at the 1919 Peace Conference, and while there was no conclusion there was agreement on trying the Kaiser, which was provided for in Article 227 of the Treaty of Versailles. The Advisory Committee of Jurists appointed by the Council of the League of Nations in February 1920 rejected the idea of an ICC on practical grounds, but affirmed its desirability. The International Law Association between 1922 and 1926 addressed a report on and drafted a statute for an ICC, and concluded its creation was essential and urgent. The Inter-Parliamentary Union in 1925 undertook to find practical solutions for the prevention of international crime and to draw up a draft International Legal Code. The International Association of Penal Law between 1926 and 1928 published considerably on the subject and adopted a draft statute for an ICC. The assassination of Yugoslav King Alexander and French Minister M. Barthou at Marseilles on 9 October 1934 led to a French proposal to the League of Nations for an ICC. The Convention for the Creation of an International Criminal Court was adopted on 16 November 1937, but never entered into force.

Similar sentiments were expressed throughout the Second World War. The London International Assembly in 1941 prepared a draft Convention for the Creation of an International Criminal Court. The International Commission for Penal Reconstruction and Development stated in 1942 that the time was ripe for the establishment of an ICC. The St James Inter Allied Declaration on Punishment of War Crimes, signed by nine governments on 13 January 1942, sought to punish war crimes through an organized system of justice rather than through vengeance.[6] This was affirmed by the United States, Great Britain and the Soviet Union in the Moscow Declaration of November 1943. Earlier, in October, the United Nations War Crimes Commission had been established as the first official body for the investigation of war crimes and their punishment by an international judicial organ. In September 1944 the Commission adopted a draft Convention for the Establishment of a United Nations War Crimes Court. Instead, the Allied Powers established two ad hoc International Military Tribunals at Nuremberg and Tokyo, in August 1945 and January 1946.

The new United Nations Organization seized the matter following the Nuremberg trials. The United Nations Committee on the Progressive Development of International Law and its Codification concluded in 1947, after discussing a French proposal for the establishment of a Criminal Chamber in the ICJ, that an international judicial authority to exercise jurisdiction over the crimes punished at Nuremberg was desirable.[7] An International Criminal Jurisdiction was discussed in connection with drafts of the Genocide Convention between 1946 and 1948. In 1947, the Economic and Social Council (ECOSOC) submitted to the legal Sixth Committee of the General Assembly a draft Convention and two draft Statutes for a permanent and ad hoc ICC for the Punishment of Acts of Genocide.[8]

In 1948, the Assembly invited the ILC to study the desirability and possibility of establishing an international judicial organ for the trial of persons charged with genocide or other crimes.[9] In its report of 1950, the ILC concluded that the establishment of an ICC was both desirable and possible.[10] Further work was conducted by two ad hoc committees which reported in 1952 and 1954.[11] These devised and revised a draft Statute for an international criminal court. However, consideration of the Statute was deferred until some conclusion could be reached on the definition of aggression and the draft code of offences against the peace and security of mankind.

Throughout this history, plans for an international criminal jurisdiction have focused on the important questions of the scope and sources of the law applicable, jurisdictional bases and the organization and procedures of a court; issues of enforcement have been marginalized. While referred to as critical, the punishment and particularly the apprehension and detention of offenders have been considered only superficially. The establishment of a court and the mechanisms to underwrite it are treated as two separate developments. The draft statutes for a genocide court relied on the territorial state where the crime was committed or another High Contracting Party by its consent to provide and detain the accused, and to execute the sentence passed by the court.[12] The reports of the Special Rapporteurs to the second session of the ILC on the draft code of offences against the peace and security of mankind[13] and on an international criminal judicial organ[14] referred to the lack of executive organs to arrest offenders or an organization to bring the accused before the Court and to execute its judgements. Some members of the ILC argued, however, that: 'Though the international community lacked a police force at this present time, it might have one in the future.'[15]

The draft statute devised by the ad hoc committees of 1951 and 1953 relied on a combination of powers of the Court and execution by individual states. Article 40 authorized the Court to issue warrants of arrest to bring the accused before it and Article 31 obliged states to assist the Court in this.[16] The assistance of states under Article 31 would also be required to underwrite the powers of the Court under Article 42 to summon witnesses and produce documents and other evidentiary material. There were three proposals for the execution of sentences provided for under Article 52. First, the Statute could impose an obligation on States Parties to execute the sentence. Second, only states that had assumed by special convention the obligation to execute sentences would do so. Third, in the absence of such a convention, the UN Secretary-General could be requested to make the necessary arrangements. In so doing, the Secretary-General might rely on states directly concerned with the trial, the state where the Court had its seat or any third-party state.

Though more comprehensive, the 1992 ILC report similarly did not envisage in this 'international order' an independent, collective enforcement capacity and was preoccupied with the broad questions of the desirability and feasibility of an ICC, its structure, jurisdiction and applicable law. Implementation was referred to in considerably less conclusive terms. With regard to bringing the defendant before the Court, reliance was placed on the state with custody to 'transfer' the accused. This was not to be considered extradition to a foreign court but an obligation on the part of the State Party arising under the Statute. The report was concerned with possible safeguards of the process and referred only in passing to the responsibility of a state to arrest.[17] Furthermore, the Court relied on the assistance of states in such matters as: ascertaining the whereabouts of persons; taking the testimony and statements of witnesses; and producing and preserving judicial documents and other evidence. The report outlined the obligations of states and their reservations to rendering assistance to the Court.[18]

Finally, the report addressed the implementation of sentences. Since imprisonment would be the most common form of sentence, the question arose as to the place of imprisonment. The report rejected the idea of an international prison facility on the basis of cost and the likelihood of an insufficient number of prisoners. It considered the idea of assigning to a particular state the implementation of sentences. The report referred to the complaining state as a candidate, but it might be possible also to designate a single third-party state with responsibility for implementing sentences generally or in specific cases under sufficient direction from and control by the UN, to render it a collective enforcement procedure. The report also emphasized the need for a supervisory mechanism to monitor the implementation of sentences by states, such as an international control commission.[19]

The finalization of the Draft Statute marginalized collective enforcement issues even more. The point of contention during the ILC's redraft between 1993 and 1994 concerned the crimes over which the Court would have jurisdiction. The work of the Preparatory Committee in 1996 focused on other complicated concerns, including: the application of national law as a source of law for the ICC; the principle of complementarity between national and international jurisdiction; state acceptance of the Court's jurisdiction by 'opting in' or 'opting out', and the development of 'trigger mechanisms' for jurisdiction; the role of the UN Security Council as a 'trigger', particularly for the crime of aggression; the powers of the prosecutor, and rejection of an authority to investigate without state consent; the inclusion of provisions for individual and corporate criminal responsibility; judicial assistance by states to the Court; culpability arising from acts of omission, negligence and conspiracy; and recognition by states of the ICC's judgements. Only one among these issues concerned processes for provisional arrest by states of persons accused of serious international crimes. Also, there was minimal discussion of such constitutional issues as punishment. The Statute does not envision an independent enforcement capability and relies fundamentally on states.[20]

There are two principal consequences of progress towards the establishment of an ICC. First, it emphasizes the need for a collective system of international prosecution and illustrates a greater political willingness since 1989 to establish one. Second, since conclusions have been reached on the mechanisms of the Court – the jurisdiction, procedures, structures and so on – attention will eventually need to turn and focus on developing independent mechanisms for: securing the presence of the accused; obtaining evidence; conducting investigations; and detaining and punishing offenders.

AD HOC PROSECUTION FOR PARTITIONED YUGOSLAVIA

UN Security Council Resolution 808 of 22 February 1993 established for the first time since 1945 a means of prosecution comparable to the Nuremberg and Tokyo trials. It decided in paragraph 2 that an International Criminal Tribunal for the Former Yugoslavia (ICTY) 'shall be established for the prosecution of persons responsible for serious violations of international humanitarian law committed in the territory...since 1991'. This was pursuant to the opinions of the UN Commission of Experts on war crimes in the former Yugoslavia, which called for a tribunal in its first interim report issued earlier in the month.[21] Resolution 808 gave the UN Secretary-General sixty days to prepare a report with 'specific proposals...for the effective and expeditious implementation of the decision'. The deadline was not met, leading to doubts about possible trials for the Balkans.[22] But on 3 May, a comprehensive report was presented to the Security Council outlining a blueprint and Statute for an International Tribunal.[23]

Security Council Resolution 827 of 25 May 1993 adopted this Statute and decided 'that all States shall cooperate fully with the International Tribunal...and that consequently all States shall take any measures necessary under their domestic law to implement the provisions of the present resolution and the Statute'. Such obligatory language of Chapter VII of the United Nations Charter incurred mandatory compliance among members under Article 25. This was an enforcement action, with all that that implied, for the implementation of international criminal law, although not justified on the basis of such law by itself but on the argument that violations of international humanitarian law occurring within the territory of the former Yugoslavia constituted a threat to international peace and security. In doing so, internal atrocities were further internationalized.[24] For instance, unlike Nuremberg the ICTY has jurisdiction over breaches of the law of war applicable not only to international but also to internal armed conflicts.[25]

Interestingly, although an enforcement measure under Chapter VII, the Tribunal was established as a subsidiary organ within the terms of Article 29 of the UN Charter and then given a degree of independence. According to the Secretary-General's report of 3 May, the ICTY was to be a subsidiary organ of a judicial nature that 'would, of course, have to perform its functions independently of political considerations; it would not be subject to the authority or control of the Security Council with regard to the performance of its judicial functions'.[26] Effectively, the Tribunal was rendered not only the first truly collective, but the first properly independent judiciary for international criminal law enforcement. As a result, the few individuals responsible for constructing the Tribunal in its early months managed to proceed aggressively, albeit slowly, even as the entire project became increasingly inconvenient for the peace process, leading to fiscal and other interference by some UN member states.[27]

The eventual inconvenience of the Tribunal was logical, given its establishment at a time when peace seemed hopeless. This was exacerbated by the very fact that the mandate to search for justice had been authorized according to the need to restore peace, and the temporal jurisdiction of the Tribunal was limited in Resolution 827 by the restoration of peace. Nevertheless, the Judges were sworn in on 17 November 1993, and on 11 February 1994 they adopted the Rules of Procedure and Evidence.[28] Unfortunately, a Prosecutor was not nominated until 8 July 1994,[29] principally as a result of hesitation by some Security Council members regarding the independent evolution of the Tribunal at that time. Judge Richard J. Goldstone of South Africa took office as the new Prosecutor on 15 August 1994.[30]

On 7 November, the Tribunal issued its first indictment against Dusko Tadic for the persecution of the Muslim population of the Prijedor area of Bosnia-Herzegovina and deportation of civilians to the Omarska, Keraterm and

Trnopolje camps, and the collection and mistreatment, including killing and rape, of civilians within and outside the Omarska camp. As such, he was responsible for grave breaches of the 1949 Geneva Conventions, violations of the laws or customs of war, and crimes against humanity. Tadic was not a senior commander of any kind targeted by the Tribunal Prosecutor, but he happened to have been arrested in Munich on 13 February 1994 after being identified by refugees. Following investigations, authorities indicted him for genocide under paragraph 220a of the German Penal Code. While the case was pending before the courts, Goldstone requested Germany to defer to the ICTY the proceedings concerning Tadic in accordance with Rule 9 of the Rules of Procedure and Evidence and under Article 9(2) of the Statute, which gives the Tribunal 'primacy' over a national court in their concurrent jurisdiction. Germany complied and Tadic was transferred to the Tribunal on 24 April 1995. His trial finally began on 7 May 1996[31] and proceeded throughout the year, until a guilty verdict was delivered on 7 May 1997.[32] On 14 July, Tadic was sentenced to twenty years' imprisonment.[33]

In early 1993, there had been several proposals for the establishment of an international tribunal,[34] but the most comprehensive of these came from the then Conference, now Organization, on Security and Cooperation in Europe (CSCE),[35] which included its own blueprint and 'Draft Convention on an International War Crimes Tribunal for the Former Yugoslavia'. It is worth comparing this proposal to the subsequent documents of the Tribunal, since it genuinely attempted to address the nature of the problem generically – and this is particularly illustrative for identifying peace-maintenance means of order – before the practicalities of the Tribunal took on a life of their own. The principal problem with the CSCE proposal was inherited by the ICTY, and in its turn the Rwandan Tribunal; that is, it did not account for an independent enforcement capacity.[36] In many regards, the Draft Convention resembled earlier plans,[37] but was more detailed and explicit, which may have been the consequence of a country-specific proposal. It still relied largely on assistance from individual states, but envisioned a cooperative role for the International Criminal Police Organization (INTERPOL) and included better-developed supervisory mechanisms than previously suggested, as well as some independent functions. Similarly, while the ICTY has primacy over national courts with regard to prosecution, Article 29 of the Statute requires the cooperation of states generally on the request of the Tribunal, and under Article 27 individual states designated by the Tribunal are to enforce sentences. This is reflected comparably in the Rules of Procedure and Evidence. The President, legal scholar and judge Antonio Cassese, quipped that the Tribunal 'is like a giant who has no arms and no legs'.

Investigation

Article 34 of the CSCE Draft Convention provided for 'criminal inquiry'. This was to be conducted in the manner of a conventional, domestic criminal investigation, and while national authorities of States Parties to the Convention could be requested to assist in the performance of this function it was to be conducted independently by a prosecutor of the Procuracy appointed by the Procurator-General.[38] The prosecutor also had the right to call witnesses for examination, request evidence and call experts. The 'criminal inquiry' was distinguished from the UN Commission of Experts, which gathered, examined and analysed information in a general way and arrived at 'conclusions' to be considered as the basis of recommendations. The report observed 'that it is a different matter to collect information in a more general way and to collect information within the framework of a criminal investigation with the intention to bring suspects to justice'.[39] Although the mandate of the Commission explicitly referred to 'investigation', in the practice of UN operations it appears that the Commission had a 'reporting' function while the inquiry of the tribunal would properly be 'investigation'.

Indeed, as it turned out, much of the information gathered by the Experts could not be used by the Tribunal, given its rules of evidence, and each case had to be re-examined and fully investigated.[40] According to Article 16(1) of the ICTY Statute, the Prosecutor is responsible for investigations and under Article 18(2) has 'the power to question suspects, victims and witnesses, to collect evidence and to conduct on-site investigations'. Indictments are prepared upon the Prosecutor's determination that a prima facie case exists. Investigations can be initiated on the basis of information obtained from any source, whether governmental, inter-governmental or non-governmental. And under Article 29(2)(b), states are to comply with requests for assistance in the taking of testimony and the production of evidence.

These provisions are expanded on in Part Four, Section 1, of the Rules of Procedure and Evidence, and particularly in Rule 39, which also refers to cooperation with such bodies as INTERPOL. Provisional Measures under Rule 40 enable the Prosecutor, in case of urgency, to request any state to seize physical evidence or to take all necessary measures to prevent the destruction of evidence. The Rules of Evidence are outlined in Part Six, Section 3, and cover testimony of witnesses (Rules 90 and 91), confessions (Rule 92) and inadmissibility of evidence obtained in violation of human rights (Rule 95). Furthermore, the Production of Evidence is governed by Rules 66–70 of Part Five, Section 3, and Rule 71 in Section 4 includes the specifics of taking depositions.

One problem that initially plagued the Tribunal concerned the protection of witnesses as called for in Article 22 of the ICTY Statute. According to Rule 75 of the Rules of Procedure and Evidence, judges may 'order appropriate measures for the privacy and protection of victims and witnesses, provided that the measures are consistent with the rights of the accused'. Such measures include the non-disclosure to the public of the identity or whereabouts of witnesses through: the removal of their names from the Tribunal's public records; the giving of testimony using image or voice-altering devices or closed circuit television; the assignment of a pseudonym; or hearings in closed session as provided for under Rule 79. Also, pursuant to Rule 34, a Victims and Witnesses Unit was established under the authority of the Registrar, who is responsible for the overall administration of the Tribunal. It is supposed to recommend protective measures for victims and witnesses.

However, the Unit does not have the physical means to protect witnesses, and certainly not in the territory of the former Yugoslavia, the location of most victims. And under Rule 67, the Prosecutor has to 'notify the defence of the names of the witnesses that he intends to call in proof of the guilt of the accused and in rebuttal of any defence plea'. Since defendants in custody are given full international telephone privileges throughout the day, and despite the non-publication of names under Rule 75, disclosing the identity of witnesses to the accused in accordance with his rights placed victims in immediate danger. Assurances were made by the Tribunal to witnesses for their protection in the course of soliciting their testimony in proceedings, knowing full well that this could not be provided.[41] Although rather scandalous, this was a casualty of a system of prosecution without an independent means of police protection that relied on security services in multiple jurisdictions. It would not have helped if the territorial jurisdiction of the Tribunal was not limited to the former Yugoslavia, and like Nuremberg adjudicated on crimes which had no geographic location. There may have been an argument for situating the Tribunal at the *locus delicti*, but this would not have made the difference either, and there were many more arguments against it. The shortcoming was structural: a court without guards necessitated the goodwill of the perpetrator or the agreement of several authorities to implement each of its decisions.

The problem was mitigated somewhat by the hearing of witnesses in Banja Luka via a teleconferencing satellite link,[42] although the judges decided that: 'The evidentiary value of testimony of a witness who is physically present [before the Tribunal] is weightier than testimony given by video-link.'[43] Also, the judges had to confront squarely the issue of protecting witnesses for the *Tadic* case, and in particular the Prosecutor's request for 'anonymity' measures, or the non-disclosure of certain witnesses to the accused. By majority vote, with one separate opinion, they decided on 10 August 1995 to assume the discretion to grant such measures in exceptional circumstances, and outlined five criteria for balancing the interests of the accused and witnesses:

1   there must exist a real fear for the safety of the witness;
2   the testimony of the particular witness must be sufficiently important to the Prosecutor's case;
3   the reliability of the witness must be satisfied;
4   'the ineffectiveness or non-existence of a witness protection programme' has to be taken into account; and
5   the measures must be necessary so the accused does not suffer any undue unavoidable prejudice.[44]

With regard to on-site investigations and documentary evidence, the ICTY is reliant on local governments. On 7 July 1996, Tribunal investigators began a series of mass-grave exhumations to corroborate witness testimony, to recover evidence related to events reported in Tribunal indictments, and to document injuries and identify the cause and date of death. While the ICTY is to be granted free access to mass grave sites under the Dayton Agreement, it requires the cooperation of Croatia, Bosnia and Republika Srpska authorities. Not only are they supposed to help identify the location of sites, but also guard them and refrain from exhuming other sites without coordinating with the Tribunal Prosecutor.[45] This places responsibility for protecting the integrity of evidence in the hands of potential defendants or even the indicted, a preposterous proposition given the rules of evidence.

Similarly, while the Nuremberg Tribunal from the beginning had in its possession thousands of documents, the ICTY does not have a paper trail, and has to rely on relevant governments to surrender documentary evidence. So, on 15 January 1997, Judge Kirk McDonald issued subpoenae which were served on Croatia and Bosnia-Herzegovina ordering them to turn over to the Prosecutor documents related to the *Blaskic* case. On 19 February, McDonald directed Croatia to resolve the matter informally with the Prosecutor and the Bosnian Defence Minister to appear before her on 24 February. On 28 February, Judge McDonald directed the Defence Minister to inform her of the exact location of the documents, to provide the Prosecutor with immediate access to them, or to appear in person before her on 7 March 'to show cause why he should not be held in contempt of court'. In turn, this led to separate hearings on the issue.[46] On the one hand, these were extraordinary powers exercised with regard to high officials of sovereign states; on the other, they lacked the kind of control on the ground that could give them full effect. And subsequently, on 29 October, the Appeals Chamber quashed the Croation subpoena, which has to be issued to private individuals and not states or their officials.[47]

Arrests

The question of bringing the accused before the Tribunal was left largely unresolved in the CSCE proposal. While there was reiteration of the general obligation on the part of states to try or extradite offenders under Article 59, and while reference was made throughout the report to the assistance required by states,[48] the delivery of persons referred to in Article 56 was inconclusive. Commentary to the article referred to the procedures for 'transfer' outlined by the 1992 report of the ILC Working Group on the ICC,[49] but left it as a matter to be resolved. Given Serbian intransigence, the 'problem of the physical apprehension of suspects appear[ed] to be the greatest obstacle at the sentencing stage of the criminal justice process'.[50] The obverse of this problem was the need to try those already in the custody of local authorities, in order to avoid the establishment of makeshift tribunals for the purpose, such as the Bosnian trials.[51]

In the absence of custody of the accused, the competence of the Tribunal was limited. Under Article 36, the Public Prosecutor could request the Court of First Instance to issue a warrant of arrest, search warrant or warrant for the surrender of the offender. General commentary on the article envisioned individual states and perhaps INTERPOL intercepting and apprehending a fugitive at border crossings or airports. Under Article 37, the Court would indict the offender, but according to Article 38(2), unless the Court was satisfied that the accused had been served with the indictment, it 'shall not proceed with the trial'. This was linked to the rejection by the Special Rapporteurs of trials *in absentia*.[52] The ILC also rejected for the ICC trials *in absentia* as being inconsistent with the right of an accused person 'to be tried in his presence' under Article 14(3)(d) of the International Covenant on Civil and Political Rights (ICCPR).[53]

However, there is a distinction between the 'possession' of a right and the 'exercise' of a right. Provided a criminal justice system guarantees this right, it is not inconsistent with international law to proceed with prosecution since the system is not responsible for ensuring the accused exercises this right. In this manner, the right to trial in one's presence is a right, but not an inalienable right. Also, the ILC rejected trials *in absentia* as being ineffective. It may be argued, on the other hand, that, once found guilty, individuals may be pursued for the rest of their lives, since jurisdiction to punish international crimes is accorded to all states and there is no statute of limitations applicable, given the UNGA Convention on the Non-Applicability of Statutory Limitations to War Crimes and Crimes Against Humanity (1968). Nevertheless, there is currently a general rejection of trials *in absentia*[54] and therefore the problems of apprehension and custody are particularly acute. In any case, an individual may be rendered a fugitive by virtue of an indictment by the Tribunal and its issuance of an arrest warrant.

Trials *in absentia* were rejected during the establishment of the ICTY in accordance with Article 14 of the ICCPR.[55] In fact, Article 21 of the Tribunal Statute is a restatement of the internationally recognized standards regarding the rights of the accused contained in Article 14. Subparagraph (4)(d) of Article 21 guarantees that the accused shall be entitled 'to be tried in his presence'. Part Five, Sections 1 and 2, of the Rules of Procedure and Evidence concerns indictments and orders and warrants to bring the accused before the Tribunal physically. The procedures for indicting an individual for a crime within the jurisdiction of the Tribunal are outlined in Rules 47–53, in accordance with Articles 18 and 19 of the Statute. Basically, following an investigation and the determination of reasonable grounds for an individual's criminal responsibility, the Prosecutor may submit an indictment with supporting evidence to the Tribunal for review. An appointed judge may confirm or dismiss each count, or the indictment as a whole. Under Rule 53, it may be decided not to publicize a confirmed indictment until it is served on the accused, for practical purposes of locating and arresting the individual and to prevent his evasion of justice.

According to Article 19(2) of the Statute, 'Upon confirmation of an indictment, the judge may, at the request of the Prosecutor, issue such orders and warrants for the arrest, detention, surrender or transfer of persons, and any other orders as may be required for the conduct of the trial.' And under Article 20(2), 'A person against whom an indictment has been confirmed shall, pursuant to an order or an arrest warrant of the International Tribunal, be taken into custody, immediately informed of the charges against him and transferred to the International Tribunal.' Rules 54–61 of the Rules of Procedure and Evidence outline the intended process of arresting the indicted, in which there is particular reliance on states to execute warrants. Under Rule 55, a warrant of arrest, signed by a judge, bearing the seal of the Tribunal and accompanied by a copy of the indictment and a statement of the rights of the accused is 'transmitted by the Registrar to the national authorities of the State in whose territory or under whose jurisdiction or control the accused resides, or was last known to be', together with instructions for the arrest. A member of the Prosecutor's Office may be present 'as from the time of the arrest'.

Rule 56 invokes the obligations of states to cooperate with the ICTY under Article 29 of its Statute. Therefore, a 'State to which a warrant of arrest is transmitted shall act promptly and with all due diligence to ensure proper and effective execution thereof'. And under Rule 58, national extradition provisions cannot be an impediment to the surrender or transfer of the accused to the Tribunal, whose Statute prevails over any such domestic laws.[56] Rule 59 concerns the failure to execute a warrant. If a state is unable to execute a warrant, 'it shall report forthwith its inability to the Registrar, and the reasons therefor'. The accused may have voluntarily eluded authorities, or perhaps he cannot be located. Alternatively, a state may simply ignore the Tribunal, in which case Rule 59 adds: 'If, within a reasonable time after the warrant of arrest has been transmitted to the state, no report is made on action taken, this shall be deemed a failure to execute the warrant of arrest.' The Prosecutor may attempt to advertise the indictment in the relevant national newspapers as a last effort pursuant to Rule 60.

Thereafter, there is Rule 61, the procedure in case of failure to execute a warrant. The indicting judge must order the Prosecutor to submit the indictment to one of the two Trial Chambers of three judges each. At this hearing in open court, the Prosecutor presents the evidence that constituted the foundation of the indictment, as well as accounts for the efforts to effect service of the arrest warrant. The Prosecutor may call witnesses to testify. This is not a trial *in absentia*, since Rule 61 does not allow for determination of a verdict, nor, therefore, can the Trial Chamber pronounce any sentence. However, it is a means of preventing the paralysis of the Tribunal as a result of non-appearance of the accused. It can at least create a historic record against the indicted:

> Rule 61 affords a formal means of redress for the victims of the absent accused's alleged crimes by giving them an opportunity to have their testimony recorded for posterity either directly if they are invited to testify or indirectly when the Prosecutor speaks on their behalf.[57]

Furthermore, if the Trial Chamber is convinced of the evidence, it must issue an 'international arrest warrant' and transmit it to all states. Again, under Article 29 of the ICTY Statute, this incurs the mandatory obligation of states to comply with the order of the court and execute the warrant of arrest. The issuance of this special kind of warrant entails a series of consequences:

- the accused will find himself publicly branded an 'international fugitive', and the country he has taken cover in will be converted into an 'open-air prison';
- the accused will become a hostage to the political changes which might take place in his country of refuge: any protection he enjoys today may turn out to be only temporary;
- should the accused hold a public, civil or military position of responsibility, his exercise thereof will be seriously affected, both internationally and domestically, by his status as a 'wanted person'.[58]

In addition, if the Prosecutor satisfies the Trial Chamber that the failure to effect an initial arrest warrant 'was due in whole or in part to a failure or refusal of a state to cooperate with the Tribunal', then the ICTY President must notify the Security Council. As a subsidiary organ established pursuant to an enforcement action under Chapter VII, non-compliance with the Tribunal is a challenge to the authority of the Council.

On 11 July 1996, the ICTY issued two international arrest warrants, against the former President of Srpska, Radovan Karadzic, and his military commander, Ratko Mladic.[59] Both had been indicted in 1995 for grave breaches of the Geneva Conventions, violations of the laws or customs of war, genocide and crimes against humanity. In a letter informing the President of the Security Council of the international arrest warrants, President of the Tribunal Cassese stated that

> the failure to execute the initial arrest warrants…was wholly due to the refusal of the Republika Srpska and the Federal Republic of Yugoslavia (Serbia and Montenegro) to cooperate with the Tribunal in accordance with article 29 of the Statute.[60]

Srpska had committed itself to comply with ICTY determinations under Article 10 of annex 1-A of the General Framework Agreement for Peace in Bosnia and Herzegovina of 14 December 1995. Under the Dayton Accords, the Federal Republic had undertaken the responsibility for Srpska's cooperation or non-cooperation with the Tribunal, as well as its own. On 8 August 1996, the President of the Security Council issued a statement reminding all states of their obligation under Resolution 827 and condemning Srpska and the Federal Republic for their refusal to cooperate with the Tribunal. Also, the Council was 'ready to consider the application of economic enforcement measures to ensure compliance by all parties with their obligations under the Peace Agreement'.[61]

Notably, the international arrest warrants were not only addressed 'to all states', but also 'to the Implementation Force (IFOR)'. The executive authorities of UNPROFOR had flatly refused the Tribunal's request for assistance on the

ground.[62] In principle, this would have placed each troop-contributor in violation of Article 29 of the Statute, leaving open to some degree, in the absence of
an explicit provision, the corporate responsibility of UNPROFOR as a whole.
While UN executives on the ground may have rejected a policing role for the
Tribunal for lack of capacity or perceived mandate, the idea that a UN peace
operation could somehow escape a binding obligation of its own master was a
travesty of interpretation. Therefore, after the deployment of IFOR, the judges
amended the Rules of Procedure and Evidence and adopted on 18 January 1996
new Rule 59 *bis* on the transmission of arrest warrants:

> on the order of a Judge, the Registrar shall transmit to an appropriate
> authority or international body a copy of a warrant for the arrest of an
> accused, on such terms as the Judge may determine, together with an order
> for his prompt transfer to the Tribunal in the event that he be taken into
> custody by that authority or international body.[63]

Indeed, in the wake of the signing of the Bosnian Peace Agreement,
President Cassese and Prosecutor Goldstone issued a joint statement on 24
November 1995 concerning its provisions that affect the ICTY. They said the
Agreement 'reaffirms that the three signatory States, as well as the Republika
Srpska, are under a stringent obligation to co-operate with the Tribunal and to
render judicial assistance'. Also, the Agreement did not provide any amnesty for
those accused of serious violations of humanitarian law, which would have been
contrary to international norms. In addition, there were several points
concerning Bosnia specifically. Bosnia committed itself to provide unrestricted
access for Tribunal investigators to persons and sites, including mass graves. It
laid down in its Constitution that anyone convicted or indicted by the Tribunal
will be barred from public office. Above all, one point concerned the creation of
a Human Rights Commission and an International Police Task Force (IPTF),
'which shall furnish information to the Tribunal's investigators', and another
authorized 'the NATO Implementation Force to arrest any indicted war criminals it encounters or who interfere with its mission'.[64]

In order to clarify the anticipated cooperation between IFOR and the ICTY,
Prosecutor Goldstone met with the Secretary-General of NATO, Javier Solana,
in Brussels on 19 January 1996. They agreed that this would be twofold. First,
IFOR would assist the Tribunal's investigators in Bosnia with logistics, such as
transportation, security and communications. Second, and particularly critical,
IFOR would 'detain any persons accused by the ICTY whom it may come
across, and will detain them until their being rapidly and directly transferred…to
The Hague'.[65] Despite a Security Council mandate and obligations incumbent
on each participating state, IFOR resisted conducting arrests, for fear of dreaded
'mission creep' and unsustainable casualty figures, particularly on the US home
front. Goldstone later 'insisted on a more robust policy from NATO with regard
to war criminals.…He said that in the same fashion that a police force arrested
criminals, NATO was expected to arrest indicted war criminals.'[66]

By the end of 1996, the ICTY had indicted seventy-four individuals, but had only seven in custody.[67] None had been delivered by IFOR and Karadzic and Mladic were still at large. The Rwandan Tribunal, for circumstantial reasons, suffered the opposite condition. Some 80,000 individuals had been detained in sub-human conditions, with a high casualty rate of up to ten deaths a day. However, there were only twenty-one indictments, and of these only thirteen individuals had been identified as being in custody.[68]

Detention

Another problem addressed by the CSCE Report was detention of the offender, either in the short term during the trial or longer-term imprisonment after sentencing. The former was left as a problem to be resolved, although reference was made to the need for a headquarters agreement between the Tribunal and the state where the seat of the Tribunal is located. This needed to include special arrangements such as 'concerning the premises necessary for keeping detained persons under appropriate custody'.[69]

An individual is understood to be in 'detention' from the time of arrest, pursuant to Articles 19(2) and 20(2) of the ICTY Statute, until the determination of a verdict and passage of sentence, at which time the execution of the punishment by imprisonment begins. Such detention is only a temporary measure, since the accused has the right 'to be tried without undue delay' under Article 21(4)(c) of the Statute. According to Rule 57 of the Rules of Procedure and Evidence, 'Upon the arrest of the accused, the State concerned shall detain him, and shall promptly notify the Registrar. The transfer of the accused to the seat of the Tribunal shall be arranged between the State authorities concerned and the Registrar.' This requires not only reliance on local governments, but also an independent detention capability, as well as standing agreements with the government at the seat of the Tribunal, in this case the Netherlands. Furthermore, under the provisional measures of Rule 40, the Prosecutor may request a state to arrest a suspect without an indictment and to take all necessary measures to prevent the escape of an accused. There ought to be some oversight for this provided by the Prosecutor's Office.

According to Rule 64, 'Upon his transfer to the seat of the Tribunal, the accused shall be detained in facilities provided by the host country, or by another country.' The accused must be brought before a Trial Chamber and formally charged without delay under Rule 62. And while the conditions of detention may be modified on request, Rule 65 does not permit the release of an accused except upon an order of a Trial Chamber. In exceptional circumstances, provisional release may be ordered if the accused is sure to appear for trial, or under such conditions to guarantee this, like the execution of a bail bond. A warrant of arrest may be issued if necessary. During detention, instruments of restraint, such as handcuffs, are not to be used under Rule 83, 'except as a precaution against escape during transfer or for security reasons'.

On 5 May 1994, the judges adopted specific Rules of Detention, and on 1

October a Detention Unit was handed over and a detention facility with twenty-four cells was provided for at a fortress-like complex at Scheveningen. There were six cells on the premises of the Tribunal and thirty security guards within the organizational structure of the Registry responsible for protection of ICTY personnel and holding the accused while there. On 22–23 April 1996, the judges adopted a new Rule 40 *bis* providing for a system of provisional detention of suspects transferred to the Tribunal's Detention Unit. By this, a suspect may be held for periods of thirty days at a time, up to a maximum of ninety days, while an indictment is being investigated and prepared.[70]

Punishment

The CSCE Report was more explicit with regard to punishment and imprisonment, which was examined more closely because the Rapporteurs could not conceive of the CSCE endorsing capital punishment. Article 29 listed the penalties that the Court had the power to impose and referred first to the deprivation of liberty; it explicitly rejected capital punishment. The Report considered the prospects of imprisonment for life and raised the question of where imprisonment was to be served. The Rapporteurs concluded that sentences should be served principally in the territory of the former Yugoslavia, but also provided under Article 46 for enforcement of the penalty by a third State Party to the Convention.

The Report acknowledged that neither was ideal and there were no guarantees that the enforcement would be just or that prisoners would be treated equally. In the former Yugoslavia, 'There is a risk that prisoners, with whom the population in the province where the sentence is served might sympathize, would be treated in an unduly favourable way, while prisoners belonging to the "opposite side" might even risk maltreatment.'[71] Also, the Rapporteurs envisioned the likelihood of the number of prisoners in the territory being considerable and noted the heavy burden this placed on the states. They concluded, however, that unless the former Yugoslav states 'are prepared to take upon themselves to accept enforcement, the Rapporteurs foresee little possibility that justice can be done in the present case'.[72] With regards to third-party enforcement, there needed to be safeguards for minimum standards of justice for prisoners, and the execution of sentences 'must not be used to circumvent the system established by the Convention'.[73]

To surmount these shortcomings the Rapporteurs proposed 'rigorous international supervision of enforcement' wherever it was to be carried out. Article 47 outlined an independent capacity for this. The Plenary Court selected both a judge from the Court of First Instance to supervise the execution of judgements, known as the Supervising Judge, and an alternate Supervising Judge. The Supervising Judge had two main functions. The first was to ensure that prisoners were treated in conformity with international obligations. 'In particular it is important to ascertain that they are not discriminated against or humiliated by other inmates, wardens or other judges who may come in contact with them.'[74]

To do so, the Judge could inspect any prison or other place of detention and communicate in private with any person subject to the supervision. In the event of complaints, the Judge would raise these with local authorities or at the appropriate higher level. The second function of the Supervising Judge was to examine and approve all national decisions concerning conditional release or alternative measures. Unless approved, such decisions could not be executed. This was a measure to ensure the equal treatment of prisoners.

The Secretary-General's report of 3 May 1993 recommended that the ICTY 'should not be empowered to impose the death penalty'.[75] Under Article 24(1) of the Statute, 'the penalty imposed by the Trial Chamber shall be limited to imprisonment', excluding, therefore, not only capital but also corporal or other kinds of punishment, although under Article 24(3), Trial Chambers 'may order the return of any property and proceeds acquired by criminal conduct, including by means of duress, to their rightful owners'. In determining the terms of imprisonment, Trial Chambers are to 'have recourse to the general practice regarding prison sentences in the courts of the former Yugoslavia'. In imposing sentences, judges 'should take into account such factors as the gravity of the offence and the individual circumstances of the convicted person'. Judgements are rendered by a majority of the members of the Trial Chamber, according to Article 23, and appellate proceedings are provided for under Article 25. Article 28 permits pardons or the commutation of sentences by a decision of the President in consultation with the judges.

The Rules of Procedure and Evidence correspondingly expand on the statutory provisions. Under Rule 101, 'A convicted person may be sentenced to imprisonment for a term up to and including the remainder of his life.' Unlike Nuremberg, the ICTY envisages the sentencing phase as distinct from the delivery of the verdict. In determining the sentence, the Trial Chamber can take into account such factors as: aggravating circumstances, mitigating circumstances, sentencing practice in the former Yugoslavia, and the period of detention to date. Also, under Rule 100, the Prosecutor may submit any relevant information that may assist in the determination of an appropriate sentence. Furthermore, Rule 105 outlines the procedure for the restitution of property and Rule 106 concerns compensation claimed by victims. Appellate proceedings are covered in Part Seven of the Rules, and pardons and commutation of sentences in Part Nine. According to Rule 125, when determining whether a pardon or commutation is appropriate, the President may consider: the gravity of the crimes of the convicted; the treatment of similarly situated prisoners; the prisoner's demonstration of rehabilitation; as well as any substantial cooperation of the prisoner with the Prosecutor. Practice in this regard will develop an international criminological jurisprudence.[76]

Contrary to the CSCE proposal, the Secretary-General was 'of the view that, given the nature of the crimes in question and the international character of the tribunal, the enforcement of sentences should take place outside the territory of the former Yugoslavia'.[77] Accordingly, Article 27 of the ICTY Statute provides that: 'Imprisonment shall be served in a State designated by the International

Tribunal from a list of States which have indicated to the Security Council their willingness to accept convicted persons.' While such 'imprisonment shall be in accordance with the applicable law of the State concerned', it is to be 'subject to the supervision of the International Tribunal'. Rule 103 adds that: 'Transfer of the convicted person to that State shall be effected as soon as possible after the time-limit for appeal has elapsed.' Rule 104 specifies that, 'All sentences of imprisonment shall be supervised by the Tribunal or a body designated by it', indicating, therefore, an independent capacity to do so.

Italy, as of February 1997, and Finland, as of May, signed agreements on the enforcement in its prisons of ICTY sentences.[78] Five other states agreed in principle to do so without reservations, although the first two were likely to be rejected given the Secretary-General's recommendation above: Bosnia, Croatia, Iran, Norway and Pakistan. Five states agreed in principle to enforce sentences subject to certain reservations: in addition to Denmark and Spain, the Netherlands did not want to be the first country selected, since it is already the Host of the Tribunal and suspects are in remand in The Hague; Germany would take only German citizens; and Sweden would take only its citizens, residents or others with strong ties to it. Countries such as Switzerland, Belgium and Austria included in their legislation provisions which enable them to enforce sentences, even though they did not express a willingness to do so.

Also, some states feel that the sentences imposed by the Tribunal should be converted into penalties under their national law with which they most closely correspond. For instance, 'Germany has stated that, with respect to the duration of sentence, the judgement of the Tribunal shall be controlling but may not exceed the maximum penalty which could be imposed under German law for that offence.'[79] There are also ten states that have indicated they are not in a position to accept prisoners: the Bahamas, Belarus, Belize, Burkina Faso, Ecuador, France, Liechtenstein, Malaysia, Poland and Slovenia.

On 29 November 1996, the ICTY pronounced its first sentence. Drazen Erdemovic was given ten years' imprisonment for crimes against humanity. He had been indicted on 29 May 1996 for participating in the massacre of Bosnian Muslims of Srebrenica on 16 July 1995, when hundreds of men aged 17 to 60 were summarily executed. During his initial appearance on 31 May 1996, Erdemovic pleaded guilty and declared: 'I had to do this. If I had refused, I would have been killed together with the victims.'[80] He was invoking Article 7(4) of the Statute, which permits superior orders, not as a defence, but as a mitigation of punishment. Erdemovic also testified against Karadzic and Mladic during the Rule 61 proceedings of 5 July 1996. Consequently, when considering mitigating circumstances, which were not in any way to diminish the gravity of crimes against humanity, the Trial Chambers took into account elements such as the fact that 'the accused surrendered voluntarily to the International Tribunal, confessed, pleaded guilty, showed sincere and genuine remorse or contrition and stated his willingness to supply evidence with probative value against other individuals'.[81]

In determining a sentence, the Trial Chamber had to consider the kind of penalties that are applicable to crimes against humanity. In national legal systems they are understood to be of extreme gravity warranting the most severe penalties. They are

> serious acts of violence which harm human beings by striking what is most essential to them: their life, liberty, physical welfare, health, and or dignity....But crimes against humanity also transcend the individual because when the individual is assaulted, humanity comes under attack and is negated. It is therefore the concept of humanity as victim which essentially characterises crimes against humanity.[82]

The Chamber did not gain any guidance from the practice of the former Yugoslav courts, inadequate as its jurisprudence was on the issue. In any case, sentences available in the former Yugoslavia included the death penalty but not life imprisonment.

So, the Trial Chamber considered the purposes and functions of penalties imposed for crimes against humanity. It accepted the concepts of deterrence and retribution, as well as reprobation: 'One of the purposes of punishment for a crime against humanity lies precisely in stigmatising criminal conduct which has infringed a value fundamental not merely to a given society, but to humanity as a whole.' The Trial Chamber ruled out the rehabilitative function of punishment because this 'must be subordinate to that of an attempt to stigmatise the most serious violations of international humanitarian law, and in particular an attempt to preclude their reoccurrence.'[83]

On the enforcement of the sentence, the Trial Chamber held the view that the President must be given a special role, additional to his statutory responsibilities, for instance in the oversight of punishment. Also, while the Trial Chamber does not have the power to designate the location of enforcement, it considered the place and conditions for execution of the sentence in an effort to ensure due process, the proper administration of justice and equal treatment for convicted persons. It further provided guidance for the execution of international judicial decisions and on the rights of the convicted person. In particular, drawing on Article 27 of the ICTY Statute, it concluded that the state designated

> will execute the sentence 'on behalf of the International Tribunal' in application of international criminal law and not domestic law. Therefore, that State may not in any way, including by legislative amendment, alter the nature of the penalty so as to affect its truly international character.[84]

Finally, the Trial Chamber recommended that there be some degree of uniformity and cohesion in the enforcement of international criminal sentences, given the principle of equal treatment before the law and considering that there should not be significant disparities between states as regards the enforcement of penalties. It formulated two essential elements which derive from the international character of the prison sentences set by the ICTY from which states should not in principle derogate. First, concerning the duration of the penalty, 'no measure which a State might take could have the effect of terminating a penalty or subverting it by reducing its length'. Second, relating to the treatment of prisoners, states must 'always conform to the minimum principles of humanity and dignity which constitute the inspiration for the international standards governing the protection of the rights of convicted persons'. Indeed, 'the penalty imposed on persons declared guilty of serious violations of humanitarian law must not be aggravated by the conditions of its enforcement'.[85]

In the vein of previous plans for international tribunals, the CSCE Proposal detailed an independent capacity for prosecution, but relied heavily on assistance by individual states. It departed from other plans in that it effectively acknowledged the need to move beyond reliance on individual states, but suggested only incremental steps. An independent capacity to supervise long-term imprisonment was more viable than a separate jail for the Tribunal. However, the adequacy of a visiting inspector-judge is questionable if pitted against the notion that the continued presence of international personnel to assist and oversee the execution of sentences is not an inconceivable project given the history of UN observers in conflict areas. Also, the donation of temporary detention facilities by former Yugoslav states could have been manned by UN or NATO troops given their presence in the area.

The most difficult problem, apprehension of offenders, remained unresolved. Unlike other proposals, the Rapporteurs were not satisfied with obligations on the part of states to try or extradite, or the procedures envisioned by the ILC in its 1992 Report for 'transfer'. By recognizing these as insufficient and calling for more study on the question, they identified the need for an independent, collective capacity to secure custody of offenders – the absence of which has limited the effectiveness of the ICTY.

SPECIAL PROSECUTION IN FACTIONAL CAMBODIA

An international tribunal to prosecute individuals for the auto-genocide that occurred between 1975 and 1979 under the regime of Pol Pot's Democratic Kampuchea (DK), or for various war crimes and crimes against humanity since, has not yet been established. However, one of the most ambitious operations in UN history, the United Nations Transitional Authority in Cambodia (UNTAC), illustrated the increasing need to develop an independent, collective capacity for apprehending, detaining, prosecuting and punishing criminal individuals.

UNTAC had a control mandate over an entire sovereign state. It was established pursuant to the 'Agreements on a Comprehensive Political Settlement of the Cambodian Conflict' signed in Paris on 23 October 1991 by the four warring factions and brokered by the five permanent members of the Security Council (Perm-5) – France, China, the United States, Great Britain and the former Soviet Union.[86] The plan of the United Nations Secretariat for implementation of the Agreements, effectively the blueprint of the operation, called for seven distinct components:

1   a Human Rights Component to promote and protect human rights;
2   an Electoral Component to organize and conduct free and fair general elections;
3   a Military Component to stabilize the security environment and build confidence among the parties to facilitate free and fair elections through the disarmament and demobilization of at least 70 per cent of each of the factions' armed forces;
4   a Civil Administration Component to ensure a neutral political environment conducive to free and fair elections through 'direct control' of five key areas – foreign affairs, national defence, finance, public security and information;
5   a Civilian Police Component to ensure that law and order was maintained effectively;
6   a Repatriation Component to facilitate the return to Cambodia of refugees and displaced persons; and
7   a Rehabilitation Component to restore the country's basic infrastructure.[87]

The operation on paper had extraordinarily wide powers. While sovereignty resided in a Supreme National Council (SNC) composed of representatives of the four factions, the UN Secretary-General's Special Representative, Yasushi Akashi, needed only to heed 'advice' from the SNC if there was consensus among its members, and even then he needed to comply only if the advice was consistent with the objectives of the Paris Agreements. Also, the SRSG had exclusive responsibility and could dictate to the SNC in such areas as the electoral process. In practice, however, UNTAC did not have an independent capacity to underwrite its powers. This was particularly apparent in the Human Rights and Civil Administration Components.

The human rights mandate was the legacy of excluding from the Agreements, for the sake of achieving a 'comprehensive' final settlement which included the Khmer Rouge, any reference to prosecution of offenders. Trials would be left for a newly elected government to carry out if it so wished. On the day the Agreements were signed, US Secretary of State James Baker stated: 'Cambodia and the US are both signatories to the Genocide Convention and we will support efforts to bring to justice those responsible for the mass murders of the 1970s if the new Cambodian government chooses to pursue this path.'[88] During the operation some UNTAC officials raised the issue internally, but were not supported by others who felt that without a clear mandate no efforts should be made in that direction.[89]

The process of exclusion occurred gradually.[90] The final communiqué of the first Jakarta Informal Meeting of 28 July 1988 referred to preventing a return to 'the genocidal policies and practices of the Pol Pot regime'. A UN General Assembly resolution of 3 November 1989 generically noted 'the universally condemned policies and practices of the recent past'. The February 1990

Australian proposal referred to 'the human rights abuses of a recent past'. Finally, the Perm-5 developed in August 1990 the formula which eventually appeared in the Agreements: 'the non-return to the policies and practices of the past'. This would be the basic task of the Human Rights Component.

Pursuant to the Paris Agreements[91] and the February 1992 Report of the Secretary-General,[92] and to foster 'an environment in which respect for human rights shall be ensured in order to prevent a return to the policies and practices of the past and to enable free and fair elections to be held',[93] the Human Rights Component was active in three main fields: (1) human rights education, training and information specifically for government officials, judicial officers, Khmer police, law students, school teachers and non-governmental organizations, and generally through a publicity campaign for the entire Cambodian population; (2) promotion of adherence to international human rights instruments and review of legal, judicial and penal standards in the light of these instruments; and (3) investigation of human rights complaints and, where appropriate, corrective action. In the event that legislation or conditions of detention were not in conformity with international human rights standards, or if the outcome of investigations warranted corrective measures, the Human Rights Component was to contact 'the relevant authorities', including the SNC, and recommend 'appropriate action'.

While Human Rights Officers interpreted their powers widely, they recognized the physical limitations placed on the Component, as the above description of its activities from its publicity brief indicates. The power of the Component was not merely to 'recommend'. According to the Secretariat's interpretation of the Agreements, 'UNTAC would naturally retain the right to order or to take corrective action, as appropriate'.[94] The problem rested with the fact that the operation did not have an independent capacity to take corrective action, such as releasing unlawfully detained prisoners or arresting, prosecuting and punishing human rights violators.

The Civil Administration Component was similarly flawed. 'To ensure a neutral political environment conducive to free and fair elections' the 'direct control' referred to in the Paris Agreements[95] did not mean that UNTAC would assume all the administrative tasks of the country – as in a *governorship* operation – but would supervise and judiciously intervene in administrative institutions. UNTAC was given the power to: issue binding directives; install UNTAC personnel in administrative agencies, bodies and offices of existing administrative structures, who would enjoy unrestricted access to all administrative operations and information; and require the reassignment or removal of any personnel of such administrative agencies, bodies and offices. According to the Component's publicity brief, in terms of implementation 'UNTAC relies heavily upon codes of conduct and guidelines for management, especially regarding ethical conduct, measures to counter corruption, measures to ensure non-discrimination and other principles of accountability including mechanisms to investigate complaints'.[96] This mirrored the Secretary-General's Report,[97] but added the word 'heavily', effectively affirming the limitations of the Component.

UNTAC Civil Administration did not function as was envisioned. The Component was unable to access, nor was it therefore able to adequately supervise, Cambodian administrative institutions. In particular, it did not have the capacity to underwrite its powers of dismissal. The authority to remove officials from office in the absence of a means to ensure compliance was reduced to a recommendatory power. Reluctance to comply, principally by the State of Cambodia (SOC) which had the most extensive administrative structures in the areas where the UN had deployed, forced issues to be handled at senior levels, usually between the SRSG and Prime Minister Hun Sen themselves. This turned an administrative problem into a diplomatic negotiation, which would be addressed in the context of the wider political landscape. Like the Human Rights Component, Civil Administration required an independent administrative capacity to physically remove the offender and prosecute if the violation was serious enough.

The lacunae between UNTAC's administrative powers and its enforcement capacity could have been mitigated somewhat by the CIVPOL Component of the operation, but it failed to meet the challenge. UN CIVPOL usually does not maintain law and order independently but supervises law enforcement by local police forces. Of policing powers – including: reporting, investigation, search, seizure, arrest and detention – CIVPOL conventionally is restricted to reporting, as in Namibia, or reporting and investigation, as in Cyprus.[98] However, UNTAC CIVPOL not only had a supervisory function, through reporting on and investigating incidents, but the power of 'control'.[99] This last provision was particularly significant since local police forces, which had become largely politicized institutions with little discipline and weak links to Phnom Penh authority, would be subject to laws drafted by UNTAC.[100] This put CIVPOL in a powerful position to challenge abuses of power and direct law and order.

In practice, CIVPOL did not even attempt to carry out its 'control' tasks. Its publicity brief[101] did not refer to 'control' as one of its functions. In fact, the CIVPOL leadership interpreted the powers of the Component very narrowly. In comparison to the Human Rights officers, it was a poor investigator. The leadership failed to comprehend the scope of the laws promulgated by UNTAC or the powers CIVPOL had to demand compliance. The subculture of the police used to a familiar environment, with knowledge of the local language and laws, and used to underwriting authority, not challenging it, meant that CIVPOL required special training for international service. Nevertheless, even if CIVPOL had taken full advantage of its available powers, it would still have lacked the manpower and authority to conduct independent policing functions, including the removal of local policemen or the arrest of serious offenders. Although UN CIVPOL as currently manifested is ill suited to the task, it does provide the basis for developing an independent law and order capability.

The absence of this capability in UNTAC was not sustainable. As the registration process proceeded through November and December 1992, incidents of politically motivated violence increased and led to twenty deaths. The principal target of the attacks was the National United Front for an Independent, Neutral,

Peaceful and Cooperative Cambodia (FUNCINPEC), the royalist party headed by Prince Norodom Ranariddh, son of the SNC Chairman, Prince Norodom Sihanouk. The inability of UNTAC to adequately address the violence led to Sihanouk's refusal on 4 January 1993 to continue cooperating with UNTAC or SOC. Ranariddh stated on 10 January that: 'We have got no results from UNTAC or investigations of political violence. We know very well…the names of the SOC officials who are behind it.'[102] Sihanouk rejoined the peace process following a meeting with SRSG Akashi on 8 January in Beijing, but 'his threats made it clear to Untac that they must institute concrete measures to address the deteriorating situation'.[103]

On 11 January, Akashi announced the creation of a special prosecutor's office and court system designed to indict, prosecute, sentence and imprison individuals responsible for political crimes. This would be additional to Akashi's powers under the Paris Agreements to dismiss officials accused of violence and intimidation. Despite new powers, there was still reliance on local authorities for enforcement and prosecution. Akashi attempted to remove the governor of Battambang province, Ung Sami, not only for his part in attacks against opposition party workers and offices, but for a long history of human rights abuses and corruption in the area. A SOC spokesman responded on 12 January: 'If UNTAC insists on removing him it will have to remove Prime Minister Hun Sen and the SOC won't cooperate with UNTAC anymore.'[104] Akashi still effectively relied on Hun Sen to remove Ung Sami since, in the run-up to the May elections, he could not afford to alienate SOC, which controlled 80–90 per cent of the population and territory of Cambodia.

The first arrests took place in January 1993. UNTAC apprehended on 11 January a member of the ruling Cambodian People's Party (CPP) who was destroying a FUNCINPEC office with an axe. Unfortunately, the suspect was placed in the custody of the SOC police who later released him. An UNTAC spokesman said UN police would try to rearrest the suspect.[105] On 15 January, a SOC policeman, Em Chan, was arrested and formally charged on 21 January with killing FUNCINPEC party official Kier Sarath in the southern port city of Kampot. The hearing, however, was delayed while UNTAC searched for a suitable magistrate. An UNTAC official said: 'The problem is finding the right court mechanism and finding the right judge.'[106] The problem was exacerbated by the arrest of a defecting Khmer Rouge guerrilla, Than Theaun, for his part in the December 1992 massacre of twelve ethnic Vietnamese and two Cambodians. A Phnom Penh court refused to hear the case. According to UNTAC officials, SOC wished 'to avoid setting a precedent in Theaun's trial which could be used against Em Chan and other government defendants'.[107] The government claimed that UNTAC did not follow proper procedures in either case as the incidents occurred outside the jurisdiction of the Phnom Penh court. UNTAC had no independent recourse.

Weaknesses of the powers of arrest were also illustrated. On 5 February, FUNCINPEC officials accused the Phnom Penh government of arresting six of its members. One was released, but UNTAC admitted it did not know the whereabouts of the others.[108] Warrants were issued for the arrest of seven government soldiers, including a captain, who would be charged with murder, causing injury, illegal confinement and infringement of human rights. On 8 March, a special UN prosecutor accompanied by Malaysian troops failed to make any arrests. According to an UNTAC spokesman, 'Despite advance notice that the team was coming, [none of the seven] accused of the abduction of FUNCINPEC members were present.' A government spokesman rejected the legality of the UN's prosecutorial powers:

> We believe this kind of power of UNTAC is a violation of existing rules and is also in violation of human rights....If UNTAC continues to insist to apply these rules of law, then the [government] would find it very difficult to cooperate with UNTAC in this field.

A UN spokesman stated: 'Without the cooperation of the existing administrative structures in the process of bringing the alleged offenders to justice there is nothing more UNTAC can do.'[109]

This SOC-UNTAC confrontation intensified later in March. FUNCINPEC reported one of its members was tortured to death after being summoned for talks with government authorities at a district office in Kompong Cham. The mutilated body of Hou Leang Bann was found in a sack after seven days. UNTAC questioned suspects and raided two SOC district offices, but made no arrests. Hun Sen was enraged by what he considered abuses by UNTAC in its investigation. On 19 March he sent a letter to Prince Sihanouk, UN Secretary-General Boutros Boutros-Ghali and UNTAC leaders stating: 'We consider recent acts by the UNTAC supervision group as abuses of its control powers....It constitutes a disgusting act which reminded me of those committed by the Pol Pot regime while in power.' He went on to say, 'We cannot endure the...terror of our people, who are suffering by threats and oppression from foreigners excessively abusing their powers like colonialists in Cambodia.'[110]

In spite of these problems, there were calls for tribunals to be established to prosecute those responsible for the massacres of ethnic Vietnamese, which had plagued the process since its beginning. For instance, on 10 March 1993, at least thirty-three ethnic Vietnamese were killed and another twenty-nine wounded in a fishing village in Siem Reap province. Among those killed were eight children and a baby. 'There were babies with their hands shot off....[Attackers] got into one houseboat and shot the kids in the head. It's that savage,' said a UN investigator. Khmer Rouge guerrillas under the command of the infamous General Ta Mok were suspected of committing the massacre.[111]

In response, UN officials raised the possibility of genocide trials. 'In human rights terms these are crimes against humanity and may well be considered acts under the genocide convention,' said an UNTAC Human Rights Officer. 'Those responsible for authorizing or who fail to take steps to prevent such acts may well be charged if not for genocidal acts then for complicity in genocidal acts.' In his confirmation hearings on 31 March before the US Senate Foreign Relations

Committee, Winston Lord, President Clinton's appointee as Assistant Secretary of State for East Asia and the Pacific, stated:

> There is a real concern here [regarding ethnic violence] that we may see another example of ethnic cleansing taking place, and we know the Khmer Rouge's history on this matter. We have urged the UN to look into this matter, to appoint special people to judge whether war crimes and other atrocities are being committed that should be brought before a future Cambodian government for possible prosecution.[112]

The case of the United Nations in Cambodia, despite its extensive shortcomings, included a number of innovations, such as the Human Rights and Civil Administration Components. Their significance rests partly on the attempts to develop for peace operations an independent, collective capacity for apprehension, detention, prosecution and punishment of individual offenders within a sovereign state. It was recognized among UNTAC Human Rights Officers that regardless of the restrictive nature of the UN military force, they could not have started functioning without the overall mission framework and presence of international troops. Nevertheless, the UNTAC experience illustrates most specifically the practical problems associated with transitional rules of law and order.[113]

NON-PROSECUTION OF AUTHORITARIAN EL SALVADOR

While not as far-reaching as UNTAC, it is worth comparing with the Cambodia experience the United Nations Observer Group in El Salvador (ONUSAL), which faced similar problems. It was established,[114] uncharacteristically, prior to a cease-fire and unlike UNTAC's Human Rights Component, ONUSAL preceded the deployment of a larger military peacekeeping framework. It was authorized to monitor all peace agreements between the El Salvador government and the Frente Farabundo Martí para la Liberación Nacional (FMLN) guerrillas, but it was specifically mandated initially to verify compliance with the San José Accord on Human Rights concluded on 26 July 1990.[115] This provided a basic set of minimum standards for human rights to be met by the belligerents and outlined the terms of reference for a United Nations human rights verification mission.

Article 13 of the Accord stated: 'The purpose of the Mission shall be to investigate the human rights situation…as from the date of its establishment and to take any steps it deems appropriate to promote and defend such rights.' Article 14 referred to the Mission's mandate, which included, *inter alia*, the following powers:

a   to verify the observance of human rights in El Salvador;
b   to receive communications from any individual, group of individuals or body in El Salvador, containing reports of human rights violations;

c   to visit any place or establishment freely and without prior notice;

d   to hold its meetings freely anywhere in the national territory;

e   to interview freely and privately any individual, group of individuals or members of bodies or institutions;

f   to collect by any means it deems appropriate such information as it considers relevant;

g   to make recommendations to the Parties on the basis of any conclusions it has reached with respect to cases or situations it may have been called upon to consider; and

h   to offer its support to the judicial authorities of El Salvador in order to help improve the judicial procedures for the protection of human rights and increase respect for the rules of due process of law.

ONUSAL launched its first phase of operations on 26 July 1991, but despite these wide powers it interpreted its mandate narrowly and relied excessively on local institutions. In his first report, the Director of the Human Rights Division, Philippe Texier, stated that

> Salvadoreans right across the political spectrum believe that the Mission will be able to prevent, or at least punish, human rights violators....[I]t is worth remembering that while its verification possibilities are considerable, it does not have the power to prevent violations or to punish violators.[116]

In an interview with Americas Watch, he further stated that regardless of the language of the San José Accord, 'we cannot do a direct investigation, but rather, do so by observing the process of justice'.[117] Others in the Mission disagreed and conducted independent investigations. 'The lack of a standard investigative procedure,' argued Americas Watch, 'has meant that it is often left to the individual employee, or to the director of one of ONUSAL's regional officers, to determine to what extent and how any given case should be investigated.'[118]

A Police Division was established[119] as part of the enlargement of ONUSAL's mandate pursuant to the conclusion of peace agreements between the El Salvador government and the FMLN. These were the New York Act of 31 December 1991 and the Chapultepec Agreement of 16 January 1992. The Police Division was to supervise the maintenance of public order by the National Police (PN), until such time as a newly created and integrated National Civil Police (PNC), trained at a newly established National Academy for Police Security, could assume law enforcement functions. To do so UN observers were to be placed in key PN offices around the country and accompany PN patrols on their rounds. Such monitoring was meant to prevent acts of intimidation or human rights violations by PN officials. As well, it 'was to ensure adequate law enforcement in order to generate popular confidence in national reconciliation'.[120]

Unfortunately, the Police Division interpreted its mandate narrowly and fulfilled its tasks only intermittently. It should have coordinated with the Human

Rights Division but did not, and cooperation was left to the discretion of individual officers. It could not operate at night. Both its inability to provide security in FMLN zones and its presence at illegal acts of the PN, such as evictions, gave both sides the image that the Police Division was biased. It should have played an independent role to avoid this. Americas Watch concluded:

> the access of the Police Division to National Police operations makes it the best suited for overseeing police investigations. Yet despite its ability to deploy personnel to monitor preliminary and ongoing police investigations, ONUSAL's Police Division has not consistently chosen to do so. This represents a tremendous waste of ONUSAL's resources and potential.[121]

Furthermore, in the absence of an independent capacity for prosecution, ONUSAL was fatally reliant on El Salvador's judicial system. Judges did not recognize the various agreements and refused to cooperate. ONUSAL officials who did investigate cases were quickly checked by the pervasive criminal justice system. One official said: 'What is called "judicial power" is not power. Nothing works, not just the judges. The defense doesn't defend, the Attorney-General's office doesn't investigate.'[122] ONUSAL called for complete reform of the judicial system,[123] but was unable to allay fears and mistrust among the general population of authority and government institutions.

Two commissions appointed by the UN Secretary-General had been accepted by the parties in 1991 to purify the armed forces and break the impunity of human rights violators. The Ad-Hoc Commission of September 1991 reviewed records of military officers in order to purge those who committed or tolerated human rights abuses. The Commission on the Truth was charged under the Mexico City Agreements of 27 April 1991 with investigating serious acts of violence committed since 1980 and 'whose mark on society demands with great urgency public knowledge of the truth'. Both required the cooperation of the government given the wide range and large number of abuses, lack of information on individual responsibility and short time-frames of operation – three and six months, respectively. Also, the findings could only result in the release of officers from active-duty service and not their prosecution.

On 15 March 1993, the Truth Commission produced its 800-page report. It had examined 18,000 cases of human rights abuse, 90 per cent of them by the army and 'death squads' of the security forces. It recommended the dismissal of forty senior army officers, including the Defence Minister, General Rene Poncé, who in November 1989 ordered the murder of six Jesuit priests, their housekeeper and her daughter. In anticipation of the report, Poncé resigned three days earlier after bitterly attacking the Commission. In response to the recommendations, President Alfredo Cristiani and the Nationalist Republican Alliance (ARENA)-controlled Legislative Assembly passed a broad amnesty law exonerating the accused. This was in spite of the fact that the peace accords had explicitly avoided amnesty as a means towards national reconciliation.[124]

The question posed by the experience of ONUSAL is whether a peace-maintenance operation specifically designated with a law and order mandate could operate independently of a coherently functioning host government or without the larger security framework of a peace process. ONUSAL did not have the authority to arrest, detain, prosecute or punish individuals, nor did it utilize fully its quite considerable interventionary powers. The question arises as to what means would be required for a peace-maintenance operation to carry out such tasks.[125]

PEACE-MAINTENANCE LAW ENFORCEMENT

Can a peace-maintenance law and order mechanism, that operates independently of the subjective interests of individual states in specific cases, that is organized and controlled by the international community as a whole or in some other joint manner, be developed to enforce an international criminal code through the apprehension, detention, prosecution and punishment of offenders? Most attempts to address the enforcement of international criminal law have focused on prosecution, and the judicial plans for this are better developed. Largely absent, or only superficially addressed, are the other practical problems which tend to be left beyond the writ of legal planners. The process of developing the ICC and the former Yugoslav Tribunal as judicial bodies needs to be connected to the policing experience from, for instance, the factional environment of Cambodia and the authoritarian conditions of El Salvador. Together, these inchoate fragments for implementing international criminal conventions constitute the basis of peace-maintenance law enforcement.

As part of the second generation concept on using limited military force, 'Internal Conflict Resolution Measures are the actions taken by a UN multinational force to restore and maintain an acceptable level of peace and personal security in an internal conflict.'[126] Peace-maintenance military forces need to be able to: provide liaison between the belligerent parties; conduct a multi-party cease-fire; regroup into cantonment areas and disarm combatants; secure and maintain custody of war supplies; and supervise the reconstruction of a national and police defence force. Such operations have a multi-functional composition: a military force and monitors to conduct the disengagement phase of the peace process; election organization and verification teams; advisers on restoration of government functions, environment and mine clearance; assistance in rehabilitation of displaced populations and disarmed fighters; and military assistance and advice in the reconstruction and reorganization of police and defence forces.

> The provision of assistance to an interim civil authority usually follows a successfully conducted cease-fire....The overall task of the UN will be to supervise or police the provisions of a peace agreement and ensure the lead up to an election or transfer of power is conducted in a free and fair manner. The role of the military element is to maintain a workable level of peace and security which allows the humanitarian, human rights and civil administration elements of the UN force to function effectively.[127]

More specifically, peace-maintenance troops need to: assist in the maintenance of law and order; assist in the provision of security prior to, and during, an election; facilitate the transfer of power from the interim authority to an elected government; help to maintain the smooth running of essential services, such as power, water and communications; assist in the planning for, and reconstruction of, the national defence and police forces; assist in the relocation and rehabilitation of displaced elements of the population; and supervise and assist in the clearance and removal of unexploded ordnance and mines.

There are a number of basic requirements if UN and multinational police forces with military assistance are going to conduct successful law and order tasks, and overcome the essential problems of apprehending international criminals in the operational area of peace-maintenance.

Apprehension

The basic aim of apprehension is to secure custody of the offender. This raises a number of practical difficulties. It may be hard to find offenders. They will probably know the area – whether urban, rural, desert or jungle – better than the newly arrived peace-maintenance authority, and will be able to hide, move clandestinely and perhaps escape. In this they may be assisted by sympathetic members of the local population, other unknown offenders or armed forces loyal to the accused. Also, local officials may not cooperate for reasons of principle, even if they are opposed to the offender, for they may be against the nature of the UN activities. They may be partial, for personal or political reasons, and they may have direct interests either in the safety of the accused or, alternatively, in severe and unaccountable retribution. Furthermore, international forces may inadvertently assist an offender who is disguised as a demobilizing soldier, and who may then be assisted by a UN repatriation or rehabilitation component to relocate within the country or emigrate elsewhere. It may be simply not known who carried out a particular offence and UN investigations may be hampered by fear of victims and witnesses or ulterior motives of others in the area.

It will be probably difficult to determine the scope of culpability: principal offenders may be notorious, perhaps even mythic, but it would be difficult to establish who directly or indirectly assisted in the crimes – such as subordinates, civilians or political organizations locally or in a neighbouring state – and who tolerated the crimes, such as superior military officers, political parties or government officials. Consequently, there may be too many offenders to reasonably apprehend all or even most of them. It may be that individuals or political parties known to be guilty of offences are afforded effective immunity through their key role in a peace process. Guilty individuals or criminal organizations may move and act freely because the political cost of apprehending them may jeopardize other UN activities or endanger the personal security of UN officials. The UN may be unable to enter certain areas, which are usually strongholds of recalcitrant forces.

To mitigate some of these problems, even if only some of the time, peace-maintenance operations require a specialized capability for the purpose. To be effective, such a competence would have a number of requirements. Initially, there should be a small permanent headquarters office maintaining a store of expertise and knowledge. A core group of officers from the headquarters supplemented with additional, sufficient manpower could be attached to UN missions as required, although the team would operate with a certain amount of independence and would not be limited by the life of a larger operation. In the field, there must be sufficient personnel, resources and a mandated authority to conduct the full range of conventional policing powers: reporting, investigation, search, seizure, arrest and detention.

'Detention' in this context refers to the period between apprehension and delivery to a place of prosecution and is not to be confused with 'detention' during judicial proceedings. Some mobile facility for the purpose is required to avoid dependence on local jails. Delivery to the place of prosecution should be carried out as swiftly as possible to reduce the period of detention in the field in order to ensure the safety of the prisoners, to prevent escape and to avoid charges of 'unlawful detention'.

There must be a right of 'hot pursuit' across international boundaries. It would have to be determined whether this extended only to neighbouring states or applied generally to the movements of the accused. Freedom of movement for peace-maintenance apprehension should be as unrestricted as possible and only limited by the decision of a particular state with custody of the accused to try or extradite in conformity with its international obligations. Special agreements with states may be required for rights of passage across territory, as well as with states if the accused should be finally located within its national jurisdiction. In the latter case, the need for agreements may be self-defeating. The right of territorial access should be based on the obligation of states to furnish any and all assistance to the prosecution of international criminals.

The inclusion of such a capability in peace-maintenance, apart from preparatory or follow-up activities, ideally should be authorized by a competent body of the UN, such as through a resolution of the Security Council. However, it is also true that a standing mandate and universal jurisdiction exist in the international criminal code described previously in Chapter 4. Additional instructions in any UN decision should be clear and comprehensive, though not so precise as to limit the flexibility or diminish the effectiveness of the mission. In the field, a law and order capability, including civilian police and specialized military units, would be operationally responsible to the peace-maintenance political authority. In this manner, political command can ensure complete coordination with military, police, human rights and civil administration components of the peace-maintenance mission. As well, cooperation with and assistance from local police and military forces should be sought at all times, but not relied upon exclusively.

Since the principal authorities for a law and order capacity are the mandate of the peace-maintenance authority, based on UN Charter provisions[128] or multinational agreements, or the universality of and obligations under international criminal law, and not the consent of territorial host states in the area of its operations, the impartiality of the operation is defined by the objectivity with which the mandate is executed or law is enforced. And, again, an objective rule of law is guaranteed by its common application to both local offenders and international personnel. As part of a peace-maintenance operation, law and order activities are jointly controlled and directed and its mission is to function as a mechanism underwriting the international criminal code. In this, it must exercise its powers equally in all cases and ensure the aim of prosecution, not persecution. It cannot act with retribution, which is a matter for the court, and must guarantee the basic minimum rights of the offender.

While peace-maintenance law and order officials may have policing, military, legal or criminal investigative backgrounds, they must be further trained in international service and the peculiarities of international criminal apprehension. For instance, police officers will be operating as part of an international institution and must be prepared to challenge local authority and domestic laws, contrary to their conventional training, and they must be prepared to operate in unfamiliar environments where they may not be able to rely on knowledge of the language. Also, they must have a strong and rapid capability for information collection and analysis. This will require effective means of acquiring information – including rapid movement to sites of crimes, inspection of relevant areas, interviewing witnesses and transmitting data to field headquarters – as well as advanced means of recording evidence. This should be supported by a well-developed research capability at the mission's overall headquarters, with which deployed personnel should have an independent, continuous communications link.

Determining who should be apprehended may be pursuant to a warrant of arrest issued by an International Criminal Court, an ad hoc tribunal established for the area or the peace-maintenance judicial mechanisms. As well, field officials should be authorized to apprehend individuals on the basis of reasonable suspicion of guilt. This will require a functional set of criteria of guilt by which to operate. Apprehension of offenders following the conclusion of a specific operation will have to be pursued by the newly established local authority, or jointly – depending upon the follow-up status of the peace-maintenance authority. In any of their activities, peace-maintenance headquarters or field officials should solicit the assistance of national security services or cooperative bodies, such as INTERPOL or the European TREVI.[129]

Detention

By far less complicated, the aim of detention is to hold in custody an accused individual until a system of prosecution has been completed and a sentence passed. Facilities for this purpose will have to be located within daily commuting distance of the place of prosecution. If an ICC is created with a permanent, fixed location then a permanent facility may be established next to it. It is unlikely that such a facility would be an entirely international venture and would require significant assistance from the host state or a group of interested states. If the place of prosecution is an ad hoc tribunal or if the ICC is created with a mobile seat, then temporary facilities for the period of existence of the tribunal or Court would be required. These would have to be provided by the territorial host state, although the financial burden would be borne by states collectively in the manner of UN peace operations.

In either case, the bulk of the resources for a detention facility should be provided by the territorial host state where the Court is established or tribunal is sitting, but the facility should be controlled by the UN. 'Control' in this sense means the power to direct the overall process of detention while the host state physically administers the premises. To ensure that prisoners are treated equally, that international minimum standards of detention are guaranteed, and to verify that the host state fulfils its obligation of detention, strict supervision will be required, particularly if the facility is located in the place where the crime was committed.

Supervision should not be limited to occasional inspection; continued international presence should be guaranteed by international prison guards. These would need to serve under an inspector of guards, who would oversee the political direction and 'control' functions of the peace-maintenance authority, and who would operate in tandem with the chief warden of the prison, effectively the international inspector's subordinate. While the warden would be responsible for the principal administrative functions, the inspector would have the authority to ensure the impartiality of the facility, including the power to dismiss local officials or guards serving under the warden. This authority would be derived from a mandate of a competent UN body, such as the Security Council, through the peace-maintenance authority. The guards should have been specifically trained in penal detention and should be further trained in international service, given the potentially hostile atmosphere in which they may have to operate in the event of an ad hoc tribunal located where the crime was committed or if they are serving as part of a peace-maintenance operation. Also, it may be possible to employ military personnel for the purpose. The guards must be guaranteed freedom of movement at least between the facility and place of prosecution.

Punishment

The aim of punishment is to execute a sentence passed by an ICC, an international tribunal or peace-maintenance judicial body. Capital punishment should not be, and is unlikely to be, authorized collectively on general human rights grounds. The value of punishment is not to exact retribution; given the gravity of the offences there is unlikely to be a punishment to fit the crime. Rather, punishment should be conceived as a means to affirm the unacceptability of the offences and to create confidence in a local population as well as the international community that offenders will be tried. Consequently, life imprisonment will be the most likely sentence. Long terms of incarceration would pose a problem of resources if a large number of prisoners is envisioned. Therefore a similar, though more permanent, arrangement to international prison guard-supervision for detention might be required. This would be so whether a prison facility was located in the territory where the crime was committed or if a third state was requested to execute the sentence, either for an ad hoc tribunal solely, generally for an ICC or for a peace-maintenance authority. In the case of the ICC, a permanent facility in a single state supervised and controlled by international prison guards might be established for the general punishment of international criminals. But in peace-maintenance there will need to be a variety of options.

Part III

The evolution of peace-maintenance

6 Peace-maintenance in anarchical Somalia

The March 1995 departure of United Nations forces from Somalia resembled more a 'retreat' than a 'withdrawal'. In fact, the exit was declared a 'master-piece' in military terms by Assistant Secretary-General for Peace-Keeping Lieutenant-General Manfred Eisele. Early in the morning of 1 February, Pakistani troops abandoned the UN compound, formerly the site of the US embassy, which was to be returned to the US after the UN had spent $160 million on it in the preceding two years. Within moments, hundreds of looters and armed men loyal to the mission's nemesis, General Mohammed Farah Aidid, swarmed into the walled enclosure and stripped it unceremoniously of every piece of wood and wire, every movable object and removable part of the five permanent buildings, including their light fixtures and chairs.

Tension rose at the airport, the final point of departure and site of the initial landing of 500 Pakistani troops in September–October 1992.[1] Just as they had then been veritably imprisoned by a hostile environment, the last UN troops too were kept in a corner by aggressive militia, with only one way to move: out of Somalia.[2] An international operation with US marines mounted to secure the UN withdrawal was one of the final acts of the international community in Somalia. A *Financial Times* editorial referred to it as 'Operation Abandon Hope'.[3] The UN left behind the supremacy of the very warlords it had hoped to tame, unchallenged by new institutions or alternatives to leadership for the Somali people.[4] While mass starvation was finally ended with the arrival of US troops in December 1992, the continuation of anarchical conflict today threatens to invoke the spectre of famine again. The impact on the country had not been positively sustaining, with the fate unknown of those Somalis who remained loyal to UN forces. Perceived as the world's 'easy option', the Somalia experience had the psychological impact of an unexpected defeat. The country's ills proved impossible to cure in the manner they were treated.

However, many reasons for this have been lost or forgotten. As much printed material as there is available on Somalia, in UN reports, press coverage, and the cottage industry of secondary source publications in academic and practitioners' journals, only a limited amount has reflected the political strengths and pitfalls of US and UN operations in the field.[5] Critical internal documents never reached UN headquarters in New York. It was, comparatively, a closed operation, certainly by the critical stage of combat operations in summer 1993. The result is that few meaningful lessons have been identified from the watershed experience of the second generation of UN operations. And a disastrous effort by the Lessons Learned Unit of the Department of Peace-Keeping Operations (UNDPKO) in 1995 compounded the problem of trying to understand what happened in Somalia.[6]

United Nations secretariat officials, including the Secretary-General, permanent representatives at the Security Council, the United States diplomatic, military and political establishment, and politicians worldwide claimed opposing, sometimes simplistic and often mistaken interpretations and conclusions about what works and what does not in politically fostering peace. These rapidly hardened as stereotypic misconceptions and charted a skewed course both for peace operations and the UN itself. The essential challenges in Somalia were deep-rooted anarchy and the apocalyptic conditions this spawned. The international community used blunt instruments to respond to the crisis, first inter-state diplomacy among warring factions, and then intensive military force. Far from encouraging retreat from multinational deployments as a whole, the Somalia experience should have indicated that the missing link in UN missions is a political capability in the field.

The phases of international involvement in Somalia roughly correspond to the three eras of peace operations generally. The First United Nations Operation in Somalia (UNOSOM I) deployed gradually throughout 1992 and was based on the traditional, Cold War concept of diplomatic *peacekeeping*. The military force employed during the US-led coalition, the Unified Task Force (UNITAF), in late 1992 and early 1993, reflected the second generation era of *peace-enforcement*. The Second United Nations Operation in Somalia (UNOSOM II) after spring 1993, albeit shifting between these two models, needed a strong *peace-maintenance* capability to succeed. The first two had their place, but, by themselves, neither could have responded to the conditions in Somalia. Aspects of both had to be employed as part of a comprehensive strategy to respond to the social and political demands of Somali anarchy.

The failure of international efforts in Somalia was the reluctance to acknowledge in the conceptual development of UNOSOM II that the mission could not have been less than a *governorship* mission. It needed to establish a political centre of gravity if the anarchical roots of the conflict were to be replaced, and not merely the symptoms of famine and violence mitigated. Instead, the thinking of planners was still dominated by familiar extremes: defensive, diplomatic peace-keeping or intensive military force. This chapter concentrates on one illustrative phase of a much longer process: the point at which a political mandate was planned with diplomatic and military tools. The lessons from UNOSOM II are reassessed in this context so the Somali experience is instructional and not destructive, as the conclusions of the UN and the US have been.

UNITED NATIONS USE OF FORCE

UNOSOM II was regarded by UN Secretary-General Boutros Boutros-Ghali, public commentators and practitioners in the field as an experiment in 'peace-enforcement'. However, this was an ill-defined concept, interpreted literally and confused with the much broader concept of 'enforcement' under Article 42 of the UN Charter.

Collective enforcement

The use of armed force was considered the ultimate sanction of the United Nations system. In the event that non-military responses to a cross-boundary breach of the peace under Article 41 proved inadequate, Article 42 provided for 'action by air, sea, or land forces as may be necessary to maintain or restore international peace and security'. The drafters of the Charter outlined a scheme for the provision and direction of such forces in Articles 43–50. UN member states, particularly the powerful permanent members of the Security Council, agreed to make available on call their armed forces and facilities for the successful conduct of international military operations. These perpetually available forces would be under the strategic direction of a Military Staff Committee (MSC) composed of the Chiefs-of-Staff of the Security Council permanent members. Translating broad political decisions into specific military instructions, the MSC was designed as a vital link between the legal legitimacy and political authority of the Security Council and the tactical effectiveness of operations in the field.[7]

In this concept of 'collective security' the word 'collective' had a special meaning. It did not refer merely to a group of states cooperating as a coalition in a particular venture, but to the subordination of military assets of at least the most powerful states to a central authority in advance of any crisis. Establishing a degree of objectivity, automaticity and consistency in responding to emergencies was the ideal of a genuine system of international law and order. Collective security had a genesis over five hundred years and the UN's version was intended to halt and reverse acts of inter-state aggression by a recalcitrant member of the international community.[8]

In pursuit of establishing such a system, the ideal was pitted opposite the prevailing anarchical system of balances of power and the wars shifts this balance necessitated. With conceptual attention focused on two extremes, the span of activity within collective security at one end of the pole was not adequately distinguished. Over time, international law and diplomacy determined a span of non-military activities to pacifically settle disputes or to negotiate the avoidance, mitigation or end of hostilities.[9] Meanwhile in war, strategies were refined for defeating an enemy. In traditional warfare a competition between territorially fixed opponents meant clear delineation on the battlefield and a single objective of subduing the vanquished to the will of the victor.[10] The United Nations was born in the wake of concepts of 'total war' and 'Blitzkrieg'. Consequently, the tools available to the new system were black and white: non-military action or the unlimited, and therefore uncontrollable, use of force; and the latter amounted to the kind of violence used in traditional warfare.

However, as pointed out in Chapter 4, international law does not regard the international aggressor as an 'enemy' nor consider it criminal in the manner that a murderer is in national legal systems. The sovereignty of states renders the crime, not the perpetrator, the enemy. Enforcement actions, therefore, are circumscribed in how they halt and reverse aggression. The use of force is to be more accountable than it can be under the laws limiting traditional warfare. A 'state of war' is unlawful in the first place and, once entered, the humanitarian laws of war at best can identify excesses of illegal force. But enforcement actions, derived from international authority, have to adhere rigorously to the rule of proportionality. They are to use only the amount of force comparable to the force used in an initial violation or not more than required to reverse the conditions that resulted from the violation.[11]

To match these legal requirements, a specific military doctrine was necessary to distinguish enforcing international rules of law from subduing an opponent in pursuit of national victory. Such a concept was not available to the international community, and although it could have been adapted from the existing arsenal of military strategies for using force, this was not done since there had not been the need: 'collective', as opposed to 'cooperative', armed forces had not been put to the test. The core scheme of the UN was stillborn, even before the signing of the Charter in June 1945 as its drafters witnessed an increasing polarization between the United States and the Soviet Union.[12] As its name suggested, to function the United Nations had to rely on the kind of cooperation that existed between the Allied nations to reverse Nazi aggression and defeat the Axis powers of the Second World War. Instead, it fell victim to the ideological stalemate of the Cold War: the two superpowers could not agree on the numbers of forces to be placed at the disposal of the UN and consequently the ideal was left to atrophy.[13] Although the MSC was established, it has existed only pro forma. There has not been an international strategic directorate to translate adequately Security Council decisions into military action. While national ministries and departments of defence had a capacity to interpret political instructions, they had to guarantee national interests and did not have an international mandate to develop objective UN strategies. Therefore, when collective armed forces were needed, the UN system had no one allocated to adapt military instruments from warfare to enforcement nor any means to command them.

There is a mistaken belief that Article 42 action can be carried out only by the instrument envisioned in Article 43 of the Charter.[14] But Article 42 does not state this[15] and action could be undertaken by forces established, for instance, under the implied powers of other Charter provisions[16] or as a subsidiary organ under Article 7(2).[17] Nevertheless, Article 42 has never been relied on explicitly as a legal basis for military deployments: armed force in Korea in the 1950s was based on 'recommendations' to member states under Article 39 of the Charter;

Security Council authorization permitting Great Britain the use of force to inter-
dict the passage of oil into Southern Rhodesia in 1966 was a kind of Article 41
1/2, or the use of force to underwrite economic sanctions; and the 1991 Persian
Gulf War was based on Chapter VII as a whole and used the language of
Article 42 without expressly referring to it.[18] In each case, 'enforcement' relied
on the willingness of individual states to act independently or participate in
loose-knit cooperative arrangements or coalitions. A single nation dominated
each action and at no time was there a high-intensity military operation functionally integrated as part of the UN system nor armed forces genuinely placed
under UN command and control for this purpose. Consequently, a commonly
accepted approach to enforcement was not developed; member states conducted
warfare as they knew how, against North Korea and Iraq.

In principle, an operation authorized by a Security Council resolution
subcontracting specific tasks to a state or group of states still may be regarded a
collective action[19] if the commander is accountable and responsible to the direction of the UN. It is more important for the political direction of an operation to
be collectively mandated than for armed forces to be multinationally composed
and collectively commanded. However, in Korea, the US command was not as
directly responsible to the UN as it should have been, but the use of force was
mostly limited geographically by the political restrictiveness of the Cold War to
the *locus delicti* south of the 38th Parallel.[20] In the Gulf, the use of force was not
limited to Kuwaiti territory nor in intensity by a Soviet check or balance. With a
carte blanche Security Council resolution arrived at by diplomatic pressure, the
United States conducted an unfettered, disproportionate military campaign.
This was subsequently criticized. Nations which voted in favour of Security
Council Resolution 678 authorizing 'all necessary means' had not expected the
degree of force used nor the interpretation of 'all necessary' to mean 'unlimited'.
There were charges that the Security Council had been unlawfully hijacked.[21]

The US Pentagon, on the other hand, found the Gulf experience to be a
model which fitted its established war-fighting strategy, embodied in the six so-
called 'Weinberger principles'. Developed in 1984 under then Secretary of
Defence Caspar Weinberger, in the wake of the marines' withdrawal from
Lebanon, they called for the use of overwhelming force against a clearly identifiable enemy.[22] The principles were military imperatives that had been turned into
foreign policy and effectively severed operations in the field from civilian political
goals in Washington until the enemy had been defeated. Furthermore, the
Pentagon felt that 'coalition warfare' was a cost-effective arrangement for
America's future military engagements.[23] In 1992, military envoys in
Washington of countries such as Britain and Australia defined cooperation as
the best way to integrate their forces under a US command. Others felt that the
Gulf War was an aberration and its scale unlikely to be repeated soon, and that
there was other activity needing attention.

At the UN, legal and political control over nations subcontracted out of
necessity was to be tightened. The distance between Security Council decisions
and operations in the field had grown too great, rendering UN resolutions mere

camouflage for ulterior motives of member states. So when the United States offered troops and leadership of another coalition in late November 1992 for Somalia, a Security Council and Secretary-General without alternatives accepted gratefully. But after the Gulf, they clarified somewhat the mission to be undertaken and tried to ensure their direct participation in operational decision-making. 'All necessary means' in Security Council Resolution 794 of 3 December 1992 was qualified with reporting and joint consultative procedures. In this manner, there was a partial convergence of international direction and subcontracted great power assets in a kind of joint operation juridically that crystallized functionally with the need of the US to withdraw in the spring of 1993 and the attempt to unite UN contingents and US coalition forces in a single operation. The overall experience of Somalia eventually led by the summer of 1994 to a complete divergence of the two and a return, more robustly than ever, to great power military expeditions in the national interest and the conscription into national service of the UN through fig-leaf resolutions authorizing such actions.[24]

By early 1993, in military circles a false distinction had been drawn between 'UN operations' and coalition operations with UN resolutions.[25] In the former, national forces helped implement UN diplomatic decisions, while in the latter military imperatives or national interests in the field determined a response first, and only then was a resolution to be sought for approval. This distinction had a historical basis, because the UN had only commanded less complex peace-keeping operations while large-scale force had been the monopoly of states. But it cannot be sustained in law: whether under the Secretariat's command and control or sub-contracted to a coalition, an operation is either a UN mission or it is not. Forces mandated by UN resolutions should fly the blue flag and not a grey combination of national flags. But this is not enough: the blue flag flew in Korea and not over coalition forces in Somalia, yet the former was less under UN direction than the latter. It is still something else to be fully integrated under UN command and control. Juridically on paper, UNOSOM II was the first experiment of such an operation with quasi-enforcement powers. But the dominance of the US in the field and the special relationship of US forces to the UN Force Commander, as well as the UN Secretary-General's direct contact with US policy-making in Washington, rendered it structurally another species of joint operation.

Joint peace-enforcement

Furthermore, the mandate of UNOSOM II was not 'enforcement' in the manner of reversing inter-state aggression. It was perceived to be 'peace-enforcement', which was something less, but it was not clear what. Paragraph 44 of *An Agenda for Peace* was a proposal more for a mechanism than a concept. 'Peace enforcement *units*' were distinguished from the large-scale forces outlined in Article 43 of the Charter. The UN, it said, had been called on to restore cease-fires that had broken down and this required something more than what the Secretariat had at its disposal. The 'units' would be available on call, undergo advance training, and be deployed under the authority of the Security Council and commanded by the Secretary-General. Their deployment was to be considered provisional measures under Article 40 of the Charter. The *Agenda* did not elaborate further on the meaning of peace-enforcement.

Not only was the *Agenda* a document drafted by committee and insufficiently detailed, but national defence bureaucracies and the UN Secretariat had conflicting approaches to the development of doctrine for multinational operations. Therefore, despite the limited Security Council check and balance on UNITAF and the UN's juridical control of UNOSOM II, US strategic domination throughout the process and the lack of a functional UN doctrine obscured the fundamental distinction between enforcement and peace-enforcement. The conceptual stage was set for a flawed and uncontrollable experiment in Somalia of historic significance. There was not to be a genuine experiment with limited uses of force. Instead, operations shifted between extremes of inaction or excessive force. Resulting false conclusions argued that the middle ground between peacekeeping and high-intensity operations failed its test.

The United States, the United Nations machinery and the UN Secretary-General all had different perspectives on the intensity of coercion armed forces in Somalia were to use. The United States brought to the field not only its Gulf War experience, its coalition model and 'new world order' peace-fighting strategy, but in fact Central Command was responsible for both missions and many of the same troops and officers were deployed from the Gulf to Somalia. United Nations officials were still rooted in the traditional peacekeeping school and carried this baggage in an overwhelmingly hostile environment. Conceptually, the Secretary-General was somewhere between these two positions. Without adequate clarity, he pushed for an extensive test of UN command and control. He later admitted that *An Agenda for Peace* had only 'touched on peace enforcement'.[26] Individually, none of these views suited operational requirements in Somalia, as the limitations of UNOSOM I and UNITAF illustrated. Together, they subverted UNOSOM II: a mission underwritten by divided perceptions fractured and was overwhelmed by a fragmented environment.

United Nations officials concluded that military force should not be used in peace operations,[27] since the degree of destruction in Somalia was not matched by achievement of many objectives. The United States decided that failure was due to the fact that not enough force was available for use.[28] And the Secretary-General returned to black-and-white options, the very conditions that had led initially to the need for a third option. He stated in his 'Supplement to An Agenda for Peace' that: 'Peace-keeping and the use of force…should be seen as alternative techniques and not as adjacent points on a continuum.'[29] He falsely declared that the most successful operations in recent years respected the traditional peacekeeping principles of consent of the parties, impartiality and the non-use of force except in self-defence. The 'Supplement's' general reaffirmation of traditional peacekeeping stood in stark contrast to the types of 'peace-keeping operations' it described.[30] The scenarios were beyond the kinds of conditions in which peacekeeping developed and inherently challenged the principles of traditional doctrine. That reliance on conventional peacekeeping in internal conflicts had repeatedly proved inadequate was ignored.

At the other extreme, the Secretary-General disregarded the essentially political framework in which legitimate peace-enforcement has to be conducted. He stated: 'The logic of peace-keeping flows from political and military premises that are quite distinct from those of enforcement; and the dynamics of the latter are incompatible with the political process that peace-keeping is intended to facilitate.'[31] This is a confusion of political activity and diplomatic processes. It is as part of the latter that peacekeeping is traditionally deployed, but exercising political authority is distinctly more complicated. Essentially, the Secretary-General divided the third option in two and relegated one part back to expanded but traditionally conceived peacekeeping, and the other to enforcement. He further regarded 'peace-enforcement' explicitly as synonymous with high-intensity enforcement characteristic of Article 42 of the Charter. In paragraph 23 he listed the 'instruments for peace and security', among which he included 'peace-enforcement'; yet Section III.F, corresponding to this, was titled 'Enforcement action' and paragraphs 77–80 described the kind of response to inter-state aggression. Anything other than peacekeeping or large-scale force therefore was obscured.

The United States is most familiar with massive force. In the wake of its experience in Somalia, the year-long inter-departmental debate in Washington about the criteria for engagement in UN operations was settled in spring 1994, one month after the US withdrawal from Mogadishu. On 3 May, President Bill Clinton signed Presidential Decision Directive 25 (PDD-25), the 'U.S. Policy Guidance on Reforming Multilateral Peace Operations'.[32] Largely declassified, except for sections on US views of Russian 'peace-creation' in the Near Abroad, PDD-25 was an initiative of the Pentagon to restrict political commitment of US military resources. It applied to peacekeeping the Weinberger principles, or 'Powell doctrine' – after the former Chairman of the Joint Chiefs, General Colin L. Powell.[33] Before departure from office in late 1993, he insisted on inclusion of the Weinberger–Powell logic in the PDD process. Therefore, US participation depended on the potential for results in a period of limited duration. It was a 'quick-fix' concept requiring clear conditions, a free hand to operate in the field and an exit strategy.

Like the Weinberger principles for war-fighting, Powell's peacekeeping formula was dominated by military imperatives, which were again transformed into a political strategy and foreign policy. A recipe for disaster, the doctrine severed political decision-making from unrestricted military operations conducted in a veritable vacuum. It amounted to the idea that once troops were deployed the political role had concluded until the military job was done. This was the development of a catch-all sledgehammer which had proved to be dysfunctional in the essentially social and political environment of internal conflicts – not least in Vietnam – where the 'enemy' could not always be identified. The Vietnam War generation of military officers perceived that decisive force would have prevented the mistakes leaders made in the 1960s;[34] yet this conclusion led them to make the same mistakes in the 1990s as they applied military solutions to political problems.[35] In reference to Bosnia but as applicable to the streets of Mogadishu, Powell conceded the limitations of his doctrine when he said: 'We do deserts. We don't do mountains.'[36]

PDD-25 was further exacerbated by partisan party politics and the introduction of legislation in the US House of Representatives and Senate in January 1995 as part of the Republicans' 'Contract with America'.[37] The 'National Security Revitalization Act' (H.R.7) and 'Peace Powers Act' (S.5) proposed repealing the 'War Powers Resolution' of 1973. This would have removed Congressional restrictions on the President's authority to go to war, as he would no longer have to report to Congress within sixty days of deploying troops unilaterally. Yet extraordinary restrictions were imposed on the Executive's role in UN peace operations. Not only had the Congress to participate in each stage of decision-making, but the President had to certify to Congress that:

1   the US participation in a UN operation is necessary to protect US national security;
2   the commander of the unit retains the right to report independently to superior US military authorities, and can decline orders judged to be illegal, imprudent or beyond the mandate agreed upon by the US until superiors override this;
3   US forces remain under US administrative command for discipline and evaluation; and
4   the US retains its authority to withdraw.

The Acts also imposed severe financial restrictions on US–UN peacekeeping relations. Holding the UN fiscally responsible for US military interventions could quickly bankrupt the organization as a whole.

The passage of parts of the legislation limited the scope of US engagement in UN operations. Relying on US forces in the field has become an unreliable proposition for the UN if units can withdraw in the grip of a crisis, exposing to danger other contributing member states' contingents. Doing so would be a contravention of obligations incumbent on the US under Article 25 of the UN Charter, which binds member states to accept and carry out decisions of the Security Council. Therefore, if the US were to be explicitly authorized by the Security Council to perform specific tasks with other member states, as it was in Somalia, it could not unilaterally withdraw against the express will of the Council. To avoid this possibility, the US may relegate itself less to a military role than a diplomatic function, underwriting peace operations with its presence in a negotiating process, fostering the political will of others – as argued in the next chapter. But can it be credibly engaged if its own commitment on dangerous ground is at best symbolic? And will other nations contributing troops accept such a role for the US? It may instead continue its attempts to use force 'on the cheap' through long-distance bombing – until otherwise compelled to deploy, as in Bosnia. As the UN Force Commander in Sarajevo, General Phillipe Morillon, argued: 'You can't have soldiers ready to kill but not willing to die.'[38]

Both UN and US options again resemble extremes. Severing both enforcement from a political process by the Secretary-General and military imperatives from political direction by the US will exacerbate the fog of peace missions. Somali anarchy emphasized the need for precisely the opposite: the subordination of diplomatic, military, humanitarian and civilian tools to a political peace-maintenance framework that could ensure functional harmonization, not merely coordination, and respond to the daily evolution of local social and political conditions. To succeed along these lines, UNOSOM II planners required a comprehensive historical and sociological assessment of the root causes of the crisis.[39]

SOMALIA'S POLITICAL ANARCHY

Anarchy, it could be said, was a principal characteristic of Somali social organization before the colonial powers' scramble for Africa reached the Horn. That is, if anarchy is understood to mean the absence of a central government, or by implication the trappings of a European sovereign state. Anarchy is not a vacuum, however: the alternative to modern sovereign government may not be disorder, but an unfamiliar order; and even when the absence of centralized authority does result in disorder, there proliferate, not stagnate, in political fragmentation social and political factions.

Fractured homogeneity

In Somalia, there was a fundamental difference between the chaotic disorder and uncertainty that followed the collapse of the Somali Republic in January 1991 and the lack of centralized authority in pre-colonial times. The conventional view holds that 'Somalia has dissolved into its traditional segmentary divisions', and rather than being anarchical, Somali society has returned to its traditional institutions of clans and sub-clans.[40] This does not explain, however, why

> At no time in the recorded history of Somalia has nearly one-third to one-half of the population died or been in danger of perishing due to famine caused by civil war. This calamity surpasses all previous ones and can be appropriately called '*Dad Cunkii*', the era of cannibalism.[41]

The successors to the Somali state were not clans and sub-clans, which were reverted to by the population as social institutions, but political factions. These armed groups, which commanded some resources and managed to control limited territorial areas and their populations, may have been divided along clan or sub-clan lines initially. But they perpetually fragmented into splinter factions and formed alliances out of convenience or by necessity that crossed clan lines. Established and led by warlords and their cronies who galvanized support through clan allegiance, factions became the repositories of power by the force of arms. However, the evolution of factional violence did not proceed according to clan loyalty, but according to the necessities dictated by the exercise of power through violence and the vicissitudes of uncontrolled warlords. This was only a recent phenomenon in Somali history. But why was there no check or balance in society to prevent the emergence of factions, as there had been in the past?

The pre-colonial Somali community extended beyond the geographical boundaries of modern Somalia to Djibouti, the Ogaden region of Ethiopia and the Northern Frontier District in Kenya. In this general area there was perhaps the most homogenous ethnic community in a single place on the African continent. Islam had been commonly adhered to since the eighth century and almost the entire population today is Sunni Muslim. Somalis spoke the same Cushtic language and shared common customs and traditions and a single culture. Of the population estimated in 1992 to be 6.5 million, 98.8 per cent were ethnically Somali and only 1.2 per cent Arab or Asian. This included the 250,000 Bantu- and Swahili-speaking groups settled along and between the Shebelle and Juba river valleys in southern Somalia.

Despite this homogeneity, there was no collective Somali consciousness. The overwhelming majority of Somalis were nomadic, probably necessitated by a change in climate in northern Africa in the third millennium BC. Fertile savannah became the desiccated Sahara and the arid desert and semi-arid savannah of the Horn. Only the Shebelle–Juba plateau afforded the option of settled cultivation. Consequently, the majority of the population were pastoral herders. This developed into the ideal of nomadic independence among the majority, who then despised settled agricultural cultivation, the formal cooperation this required, and the hierarchy, authority and governmental organization that resulted. In fact, the all-pervasive Koranic jurisdiction was distinguished from any kind of centralized civil law, which was popularly referred to as 'Al-Jabr' – 'the tyranny'.[42] A traditional Somali proverb stated: 'Me and Somalia against the world, Me and my clan against Somalia, Me and my family against the clan, and Me against the family.'[43] Groups that were not pastoral herders were either denigrated or excluded from a kind of existing caste system. In the nomadic habit, there was not a sense of individual possession of measured parcels of land, nor of any inherent linkage of the whole Somali population to a geographical area or a central authority to regulate this.

Instead, characteristic of nomadic social organization, Somalis did not identify with other ethnic Somalis regardless of origin, but differentiated themselves from other Somalis according to their patrilineal genealogical origins. Extended family groups formed by finding a common heritage in a common ancestor. These clans further divided into sub-clans and eventually immediate families. Families constituted the basic building block of society and the household the basic unit of production. With such complete fragmentation, and given inequalities between clans, sub-clans or families, even within the equalitarian nature of Somali society, and given the appetites of the strong or the weak that invariably feed on this inequality, there is no reason to suggest why Somalis should not have descended into perpetual and internecine violence of the kind that characterized 1991.

Except that in pre-colonial times there prevailed a kind of pan-Somali code of conduct called the *Xeer*. This was 'a set of rules and norms...socially constructed to safeguard security and social justice within and among Somali communities', to which Muslim values were added as Islam spread throughout the area.[44] Clans and families could not muster enough resources and were not sufficiently centralized to exploit inequalities. The communitarian nature of Somali society prevented classes being stratified according to wealth. As a social contract, the *Xeer* regulated conflicts 'in the absence of centralised coercive machinery' through the generally accepted ethic of 'the absolute necessity of relying and living on one's labour/livestock rather than exploiting others'. It was a self-regulating system in which one was prevented from dominating others.

The source of individual authority, then, was not the capacity to control others, but the capability to ensure others were not controlled. Most individuals were involved in productive activity, and the effectiveness of one's household management in this regard was a prerequisite for leadership. Leaders would be elected by majority votes of informal councils or assemblies known as the *Shir*, composed of any member of a particular lineage. *Shirs* also made most political and judicial decisions, limiting the exercise of leadership powers. Decisions were implemented by committees of elders appointed for a specific purpose by the elected leaders. In this manner, the ideal of decentralization was guaranteed and checks and balances against exploitation were safeguarded.

Colonial centralization

Under colonial administration, a new set of relations developed. The Somali nomadic space was divided into five parts. To protect the trading links of its colony at Aden from other powers such as France, in 1886 Britain declared northern Somalia a protectorate (British Somaliland). In 1888, France established its own colony at Djibouti (French Somaliland). The Ogaden was ceded to Ethiopia in 1897 and later the Northern Frontier District became part of British colonial Kenya. Italy claimed southern Somalia in 1905 and consolidated its control by 1927 (Italian Somalia). Despite Somali indignation, political, social and above all psychological or perceptual fragmentation meant there could not be any immediate concerted response to the arrival of European powers.

Colonial administration necessitated centralization of authority if a European minority was to govern an indigenous majority. This was partly the imposition of the centralizing characteristic of sovereignty and the nation-state system that had originated on the European continent over several centuries, and which operated in a context of checks and balances on power which were lost when exported. One legacy of the colonial venture and the cost of independence would be retention of the nation-state system as a means of ensuring international acceptance of the fact of self-rule. Centralization was also the nature of imperial policy, and, as outlined in Chapter 2, politically organizing disparate groups, cultures or nationalities and their resources under a paramount authority had an older history than did the nation-state.[45]

Colonial centralization necessarily challenged the traditional source of authority in the pastoral political system. It introduced into daily life commercialism and therefore the domination of the pastoral producers by non-producers – the merchant or the colonial state-enterprise – which claimed control of pastoral surplus production. The communitarian social order without resource-based classes 'was superseded by an economy in which the competition for access to commodities, the consumption of objects beyond one's productive capabilities, and the accumulation of wealth in the urban centres were paramount'.[46] The establishment of a class of Somalis not engaged in production but with means of authority in turn generated in the colonial state system a Western-educated and acculturated élite capable of participating, not just in commercial enterprises, but in political life as well.

In the cities, the legitimacy of authority no longer relied on an individual's productive capability. Commercialism and the predominance of a new culture which sought to concentrate capital through exploitation displaced the *Xeer* ethic of mutual non-exploitation. By this the fundamental check and balance on power was discarded without there being available a replacement: an independent state-system with foreign origins could rely on neither European nor indigenous restrictions on power. Clan assemblies and committees of elders no longer made sense as a political system; they continued as social institutions in the face of state centralization.

The focus of Somali concerns centred, not on Somali exploitation of Somalis, but on European exploitation of Somalis. There was the natural desire of an indigenous people to expel foreign powers; but there was also the desire to attain the resources and exercise of authority of the colonial administrators. This was one consequence of the *Xeer*'s displacement and the absence of new rules of political behaviour distinguishing, if not separating, commercial and political enterprises. In fact, resisting colonial domination meant mustering the resources to do so, competing for control of produced surplus in the manner of the colonial master, and in so doing accelerating the replacement of Somalis' own pastoral nomadic culture. Most significantly, developing the means to challenge colonial authority meant Somalis had available the tools to fight one another. This dissolved the *Xeer* glue that regulated conflicts and held Somali society together in some kind of anarchical order. It laid the roots of future chaos when the independent Somali state finally collapsed.

Resisting colonial administration displaced the primacy in Somali society of the clans; divided as they were, it was easy for them to be ruled. Islam was a unifying force and indigenous leaders based their cause on the concept of *jihad* against the 'infidels'. There developed a kind of proto-nationalism in which the concept of clan was extended to all Somalis. This pan-Somali identity was linked to territory in the geographic nationalism that emerged after the Second World War. The notion of the Somali community being tied to territory, the notion of settlement, contradicted a nomadic past. It was another feature that at once was a centralizing tendency and served to fracture traditional institutions. Order now relied almost exclusively on the capacity of the state structure to take root and govern effectively.

Independent dictatorship

This was not to be.[47] In 1960, British Somaliland and Italian Somalia gained independence and joined to become the Somali Republic. The new country comprised only two of the five parts of the Somali ethnic population. Since the people were now identified with a geographical area, the notion of a 'Greater Somalia' developed, including the Somali communities in Djibouti, Ethiopia and Kenya as rightful members of the Republic. Foreign policy in independent Somalia aimed in part to 'liberate' Somalis in neighbouring territories, and the five-pointed star on the national flag, which symbolized the colonial division, was a reminder that the homeland could be united. In the absence of a *Xeer* to check or balance the exercise of government authority, the will to dominate extended beyond the borders of the state. Secessionist movements were supported in the Ogaden and the Northern Frontier District. Somalia fought violent wars with Ethiopia in 1961, 1964 and 1977–8. Hostility between the two continued throughout the 1980s. A war with Kenya lasted from 1963 to 1967.

Internally, unchecked exercise of political authority and imbalanced economic exploitation had its consequences. Despite the inheritance of democracy, the multi-party parliamentary state was supported by a weak civil society with fragmented institutions that had not been reconstituted to sustain representative government. The economy was stagnant: there was intense competition among élites for resources while there was not enough surplus to be reinvested to expand the productive base. Instead, resources were obtained through overseas loans. This 'made the state the most lucrative source of funds. It was the competition among the élite for these resources that ultimately led to the degeneration of the major political parties and the demise of parliamentary governance.'[48] The number of political parties and candidates for parliamentary seats increased dramatically between 1964 and 1969, since the best access to state resources was as an elected official, and, once elected, officials had the resources to get re-elected.

These were the conditions that led to dictatorship. The ruling clique was drawn from the two organizations that had agitated for independence, the Somali Youth League (SYL) and the Somali National League (SNL), established in 1945 and 1947, respectively. It was able to consolidate its control over state resources. However, since even state resources were limited, and since the parliamentary system enabled a majority of members denied their share to defeat the Government, it was imperative that important changes in the political process be brought about to save the system from consuming itself. In essence this meant shedding the 'democratic,' if not the electoral, paraphernalia, and imposing a petit-bourgeois dictatorship on the Somali society that required the support of the army.[49]

After the assassination in October 1969 of the President, Abdulrashid Al Sharmarke, who had been previously Somalia's first Prime Minister, the army stepped into the confusion and established a military government, the Supreme Revolutionary Council (SRC). Under the chairmanship of the army's senior officer, Major-General Muhammed Siad Barre, it dismissed Parliament, banned political parties, cancelled the 1960 Constitution, renamed the country the Somali Democratic Republic and adopted an ideology of 'scientific socialism'. In 1976, pressured by his Soviet patrons, Barre established the Somali Revolutionary Socialist Party and proclaimed himself Secretary-General.

Under Barre's dictatorship, the Somali state came to an end.[50] The SRC was initially welcomed by the public as a means of ending the scramble for resources in government, but it soon became apparent that Barre was the greatest looter of all. The regime lost credibility following the 1977–8 defeat in the Ogaden. The ideology of scientific socialism was discredited following US replacement of Soviet patronage. A new competition for power among the élite and members of government was triggered, but this time armed force replaced electoral manipulation. Barre responded by rewarding those loyal to him with more and more state resources, and any opposition was persecuted and violently punished. Somali nationalism and the need for popular legitimacy were discarded. Instead, to replace those he purged from his administration and the military, Barre sought loyalists in his immediate family, his Marehan sub-clan and Darod clan. State institutions became instruments of Barre's executive and were no longer Somali institutions that could survive a change of power: the remnants of the state either followed Barre out of Mogadishu or were picked apart after his downfall.

Factional warlords

Since the face of Barre's rule came to be associated with his clan, opposition to his power was also organized along clan lines. But this was not the re-emergence of the *Xeer*-bound clan led by the *Shir*, its chiefs and the elders. The fact of lineage had not been altered by the displacement of clans during the struggle for independence. So, in the 1964 and 1969 elections, candidates motivated by profit and not ideology were distinguished from one another by their clan affiliation; and in turn, voters were mobilized on this basis. But the candidates had not emerged from the leadership process of the clan; they were members of the surplus-controlling élites who now employed lineage connections for electoral gain. In this manner, the clan was becoming a basis for individually led, power-motivated factions.

Barre's own regime fed on itself and increasingly fragmented as independent centres of power emerged along sub-clan and family lines. Public law and order had long since collapsed; Barre's cabinet functioned as a hierarchy stratified along clan lines and by degrees of loyalty; and finally, one of Barre's main pillars of power, the military, disintegrated into clan militias, dividing and ruling itself in the manner the rest of the country had done for two decades. As the only defence against Barre's regime and in the institutional collapse that followed, people turned to clan connections as a support mechanism. Armed leaders managed to exploit this and create constituencies for their political and personal agendas.

Opposition factions emerged gradually, then proliferated until Barre's collapse. Following Somalia's defeat in the Ogaden in 1977–8, a group of officers, mostly from the Majerteen sub-clan of the Darod that had been denied access to central power, led a failed coup attempt in April 1978. They subsequently established the Somali Salvation Democratic Front (SSDF) in 1981, which was given sanctuary in Ethiopia and operated in central Somalia. In the north, populated by the Issaq clan, the Somali National Movement (SNM) was established in 1981 to challenge the supremacy of the south. The south had dominated political life since independence: the first three Prime Ministers were Darods, and while the fourth was an Issaq, he was overthrown by Barre, another Darod. They operated in the north with Ethiopian support and in 1988 eventually attacked Hargeysa, the regional capital, which was then razed to the ground by Barre in response. In 1989, the Hawiye of central Somalia, the largest clan, established the United Somali Congress (USC). Although it emerged late in the process, it managed eventually to overthrow Barre in 1991. By this time, there were more than fifteen armed factions operating in Somalia, nominally representing parts of all six Somali clans.[51]

The minimal association between faction and clan was second to political expedience. Factions such as the USC and SNM were loosely based on clans, others on sub-clans, such as the Somali Patriotic Movement (SPM) established in 1989 to represent the Ogadeni sub-clan of the Darods. Sometimes clans spawned more than one faction other than along sub-clan lines: the Somali Democratic Movement (SDM) of the Rahanwin clan split into two sub-factions in early 1992 and supported opposing sides in the post-Barre civil war. Sometimes sub-clans split into splinter factions: the SPM of the Ogadenis split to support other opposing sides in the war. Furthermore, despite factional identification with clans, many factions were composed of individuals from a variety of clans and sub-clans: there were Hawiye guerrillas who had operated with the Issaq SNM in central Somalia, for instance.

Most significantly, alliances emerged between factions, sub-factions, clans and sub-clans and splinters of each. For instance, the USC split in 1991 between the Abgal sub-clan led by Ali Mahdi Mohamed and Aidid's Habr-Gedir. Both allied themselves with other clans and factions, and in 1992 Aidid formally established the Somali National Alliance (SNA). It included his Habr-Gedir USC, a sub-faction of the Rahanwin SDM, a splinter of the Ogadeni SPM, and the Southern Somali National Movement (SSNM), a southern coastal faction. While

Mahdi was courting the SSDF and the pro-Barre Somali National Front (SNF), his own sub-clan split into three factions, leaving him a narrow base of support.

The mob had replaced tyranny and it could be said, not that Somalis had returned to the anarchical order of the clan, but that factional warlords had unravelled the last shreds of the Somali social fabric. Without the *Xeer*'s check and balance, the collapsed state meant that transferred to the warlord was the appetite of sovereign power, unrestricted by political institutions or a social order. The individual and the faction were free to dominate all other Somalis. The opposition had not intended to liberate Somalia from Barre's dictatorship, but to replace him with themselves. So the opposition, not so much fragmented along clan lines but by factional self-interest, could agree only on the removal of Barre and nothing else beyond. In a state institutional vacuum, the factions were poised for mutual destruction in an unprecedented chaotic anarchy.

By 1992, Somalia resembled an apocalyptic image in which the four horsemen emerged in something of a vicious cycle. As a result of anarchy, war and famine and death plagued the country in an increasingly uncontrollable dynamic. Anarchical conditions, and the inequalities inherent in the absence of a rule of law, perpetuated civil war and caused in turn increasing fragmentation, which in turn again caused more competition and conflict. The destruction of the means of food production and the wilful use of food as a weapon led to famine. The conditions of internecine violence that led to the famine also limited the access of international humanitarian responses. This intensified the famine and exacerbated in turn the security conditions that led to it, as fighting over power and fighting over food for survival became increasingly connected. Even the limited control over their members that factional warlords exerted at any given time could not prevent self-interested looting by individuals.

The roots of the vicious cycle were the anarchical conditions and the prolifer-ating, hydra-like warlords; the vast numbers of armaments and the famine were symptoms of this illness. The warlord was best challenged by another warlord: local civilians were not strong enough, unless they too were willing to engage in a ruthless competition for power; and the international community did not have the finesse to displace him. These were the two attributes needed to counter the warlord: strength and finesse. In the absence of this combination at any given time, the warlord survived, appearing invincible, and incited others locally to proclaim themselves warlords.

Responding to this 'warlord syndrome' was the ultimate challenge of the international community, and it should have been the basis of the overall frame-work in which a comprehensive peace-maintenance approach disentangled the self-perpetuating dynamic. Instead, there was a tendency to respond primarily to the symptoms of the problem, and to minimalize overwhelmingly the essentially political tasks or to exclude them in all but name. In a traditional peacekeeping manner, UNOSOM I attempted to halt violent conflict by establishing a cease-fire through diplomatic agreement. But treating factions within a state as territorial sovereign entities formalized the fragmentation of Somalia rather than helping to unify it. With a peacekeeping operation deployed between areas of factional control, cease-fire lines functioned as international boundaries. Defined boundaries intensified rather than reversed the evolution of violence.[52] The military force of UNITAF successfully delivered humanitarian assistance, albeit after the peak of the famine, and helped disarm the role of food as a weapon. But it could only have limited impact on the Somali environment.[53] It was left to UNOSOM II to address the root of the problem. It too failed the conceptual test.

CONDITIONS FOR ORDERING ANARCHY

A transitional phase from UNITAF to UNOSOM II had effectively begun by the beginning of March 1993, as the US became impatient about withdrawal. It ended on 4 May 1993, when US forces formally returned Somalia to the UN. There was supposed to be a seamless interface in the transition from one operation to another. It was to be a process of painting UNITAF blue through proportional US withdrawal and UN deployment. The principle was a piece-by-piece transfer of authority to UNOSOM. When UNOSOM was in place after a general transfer, the US would pass the hat of command to the UN. However, the US withdrew more quickly than UNOSOM could deploy, therefore creating a gap. The US was forced to respond to the resulting vacuum, since UNOSOM could not. The physical gap on the ground drew the US back into Somalia for its assets. This in turn led to increased US dominance of the UN force, as well as military domination of the overall mission because of reliance on troops to fill the geographic gap. Inertia from the ground experience of UNITAF dictated to a large extent the May 1993 first operational plan (OPLAN 1) of UNOSOM II. UNITAF's leadership dominated the means of their withdrawal.

The seamless strategy had been a US proposition which the UN accepted. With the experience of a fragmented deployment to Cambodia one year earlier, and similar ineffective deployments elsewhere, the US should not have expected the UN to have been able to deploy quickly. The UN should have known it could not have. Yet, there was the belief that the population ought not to notice the difference on the ground between the two operations. This was a critical mistake: the transition was from one mandate to another, from one mission to another, and from one flag to another. The shift should have been dramatically marked for the population and NGOs. There was a wider mandate with more tasks to be accomplished. The political nature of the mission and the force was altering. However, in the minds of the population it was the same operation, particularly since the flags did not change significantly, nor did the mission turn very blue. Although never explicitly stated, as a *fait accompli* much more would have to be accomplished with far fewer resources. The effects of this caused frustration among Somalis and NGOs, who had the impression of a failing mission rather than the slow start of a new operation.

The scope of peace-maintenance

The experience of a one-dimensional military operation serving as the basis of a design for a multidimensional political operation meant that the military tasks would be disproportionately important. Their primacy was logical in UNITAF but dysfunctional in UNOSOM II, which required a concept for responding to anarchy. Establishing 'a secure environment' under UNITAF's mandate had been interpreted narrowly, in the short term for specific tasks. Although the mere presence of troops had some impact on improving overall security, without a political link UNITAF could not have had the long-lasting impact desired by the Secretary-General. Similarly, UNOSOM II was doomed from the beginning until its departure to having only a superficial impact on the anarchical roots of violence. Confusion of political authority with diplomacy by the UN Secretariat, and the perception among UN officials of greater familiarity with executive power than with military enforcement, constituted a failure to appreciate the need for some clarification of how UN political authority can or ought to be exercised in the field and its relationship to military force, diplomatic activity, humanitarian assistance and local conditions as the basis of achieving sustainable results.

Conflict between these limited perspectives led to a contradiction in the logic of UNOSOM II: while it was authorized under Chapter VII of the UN Charter and endowed with enforcement powers in the absence of local consent, the premise of its presence in the country was conceived as 'assistance'. But legitimate 'assistance' in law, such as the lawful assistance one government can render another, implied local consent, since assistance would have been given on request of a local authority.[54] UNOSOM II had more powerful military forces than the UN had in Cambodia, was deployed with a less intrusive premise of 'assistance' in a more divided society among weaker factions. Therefore, it could have been expected that an excess of assets would mean the sure success of its mandate. But this was not the case. Precisely because of the imbalance of military assets and political authority, troop contingents did not have strategic, political direction proportionate to their strength. The premise of the operation, the assets available and the objective requirements on the ground needed to be comparable and matched. Not enough assets with too intrusive a premise leads to dysfunction; an insufficient premise for the available assets leads to lack of direction. Consequently, insufficient assets to meet ground conditions leads to submission to local factions; and an insufficiently intrusive premise to meet local requirements causes reactive responses to factions, who then gain the initiative militarily and politically.

More than 'assistance' was needed to respond to conditions of anarchy. UNOSOM II could not resist doing more. It did so intermittently as it shifted back and forth between its mandate and ground needs, almost unconsciously, and fulfilled neither. It had to conduct political and law and order tasks independently of Somalis in the absence of functioning indigenous institutions. And when UNOSOM II in its later phases finally began to help build Somali institutions, officials had to do so in a *control* manner precisely because of the weakness of the institutions being established. That they had been fostered by the UN in the absence of an existing infrastructure meant that the UN had effectively the power of a governor-in-trust. Yet the refusal to acknowledge this and design a comparable mission framework meant that the mix of *assistance, control* and *governorship*, exacerbated by the domination of military assets and structures, fragmented UNOSOM II's political potential and directional capability.

Beyond consent

It was affirmed at last in public statements that UNOSOM II was not restricted by Cold War peacekeeping principles. On 19 April 1993, both Kofi Annan, then Under-Secretary-General of UNDPKO, and the Canadian Permanent Representative to the UN, Louise Fréchette, spoke at the opening session of the 'Committee of 34' meetings on peacekeeping. They stated that consent was no longer a *sine qua non* of UN operations. This was a direct reference to the impracticality of obtaining diplomatic consent in Somalia. The warlords were numerous, did not represent the country as a whole and their agreement to cooperate was inconsistent from day to day. Voices of the UN Secretariat and a traditional troop-contributing nation, which consistently resisted expanding the 'UNEF II Rules', signified a recognition among the parish of peacekeeping purists of a wider scope of operations.[55]

Local consent to deployments in the past had constituted something of a legal basis. In its absence, the independence of the UN in the field required clarification of the constitutional provisions underlying its missions. The problem turned on what constitutes a 'threat to international peace and security'.[56] Chapter VII is relied on to authorize the use of force because responding to a threat to or breach of the peace is an exception to the prohibition on force under Article 2(4) of the UN Charter. It is also an exception to Article 2(7), prohibiting the UN from interference in internal affairs of states. After the Cold War, the powers under Chapter VII were extrapolated and applied to internal conflicts, whose spread could constitute, it was argued, a threat to international peace and security. It was not entirely clear how Somalia's anarchy threatened international peace and security, but both Resolution 794 authorizing UNITAF and Resolution 814 of 26 March 1993 authorizing the deployment of UNOSOM II determined that it did.

If Chapter VII obliquely authorized the use of force, what was the legal basis for international occupation of the country and engineering authority locally? This was not an explicit part of the exception to Article 2(4). The procedural provision under Article 25 requiring member states to adhere to decisions of the Security Council served more as a basis for action than a substantial part of the Charter. However, action could have been based on the under-utilized parts of the Charter, such as the implied powers under Article 1(1). Given the nature of conditions in Somalia, including mass human rights abuses, the wilful use of violence, withholding of food as a weapon and warlordism tantamount to piracy, the legal case for intervention could have been strengthened if reference had been made to human rights conventions, international criminal conventions and customary law.[57] Instead, the Security Council stretched the definition of threats to and breaches of international peace and security. In the grip of crisis, less appropriate but well-tried provisions take precedence over more appropriate but less-established bases of authority.

Expanding the definition of security had been given impetus following the Gulf War by Security Council Resolution 688 of April 1991, authorizing humanitarian assistance in Iraq because the plight of civilians was regarded a threat to international peace and security. In Somalia, was recognition of the non-military sources of instability and the resulting violence as a threat to international peace and security a sufficient replacement for consent of a host authority? Or had the definition of an international threat been stretched beyond its limit? What was this limit? Without answers to these questions, UNOSOM II was deployed in something of a legal vacuum. While it acted under the authority of the Security Council, the parameters of many of the powers UNOSOM II would exercise in the execution of its broad mandate were unclear. These included extensive policing powers of search, seizure, arrest and detention coupled with destructive uses of military force that in fact breached applicable humanitarian laws of war. This could have been mitigated in the field by stricter adherence to humanitarian instruments and extensive UN conventions on treatment of prisoners and emergency powers.[58]

Instead, the Legal Advisor to the Special Representative of the Secretary-General argued that as an international organization the UN was not a party to the Geneva Conventions and therefore was not bound by its provisions. This perverted argument contradicted the UN's own standard-setting in the past and the reaffirmation by the ICTY of the Conventions as customary international law. It was also a contravention of the UN Charter: the powers of the Security Council are circumscribed under Article 24(2) by the purposes and principles of the UN, including respect for human rights and fundamental freedoms under Article 1(3). Furthermore, the Legal Advisor referred to detentions of Somalis arrested during US and UN combat operations as 'preventive measures'.[59] However, in the absence of a means of prosecution and due process, this was rejected as a contravention of Article 9 of the International Covenant on Civil and Political Rights by the Independent Jurist, the Honourable Enoch Dumbutshena, former Chief Justice of Zimbabwe, dispatched by the Secretary-General to investigate the grounds for detention.[60]

A political mandate

There was also needed an appropriate and specific mandate. The mandate had to identify more distinctly political objectives and could not afford such a vague notion as 'creating a secure environment'. It was reminiscent of traditional peacekeeping mandates incapable of implementation, such as in Lebanon where troops were responsible for 'restoring international peace and security' without clear guidance as to the meaning of this.[61] Also, the degree of attention and continued support by the Security Council of the mission needed to be increased. Monitoring from afar, however diligently, was inadequate. Now required was decision-making in the field through political peace-maintenance, with the kind of input available to the Security Council, as well as representation from a wide spectrum of international, regional and local interests. The absence of this, coupled with the kinds of assets already deployed and further expected, meant issues of command and control would be acute. The perpetual need to balance effectiveness and legitimacy was tested in Somalia, with US assets and a UN mandate, but the correct command and control formula could not be found.

The military–political imbalance was apparent in the Secretary-General's report of 3 March 1993, concerning recommendations for the transition from UNITAF to UNOSOM II and the latter's concept of operations.[62] In the Secretary-General's opinion, 'a secure environment' had not been created in Somalia, despite improvements in security and humanitarian conditions. Although the reason for this being that the root causes of conflict had not been tackled, he too focused excessively on the atmosphere of violence. He affirmed that there was still no effective functioning government in the country, no organized civilian police force and no disciplined national armed force. The security threat to the UN, its agencies, UNITAF, the ICRC and NGOs was still high in Mogadishu and elsewhere. Furthermore, there were no international deployments in the northern 60 per cent of Somalia or along the Kenyan border, where security continued to be a matter of grave concern.

The Secretary-General concluded, therefore, that UNOSOM II should be authorized with sufficient powers to establish a secure environment throughout Somalia. While such powers were necessary, they had to be employed strictly to underwrite political objectives of attending to the root causes. But the lack of this disciplined linkage of military force to specific political goals resulted in each aspect of the operation functioning in a certain degree of isolation, exacerbated by the disparity in size and structural development between the military and civilian leadership and personnel. This in turn resulted effectively in military leadership of political strategy. Nominally connecting enforcement powers and a political mandate could not produce an operational concept for a peace-maintenance authority. The two had to be integrated and a limited-force concept devised and subordinated to political decision-making and applied to specific tasks identified.

Instead, two approaches relied on by Boutros-Ghali to tackle the Somali apocalyptic dynamic were military disarmament and diplomatic reconciliation. The mandate would empower UNOSOM II to provide assistance to the Somali people in: rebuilding their economy and social and political life; re-establishing the country's institutional structure; achieving national political reconciliation; recreating a Somali state based on democratic governance; and rehabilitating the country's economy and infrastructure. These were intensely social and political tasks addressing the heart of the vicious cycle, but they were still being approached with military and diplomatic instruments. If such tasks were to be accomplished, there had to be political transformation, not merely reconciliation between factions. Could international bureaucracies be honest about or even realize what state-building entailed, being as they are the product of that process, yet entirely outside it? Bureaucracies maintain the status quo but are unused to creating it. In the dehumanized world of inter-state relations, the social substance behind state institutions – the executive, the legislature, the military, the police, the courts – can be forgotten. Once in place, bureaucracies communicate with similar institutions and can neither relate to nor envision alternate arrangements of organization. Therefore, the international community's ideal response to Somalia would be based on the familiar institutions of the nation-state, alien as it was to the local environment. Somalia continued to be regarded as a sovereign state in international law despite the loss of such critical criteria as a legitimate and effective government.[63] Therefore, the UN approached institution-building on the basis of the final pattern of structures rather than on the social life behind them.

Political institutions cannot be constructed in a social vacuum. The social fabric of the *Xeer* had dissolved and been replaced by the rule of arms. If guns were to be confiscated under a programme of disarmament, what then would replace arms as the basic glue of society, the means of its evolution and distribution and redistribution of authority? This was a particularly pertinent question if political institutions were to be built without the factions in order to displace them. If 'the Somali people' were to be any kind of replacement of the warlords, the population would have to be reconstituted as a society. Without being armed, the Somali people would have to be sufficiently unified and more powerful than any other single faction, or even all of the factions combined. This may have been possible if enough momentum could have been initiated and intensified to subvert support of the factions. To isolate factional leadership as a phenomenon, the balance of influence from popular consent would have to be in favour of a new, united Somali order.

Was this possible? How could Somalis be united without a historical culture of unity, and with their only experience of centralization having failed? How could unification be achieved with few resources in the context of perpetually fragmenting forces of anarchy? Social divisions along clan lines persisted as one of the few social reference points left. Under whose leadership, then, could unity be maintained? Most of the middle-class intellectual élites had left Somalia for neighbouring countries or had gone farther abroad, to Europe and North America, and refused to return despite repeated requests from UNITAF and UNOSOM II.

INGREDIENTS OF PEACE-MAINTENANCE

Was Somalia at a historical juncture requiring a statesman to rebuild it, a Peter the Great, a Kemal Atatürk or a Bismarck who could bring the country into a new century? To succeed, would a statesman have to militarily defeat the other

factions first and then build a new order? Many of the factional leaders considered themselves such statesmen, as did their supporters. This term was most
commonly attributed to Aidid; was an 'Aidid' the right man for such a Somalia,
despite the blood on his hands? Alternatively, could a nation be built in an institutional manner? And when it came time to construct a new order, how would a
social fabric be engineered? Or would such a project be abandoned in favour of
tyranny, of absolute individual power in the midst of a destitute mass, of the
kind characterizing Siad Barre's rule or the mini kingdoms of each faction?

Could a third party play such a role? With an 'assistance' mandate the UN
was unprepared to play 'statesman'. Yet the tasks it assumed were precisely those
with which a statesman would have to contend. This fact is at the core of appreciating the role that a governorship category of political authority would have to
fulfil, either itself or by fostering a local equivalent. But how?

Deploying powerfully and decisively

First, there had to be a decisive, powerful deployment, quickly and comprehensively. Initially, it would have to cover the troubled areas and ultimately the entire
country, but not at the cost of becoming a vulnerable, thin blue line. After the
announcement of the pending arrival of a new force, there is on the ground a
moment of unsureness among factions and the local population as to the consequences of this development in the historical evolution of a conflict. This
wariness, and the defensiveness that results, creates the political window of
opportunity which an operation can employ to its advantage or fail to employ to
its disadvantage. If a force arrives in strength, controls ground conditions and
does not submit to the momentum of the conflict, it can win the confidence of
the local population. They will consider the force a reliable and effective
authority, and in turn will strengthen the influence of that authority. Provided it
does not behave rapaciously, it can further win the trust and active support of
the population as a legitimate authority. If it arrives in a fragmented and weak
manner, it will alienate the local population, whose expectations of the saviour
are disappointed and who will become more resentful of the force than if it had
not had any expectations or had actively opposed it before its arrival.

Furthermore, if an operation arrives effectively, its appearance of strength
can avoid the need to use much force. And if it backs this strength credibly with
appropriate, limited, occasional force, it can significantly weaken the primacy of
the factions and begin to create an alternate centre of gravity. This can lower the
level of relations between the operation and factions from military opposition
and political competition to diplomatic relations as an administrative function of
an overall framework. If the force is weak and fragmented, local factions will
gain the initiative and in no case when this has happened has the UN managed
to regain the initiative and overturn the domination of the will of local factions.
Success or failure in this manner can be determined at the beginning of an operation and the tendency of the UN to deploy slowly and ineffectively, as in
Cambodia, has usually ended in the latter.

The powerful arrival and deployment of UNITAF caused something of a factional retreat, yet the restrictive exercise of its powers led to the renewal of a factional offensive. The principles of seizing the moment and snatching the initiative are as important politically as the element of surprise is in conventional warfare. The US strategic tendency of overwhelming situations would be best employed at this beginning point, but it cannot be retained as the principle strategy thereafter. An anathema to the US military is the idea of being a policeman one day, a soldier the next, and a policeman the day after that. The problem is precisely because of the US options for force, using either none or alternatively all; and once all force is used, it is considered difficult to return to using none. In fact, this is the everyday challenge of a policeman on the streets, whose mere presence is relied on most of the time, but who uses force at other times, then must return to a passive role. Military forces, too, must have a scale of limited force that they can regularly move up and down, as described in Chapter 1.

Ensuring legitimacy and local participation

Military forces need to be prepared to behave as policemen, as well as soldiers, if the centre of gravity created by a decisive deployment is to be consolidated. This is because of the second requirement of responding to a social and political malaise, namely the establishment of a political presence and the need for subordinated assets to implement decisions independently of local conditions. 'Independent' does not mean making decisions in an organizational vacuum in a headquarters isolated from the population; only that peace-maintenance must not be dictated by the will of the factions, the very problem with which the operation has come to contend. On the contrary, an independent political authority must have as many contacts and make as many joint decisions with local players as possible. This will increase in incidence as legitimate local authority structures are identified and established. Limited as the diplomatic instrument is by itself, it is critical throughout the deployment and consolidation phases to strengthen links as much as possible with factional leaders and other local figures in order to mitigate as far as possible the problem of lack of overall consent to the mission. This should reduce opposition, build bridges and confidence, open channels of communication to facilitate joint functioning and avoid misunderstandings, and foster support and the image locally of legitimacy of the intervention. It will also help ease deployment and the quick positioning of effective political authority.

Securing power

If there is to be genuinely a transition in a country from one set of conditions, such as anarchy, conflict and famine, to another set of conditions, resulting in order, peace and health, and whether a UN mission is a supervisor of this or a catalyst for it, the operation must secure the reins of power first. How else can the power that is driving the existing problems be transferred to a new authority? Missing this middle step leads to a transformation that occurs by itself, the continuation of conditions as they had been before, or a slight realignment of this in which the international community permits itself the luxury of treating the existing power structure as legitimate, having been rubber-stamped by a UN operation. Therefore, in the wake of a decisive arrival, an operation needs to declare its jurisdiction and raise the single flag of a new, transitional authority. It should clarify to the public that it has decision-making power over the local territory and population, that there are military and police forces to implement these decisions and judicial mechanisms applicable to all.

Transferring power to a local authority

Then the question arises pertaining to the transfer of this centre of gravity to a local authority. Over time, local individuals should play an increasingly greater role in the international operation's political, legal and security institutions, thus creating a trained cadre that can inherit the shell of each institution as the international personnel disengage from it. However, while these institutions may be appropriate for the tasks of the international operation and a consequence of member states' cultural style of governance, they may not be ideally suited for the country in question. On the other hand, they may serve as a means to an end, which displaces fragmented factions and can be transformed subsequently into something more indigenous. This may not be possible if the logic varies too greatly between the internationally established institutions and local cultural traditions. In fact, another collapse of newly established but alien and rootless institutions may occur. In Somalia, had the logic of the centralized and artificial European state concept failed, or had it been simply mismanaged? In the absence of the indigenous *Xeer*, was there an alternative to state institutions or were they doomed to failure? Simply, what was the ideal basis for institution-building in Somalia?

Determining the basis, source and structural logic of a new authority was very much an anthropological project and operations of the type and magnitude of UNOSOM II require strong components with cultural, sociological, psychological and other kinds of area expertise. Was democracy, for instance, exportable to Somalia? Being a Western imperative, what form could it take? As pointed out at the end of Chapter 3, one limitation of elections, an unstated ideal objective of the UNOSOM II political process, was that they would not have been necessarily conceived by Somalis to have a winner, loser and transfer of power.

If there was any doubt about this, it was expressed very clearly in Aidid's book.[64] He described democracy historically in Somalia over 4,000 years as a system in which all parts of the society participated, regardless of leadership. In the future, he said, there should be the ideal of 'Autonomous Democracy':

> We have to realise that the model of healthy and functional democracy that we are planning to adopt in Somalia is such that every one will have perfect autonomy and satisfaction of serving the nation whole-heartedly, and no

one will be able to exploit the people by becoming President, Prime Minister or a big boss.

This meant that

> After the fair elections to the Parliament, a truly national government should be formed by inviting members from all the national parties and not just by the members of the majority party....Therefore, the idea of the formation of National Government inviting members from all the national parties should satisfy all the voters – no matter which particular party one has voted for.

By implication, then, regardless of who won an election, Aidid would be part of the government.

If elections were not chosen as the basis for a transfer of power, what alternatives could there be? Would a constituent assembly of clans and other social group leaders, with or without the factions, have been able to answer this question? Whatever the most sustainable model of governance, it would have to be devised in the context of an international caretaker administration of the territory. Somalia was no longer pre-colonial or post-colonial, but something else in the absence of the *Xeer*, an alternative social fabric or effective alien or indigenous institutions. Without an interim authority, any ideal model could not be put in place, prevented as it would be by the tyranny of the factions threatening any transition.

Pacing the withdrawal

Furthermore, if a new indigenous authority was to survive, it could not be abandoned as soon as its legitimacy was affirmed. Since elections constitute for the UN an exit strategy, there is a tendency to withdraw too early. The juridical transference of power from an effective international political authority to a newly established indigenous authority may occur instantly, with the stroke of a pen or the lowering and raising of flags, but in practice withdrawal and devolution of functions should occur gradually. And if there is genuine interest in sustainability of results, operations cannot be conceived as a one-way process, entering and departing. If new institutions weaken for one reason or another, there may be need for increasing international personnel and resources to buttress them. In this manner, a *governorship* or *control* mandate can become an *assistance* mandate, under which an international presence can expand or contract as required. This can serve a preventive function as well, to avoid the resumption of hostilities or the repeated collapse into anarchy as a result of competition between new factions or old ones that may have been displaced but survived the transition. Without this kind of follow-up to institution-building, post-withdrawal conditions can resemble the pre-deployment environment; the operation is interpreted by the international community as a waste of time, effort and resources; international willingness to respond to emergencies erodes; and nations conclude that such missions are unworkable, since 'I guess they've got to work it out themselves'.[65]

Understanding the local population

Effectiveness rests much on appropriate instruments, appreciating the dimensions of requirements of tasks mandated, and above all a clear understanding of the nature of the place and people which a political authority has to administer-in-transition. Unlike policemen, who function as part of the structure of a civil society and are integrated as part of the population, the military tend to function separately from existing local institutions. They are usually opposing an enemy's institutions and carrying with them organizationally their own institutional culture and structures. But in political missions, policing must be conducted more independently, so as not to be subjected to local conditions, and the military must interact more closely with local institutions and the population.

Used to the luxury and habit of operating at arm's length, affordable on a battlefield, troops in UNITAF and UNOSOM II were insufficiently briefed on local social and political phenomena. There tended to be in the field the perception that Somalis had lost their value of human life; infinitely more important was the currency value of a plank of wood, a piece of corrugated sheet metal, livestock or a camel. Soldiers witnessed killing as a means of dispute settlement at mundane levels of disagreement. Killing had become a normalized form of social behaviour. Intense aggression in anarchical conditions, that favoured whoever was the physically stronger in the case, led international troops to conclude: 'The Somalis don't want our help.' Their view of Somalis was similar to Burton's nearly a century and a half earlier: they are 'constant in nothing but inconstancy – soft, merry, and affectionate souls, they pass without any apparent transition into a state of fury, when they are capable of terrible atrocities'.[66]

This fed a behaviour and perception of opposition and exclusion, rather than integration between international forces and local Somalis, and set a psychological stage for conflict. It was expressed by the high walls around the airport and UN compound in Mogadishu behind which UNOSOM II kept. In another miniature vicious cycle, the more hostility there was between Somalis and the UN, the less freedom of movement international troops had in Mogadishu; the less freedom of movement there was, the greater the gulf between the two grew. This narrowed the social basis for communication and established an environment ripe for misunderstanding – a factor which would have a cataclysmic political consequence in UNOSOM II's relationship with Aidid.

MISSING THE POLITICAL LINK

Dominant military objectives

Instead of a complex social and political approach to Somalia, the core of the operational concept outlined in Boutros-Ghali's 3 March 1993 report was a series of military tasks.[67] When political reconstruction did begin, it was too little too late and ill-defined, resulting in political failure and military retreat. If there was any attempt at clarity, it was in the areas of disagreement between Washington and the UN Secretary-General that had plagued UNITAF. UNOSOM II would provide security by:

1 monitoring that all factions continue to respect the cessation of hostilities and other agreements to which they have consented;
2 preventing any resumption of violence and, if necessary, taking appropriate action against any faction that violates or threatens to violate the cessation of hostilities;
3 maintaining control of the heavy weapons of the organized factions which will have been brought under international control pending their eventual destruction or transfer to a newly constituted national army;
4 seizing the small arms of all unauthorized armed elements and assisting in the registration and security of such arms;
5 securing or maintaining security at all ports, airports and lines of communications required for the delivery of humanitarian assistance;
6 protecting the personnel, installations and equipment of the United Nations and its agencies, the ICRC as well as NGOs, and taking such forceful action as may be required to neutralize armed elements that attack, or threaten to attack, such facilities and personnel, pending the establishment of a new Somali police force which can assume this responsibility;
7 continuing the programme for mine-clearing in the most afflicted areas;
8 assisting the repatriation of refugees and displaced persons within Somalia; and
9 carrying out such other functions as may be authorized by the Security Council.

The report stated that further to the disarmament provisions of the 8 January Addis Ababa agreements, a planning committee composed of senior officers from UNITAF and UNOSOM had developed a 'Somalia cease-fire disarmament concept'. This required the establishment of cantonment locations, for storage of heavy weapons, as well as transition sites for temporary accommodation of factional forces while they turned in their small arms, registered for future governmental and non-governmental support and received training for eventual reintegration into civilian life. Cantonment and transition sites would be separated from each other to prevent any possibility of factions or groups seizing the heavy weapons. Those failing to comply with timetables or other modalities of the disarmament process would have their weapons and equipment confiscated or destroyed.

UNOSOM II was envisioned to be conducted in four phases of military operations. Extensive military activity in the beginning would gradually decrease as civil authority was established in a linked evolution. Phase I concentrated on the transition of operational control from UNITAF. Military support to relief activities and the disarming of factions would continue throughout the transition. Phase II focused on consolidating UN operational control and would conclude when UNOSOM II had deployed and was operating effectively throughout Somalia and the border regions. In Phase III, efforts would be made to reduce UNOSOM II's military activity and assist civil authorities in exercising greater responsibility. This phase would end when a Somali national police force became operational and major UN military operations were no longer required. Phase IV concerned redeployment or reduction of UNOSOM II forces.

The logic of the four phases was a result of the existing military domination by UNITAF in the field, the desire of the Secretary-General for a UN peace-enforcement operation and the lack of consideration of UN political authority. While transition from phase to phase was supposed to be dictated by parallel reconciliation efforts and rehabilitation programmes, stages were defined by diminishing degrees of military responsibility. By subordinating political imperatives to the extent this did, civil authority could not develop meaningfully. The political process was disconnected from and overwhelmed by the military, which therefore could not devolve its tasks to a civilian counterpart. Since international military activity decreased as Somali civil authority grew, UN civil authority could serve only to negotiate among Somalis to foster local agreement. The UN political office was not large enough or conceptually structured to serve as a link for this progression. It was a vestige of the diplomatic activity of UNOSOM I that approached reconciliation through negotiations rather than by institution-building.

Consequently, each development on the ground, political or otherwise, was addressed militarily, thus drawing the military more deeply into the conflict, rather than the reverse. Initially, until June 1993, there was some diplomacy and reliance on military deployments. Diplomacy disappeared thereafter as combat operations monopolized UNOSOM II and US resources. Minimal institution-building followed in late 1993 as a means of military scale-down and withdrawal during a strategic reset. Diminishing both military and civilian activities led to complete withdrawal and the consumption of anything left in its wake by Somali anarchy.

Although the central goal of UNOSOM II was to assist the people of Somalia to create and maintain order and new institutions for their own governance, any degree of detail in the 3 March report was devoted to the military tasks of Phases I and II. Only one broadly worded paragraph pertained to the critical Phase III that was the purpose of the exercise. The standard of measurement of the end of this phase was itself a military imperative, since a functioning police force was the exit strategy for the military. Just as the military dominated the operation, so too the establishment of police forces dominated the prioritization of institution-building. In the beginning, this was true partly as a result of UNITAF efforts: by mid-May it was reported that 2,840 police were directing traffic, controlling crowds and protecting feeding centres; while another 2,000 performed similar duties in other cities.[68] The importance of the police increased dramatically during the strategic reset at the end of 1993 to justify military withdrawal of Western nations.

Establishing police forces in a vacuum could not be sustained, particularly in spring 1993. There was no government or court system of prosecution, nor any law for the police to enforce. Eventually the 1960 Constitution and 1962 Criminal Procedure and Penal Codes were resuscitated and mixed with Islamic Sharia law, but these were utilized more by the fledgling courts from the end of 1993 than by the police before. To link functioning police forces, without an established civil authority, to the reduction of military operations, was artificial. There would be violence for as long as there was no political authority, and probably afterwards as well. A police force did not imply the existence of a political authority or factional reconciliation.[69]

Civilian staffing misjudgements

The Secretary-General called for a military component of 20,000[70] all ranks to carry out the assigned tasks and an additional 8,000 personnel to provide the logistic support. The latter would be the first US troops to serve under UN command, even if in a non-combat role. He further indicated the capability required by the combat forces. These included: patrolling and close combat; information gathering and interpretation; indirect force; anti-armour fire; all-weather night-and-day operations; casualty evacuation; tactical communications; and air support (fire-power and transport). In addition to the UN force of 28,000, the US agreed to provide a tactical Quick Reaction Force (QRF) of 1,000 troops positioned off-shore, which ultimately became the spearhead of combat operations, for which it had not been designed.

According to the UN figures, of a force of 28,000, about 29 per cent would support the active work of about 71 per cent. But the environment turned out to be more hostile than such numbers anticipated. For instance, UN headquarters in Mogadishu estimated that for a contingent to be self-sufficient in the field it required a minimum of 1,400 personnel to provide the means of survival in Somalia. At the height of its strength in late 1993, the German contingent deployed at Belet Uen numbered about 1,700. It was a logistics unit that was supposed to support the Indian contingent of 5,000, which only began to arrive in October 1993. Consequently, it was one of the best-supplied units in the country. By these figures, however, it was taking some 83 per cent of the whole German contingent to keep its troops alive, leaving a little more than 17 per cent to focus on Somalia. This was symptomatic of a mission that spent more time surviving than saving the country. Furthermore, troops were concentrated in

Mogadishu. While about one-third of UNITAF was deployed in the city and the rest in the countryside, more than half of UNOSOM II was deployed at the airport and UN compound with access only to Mahdi's area of control in the north of the city

In contrast, a civilian staff of approximately 2,800 was proposed, though their tasks and distribution were not indicated. Specialized civilian components required for institutional reconstruction were not identified. A small civilian headquarters staff had to be subdivided into small offices with only a few individuals in each to manage a process more complex than were the military tasks. As late as February 1994, in a civilian-reliant, institution-building phase, UNOSOM II had only 400 international civilian personnel, of which only 200 were substantial and 200 administrative.

Boutros-Ghali's report outlined UNOSOM II's conventional peacekeeping chain of command, extending from the Security Council to the Secretary-General and then to his Special Representative and Force Commander in the field. The Special Representative, US Admiral Jonathan T. Howe, was appointed on 5 March 1993 with the broad writ of overseeing the transition from UNITAF to UNOSOM II, and continuing the tasks of: promoting reconciliation, coordinating humanitarian assistance and paving the way for rehabilitation and reconstruction of the country. However, OPLAN 1 designated dual US–UN command roles for two officers: the Commander of US Forces in Somalia was appointed Deputy Force Commander of UNOSOM II; and the Deputy Commander of US Forces in Somalia was appointed Commander of UNOSOM II Logistics Forces Command. Furthermore, the US Commander-in-Chief of Central Command in the United States retained command of all US Forces assigned to UNOSOM II and would assign operational control (OPCON) to the Commander of US Forces in Somalia. When directed, the Commander of US Forces in Somalia would assume tactical control (TACON) of the US QRF.

The contradictory logic of consent to enforcement

The Secretary-General noted that the deployment of UNOSOM II would not be subject to the agreement of any local factional leaders; yet he also reiterated his belief that

> Notwithstanding the compelling necessity for authority to use enforcement measures as appropriate…the political will to achieve security, reconciliation and peace must spring from the Somalis themselves. Even if it is authorized to resort to forceful action in certain circumstances, UNOSOM II cannot and must not be expected to substitute itself for the Somali people. Nor can or should it use its authority to impose one or another system of governmental organization. It may and should, however, be in a position to press for the observance of United Nations standards of human rights and justice.[71]

This perception was correct at one level, since no system can rely on enforcement exclusively. However, stated in this manner it was dangerously contradictory. There was too much of a gap, expressed by the ill-conceived Phase III, between rejecting the need for factional consent to the operation on the one hand, and, on the other, the reliance on Somalis' political will to achieve peace and security. If Somalis could be expected to 'do it themselves', then what was the need for such a large and intrusive mandate? To assume political control in fact, to match the powers assumed on paper, would not be a substitute for the Somali people but a transition from factional tyranny *to* the Somali people's self-rule. Nor would creating a centre of gravity that could be securely transferred to the Somali people be any more of an imposition than was the operation as designed or were the goals as set, which after all were precisely the creation of a new government. And doing so was no more of an alien intrusion than demanding compliance with human rights standards. The Secretary-General's guarded reservation to such an extensive operation, relegated to a single paragraph in a minimalist manner, was insufficient to clarify UNOSOM II's legitimacy. Instead, it represented a point of view among some developing nations and individual observers that still hesitated about such interventions. Ultimately, disagreement among contingents about the logic of the operation condemned the mission to failure.

The flaws, inconsistencies and misconceptions of the 3 March plan were approved on 26 March by Security Council Resolution 814. Acting under Chapter VII, the Council decided to expand the size and mandate of UNOSOM in accordance with the Secretary-General's recommendations for a period extending to 31 October 1993. Emphasizing the security aspects of the plan first and foremost, the resolution demanded that all Somali parties comply fully with the commitments they had undertaken, and in particular with the Agreement on Implementing the Cease-fire and on Modalities of Disarmament,[72] and that they ensure the safety of the personnel of all organizations engaged in humanitarian and other assistance to Somalia. It called for all, and particularly neighbouring, states to cooperate in the implementation of the arms embargo under Resolution 733 of 23 January 1992.

Thereafter, the considerably more complicated provisions of the plan were approved in a broad brush-stroke. The Council requested the Secretary-General, through his Special Representative, and with assistance from all relevant United Nations entities, offices and specialized agencies, to provide humanitarian and other assistance to the people of Somalia in rehabilitating their political institutions and economy and promoting political settlement and national reconciliation. Such assistance would include economic relief and rehabilitation of Somalia; the repatriation of refugees and relocation of displaced persons within Somalia; the re-establishment of national and regional institutions and civil administration in the entire country; the re-establishment of Somali police; mine-clearance; and public information activities in support of the UN activities in Somalia.

Unrealistic expectations at Addis Ababa

The stage for conflict crystallized at the Conference on National Reconciliation in Somalia, convened in Addis Ababa between 15 and 28 March 1993. This was further to the January agreement at the Informal Preparatory Meeting in Addis Ababa.[73] The Conference was chaired by the Secretary-General's Deputy Special Representative for Somalia, Ambassador Lansana Kouyate of Guinea, and attended by the leaders of fifteen Somali political movements, as well as representatives of the regional and other arrangements that had attended the January meeting – the League of Arab States (LAS), the Organization of African Unity (OAU), the Organization of the Islamic Conference (OIC), the Standing Committee of the Countries of the Horn and the Non-Aligned Movement. After two weeks of intensive and intermittent negotiations, on 27 March the leaders of all fifteen Somali political groups signed the Agreement of the First Session of the Conference of National Reconciliations in Somalia.[74] At the closing session of the Conference on 28 March, the Agreement was unanimously endorsed by all the participants, including representatives of women's and community organizations, as well as elders and scholars.

The Agreement comprised four parts: disarmament and security; rehabilitation and reconstruction; restoration of property and settlement of disputes; and the establishment of a Transitional National Council (TNC) vested with administrative and executive authority. The parties agreed to consolidate and carry forward advances in peace, security and dialogue made since the beginning of 1993. They reaffirmed their commitment to comply fully with the cease-fire agreement that was signed in Addis Ababa in January, including the handing over of all weapons and ammunition to UNITAF and UNOSOM II. There was to be disarmament of the factional militias within ninety days.

This was an unrealistic proposition. Since UNITAF had disarmed only sporadically, as a matter of convenience rather than as a concerted programme, there was little institutional framework UNOSOM II could inherit, such as coherent procedures, identified cantonment sites or generally agreed target locations or elements of factions to be disarmed. All of this would have to be established as UNOSOM II was deploying, acclimatizing to Somalia and organizing internally. It would approach disarmament not as a comprehensive programme but arbitrarily and haphazardly.

Furthermore, there was too great a gap between the nominal agreement in Addis Ababa, genuine consensus between the factions and understanding between the factions and the UN. Since there had been a difficult process of negotiation, characteristically broad provisions were drafted to achieve consensus. Terms of agreement in the conference hall tend to be capable of multiple interpretation. Different expectations lead to confrontation and conflict in the field, usually at the cost of the UN's effectiveness, such as in Cambodia, or to violent conflict if the UN makes a stand, as it was preparing to do in Somalia.

Of the fifteen 'political movements' at Addis Ababa, only four or five were very influential, such as Aidid's SNA, General Mohamed Said Hersi 'Morgan's'

SNF, Colonel Ahmed Omar Jess's SPM, and the SSDF allied with Mahdi. Each felt they could interpret the Agreement to their advantage on the ground. The balance of forces in the field would dictate the details of the terms accepted. All had self-confidence in their physical strength and expected to defeat the others. Also, as one UN official observed at Addis Ababa, 'It is a Somali habit: they are friendly together abroad, but at home they realize they are worse off than they thought when they made an agreement. So conflict ensues.' This contradicts the culture of inviolable contractual arrangements relied on by the UN in its operational calculations, which result in best-case-scenario preparations for worse-case-scenario conditions.

There was a difference of opinion about how to approach the factions after the Conference between UNOSOM II political officers and other civilian and military officials. Some felt the importance of Addis Ababa was that it gave UNOSOM II a local mandate that matched its international mandate of disarmament and national reconciliation – a form of consent that had not been generally obtainable. But it was artificial consent, without agreement on specifics or on a concept of operations which required cooperation. Nominally, UNOSOM II could claim some legitimacy in its actions on the basis of Somali acceptance of its mandate, but this was not enough.

Political officers recognized the limitations of the Addis Ababa Conference. In hindsight they posed the question about the right moment to bring all the people together, both factional leaders and other social groups. One UNOSOM II official described the need for political momentum before local diplomatic reconciliation should proceed:

> There is no point holding a conference for the sake of a conference. The Addis Ababa Conference was meaningless as a conference, regardless of the good will....There cannot be agreement in Somalia without a conference, but the pieces must be in place first and then a conference can formalize what is in place. Therefore the conference must be well-prepared.[75]

Until a local political authority was created by the UN, which could be formalized by a conference as the basis of a transfer of power, any reconciliation meeting convened would be no less a battlefield than was Mogadishu or the Somali hinterland.

Disagreement over enforcement and negotiation

At UN headquarters in Mogadishu, there were opposing views on disarmament through diplomacy and disarmament by force. Seasoned UN officials with experience rooted in traditional operations were used to presenting the UN view to the parties and then proceeding according to agreements that could be reached or disagreements that limited options. In this manner, accountability of parties and terms of agreements evolved. The opposing view was held by other civilian officials, the many US advisers from the Pentagon and the National Security

Council (NSC), and the military. If the Somalis did not live up to their commitments then, it was felt, 'we can force them to do it'. The diplomatic view charged such attitudes as being the 'arrogance of power', and criticized the reluctance to meet with those considered 'criminals'.

The enforcement view dominated because of the greater number and influence of those who supported it, including the UN Secretary-General. But the use of force to respond to multiple diplomatic gaps was an ineffective approach in anarchical conditions. While it is true that military strength backing diplomatic efforts can influence parties and lead towards agreement, under the complex circumstances this could not create an alternative to the factions nor transform the conditions of anarchy. On the other hand, an exclusively diplomatic approach was not possible. To broker a power-sharing agreement between the factions could easily fracture; to favour one faction over the others would be a partisan approach and render the UN a belligerent; or alternatively the UN might become a victim of the factions.

The failure to establish Somali authority

The process of establishing Somali authority suffered the same gaps and flaws of an artificial agreement. At Addis Ababa there was a strategic manoeuvring between factions and the UN to create a framework which could be employed to their respective advantages. The TNC would consist of seventy-four members, with two men and one woman from each of the eighteen regions of the country, one from each of the fifteen political movements, and five from Mogadishu. This would serve as an interim government before elections could be held in 1995. The Agreement referred to the drafting of a provisional constitution, or 'charter', and the establishment of an independent judiciary. Most significantly, arrangements were made for autonomous councils on the regional and local levels. This was a kind of revival of the 'regionalization' strategy attempted during UNOSOM I by then SRSG Mohamed Sahnoun, who tried to shift the focus of UN efforts away from the conflict in Mogadishu.[76]

Competition between the factions and the UN focused on the timing and location of the centre of gravity to be developed. The factions wanted to create a TNC first, as soon as possible, because this gave them primacy. While they were united on this, in the manner that opposition factions had agreed on felling Barre but could not agree on anything else, the factions perceived the TNC as one more battlefield. This was a top-down approach, while the UN, on the other hand, jockeyed for a bottom-up approach. According to a UNOSOM II political officer, 'At Addis we planned to establish the District Councils (DC) and Regional Councils (RC) only; and only after that was complete, then on the basis of the DCs and RCs and the experience of this, create the TNC.'[77] If the TNC was to be vested with administrative and executive authority, and if the UN was trying to control the process of establishing executive authority, then this was a clear affirmation that the UN could not merely 'assist' but was assuming executive authority as a fact.

Discussion should not even have arisen about the centre of gravity if it was to be effectively established and controlled by the UN. Negotiation elevated the issue to a political confrontation between the UN and the factions instead of relegating it to an administrative level. This turned the question of 'how' to maintain the centre of gravity under international control to 'whether' it would be under international or local control. The strategy was to displace the factions by establishing an alternative authority on the basis of the Somali people, emerging from the elders, women, the social institutions rooted in the clans or any other constituency not assimilated in the factional competition. But building an authority on the basis of such disparate fragments with only few diplomatic resources could not compete with the power centres of the factions. As it happened, the factions established the TNC prematurely, though, predictably, continued to fight, rendering the TNC a fiction but out of the control of the UN. As one official stated, 'The TNC was not a consequence of the UN at that point.' The DCs and RCs evolved painfully slowly, the UN lost the political initiative and was left with military force as its only response.

The battlefield was being delimited: Aidid miscalculated at Addis Ababa. He had conceded to the Agreement because he believed that not only could he compete for control of the top-down TNC process as part of the overall factional conflict, but that he could out-manoeuvre the UN in the countryside by controlling the bottom-up process as well. There were several fronts emerging on which Aidid and the UN would confront each other irreconcilably. There was insufficient detail regarding disarmament, and the opportunity for misunderstanding and disagreement; there would be disagreement about the primacy of the TNC and the process of regionalization, and competition for the latter.

Aidid's intransigence evolved progressively after UNITAF's arrival. With each milestone – a second phase of limited rehabilitation efforts under UNITAF, the January Informal Meeting and the March Conference – the gap widened between Aidid and the UN and the US. Conflict over the regions had begun during UNITAF, but as UNOSOM II explicitly focused on the RCs and DCs, the competition became more acute and volatile. In his perpetual redrafting of history, Aidid described from his point of view how this developed:[78]

UNITAF extended its operation after one month by [its commander] General [Robert] Johnston, who became more involved in Somalian affairs. The UN and the US started to call the leaders of the liberation movements 'warlords' and only wanted to talk with the elders. I met with [Robert B.] Oakley [former US Ambassador to Somalia and special presidential envoy] and asked what was the interest of the UN and US in Somalia, but did not get an answer. What became evident was that the UN and the US had converging interests. The humanitarian mission was transformed into a military operation. The UN and the US both understood that the SNA was the only obstacle in their efforts to take control of Somalia. At that time SNA controlled 11 out of 18 regions of Somalia, and 75 per cent of the population. But the UN used lack of government and local authority structures as an excuse for wanting to take control. A political gap existed, and the UN took advantage of this by contacting the elders and playing on them. Thereby they ruined my attempt to build local structures. SNA's programme was regional autonomy, and the people were happy with this.

He added that UNITAF behaved abusively and lost the support of the population. They

> began to disarm in December without our agreement. They forcefully inspected houses, they looted and they raped. SNA demanded to be present when they made their inspections, but the US ignored this. Many claims were filed against UNITAF, but nothing happened. In February 1993 the biggest demonstration in Somalian history took place against UNITAF. This was not adequately mentioned in international media...UNITAF forces were isolated for 3 days by women and children due to their misbehaviour.

Such 'demonstrations' with women and children foreshadowed the events of 5 June, in which the mob literally tore apart twenty-four Pakistanis. Aidid also charged that the US had returned Morgan to Kismayu in February, which was another point of contention that erupted in May.

By the time of the Addis Ababa Conference in March, the forces in anarchical Somalia were predominantly arrayed between two sides. The UN was pitted against a faction in the manner of another faction, rather than displacing the phenomenon of factionalism in the beginning altogether. Aidid's charge that the US and the UN 'would effectively re-establish Somali sovereignty' reflected the location of the front line. These prevailing political conditions meant the operation was over before it had begun. The events just had to play themselves out, logically, inevitably. There was nothing that could alter at this stage the trajectory and momentum of interconnected factors.

7   Peace-maintenance in divided Western Sahara

'Africa's last colony' was an unfortunate distinction attributed to Namibia until its independence in 1990. The title was inherited by the old Spanish stretch of North Atlantic desert then remembered to be still occupied by Morocco. With mantric regularity, the 1975 opinion of the International Court of Justice on Western Sahara continues to be cited as one of the defining cases of self-determination, a reminder as the twentieth century closes of a persistent relic of nineteenth-century conquest. Divorced from the textbook, though, the indigenous population has been unable to decide the future of the territory.

UNTAG in Namibia set as a standard 'free and fair' elections and helped encourage the new generation of peace operations, but was not to be repeated by an encore in Western Sahara. Observers anticipated that once the UN deployed, this conflict, too, would become a historical footnote. But towards the end of the decade, its Mission for the Referendum in the Western Sahara (MINURSO) is still listing in the sand. It has gained little from costly peace experiments worldwide, as 165,000 Sahrawis seem not to have benefited from the lengthy struggles of their continental neighbours.

Beginning in autumn 1996, however, an opportunity unfolded for open and direct talks between the Kingdom of Morocco and the Frente Popular para la Liberación de Saguia el-Hamra y de Rio de Oro (POLISARIO) to finally resolve their dispute. Contacts between the two were renewed and both the General Assembly and Security Council called for more dialogue. If this fragile momentum is to be sustainable and to have any results, a specific code of conduct for the parties and guarantees by UN member states are indispensable. Direct engagement will be needed whether the proposed referendum succeeds, for the results to be accepted by each side, or whether it fails, to avoid the resumption of hostilities.

A joint political mechanism can help to guarantee the legitimacy and effectiveness of the Western Sahara settlement plan. Developing this became possible with the appointment of former Secretary of State James A. Baker III – and with him the implicit authority of the United States – as Secretary-General Kofi Annan's Special Envoy for completing the UN's mission. An unparalleled event since MINURSO's deployment, such a prominent representative provided the best, if still limited, chance for relaunching implementation of the peace process.

If sufficient will in a collective political body can be generated to do so, in the midst of equal measures of optimism and doubt, then it may help refine the means of ensuring from the start the good faith and genuine commitment of combatants and mediators.

While a military stalemate on the battlefield had led to the possibility of a settlement, a subsequent diplomatic stalemate over its interpretation prevented its implementation. This chapter describes the problem of incomplete consent of the parties to a complex decolonization operation and the divisive impact of a sort of international gerrymandering. With unaccountable proximity talks as the only recourse, it considers the type of peace-maintenance framework that can guarantee the terms agreed to and outlines the evolution of this in the context of Western Sahara. To reorient a dysfunctional mission, approval from the multilateral fora of the General Assembly and Security Council can provide necessary legitimacy. This needs to be underwritten, however, by the kind of effectiveness that US authority can provide. In combination, these ingredients constitute a formula for integrating lower-level troop deployments with firmer, multinational, political control of conflict resolution.

CONDITIONS OF STALEMATE

It was a cardinal principle of Sun Tzu's *Art of War* that war must be finished quickly: 'In all history, there is no instance of a country having benefited from prolonged warfare. Only one who knows the disastrous effects of a long war can realize the supreme importance of rapidity in bringing it to a close.' Yet protracted conflict has been a perpetual feature of warfare in recorded history at least since the Trojan wars. And the nihilism that seemingly pointless stalemate engenders appears to have reached its apex in the twentieth century.

Camus captured this in *The Myth of Sisyphus*, a written response in the midst of the darkest days of the Second World War to a generation's despair that emerged from endless trench warfare in the First World War. It was certainly characteristic of the zero-sum superpower rivalry of the Cold War and of another generation's reaction to perpetually impending nuclear doom. The human condition appears a kind of paralysis given the desperate desire to eradicate war altogether and the inability to do so. The senselessness of war seems inescapable; Wilfred Owen observed 'None will break ranks, though nations trek from progress.'

Protracted warfare

Conditions in twentieth-century conflicts have specifically fostered the phenomenon of stalemate. The increased sophistication of weapons technology has enabled the flea to take up arms against the sovereign. Not only have small but powerful weapons tended to equalize the battlefield between the numerically weak and strong, but they erased the clear lines between state armies and shifted the theatre of war to pervasive insurgencies within states. To keep pace, the tactics of guerrilla warfare evolved rapidly throughout this century.

In particular, the Clausewitzean doctrine of war as an extension of politics, as integrally linked though still somewhat separate, was replaced by the notion of conducting simultaneous military and political campaigns, by the idea of war *as* politics. T.E. Lawrence considered guerrilla warfare not merely a tactic to support conventional warfare but a political process in which irregular warfare was one tactic. Both V.I. Lenin and Mao Tse-Tung recognized the linkage of the political and the military in revolutionary warfare, and distinguished between 'the party' and the armed cadre. Vietnamese General Vo Nguyen Giap and Ernesto Che Guevara took this one step further and unified the political and the military. Giap referred to 'the people's war' in which the population was the army. Che's *focismo* strategy in Cuba, which the Sandinistas employed in Nicaragua, unified the party, the people and the army.[1]

An essential feature of war of the weak against the strong was that it took a long time. Lenin called it 'protracted revolutionary warfare' and Mao divided this into stages of preparation, direct action and defeat of the enemy. In turn, counter-revolutionary warfare and the tactics of counter-insurgency developed by governments to combat guerrilla movements, such as by European powers withdrawing from overseas possessions in the 1950s and 1960s,[2] included the same politico-military approach adopted by revolutionaries. Support of the local population was the currency of the conflict, over which governments and guerrilla movements fought. Winning the so-called 'hearts and minds' of local people meant transforming the psychology of the population and therefore publicity, controlling media and issues of legitimacy increased in importance. Battles with this kind of weaponry took decades to fight and fostered the conditions of stalemate.

One tactic of revolutionary warfare during the Cold War and since has been the diplomatic campaign particularly waged by national liberation movements. This tended to minimalize the importance of military victory in the field. Armed struggle was an important means of maintaining the presence of a movement among a local population and in the international imagination, but final victory lay in diplomatic circles among friends more powerful than the opponent.[3] While this kind of patronage by the powerful tended to be abused by both East and West during the Cold War, it also enhanced the role of the world community and inter-governmental organizations in such internal conflicts.

The South West Africa People's Organization (SWAPO), for instance, did not control any part of Namibian territory during its struggle for independence, but it was recognized by the UN General Assembly as 'the sole and authentic representative of the Namibian people' and assisted by a special UN Council and later Commissioner established to facilitate Namibia's self-determination. International condemnation of apartheid meant the international community had united diplomatically, if not genuinely domestically, against SWAPO's opponent.

To capitalize on this support, as a recognized observer at the General Assembly SWAPO maintained a presence at UN fora where South African diplomats were not permitted. It was here that a strategy for victory was devised, in the context of legitimacy, publicity and international law, rather than through military power. Armed units conducting operations in the field reinforced this diplomatic activity as part of a larger political scheme. When the international constellation of factors was ripe for Namibian independence, SWAPO was able to win the electoral contest decisively since diplomatic and electoral campaigns required some of the same expertise in winning public support.

Politico-military revolutions by attrition often relied on conditions of stalemate to proceed. Time and sustainability were critical weapons. For this reason, outside interventions supporting one side found quick victory elusive. Long-term commitments tended to favour more cost-effective tactics of guerrillas, and home constituencies of third-party interveners tended to tire increasingly quickly from the time America went to Vietnam to the more recent rapid interventions in Grenada, Panama and the Persian Gulf. Constituencies of local governments combating revolutionary movements tended to be divided, not only further perpetuating conditions of stalemate but breeding the internecine struggle itself for control of popular support.

MINURSO

The UN has proved incapable of sustaining a meaningful diplomatic presence in political stalemates. A joint political mechanism has been needed perhaps most during the peace process in Western Sahara. According to US State Department officials, MINURSO was the first test case for the PDD-25 policy, threatening termination of the operation in the absence of results.

MINURSO was deployed with one of the greatest missing links of recent UN operations. It suffered from an unprecedented gap between the powers of the UN assumed on paper and the means to exercise this authority in the field. Consequently, the process faltered at each critical phase of the timetable, during the cease-fire and the identification of voters, and is likely to stick during the referendum and the acceptance of electoral results if hostilities do not resume first.[4]

The architecture of MINURSO was that of a *governorship* operation, responsible for administering-in-transition the territory of Western Sahara. As a decolonization mission it was to guarantee the exercise of the right of self-determination of the indigenous population. The Special Representative of the UN Secretary-General had sole and exclusive responsibility over all matters relating to the referendum, its organization and conduct. MINURSO could promulgate and repeal laws in the Western Sahara, maintain law and order independently of local security forces, and assume the role of territorial authority.

Indeed, if it was to transfer power to the winner of a free and fair referendum, then it would have to first wrest that power from the *de facto* authorities in the area, namely the two parties. This MINURSO could not do, since the more powerful party refused to cooperate or even permit deployment of the operation or its freedom of movement: of the 1,695 military and 1,600 civilian personnel called for, throughout most of the Mission not more than 375 military observers, headquarters and support unit staff reached the field.[5] Instead, cooperation of the weak, with the UN held hostage by Morocco, meant the UN served to strengthen the hand of the strong.[6]

With these paper powers MINURSO was to conduct a series of complex tasks. Before the main force arrived, an Identification Commission was to prepare a list of voters. Advance deployments of civilian administrative, signals, medical and air support units, as well as a logistics battalion, would begin. After the Special Representative established a presence, 'D-Day' marked the coming into effect of the cease-fire and the beginning of the transitional period. Combatants were to be confined to barracks, and political prisoners and prisoners of war released. Only then were infantry battalions and police units planned to arrive. Voter registration would be completed and local paramilitary units in existing police forces neutralized. Laws contrary to free and fair elections were to be repealed and the repatriation of refugees completed. The referendum would be held, its results proclaimed and MINURSO would begin withdrawal. If Morocco lost, it would withdraw; and if the POLISARIO lost, it would be disbanded under UN oversight. The operation at this point would end.[7]

Instead of this 'order of battle', the operation began deployment reactively and therefore haphazardly. In August 1991, Morocco supplied a list of voters two and a half times the size of the population of the territory, effectively halting the identification process. Although a *de facto* cease-fire had been in effect since 1989, Moroccan fighter jets levelled the POLISARIO-held towns closest to the front, Tifariti and Bir Lahlou, and razed new facilities built by the POLISARIO for UN observers. The attack was meant to signal to the UN that there was no peace to be kept and that the operation should not deploy. Secretary-General Javier Pérez de Cuéllar considered three options: (1) postpone deployment and possibly destroy the momentum in the process achieved to that point; (2) deploy the Mission according to the planned timetable, which was not possible because Morocco had halted UN logistic supplies in Agadir, southern Morocco; or (3) authorize a limited deployment, which was done on 5 September. On the 6th, a formal cease-fire came into effect with a premature and unprepared arrival of military observers. They were harassed by the Moroccan army at gunpoint, and had to survive in life-threatening conditions without the requisite diplomatic support from New York.

The cease-fire has effectively held since. There has not been freedom of movement for UN observers in Moroccan-held territory and there were numerous Moroccan violations of the cease-fire until the test of verifying violations reported became more stringent in 1993 and the number effectively decreased. In response to Moroccan intransigence, the United States Congress voted to reduce military assistance to Morocco from $144 million to $52 million.[8] However, there were no casualties reported as a result of hostile action and this fact sustained the stalemate in the field.

In the meantime, on home fronts and in New York, attention turned to the issue of voter identification. The parties waged diplomatic campaigns which together created a seemingly inescapable quagmire for them both, as well as for the UN.

FRACTURED POLITICAL WILL

As a final act of decolonization, the referendum was to shed more than a century of military rule by metropolitan Madrid and then 'greater' Rabat. After a long history of contact, reaching back at least to the fifteenth century, Spain declared in 1884 a 'protectorate' over most of Western Sahara. By 1915, the area was largely pacified, its boundaries delimited and administration regularized. After Morocco achieved independence from France in 1956, a regional guerrilla Army of Liberation began to challenge Spanish authority, and the question of Western Sahara's status drew international attention. Two years later, Madrid converted its possession into a 'province' of Spain. But this did not prevent the UN including it on its list of non-self-governing territories in 1963. Thereafter, the General Assembly passed annual resolutions calling for the self-determination of Spanish Sahara.

Self-determination

Self-determination, expounded by Lenin and Woodrow Wilson after the First World War, was considered a political concept until its inclusion explicitly in Articles 1(2), 55 and 56, and implicitly in Chapters XI and XII of the United Nations Charter. Thenceforth it was a legal concept, yet its scope of application remained unclear until on 14 December 1960 the UN General Assembly passed Resolution 1514(XV), the 'Declaration on the Granting of Independence to Colonial Territories and Peoples'. This stated that all non-self-governing territories had the right of self-determination and that 'immediate steps shall be taken…to transfer all powers to the peoples of these territories'. While 'all peoples' had the right of self-determination, who were the peoples and what was the 'self' that had this right?

The scope of self-determination was linked to the territorial integrity of the boundaries delimited by the former colonial power, an expression of the so-called notion of *uti possidetis*. Therefore the boundaries of the Spanish Sahara identified the territory whose future was to be decided. Two Advisory Opinions of the ICJ regarding the Namibia and the Western Sahara cases concluded that the peoples belonging to the territory had the right of self-determination. And by 'belonging' was meant the indigenous population living in the area at the moment from which *uti possidetis* was to take effect. It was a geographic definition of the peoples, not ethnically or historically determined, to avoid the chaotic conditions in the international system self-determination on these other bases would imply.[9]

In fulfilment of its obligations under the Charter, the Declaration and subsequent General Assembly resolutions, Spain prepared to hold a referendum in 1975 under UN auspices. In 1974 it completed a census of the territorial population, whose figures did not represent a marked departure from previous counts, at least since the 1940s. The 1974 census stated that there were at the time 95,019 individuals resident in the Western Sahara, of which 73,497 were indigenous Sahrawis, 20,126 were of European extraction and 1,396 were from other

African countries. Estimates of the number of indigenous Sahrawis living temporarily in neighbouring countries ranged from the Spanish figure of between 7,000 and 9,000 in total to the official Moroccan estimates of between 30,000 and 35,000 in southern Morocco.

Before elections could be organized, Morocco announced on 16 October 1975 its 'Green March' to reclaim the Sahara, during which 350,000 'volunteers' would cross into the desert briefly, to be replaced by 20,000 Moroccan soldiers. Rabat interpreted in its favour the ICJ decision delivered hours earlier. It had contended that relations since antiquity between Morocco's sultanates and Sahrawi tribes entitled it to the territory. The Court, however, argued that such historical ties were insufficient to constitute the kind of Western-style sovereignty by which it had to adjudicate.[10]

This was a rarefied subtlety in comparison to Hassan II's strategic motives. Asserting recovery of a 'lost Saharan province' would shift focus away from domestic dissension. Popularity of the Alawite monarchy was at its lowest ebb, the King having narrowly escaped two assassination attempts in 1971 and 1972. The threat came from the army, which could be neutralized by its deployment. Furthermore, an external adventure would unite competing social and political interests at home, not least because expansionism had been a principal element in the nationalist opposition platform of the Istiqlal Party.

Despite international condemnation of the invasion,[11] Spain withdrew, signing away its administrative powers in the Madrid Accords as Generalissimo Francisco Franco lay on his deathbed. Refugees flowed into Algeria and twenty years of conflict followed between Royal Armed Forces (FAR) and the POLIS-ARIO – which had been formed first to force Spain to quit the Sahara.[12] Battles were prosecuted well into southern Morocco, until Rabat's engineers managed in the 1980s to build a 2,700 kilometre wall of sand and stone that divided the territory in two. The occupation swelled to 120,000 troops, and with comparatively high-technology weaponry from some fourteen countries, its presence was estimated to cost more than $2 million per day.[13] Matched by POLISARIO's cost-effective tactical offensives, the war ground to a contest of attrition. By 1988, military exhaustion led to settlement proposals that included an over-reaching peace operation.

Determination of the 'self'

The starting point for the 1988 agreement terms of the UN and Organization of African Unity and the 1990–1 implementation plan of Pérez de Cuéllar was the legal, territorial formulation of the 'peoples' and the 'self'. The King had accepted this as early as 1981.[14] However, the subsequent identification process departed radically from it and led to paralysis of the entire peace process. According to the original plan, the Identification Commission was to

implement the agreed position of the parties that all Western Saharans counted in the 1974 census undertaken by the Spanish authorities and aged

18 years or over will have the right to vote, whether currently present in the Territory or outside as refugees or for other reasons.[15]

This was later clarified and the Commission's mandate to update the 1974 census was to include '(a) removing from the lists the names of persons who have since died and (b) considering applications from persons who claim the right to participate in the referendum on the grounds that they are Western Saharans and were omitted from the 1974 census'.[16]

In August 1991, taking advantage of this second clause, Morocco presented a list of 120,000 voters additional to the 1974 census of 74,000. In a letter to Pérez de Cuéllar dated 15 September, King Hassan stated that Morocco would begin moving its 170,000 'Sahrawis' into the territory to facilitate the process of identification *in situ*. The King hoped that the UN would appreciate the logistic and financial contribution of $40 million, which it was estimated this operation would cost. In protest, the Secretary-General's own Special Representative for the Western Sahara, Johannes J. Manz, resigned in December. In a letter to the Secretary-General dated 13 December, he wrote:

> Concerning the non-military violations, the movement of unidentified persons into the Territory, the so-called 'Second Green March,' constitutes, in my view, a breach of the spirit, if not the letter, of the Peace Plan. It was, therefore, with great sadness that I took note of the contents of your letter on this subject to the King of Morocco dated November 18, which was sent without my prior consultation or my knowledge, although I had made very clear recommendations on this matter.

On 19 December, immediately before his retirement from office, Pérez de Cuéllar issued a final report on the subject in which he identified five criteria for determining voter eligibility:

1   persons whose names are included in the revised 1974 census list;
2   persons who were living in the territory as members of a Saharan tribe at the time of the 1974 census but who could not be counted;
3   members of the immediate family of the first two groups;
4   persons born of a Saharan father born in the territory; and
5   persons who are members of a Saharan tribe belonging to the territory and who have resided in the territory for six consecutive years or intermittently for twelve years prior to 1 December 1974.[17]

On 31 December, carefully worded Security Council Resolution 725 refused to approve the Secretary-General's report, which it was felt was a unilateral modification of the peace plan not based on the will of both parties or the views of the co-sponsor, the OAU; nor was full account taken of the work of the Identification Commission that autumn. It called for another report from incoming Secretary-General Boutros Boutros-Ghali.

Furthermore, the international press in January 1993, following their discovery of his appointment upon retirement with a Moroccan holding firm, Omnium Nord Africain, charged that Pérez de Cuéllar for personal reasons developed criteria that favoured Morocco's position. In response, the former Secretary-General denied accepting the offer.[18] Later, in his memoirs, he conceded his partisanship: 'I was never convinced that independence promised the best future for the inhabitants of the Western Sahara.'[19] Indeed, his own Acting Special Representative, Zia Rizvi, was blamed for tipping the balance of power on the ground by passing troop-strength figures and the locations of POLISARIO bases to Morocco.[20]

The new Secretary-General had, as Egyptian foreign minister, actively opposed the 1984 seating of the self-declared and increasingly recognized Sahrawi Arab Democratic Republic (SADR) at the OAU. He was not expected to be impartial, and the appointment as his Special Representative of former Pakistani foreign minister Sahabzada Yaqub-Khan, a friend of King Hassan, confirmed this.[21] Boutros-Ghali issued a report on voter identification a year after his arrival.[22] This outlined the views of the parties presented in August and September 1992 during negotiations on Pérez de Cuéllar's December 1991 criteria. Disagreement centred on the fourth and fifth criteria, as well as tribal affiliation and sources of evidence to be relied on to determine the identity of individuals applying to participate in the referendum – whether official documents, oral testimony or both. In principle, the parties agreed that a basis for voter eligibility was provided by the first three criteria and that authentic documents issued by the Spanish colonial authorities were acceptable sources of evidence attesting to the identity of an individual.

The source of disagreement was the general approach taken by the two parties: Morocco wished to expand the electorate as much as possible, to include populations linked directly or indirectly with the territory who would be disenfranchised by a strict interpretation of the criteria; the POLISARIO hoped to maintain the basic integrity of the 1974 census as the only accurate statement of the *status quo ante bellum* and definition of the people with the legitimate right of self-determination.

Particularly, the parties disagreed on tribal affiliation as a basis for voter eligibility. While both parties agreed that membership of a tribe does not by itself entitle an individual to vote, and that the individual must meet one of the criteria above, they disagreed on membership in a sub-tribal family grouping, or subfraction, as a basis for eligibility. More specifically, the POLISARIO argued that membership in a subfraction establishes eligibility for an individual outside the territory only if the majority of the members of the subfraction were counted in the 1974 census and can legitimately be regarded as 'belonging to the territory'. Otherwise, it argued, populations not linked with the territory would decide the future of its true inhabitants. This would be comparable, according to one example, of the Masai in Kenya voting in a Tanzanian election because of the existence of Masai in the latter. Morocco rejected this interpretation and argued in favour of including the subfraction as a whole regardless of the numbers linked with the colonially defined territory, as well as other subfractions excluded from the census because of unrepresentative boundaries.

In order to speed resolution of the disagreements, the Secretary-General listed three broad options on how best to proceed: (1) continuation and intensification of talks; (2) immediate implementation of the criteria without the cooperation of one of the parties; and (3) adoption of an alternative approach not based on the settlement plan. The Secretary-General disregarded (1): 'It is my considered opinion…that the chances for success under this option are very slim.' On 28 January, France tabled a draft resolution which favoured the Secretary-General's second option. It confirmed the Council's support for the 19 December 1991 report and annexed criteria; set an October 1993 deadline for the referendum; invited the Secretary-General to take the necessary measures for the organization of the referendum; and urged the parties to cooperate fully with the Secretary-General.

The United States countered this, favouring instead the first option. A series of draft resolutions culminated in proposals by New Zealand and Spain, which were accepted as Resolution 809 on 2 March. This stressed the desirability of ensuring the full cooperation of both parties for the implementation of the settlement plan; invited the Secretary-General to intensify efforts with the parties to resolve outstanding issues, particularly relating to the criteria; and further invited the Secretary-General to make the necessary preparations for the organization of the referendum and to consult accordingly with the parties for the purpose of commencing voter registration on a prompt basis starting with the updated lists of the 1974 census, regardless of disagreement on other criteria.

At the beginning of June 1993, the Secretary-General toured the area and presented to the parties a 'compromise' interpretation of the five criteria and bases for evidence. He requested from the parties a 'yes' or a 'no'. However, the interpretation was not a fundamental alteration of the permissive criteria and was unlikely to be accepted by both parties without reservation. He also warned the parties that with international attention focused on UN operations elsewhere, in the former Yugoslavia and Somalia, there was a desire among member states to conclude the Western Sahara process as swiftly as possible.

To ensure US support, the POLISARIO eventually accepted the fourth and fifth criteria but rejected the 'compromise' interpretation, and the parties continued to disagree. After failed attempts at direct talks between the two and on the eve of Morocco's departure from temporary membership of the Security Council, the Secretary-General issued a strongly worded report.[23]

The report addressed the disagreement over genuine tribal connection to the territory as a basis for voter eligibility. The Secretary-General's opinion was presented as a compromise but was perceived by observers to favour the Moroccan stand. While he restricted the subfractions to be counted to those represented in the 1974 census, he nevertheless accepted unlimited numbers of each subfraction, regardless of however small the number connected to the territory by the census. He recognized that the 'Frente POLISARIO does not agree with the compromise, as it remains concerned about the possible inclusion, in the electorate, of members of some tribal units which it does not consider as existing in the Territory'. The POLISARIO further argued that if this reasoning is to be accepted, then subfractions the majority of whose members are located in Algeria and Mauritania should be counted as well. An agreement was reached at the Permanent Mission of France to the UN between France and the United States to accept the 'framework' of identification outlined in the Secretary-General's report.

The reaction of the POLISARIO was to lose much faith in the peace process. It had looked to the US for hope and remained confident in the process principally in anticipation of this support. Disagreement within the POLISARIO, between those in favour of a pacific process and those calling for a return to hostilities, had been settled in part by expectation of US help. Since this seemed no longer forthcoming, it was felt that hostilities might be the only means of breaking the stalemate. Whether or not the POLISARIO could sustain more fighting has remained an unanswered question among UN military observers in MINURSO. It would be for states taking a chance on this not occurring to find out. The POLISARIO began preparations for war, withdrawing weaponry from cantonment and mobilizing combatants. Secretary-General of the POLISARIO Mohamed Abdelaziz communicated this willingness to return to hostilities to Boutros-Ghali in Geneva in January 1994 and to the US Administration during a visit in February.

The next report of the UN Secretary-General in March was less firm yet presented more stark options: either (1) proceed without the parties' consent; (2) proceed on the basis of the 'compromise' framework, attempt to obtain the cooperation of the parties and review the results after a prescribed period; or (3) phase out the whole operation since the cooperation of the parties was not forthcoming. Fatigue among member states led to quick acceptance of the framework in option (2). To obtain the cooperation of the parties, it was suggested that they could reserve their right to reject the results of identification but that they should permit the Commission to proceed in the meantime.

While this was accepted by the parties it could not produce the kind of results hoped for. Identification began on 28 August 1994, but it proceeded painstakingly slowly. It was already two months delayed because in June Morocco was not permitting OAU observers entry to identification sites. It also tried to prevent visits by the press. These issues were overcome through convoluted mediation rather than administratively. The Commission staff began to gather rules for identification in a loose-leaf binder as they developed. There was no room for transparency, given overlapping areas of disagreement between observers of the parties and the subordination of UN officials to their will. Provisions had not been established regarding visits by non-governmental organizations. Identification was proving not to be publicly accountable in the manner that the registration of voters was in Namibia in 1989, Cambodia in 1992–3 or El Salvador in 1994. A draft code of conduct for the referendum was sent by the UN to both parties on 14 December 1994, but it suffered from flaws corresponding to disagreements over identification. It would foster more procedural trench warfare and was not discussed in the new year.

In the meantime, the Deputy Chairman of the Identification Commission, former US Ambassador to Equatorial Guinea, Frank Ruddy, became frustrated with the process. The UN terminated his contract in December 1994. In January, Ruddy testified before the US Congress about Moroccan irregularities and UN mismanagement of the Mission.[24] In blunt language he described the 'atmosphere of terror' in Western Sahara and the 'Mafia-like behaviour' of Rabat's officials. He called the Moroccans 'gangsters'[25] and stated that the 'UN has lost control of the mission'.[26] Due to its mismanagement, MINURSO was incapable of asserting itself against Moroccan pressure. In El Ayoun, Sahrawis registering to vote were filmed and photographed and their registration cards taken away after being identified.[27] Ruddy concluded, 'This isn't going anywhere.' According to officials in the UN Legal Office, the UN response to the allegations was largely 'white-washed'. A report was issued by the four-month-old Office of Internal Oversight Services that focused only on mundane bureaucratic procedures.[28] This was the first investigation of the 'watch-dog' office and indicated its lack of independence within the system.[29]

On 25 October 1994, 233,000 applications for identification had been completed; by June 1995, nearly a year after the start of the process, only some 42,000 individuals had been identified.[30] In contrast, although strict comparisons cannot be drawn, the registration of 4.76 million voters in Cambodia was measured in months, and in Namibia of 700,000 in weeks. On 5 June, the Security Council dispatched a special mission to assess MINURSO's progress. Chaired by Botswana, it was composed of representatives from Argentina, the US, France, Oman and Honduras. An attempt to clarify evidence of criteria for eligibility to vote was confounded by drafters from the Identification Commission. Paragraph 3 of the report stated:

> In the event that an applicant is not included in the Spanish census, does not present any documentation confirming his/her identity and substantiating his/her claim for admission under one of the remaining criteria, and if the two sheikhs who are called upon to provide the relevant oral testimony disagree, the burden of proof will rest with the respective applicant to offer convincing evidence to the Identification Commission that he/she qualified for inclusion in the electoral roll.

According to the settlement plan and subsequent criteria, in the absence of the species of evidence referred to an individual is supposed to be excluded from registration. This paragraph seemed to state that if a person did not have the agreed kinds of proofs of identity, then it was incumbent on them to find other bases, without clarifying what they were. Furthermore, it gave authority to the Commission to judge the issue without reference to observers from the parties. This could have opened a never-ending loop of identification in which those rejected by the existing procedures could reapply directly to the Commission.

By the time the draft report was presented to the Security Council, paragraph 3 had become holy writ. Although Argentina and Germany strongly criticized the issue in a closed session of the Council, not one country was willing to state publicly that paragraph 3 should be interpreted in accordance with the existing understanding of identification. This included the US, which explicitly refused to do so. It was the nadir of member nations' commitment to the peace mission. In a final drafting process, dominated by France in consultation with Morocco, the report was accepted by the Security Council.

Coincidentally, a Moroccan military court sentenced eight Sahrawi youths to between fifteen and twenty years' imprisonment for participating in a public demonstration in El Ayoun on 11 May. The POLISARIO suspended its participation in the identification process. After pressure from the US, the King reduced the sentences and, accepting what was considered a gesture of confidence, the POLISARIO returned. However, the US Mission at the UN issued a strongly worded statement warning the parties that if delays continued, the operation would be terminated. A new, unrealistic deadline for the referendum was set for early 1996.

Instead, on 29 May, the Security Council adopted the Secretary-General's recommendations to suspend voter identification altogether, in the absence of convincing political will from the parties.[31] Little more than 60,000 applicants had been accepted, with another 156,000 remaining to be processed. The Council also accepted the proposed reduction by 20 per cent of MINURSO's military component, from 288 to 230 observers. Only a few of the forty UN civilian police would not be withdrawn and a political office would be retained to continue a dialogue between the two sides in order to resolve their differences. The mandate of the mission was renewed for another six months, until 30 November 1996, and Boutros-Ghali was asked to report to the Council on the stalemate on 31 August and on the overall situation by 10 November.

In fact, the problem was rooted in the Identification Commission. It lacked transparency and accountability and was challenged as such. Contrary to the settlement plan, it refused to publish the approved names on the electoral list, as well as the criteria and evidence relied on for each individual – which had been the source of so much disagreement. What happened in disputed cases was not clear and an additional Legal Review Unit was serving as an undefined layer of identification. Boutros-Ghali's Acting Special Representative, Erik Jensen, functioned by himself and excluded, when he could, the parties or OAU observers. Before the Security Council in October 1995, the Secretary-General argued that identification was only a means of provoking negotiations between the parties, suggesting that it was never intended to be completed.

The issue was raised at the beginning of 1996 with then Special Envoy, Ambassador Chinmaya Garekhan. He concurred with the importance of transparency in identification, and the next report of the Secretary-General stated that

> this could contribute to reducing mistrust and suspicion and serve to instil more confidence in the process. To that end, it was agreed that the

Commission would...share with both parties...lists of applicants identified...as well as a list of applicants still to be identified.[32]

But such an open door was incompatible with the closed procedures established.
Consequently, cancellation of identification was easier than reconciling the two.

UNACCOUNTABLE PROXIMITY TALKS

It had been clear from the earliest years of the UN's deployment that there could
be distinguished seven pillars for ending the impasse between the parties. They
formed the core missing link of political will in MINURSO, and together constituted the premise for bridging this gap:

1   Consistency: reliance on the UN/OAU plan meant that for it to succeed it
    had to be applied equitably and consistently to both parties and at each
    stage of the process.
2   Consent: the peace process was based and had to continue to be based on
    the consent of both parties.
3   Census: the 1974 Spanish census constituted the basis of the settlement plan
    and determined who could vote in the referendum. While subsequent quali-
    fication was necessary in its practical application, this could not be such an
    unreasonable departure from the plan as to alter its intent.
4   Cease-fire: priority consideration was to be given to the continuation of the
    cease-fire. The United Nations needed to plan and prepare for the worst-
    case scenario if it was to hold.
5   Corroboration: if the referendum results were to be recognized and
    accepted as 'free and fair', as called for in the settlement plan, then the
    process had to be transparent in procedure and intent.
6   Communication: the parties required encouragement to meet directly.
7   Containment: as there was broad international interest to contain manipula-
    tion of the settlement plan, each stage of the multilateral process needed to
    be underwritten by bilateral support. Bilateral efforts were not to interfere
    with but support UN objectives seeking to confine the dimensions of the
    conflict.

Essentially, these requirements reflected the fracturing of minimal consent given
by the parties to the initial settlement plan. There had not been enough willingness to sign a formal agreement, only a nod by each to Pérez de Cuéllar that the
terms were acceptable. But many provisions were riddled with holes, which would
have to be filled in the breach of the operation. Despite the powers it assumed on
paper, the UN was entirely reliant on the consent of the parties in the implementation of the plan. It was a poor application of the traditional peacekeeping
formula to a non-peacekeeping scenario. Still, if consent was to be relied on, then
the political will of the parties had to be fostered on a continuous basis.

Rather than serving as a catalyst for agreement, MINURSO divided the parties almost irreconcilably. In fact, both sides lost the capacity to discuss substance; raising any issue meant automatic disagreement because of the approaches to the process as a whole they had developed. To overcome this, an avenue had to be found back to the point when consent that was converging began to diverge. That point was the letter and original spirit of the implementation plan. Guaranteeing further consent required the direct and comprehensive engagement of the parties, the UN and member states in a joint arrangement. Instead, there was only indirect contact.

'Many countries and observers believe that direct talks represent the best avenue for reaching an agreement concerning the conditions for holding a referendum.'[33] An OAU summit adopted on 11 June 1983 Resolution AHG/Res. 104, urging the parties 'to undertake direct negotiations...to create the necessary conditions for a peaceful and fair referendum'. On 2 December 1985, the UN General Assembly adopted Resolution 40/50 to persuade the parties 'to negotiate, in the shortest possible time...the terms of a cease-fire and the modalities for organizing the said referendum'. In 1988, the General Assembly passed an unopposed resolution calling for direct negotiations.

Morocco could not accept the term 'negotiation' but nevertheless 'direct talks' of one kind or another were held throughout this period. In Bamako in October 1978, in Algiers in April 1983 and in Lisbon in January 1985, meetings were held between POLISARIO officials and advisers to King Hassan, usually Royal Counsellor Ahmed Reda Guedira; Abdelatif Filali, the current prime minister and foreign minister; and Driss Basri, the current interior minister. In April 1986 in New York, indirect talks were held through the UN. In 1988 in Taëf, Saudi Arabia, secret discussions were held between 12 and 22 July. These were unsuccessful because they were not between the POLISARIO and the Government of Morocco. They were significant, however, because they represented the emergence of the Moroccan tactic of presenting talks as being between two sides of a Sahrawi divide, rather than between Rabat and anybody else, insinuating therefore that the Western Sahara conflict was an internal Moroccan affair.

The highest-level meeting occurred in Marrakesh on 4 and 5 January 1989. This was a 'direct discussion' between senior POLISARIO representatives and the King himself. International pressure in preceding months had forced what was a major breakthrough:

> Despite Moroccan insistence that the meetings consisted of talks, the substance of the discussions could well be described as quasi-negotiations, because not only were the details of the referendum raised, but truce arrangements and the exchange of prisoners were also at the center of the talks.[34]

The King issued contradictory statements to the press: before the meeting he announced he would talk with POLISARIO representatives; after the talks he reassured Moroccan opposition parties and claimed he had met only with Moroccan Sahrawis who had 'gone astray'.

The King never reconvened talks with the POLISARIO, and once the UN was fully seized of the issue, indirect contacts through the Special Representative became the sole repository of consent. Although Pérez de Cuéllar managed to arrange a meeting in Geneva in June 1990 of tribal chieftains, though perhaps of dubious legitimacy, he was unable to convince the parties to meet directly. Morocco would not meet with the POLISARIO and the Secretary-General had to shuttle between delegations. With Manz's resignation and the appointment of Yaqub-Khan by Boutros-Ghali, outstanding issues such as identification were addressed through 'indirect talks'.

This was an inadequate means of ensuring agreement that instead further entrenched opposing positions. The Security Council was divided about the freedom and fairness in the conduct of one of the first UN missions in which all of its five permanent members were participating. The political will under-writing MINURSO had become like a ping-pong match between the fragile consent of the parties, the challenged objectivity of the UN and the individual interests of Council members. In particular, France and the US played by different rules.

Its post-colonial relations with Morocco, Algeria and Mauritania were a balancing act for Paris upset by disagreement between Rabat and Algiers over Western Sahara. Some 40,000 French citizens in Morocco, a friendly govern-ment in a geostrategic location, and financial investments had to be balanced with hydrocarbon opportunities in Algeria. A rapprochement with Rabat after 1988 divided the political heads and military hearts in Algiers over support of the POLISARIO. But by 1995, relations with Morocco had cooled again and the election of President Liamine Zéroual, a former commander of the sensitive Tindouf region and SADR base of operations, reinforced backing from the capital despite the drain of fighting Islamic fundamentalism and a vicious civil war. For France, what was being treated as a sphere of influence would be inter-rupted by an independent Sahrawi state in the middle of it. Throughout the peace process, the Quai d'Orsay pursued an aggressive diplomatic campaign of Moroccan support in the Security Council.

Washington's policy seemed to have contradictory sides. On the one hand, Hassan represented a staunch ally and a stable, moderate regime in the region. Morocco provided a military staging area for US operations, and it supported American diplomatic initiatives in the Middle East and south of the Sahara. On the other hand, the US more than once blocked French actions in the Council, including the redrafting in February 1993 of what passed as quite a different Resolution 809. It pressured Morocco in emergencies that threatened collapse of MINURSO, as in summer 1995 when Rabat imposed severe sentences on the Sahrawi demonstrators. But this intermittent response was never translated into perpetual influence on the parties to fully implement the settlement plan. As a result, the permanent five could only agree to issue mandates in the Council, but not act to fulfil their terms.[35]

These disparate fragments could not be expected to produce cohesive results. The 'UNEF II Rules' were broken without replacing them with a new paradigm.

Opposing elements needed to be fused together. The first step was to foster 'direct talks' between the parties. On the insistence of the United States, the parties met between 17 and 19 July 1993 in the capital of Western Sahara, El Ayoun. The UN brokered the conditions of the meeting, which was to be between senior POLISARIO officials headed by the organization's number two, Bachir Mustapha Sayed, and a delegation of the Moroccan Government under the leadership of a close friend and adviser to the King, Morocco's Permanent Representative at the UN, Ahmed Senoussi.

However, included in the Moroccan delegation were representatives of Sahrawis from Moroccan-controlled Western Sahara. At the meeting, Dr Mohamed Cheikh Biadillah, a Member of the Royal Consultative Council for Saharan Affairs, arrived as Chief of Delegation, with Senoussi only his adviser. Moroccan press reports presented the meeting as being between two groups of Sahrawis. Issues of substance were reduced to a Moroccan invitation to the 'other Sahrawis' to integrate into Morocco. The parties agreed only to meet again.

The second and third attempts failed altogether. In New York on 25 October 1993, the POLISARIO refused to meet with the Moroccan delegation since it included Brahim Hakim, a former POLISARIO Foreign Minister who defected to Morocco in 1992 when he was Ambassador in Algiers. Although there had been a written 'Memo of Understanding' for the meeting, an additional provision was included late which Morocco could take advantage of: 'The composition of each delegation is deemed to lie within the exclusive competence of each Party and would not be open to any objections by either side.'

In Geneva on 16 January 1994, Boutros-Ghali invited the President of the POLISARIO, Mohamed Abdelaziz, to a secret meeting with the Moroccans. It was intended that the parties would be left alone to talk. However, the Moroccan delegation was composed of Senoussi and General Khadiri, in charge of police intelligence. The highest authority in the POLISARIO could not meet in such a diplomatically asymmetrical manner, but suggested a meeting with the Moroccan delegation's counterparts. This was refused and signalled the failure of secret or 'closed direct talks'.

A new concept of 'open and direct talks' was needed. Boutros-Ghali formally approved of this in January 1996,[36] and the Security Council reacted positively.[37] However, another round of 'secret talks' without witnesses was resorted to in August 1996. Delegations met in Geneva, and then talks were held in Morocco between a POLISARIO Front delegation and the highest authorities in the country, including Crown Prince Sidi Mohamed and Interior Minister Basri. Predictably, the meetings resulted only in a restatement of the parties' positions, in what Mouloud Said, the POLISARIO representative in Washington, called a 'dialogue of the deaf'.

GUARANTEEING AGREED TERMS

At least since 1993, there has been a peace-maintenance framework proposed for breaking the stalemate in Western Sahara.[38] Linking strategic decision-making at the Security Council with operational interpretation and tactical directives through a joint interim authority established for the purpose, it properly connects negotiated peace-making with functional implementation. As part of this, a mechanism that is based on 'open and direct talks' and that can perpetuate continuous dialogue between the Government of Morocco and the Frente POLISARIO, the UN and OAU, as well as secure the active engagement of a core group of member states, may be able to provide the kinds of political guarantees mutually required by the parties in Western Sahara. This was the concept outlined on 7 October 1996 before the Fourth Committee of the General Assembly, concerned with Special Political and Decolonization questions. The Assembly was called on to affirm the need for open and direct talks and to accept the proposed principles of a code of conduct for the parties.[39]

Specific ingredients for the plan were further elaborated on 15 November at the establishment of an International Association of Jurists for Western Sahara in Barcelona. This so-called 'Agenda for Western Sahara' included a complete judicial and operational review of MINURSO, a formal agreement between the parties and a joint guarantor body.[40] Since there had been a significant departure from legal norms and past practice in identification, it was thought necessary to preserve the lessons that MINURSO's mistakes could teach, and at the same time ascertain what could be remedied. A modified Truth Commission, slightly different from those intended to discover human rights abuses by government officials in El Salvador and South Africa, might have managed this task. Alternatively, a Commission of Inquiry could have been authorized as a subsidiary organ of the Security Council, of the kind that investigated armed attacks against UN personnel in Somalia.[41] But acknowledging the dysfunction of MINURSO still required the capacity to do something about it.

It is worth considering in this context the Namibian Joint Monitoring Commission described in Chapter 1. A politico-operational unit, the JMC was additional to the diplomatic Contact Group helping to increase the numbers of interested states and widen the strategic sources of influence during mediation. As a generic model, a joint mechanism could provide the basis of a framework for Western Sahara. A supervisory cell would need to be composed of the parties; the UN and OAU, as co-sponsors of the settlement plan; neighbouring Algeria and Mauritania; interested states, like Spain and France – the former colonial powers in the area; disinterested support from such traditional peacekeepers as Canada and the Scandinavian countries; and above all, American authority to combine individual interests and impartial goodwill. This combination would represent the constellation of diplomatic factors affecting the stalemate and foster political will through confidence and leverage. It could embody the seven pillars of peace and better integrate decisions and action, as well as test peace-maintenance ideas for resolving other seemingly intractable conflicts.

There have been several kinds of arrangements worth contrasting:

1   In Cambodia, during the interim peace process, the Supreme National Council composed of the four factions served only as a forum for disagreement, because there was no outside authority genuinely fostering and guaranteeing decisions.[42]
2   The International Conference for the Former Yugoslavia was only a kind of diplomatic forum and had no pretence of guaranteeing results directly.[43]
3   The 'Friends of' groups for different countries, such as Haiti and Guatemala, can have an influence on conflicts, but their impact varies according to the degree of commitment of the membership. In the case of El Salvador, this was enhanced by the personal and direct role of the UN Secretary-General. These groups are ad hoc and there are not any consistent criteria for ensuring an effective model.[44]
4   The Russian Joint Control Commissions, composed of Moscow's officials and the local parties in conflict, are certainly effective but by no means impartial. They serve avowedly the interests of Russia and do not operate according to an objective legal standard.[45]
5   The United States has had experience since the Gulf War in building military coalitions, which illustrate the unifying influence the US can have. However, while there is a diplomatic landscape behind such joint ventures, this still needs to be translated in each case into a civilian standing body as political guarantor.[46]

A politically effective mechanism with an authoritative member must be distinguished from a diplomatic meeting of equals. While a multilateral composition may account for its legitimacy, to have the capacity to control ground conditions and direct a peace process, the body must have a centre of gravity more compelling than the sum of the other parts. With a credible guarantor like the US in a Western Sahara JMC, the parties and member states may be able to exercise political authority together as the will to implement each decision is generated on an on-going basis. Sometimes the mere presence of the US in such a setting can avoid the need for cumbersome deployments later. Minimal but committed engagement may be one of the most cost-effective tools in Washington's arsenal for preventive diplomacy to avoid the outbreak or resumption of hostilities, or to lubricate processes paralysed by differing interpretations of agreed terms. A joint initiative for Western Sahara may not only avoid total collapse of the cease-fire and regional instability, but it will indicate how the US can underwrite peace missions more with powerful diplomatic software than expensive military hardware.

While there are some generic principles for international political coalition-building, each framework needs to be tailored to the specific conflict. Considering the experience of talks between Morocco and the POLISARIO, and the reasons for their breakdown in the past, there are certain guidelines that would need to be included as a kind of code of conduct governing the behaviour of JMC members:

1   Talks need to be both 'open' and 'direct', and should be understood to be between the parties, the Government of Morocco and the Frente POLIS-ARIO.
2   The talks should be convened in the presence of member states, particularly from the Security Council. Member states would preside at the talks and participate in their capacity as 'active observers'.
3   The number of representatives in and list of each delegation participating in a meeting should be agreed to by both parties in advance. Any party or member state should be able to suspend a meeting with delegations not composed in good faith.
4   It may be agreed that private individuals could be chosen by each of the parties and member states to attend the meetings. While these 'passive observers' may be present, they should not participate in discussions.
5   At the discretion of member states, 'individual petitioners' may be called to address the meetings in their own capacity.
6   In order to ensure the talks are meaningful and constructive, an agenda with a limited number of items should be established prior to the meetings.
7   The parties should provide full support and cooperation in ensuring the orderly and proper conduct of meetings. They should act in good faith when hearing or making presentations and avoid undue provocations – including the display of symbols representing the delegations.
8   The parties should show moderation and self-restraint in their statements to the media. Public statements must not misrepresent the conduct or results of the talks.
9   Following each meeting, member states would report the results to the Secretary-General and the President of the Security Council.

In April 1994, at a gathering in Madrid to support the United Nations peace plan, Mohamed Abdelaziz called for an international conference with partici-pants representing the necessary political constellation for a Western Sahara JMC. Certainly, convening a meeting could have been, and still can be, the first step in the establishment of a more formal standing body. In a letter dated 30 April 1994, Abdelaziz suggested the idea to Boutros-Ghali. In his responding letter of 25 May, the Secretary-General accepted the importance of that kind of approach, and expressed his intention to follow up on it with the suggested UN members. Despite its consideration by some Norwegian diplomats, this avenue did not come to fruition in 1994. However, it became clear that the role of the United States would be particularly critical: Norwegian integrity had to be matched by US influence over the parties.[47]

Since then, the OAU and NGOs have subscribed to the notion of a peace-maintenance mechanism. Solomon Gomes, the Deputy Permanent Observer at the OAU Mission to the UN, has recommended the establishment of a 'Friends of Western Sahara' group of states to restore credibility to MINURSO, embrace dialogue and mediate with leverage.[48] In addition to demands by Human Rights Watch for transparency and accountability in identification,[49] the Canadian Lawyers Association for International Human Rights has favoured direct talks between the parties as a way forward and encouraged the creation of a 'Contact Group for the Western Sahara' that could include the Canadian and South African governments.[50]

LEGITIMACY AND EFFECTIVENESS

Similarly, at the United Nations in autumn 1996, after a two-and-a-half-year gestation period, the context of the 51st General Assembly seemed to have ripened for the prospects of a legitimate and effective joint framework. As it annually does, the Fourth Committee decided to consider the status of self-determination in Western Sahara. In response to the peace-maintenance proposal for open and direct talks, El Hassane Zahid, Deputy Permanent Representative from the Moroccan Mission, questioned the objective of such a dialogue. The POLISARIO representative, Boukhari Ahmed, stated that: 'We frankly do not see any other means to overcome this dangerous impasse than a process of direct, serious and responsible negotiations between the two parties.' He asked governments not only to give the parties their encouragement, but to provide an 'active presence' in the dialogue to guarantee its integrity.[51]

Reacting to the individual petitioners, member states repeatedly called for direct talks. Tanzania and Zimbabwe openly criticized the Security Council's gradual abandonment of the long-suffering drama. The General Assembly approved financing for the prolongation of MINURSO's mission, indicating to the Security Council its desire for a renewal of the mandate. The Fourth Committee circulated a draft resolution stating that the Assembly

> Declares its conviction of the importance and usefulness of the direct contacts between the two parties in view of overcoming their differences...and encourages the Kingdom of Morocco and the Frente [POLISARIO]...to start, as soon as possible, these direct talks.[52]

Sponsored by some fifty-two member states, the resolution was something of a response to the Security Council's suspension of the identification process and reduction of MINURSO. By demanding direct talks, as an infrastructural element to strengthen the existing settlement plan, the Fourth Committee was in effect challenging the Council's performance in Western Sahara. Not only was this a noticeable departure from the past, after years of silence in tacit support of the peace process as a whole, but it might have been interpreted as a willingness to disregard Article 12(1) of the UN Charter, which prevents the General Assembly from making any recommendations with regard to a dispute seized by the Security Council. This could have led to a small constitutional crisis had the reaction of the Council been confrontational. Instead, on 27 November, it passed Resolution 1084–1996, which supported the continuation of the dialogue to facilitate, in the context of the settlement plan, other efforts towards an agreeable formula. Subsequently, the Assembly plenary adopted its draft on 10 February 1997 as Resolution 51/143.

With significant statements of political will from the Security Council and General Assembly, the new Secretary-General presented his first report on Western Sahara in February. This rapid timing, so soon after Kofi Annan's election, indicated the new place the issue had on his agenda. On the one hand, he reaffirmed that: 'From a technical point of view, it is entirely possible to resume and finish identification.' On the other, he added that progress is possible 'only if both sides commit themselves fully, in deed as well as in word, to implementing the settlement plan'.[53]

Hinting at his next move, the report concluded with three significant questions:

1   Can the settlement plan be implemented in its present form?
2   If not, are there adjustments to the settlement plan, acceptable to both parties, which would make it implementable?
3   If not, are there other ways by which the international community could help the parties resolve their conflict?

Each question represented a different voice in the UN Secretariat regarding the feasibility of fully implementing the agreed provisions of the peace plan. Fearing what an alternative might mean, Senoussi addressed a letter to the President of the Security Council stressing Morocco's attachment to the settlement terms:

> It considers that the drafting of the plan was a long and arduous process and that altering it, which would necessarily entail altering all the implementing measures adopted by the different organs involved in the process, could prove to be an even longer and more complex process.[54]

Suddenly, on 17 March, it was announced that former US Secretary of State James A. Baker III had been appointed as Annan's Special Envoy for Western Sahara. The two parties were mystified. Why had Baker been chosen? More extraordinary still, why had he accepted? Was Baker the man intended to functionally save or palatably terminate the costly peace process – the shorthand implication of the third question? In a press statement, he explained that his instructions were to make a fresh assessment of the conflict and explore all viable options, including implementation of the present settlement plan or any new initiative that might bridge the current impasse.

Between 23 and 28 April, Baker visited the region and met with the parties and neighbouring governments.[55] Appropriately, he travelled with Chester A. Crocker, former Assistant Secretary of State for African Affairs, who had been the architect of the Namibian JMC. Disinformation seemed to trail the event.

The message from UN officials speaking on condition of anonymity was that Baker had come to arrange autonomy for the Sahrawi, as a third option between integration and independence. It was widely reported that the POLISARIO would have to consider such an offer from the King.[56] This was false. Baker explicitly told the parties that he was not interested in overcoming only the problem of identification. He wanted to know what it would take to implement each and every stage of the settlement plan, including the repatriation of refugees, the confinement of troops, the conduct of the electoral campaign and the final transfer of power to the newly elected authority. Baker was linking his involvement to the process as a whole, and not to any single part of it. But there was never serious consideration of autonomy.

In Rabat, Interior Minister Basri spent some time lecturing Baker on the fact that Morocco would win the referendum. This was to be interpreted to mean, not that the numbers were in its favour, but that Morocco would do everything in its power to win at all costs. He was later quoted as saying that there would be 'neither an extended, nor a medium nor a small autonomy' for Western Sahara. 'There are no negotiations on autonomy, the referendum is about integration or independence.'[57]

In meetings with Abdelaziz near Tindouf, it was clear that autonomy was not and could not be on the table. A banner welcoming Baker read 'Remember Big Fish versus Small Fish'. This was a reference to his memoirs, which described a Mongolian sentiment when Iraq invaded Kuwait about the perilous position of small countries swallowed up by larger neighbours.[58] The comparison between the 1990 aggression and Morocco's occupation of Western Sahara should have been clear. Another banner asked 'Iraq No, Morocco Yes. Why?'. And still another complained 'UN no credibility; only complicity'.

Further papers were forwarded to Baker clarifying the parties' final positions. It remained to be seen whether Baker would marshal his coalition-building skills to establish a joint guaranteeing mechanism. With him came at least the implicit authority of Washington, as well as the explicit support of the Clinton Administration, and therefore the opportunity to harness the unifying influence of the US. So it was significant that in London on 11–12 June, Baker convened the parties and the governments of Algeria and Mauritania as 'observers' to consider how to implement the settlement plan. The meeting was organized with the United Kingdom Foreign and Commonwealth Office, thereby engaging a largely impartial state that was also a permanent member of the Security Council and representative of European interests. Here were the nascent ingredients for establishing a peace-maintenance mechanism for decolonizing Western Sahara.

Indeed, even this inchoate combination produced a breakthrough in form, if not substance. Baker met separately with Foreign Ministers Filali and the recently appointed Sayed, as well as their Algerian and Mauritanian counterparts. While there was no actual contact, Baker advised them that the referendum could only be the result of direct 'negotiations' under his auspices. He explained that there needed to be a point-by-point discussion. With their consent, he invited the parties and 'observers' to meet in Lisbon on 23–4 June. In a press statement on the night of the 12th, Baker confirmed that limited autonomy was not on the table.[59] Rather than initiating an alternative, he was defining the measurement of success according to the concrete fulfilment of the settlement plan. In Lisbon, during face-to-face negotiations between the parties, he presented 'bridging proposals' for achieving this, and on 19–20 July in London, a 'compromise' on voter identification was adopted. In exchange for POLISARIO acceptance of oral testimony additional to documentary evidence of individual identity, Morocco agreed to defer consideration of 50–60,000 disputed names. A week later, back in Lisbon, discussion began on a code of conduct for the referendum, which was finalized and culminated in a set of agreements in Houston on 14–16 September.[60]

To implement these Accords, a technical assessment mission was dispatched to the UN's area of operations between 7 and 15 October. This was the first time since deployment that a comprehensive review of the requirements for fulfilling MINURSO's mandate was possible. However, the resulting approach to implementation and proposed timetable was 'based on a best-case scenario' kind of planning.[61] Assuming the likelihood of favourable conditions proved disastrous, not only in MINURSO's history, but in most other UN operations as well.

Indeed, statements in October and November by Driss Basri, the Istiqlal and other political parties, and King Hassan, all continued to treat the referendum as a means of confirming Morocco's right to the territory. Also, a rigorous effort was under way to prepare the sheikhs under Moroccan control to take advantage of the newly agreed admissibility of oral testimony. This posed yet another hurdle for the completion of identification. In the chemistry that evolved at the negotiating table, Moroccan officials were unwilling to challenge the personal authority of Baker. In the field, however, Morocco continues to have a better chance of manipulating and undermining the broad terms agreed to – in the manner that it had proved so successful in doing in the past.

If the Houston Accords were to be implemented effectively, there needed to be a reconstruction of MINURSO on the ground and fresh staff appointments made, particularly since the interpretation and application of the parties' code of conduct now rested fundamentally in the hands of UN officials. A new Chairman of the Identification Commission, Robin Kinloch, replaced Jensen, and former US State Department Arabist Charles Dunbar became the new SRSG in December 1997. However, without a peace-maintenance framework to embody the centre of gravity created by Baker's involvement, it was predictable that the parties' intransigence could quickly derail the process again. Identification was temporarily halted at the end of February 1998 due to continued disagreement over contested tribes, undermining the set timetable. By March, Baker had to consider reconvening the two sides to reassert the provisions committed to only months earlier.[62]

Part IV

Conclusion

8   Peace-maintenance puzzles

Lebanon was considered to be a religious war; the former Yugoslavia, an ethnic conflict; Somalia, with perhaps the most homogeneous community in Africa – linguistically and culturally – appeared to fracture along patrilineal clan lines; and Rwanda, Burundi and Zaïre, although at times labelled 'tribal' disputes, were believed, instead, to be more the result of social, economic and class discrepancies. Whatever their basis for differentiation, all of these cases developed comparable conditions of violent competition for control over territory, population and a central government.

It is gradually being acknowledged that these kinds of conflicts are not innately religious, ethnic or tribal, and in some way, therefore, inevitable. Rather, they are the consequence of conscious mobilization of the many by the few. In this manner, even hollow and spurious justifications for differences can be packaged and sold to societies, that divide to confront mutually manufactured enemies. The initial weapons are the advertising of the cause and the marketing of an exclusionary ideology. The struggles are set in a historical cast, to crystallize their immemorial possession. In some instances, there may have been brutal exchanges in the past, in others not – but the result is the same. In each place, a warlord consolidates a dominant position over a shattered society, no longer able to challenge the new supremo as the natural course of internecine killing devastates its capacity to withdraw from a battlefield that has engulfed home and hearth, and pitted kith against kin.

The weakened resolve of a tired and divided international community, like the victim population, has proved unable to effectively counter the emergent generalissimos who have employed military aggression, ethnic cleansing and genocide in their pursuit of power. Failed UN efforts and falsely proclaimed successes have further fatigued the bureaucratic world, nationally and in international organizations. Consequently, the Aidids and the Karadzics have won the day and been strengthened as against the weak that were intended to be helped. In the 1990s, being a bully has been good business, and the profession has spread, virtually unchecked.

Can the 'unified concept' of political peace-maintenance help counter this in a manner that diplomatic peacekeeping and military peace-enforcement could not by themselves? Could it do any worse, after all? Since its appearance in the literature and in the dialogue among the peace operations cognoscenti, a number of points have been raised about peace-maintenance, including its feasibility, sustainability, selectivity, capability, morality and future.[1] This conclusion is something of a response.

THE FEASIBILITY OF PEACE-MAINTENANCE

Will it be possible for the UN or member states to conduct effective peace-maintenance operations? At times, they have not fielded wholly successful peace-enforcement missions, as during UNOSOM II in the summer of 1993, and even failed in simpler peacekeeping, as in the early stages of UNPROFOR in 1992. But it is also true that the UN has an accomplished history of peace-keeping, in the Sinai and elsewhere in the Middle East, for instance. And it can be said that the decisive arrival and deployment of UNITAF in its first phase, between December 1992 and February 1993, was a useful example of peace-enforcement – in some ways more so than the considerable might available in IFOR for a task configured as conventional interposition between belligerents.

Similarly, without resources, willingness or vision, the UN may be unable to conduct the entire scope of peace-maintenance in multiple countries simultaneously. But it is also true that the UN has already assumed the full range of political powers in peace-maintenance, sometimes only on paper and occasionally in fact. There has been a *governorship* mandate in Western Sahara, *control* in Cambodia, *partnership* in Namibia and *assistance* in El Salvador. Often the UN fails to fulfil its mandate, but exceptionally it cannot help doing more: it proved incapable of controlling in Cambodia and instead only assisted, while an assistance mandate in Somalia, with enforcement authority, was effectively transformed into control, and was expected by parts of the local population to meet the needs of governorship. It is important not to disregard altogether the prospects for a political mechanism, but to assess what has worked and what has not, in order to strengthen our ability to genuinely respond to the nature of the problem on the ground. Defining an ideal solution exclusively according to what governments are willing to do will lead to more, perhaps significantly greater, disasters.

More is not necessarily better in peace operations of any variety. The critical factor determining success is the tailoring of a mission to its intended operational environment, and the continuous adjustments to the campaign plan that ensure a secure fit. Reliance on military overkill is a precarious strategy; it may suit the peacekeepers' dictum of deterrence – a maximum show of force can avoid the need to use force – but we know from Mogadishu that the sledgehammer is not enough. Moving the operational stage from the Gulf theatre to the sideshow in Somalia had limited results. The gains of UNITAF's effective deployment could not be consolidated between February and May 1993, as large armed forces could not reconstruct civil institutions in a sustainable manner; and during the combat phase of UNOSOM II, attack helicopters and tanks could level parts of the capital, but the city and its inhabitants could not be controlled in any meaningful sense.

In Bosnia, too, NATO forces have halted the violence, but fallen short on civil reconstitution necessary for a sustainable peace. In a grand fashion, they have replicated the peacekeeping dilemma in which a perpetual presence prevents the resumption of hostilities, but also inhibits resolution of the conflict. More troops would not have helped; only the operational design could have made a difference – and for this reason, the fate of IFOR was easily anticipated from the Dayton Accords in late 1995, even before its deployment.

What happened in Cambodia? It was not a question of needing more than the 20,000 UN troops to do more. The fatal flaw of UNTAC was its inability to deploy decisively into the Khmer Rouge-held Sector One along the Thai border. The previous time distant armies came to Cambodia was with US B-52s that bombed the country apocalyptically. In spring 1992, there was a moment on the ground when the factions – which had already interpreted the terms of the October 1991 Paris Agreements separately from the UN Secretariat's operational blueprint of February 1992 – were unsure of the impact on the self-developing balance of power that the arrival of outside forces would have. Rather than appearing stronger than the sum of the factions, Dutch and Pakistani troops arrived at Sector One as 'peacekeepers' relying on the consent of the local authority and disregarding or misunderstanding the civil 'control' powers of UNTAC.

Following the line of least resistance in a factional competition meant not only that the Khmer Rouge prevented the UN's freedom of movement and deployment – because it realized it could – but also the refusal, consequently, by the State of Cambodia in Phnom Penh to accept international control of its ministries. This led to overall failure of the disarmament and demobilization Phase Two of the operation, which in turn resulted in an insecure environment and violence during the electoral campaign and May 1993 voting. A decisive deployment in Sector One, when it was possible to do so without using notable force, and civil consolidation throughout the country immediately afterwards, would have ensured that subsequent sticking points in implementation were kept at a technical and administrative level, and would not consistently reach the SNC. Again, with more troops the mission would not have avoided spinning out of control in its earliest stages. It was a question of identifying and taking complete advantage of a window of opportunity, of exercising authorized powers, and both having the means ready and being psychologically prepared for this type of mandate.

As any strategic analyst knows, the effectiveness of military forces is determined by their quality and not just their quantity. So too in peace operations, the characteristics of a mission and not just its size dictate its ability to function. It is the balance in the formula, the relative proportions in the mixture of military forces, civilian administration and humanitarian assistance, measured according to the needs in the field, that distinguishes the basis for a successful operation. Above all, a correct combination and its usefulness relies on central direction of the separate components. This is a matter of structure, not numbers. And peace-maintenance is very much about structure.

THE TEMPORAL QUESTION

As in wars past, the troops in peace missions tend not to be home by Christmas. Deployments measured in months are unlikely to have sustainable results. Rapid interventions, as in Grenada and Panama, can topple governments, but they cannot put countries like Bosnia or Somalia back together again. Decisiveness should not be confused with 'quick fixes'; the one creates windows of opportunity, like the element of surprise in warfare, and momentum towards a long-term impact, while the latter is a means to an early withdrawal.[2]

One perceptual shift that needs to take place concerns the spatial dimension of 'intervention', which separates inside and outside. It is this factor that emphasizes so much a beginning and an end, arrival and departure. It leads to the preoccupation with 'exit strategies' and fears of 'mission creep' in the peace bog. There has been a significant difference between the geography of limited deployments along narrow lines of separation between state belligerents and the requirements of a pervasive presence within countries as a whole. Similarly, there is a distinction between periodic, 'all-or-nothing' interventions and the notion of continuous 'policing' of volatile areas, with a capability that can contract to a single individual or expand to multiple military forces according to the prevailing threat assessment. The advantages of 'maintaining' peace in this manner, consistently, rather than fixing it after it is broken, were recognized within national societies long ago. The best means of conflict prevention is a rule of law, with all that that suggests in terms of political legislation, judicial interpretation, social compliance and law enforcement.

Internationally, this would imply that the next step in organization had been reached, which it certainly has not. However, in the interim, by providing an on-going decision-making capability in the field, political peace-maintenance can better adjust the international resources required as ground conditions improve or worsen. As such, it can alter the dynamic of a mission that is all-deploying or all-withdrawing, and extend its life by facilitating the kind of national commitment that can be sustained realistically on home fronts of troop-contributors, financially and emotionally. It shifts the focus to the evolving character of the presence, and away from its duration and its start and finish. This would be a first step towards understanding peace as perpetual business, as a process, and not a single event. In particular, establishing a locus of decision-making on the ground would reduce reliance on the one-time Security Council resolution that begins missions and the sometimes biannual resolutions that reluctantly extend but seek to halt operations. In turn, as another factor of sustainability, the local population could be better integrated in making international decisions – enhancing their social vitality and legitimacy – and it should assume as many tasks of implementation as practical at any given time.

Furthermore, such peace-maintenance, arguably with the capacity for a longer-term presence, might well shorten the periods of deployment, given the impact on conflict resolution political decision-making in the field can have. The United Nations Peacekeeping Force in Cyprus (UNFICYP) is an example of a traditional peacekeeping operation that has frozen a conflict as a consequence of a diplomatic framework that concerns the static preservation of a status quo, to avoid hostilities, rather than the dynamic development of fundamentally new and different conditions that can resolve the dispute. There was enough consent from the two sides to permit deployment, but not enough to overcome their differences. In a peacekeeping manner, UNFICYP could only follow the will of the belligerents, and while a mission can sometimes act as a catalyst for conflict resolution, in Cyprus the UN could not guarantee this happening.

Depending upon whether it is assisting, in partnership, controlling or acting as a governor-in-trust in a constitutive, constructive, consolidative or chaotic environment, a peace-maintenance operation within a state would be participating in or making decisions concerning the territory and its population. It would be redirecting the local competition, and therefore playing more a leadership role than submitting itself to the will of the parties. By being politically effective, in this way, it may be able to translate violent conflict into electoral competition, or at least reduce tensions to the level that they can be managed by pacific means of dispute resolution. This will be possible only as the result of the re-establishment of law and order, with a functioning judiciary and police, which in turn will have necessitated an interim political authority. Altogether, this kind of international political engagement in the beginning will lead more quickly to reduced security and other needs.

Long-term commitments are still very much the exception. But there are examples of forward thinking. Shifting from observers to whole armadas and back, the deployments of Gulf-coalition and particularly US forces around Iraq, since the end of the 1991 war, reflect the kind of constant policing that could underwrite an international rule of law – although it would need to be less unilateral in its aims and interests. Also, within a state it would need to be more subtle and sensitive, and not so exclusively reliant on military force. It can be argued that the decisiveness of IFOR should have handled the former Yugoslav crisis years earlier, but it was nevertheless an attempt to avoid an eventual and greater European imbroglio. And UNPREDEP in Macedonia has been, if not an automatic trigger mechanism, at least a means for early warning of Serbian expansion and Albanian civil unrest in Kosovo and around Skopje.

So there is some sense of concern for tomorrow's problems. But, sadly, it is more so that in the history of international organization each stage has been reached as the result of a cataclysmic breakdown of the previous order. It may be no less true of the wisdom lacking in this generation that a psychologically devastating event may be required before there is acceptance of an international system with full and permanent commitment to maintaining peace, rather than trying to fix it in the midst of war.

THE DILEMMA OF SELECTIVITY

The international community at this time cannot do everything everywhere, nor can it justify being nowhere; somewhere in between it has done relatively little well. In Cambodia, there are still Khmer Rouge in the hills and the election never really transferred power from the loser to the winner – the former now having regained the whole government. The existence of the National Union for the Total Independence of Angola (UNITA) still lingers, endangering the prospects of a coalition government, as death squads continue to roam and threaten the peace process in El Salvador. Civil society is still fragile and vulnerable in Haiti and Mozambique. Violence in Liberia is widespread and, tragically, fighting in Somalia has intensified. Preoccupation with face-saving withdrawals, either through elections or bold abandonment, has left the problems behind.

Like the 'warlord syndrome', or as a result of it, war zones have multiplied, darkening significant parts of the globe. Comparatively advanced levels of economic development, as in former Yugoslavia and Rwanda, could not withstand the irresistible forces of malevolent mobilization. It is as if there are two worlds, not North and South, but the 'diseased' and the 'comfortable', or perhaps, more cynically, the 'violently contested' and the 'not-yet-violently contested'. There is a kind of 'clash of conditions'. East Africa is a microcosm: first there were wars northwards in Somalia and southwards in Mozambique, then westwards in Rwanda, Burundi and Zaïre. The 'domino theory' may not have applied to the spread of ideologies, but it may to the spread of conflicts. With large refugee populations in northern Kenya and western Tanzania, will these two countries be able to resist the violence that now encircles them?

Objective criteria for automatic peace-engagement would be the hallmark of an international rule of law and an ultimate ideal of order. It is difficult to develop these in the grip of crisis, while so many conflicts have erupted that at least appear different. There is also the danger, that has plagued unenforced international laws, of defined criteria that cannot be matched by a comparable will to act. They can become empty principles and undermine the credibility of those that tried to respond. This is not an argument against what is a critical process.

But the answer may lie, as with problem-solving generally, in choosing a 'soft option' that can be genuinely achieved and sustained, and which can serve as a staging platform for the spread of peace to neighbouring areas. The world needs a real peace-maintenance success story. Unfortunately, there is no international laboratory in which to experiment under controlled conditions. It may be unpalatable to speak in such clinical terms when considering the fate of peoples and territory. But more unpalatable still is the fact that what we know now about how to rebuild fractured societies does not match the effort and cost of the activities of recent years. The few lessons identified have not been learnt and digested, or, worse, have been misconstrued or purposefully discarded altogether. The scandal of the Lessons Learned Unit of the UN's Department of Peace-

Keeping Operations is a testament to the choice of some individuals in bureaucracies to obscure rather than clarify.

The issues of transmission, of general learning and remembering, though,
are still additional to research and investigation, to finding and understanding
the answers in the first place, and above all to acknowledging them generally.
Therefore, investment in a single success or a few will help tackle other cases
with greater effectiveness and efficiency. Choosing in this manner requires
broader vision than is affordable in a sort of emergency 'triage'. The question of
where to start is partly about criteria again. But it should be, first, a place with
problems that are conceivably solvable, or at least manageable enough to
generate the skills for future use and create the confidence to pursue similar tasks
in other locations. Second, the conflict should be situated strategically so that its
spread could have or has had serious geographic consequences. Third, the effort
must have sustainable results and the impact guaranteed over time, or it will be
self-defeating. Fourth, it should be possible to similarly contend with neighbouring areas, so that a kind of 'zone of tranquillity' can grow.

An evolutionary approach is always problematic, but also probably unavoidable. On the one hand, it cannot be argued that a step should not be taken
because not all the steps can be taken at once. On the other, excessive attention
to one place and insufficient care elsewhere may cause the maturing of nascent
disputes. Focus on one problem may lead to being overwhelmed by a number of
others. But this is a perennial tension in any form of organizational management, and a comparable sense of balancing the priority with other demands is
no less necessary in global management. This is one advantage of distinguishing
categories of peace-maintenance varying in degrees of commitment: If one area
calls for governorship, others may need only assistance. Therefore, multiple
fronts can be handled in a careful balance. Ultimately, it will be better for all
everywhere if one or two steps are taken somewhere than if none are taken
anywhere.

THE UN'S CAPABILITY

The peace-maintenance concept has been cast largely in the UN context for the
sake of simplification of the argument. However, it has never excluded the possibility of other arrangements, including varying combinations of a group of
states, private enterprise, non-governmental organizations and expert individuals. In fact, critical to peace-maintenance is the instrument of political
authority in the field, which really should not be exclusively a UN bureaucratic
appendage, regardless of whether it is minimally assisting or comprehensively
governing. Like the Joint Monitoring Commission that provided leverage and
confidence during the Namibian process, or the Russian-dominated Joint
Control Commissions in the former Soviet Near Abroad, similar bodies,
composed of effective guarantors and the configuration of interests on the

ground, can provide on-going political will and either help UN operations function more effectively or serve as more independent directorates.

Chapter VIII of the UN Charter provides for such ad hoc regional arrangements, although it still requires Security Council approval in the event of enforcement action. Peace-maintenance relies on a number of generic tools, which could be used by individual governments or even private organizations. However, its legitimacy will be less in question if there is a Security Council mandate or some connection with the UN, even if nominally. At the beginning of this decade, I would have been loth to consider cooperative rather than truly collective ventures. But the chronic disability, and even abuse, of UN management, and the chasm between ground demands and what the UN can supply, as well as its subsequent, disagreeable, snatching of laurels to hide defeats, has forced the need to reconsider. This is particularly required given the reluctance of governments and the UN to do more, while violent crises multiply and private 'security forces', like Executive Outcomes or ex-Ghurka services, fill the gap unaccountably, but unavoidably, in a kind of 'privatization of enforcement'.[3]

In Cambodia, the deficiency was not just the shortage of civilian staff, though, as in Somalia, it was this too, since the Civil Administration component was not at functional strength until September 1992, some seven months after the start of deployment. Nor was the shortcoming just the quality of the staff, although a specifically trained cadre of international administrators is very much needed in such operations. In Phnom Penh and other population centres, the critical failure had to do with the UN's inability to enter and control the SOC government ministries, which resisted partly as a reaction to the UN's failure to deploy in Khmer Rouge territory, but more significantly as a consequence of another reason. As the new Secretary-General, Boutros Boutros-Ghali, prepared to take office at the end of 1991, he passed over Rafeeuddin Ahmed, who had negotiated with the Cambodian factions over the preceding eight years, in favour of Yasushi Akashi as his Special Representative.

Ahmed had intended that, in addition to the text of the control mandate, an unwritten means of implementation would rest in a cell composed of the factions and the UN. It was this unit that would ease its way into the existing administrative structures, in each case acting with a representative from the faction to be controlled. It would not be up to the UN to single-handedly knock on the ministry door, which would predictably remain closed without some inside contact to open it. This is the kind of instrument, representing the configuration of the political body at the functional level, that could ultimately make peace-maintenance work. With the appointment of Akashi, this understanding was lost, and the staff that eventually reached Cambodia were left wondering why the factions were not contractually fulfilling the signed agreements line-by-line.

In addition to this factor, the flaw of civil administration in the provinces, endemic to other UN exercises, first in Namibia and later in Somalia, had to do with the structural design, as well as command and reporting procedures. The Provincial Directors were supposed to be first among the equal military, humanitarian and other component heads. In reality, they were at best equal, and when security conditions worsened before the elections, as in Battambang and Siem Reap in spring 1993, they tended to be subordinated to military imperatives – by virtue of necessity, for safety. This was the result of a chain of command in which each component in the provinces reported to their component headquarters in the capital, which then reported to the SRSG. The Provincial Director needed to have full authority over all the components in the area. The principal line of communication should have extended from this individual to an overall administration headquarters in Phnom Penh, the functional bureaucracy responsible to the political body, which in this case was Akashi and his relations with the four factions in the Supreme National Council. For unity of purpose, the other components in the provinces ought to have been restricted to direct reporting to headquarters for only certain issues, including staffing, logistics and other specialized needs – but certainly not regarding operational directives.

A combination of general conceptual and specific historical factors undermined civil administration in Cambodia. This does not condemn the practicality or possibility of international administration of territory. Its evolution and future effectiveness will rely on clearly appreciating the reasons for failure, and an honest assessment of whether they can be overcome, as well as recognition of what proved useful. Designing an appropriate operational model is the first step, against which available resources and competence of implementation can be measured in context. Otherwise, it would be like concluding that today's battle cannot be won because the tactics from yesterday's war are inapplicable. Surely the answer is to devise the necessary strategies for the new obstacles.

THE MORAL DIMENSION

Supranationality is not an evil, but an ideal of the peace plans over the last five centuries. Without this, the UN would never have come to be. Its original formulation in the thinking of its creators was fundamentally supranational. Although scaled back by compromise, it nevertheless retained majority voting in the Assembly and the veto power in the Council, in addition to other mandatory commitments, such as an obligation to support collective decisions under Article 25 of the Charter. Fringe groups in America or national elites claiming sovereignty for themselves at the cost of their populations do not understand or want to reject the limited form of supranationality that is the defining feature of the current form of international order. Nations that rapidly acceded to UN membership, to affirm their independence, cannot disregard after the fact the non-consensual obligations they accepted in advance.

Furthermore, the colonialism vitriolic, while a rallying call for someone like Aidid, is more a luxury in the universities among angry scholars who want to 'construct narratives' or 'engage in a discourse' rather than tackle the doctrinal puzzles of peace operations. While some academic or news articles have called for a return to colonialism, their flaws can be easily exposed – like their forgetting to mention why conquest and occupation may have been ill-intentioned, self-interested and worse.[4] But responding to careless proposals with significant intellectual energy has resulted in an artificial dialogue utterly removed from the functional debate among peace operations aficionados.[5] National field manuals that have been issued are not 'how-to' books on neo-imperialism. Recolonization has not been one of the contentious issues; it is a rhetorical bogey.

In any case, why is stopping war tantamount to colonialism? It is indefensible to argue that fear of illicit domination justifies the right to violate non-derogable laws against aggression, grave breaches of human rights and genocide. To choose to reject international assistance, and to accept or even perpetrate oppressive violence, all for the sake of sovereign pretensions, is not only impermissible under international criminal law, but surely odious morally. This is particularly so since it is often the perpetrators that are rejecting intervention at the cost of their people's suffering. For UN members to accede to such dismissal is precisely what has strengthened the warlord and contributed to the spread of conflict. Instead of fortifying efforts to guard against a new age of imperialism, the concerned should join the current struggles against cases of blatant injustice in Western Sahara, East Timor and Tibet. Yesterday's victims, after all, are not immune from victimizing today. The 1996 Nobel Peace Prize winner, José Ramos-Horta, has said: 'The colonial power is no longer European.'[6]

As argued in Chapter 1, peace-maintenance is the opposite of colonialism, serving as it does the local population rather than taking advantage of it economically, or obliterating it culturally. It is by no means the idea of rich Westerners governing poor Southerners. Peace-maintenance, as a principle of traditional peacekeeping generally, includes in its operations or its direction the participation of a wide geographic spectrum. It is precisely a means of engaging both the South and the West in a shared response to threats common to all. This is the logic of a collective mission. And even in other specialized arrangements, the inclusion of interested and disinterested but willing states from the relevant region or elsewhere is a practical requirement. Peace-maintenance is not about limiting participation, but fosters it for the sake of legitimacy and effectiveness. To be inclusionary, effectiveness does not have to be sacrificed to anonymous universality, as sometimes happens at the UN.

By far the greater problem is convincing the rich West to pay for something in the general interest. Efforts should be spent on explaining to such populations and governments why seemingly obscure, unpronounceable conflicts are really direct threats, and responding is in their self-interest. For their part, the afflicted nations should not confuse the protection of their territorial integrity and political independence with capitulation to the abusive will of the warlord.

In contrast, it is true that corruption has accompanied peace operations. Unfortunately, fractured societies provide ugly business opportunities, whether it is the aphrodisiac of hunger and poverty, by which prostitution proliferates, or black-market activities in much-needed supplies, or basic pilfering from UN coffers and stores. There is also a kind of 'structural corruption', in which the international official chooses not to be dynamic in the field in order to safeguard a career and survive the bureaucratic manoeuvring within the UN system. This final point is a sub-cultural tendency that is unlikely to be reformed.

But these other criminal acts can be addressed. The difficulty is that there has not been a means of prosecution for UN staff and nations have never agreed to subordinate their military contingents to a common disciplinary procedure. There has been only nominal approval in Status of Forces Agreements of cooperation between national commanders and the UN in such matters, or national inquiries into the behaviour of individual soldiers. A part of peace-maintenance, however, is the inclusion of rules of behaviour, codes of conduct and measures for compliance and redress. If an operation has assumed law and order tasks, with police powers and means of judicial prosecution, it will be self-damaging to place the operation above its own law, as has happened in the past. It was farcical, for instance, for the UN to teach Cambodians about independence of the judiciary while UNTAC's executive undermined its own Special Prosecutor. Legal unaccountability will definitely lose for a mission the support of the local population. With a political authority there is the possibility of judicial competence and the opportunity to counter corruption.

It does not follow that the more intrusive the UN is the more corrupt it will be. In a small peacekeeping operation there could be more abuse than in something larger; it depends on the context, leadership and staff personalities – in the same manner that the likelihood of criminality varies from contingent to contingent. Therefore, quite the contrary, a more political operation could provide the means of stopping corruption, no less than it could devise a sound economic policy to limit inflation caused by its presence. That logic would flow naturally from a mission designed to have more control. And any damage done must be placed in context: while there is a Hippocratic rule claimed by negotiators and planners to 'do no harm' in areas where conflict is being resolved, it is also a fact that, as busy as recent years have been, the most common form of harm has resulted from international inaction.

THE VIOLENCE OF NON-INTERVENTION

The hurdles in successful peace-maintenance are many, as they continue to be in conventional peacekeeping and effective peace-enforcement.[7] But seeking a political option is a product of witnessing the trauma on the ground and asking the honest question: What then must we do? Silence and avoidance are not means of defending the moral high ground of non-intervention. Instead, they establish culpability, not because of being remiss in some duty to intervene, but because toleration of international crimes for the sake of convenience is an obvious kind of complicity. Refusal to surmount the challenges of political peace-maintenance is to betray an unwillingness to meaningfully address the warlord syndrome, halt the spread of conflicts or rebuild fractured societies. Denial is known, individually and internationally, only to compound problems.

Development of a concept like peace-maintenance can serve as a standard of measurement for the job to be done. It can reveal the hand of nations only cosmetically meeting their international obligations, of governments concerned more with being seen to be doing something than acting in good faith. Clarity about the nature of the tasks that need to be accomplished is the first step towards fostering the political will to act. It can avoid misconceived and costly deployments which, like any defeat, drain morale and cause retreat. Without knowing what to do, how can a step be taken towards the solution? A more open debate, whether between governments or in the court of public opinion, can help determine an acceptable and functional alternative to what is a kind of paralysis in the midst of crisis. There are considerable technical issues to be resolved, but with sufficient interest generated these would remain administrative details, comparable to those long since overcome, in twenty-first-century warfighting and governance of national societies.

The 1930s illustrated how ambivalence led to world war; the 1990s indicate a similar link between apathy and the anarchy of the bully. Whether the current decade, ferocious as it has been, will have consequences comparable to the 1940s remains to be seen. In the interim, however, if inaction is justified by some bizarre ideology, it will lead to the acceptance of a doctrine of 'the violence of non-intervention'. Peace-maintenance is the other response.

Notes

1 PEACE-MAINTENANCE

1 Dan Smith, 'Towards Understanding the Causes of War', in Ketil Volden and Dan Smith, eds, *Causes of Conflict in the Third World* (Oslo: North/South Coalition & International Peace Research Institute, Oslo, 1997), pp. 9–10.

2 John Mackinlay and Jarat Chopra, 'Second Generation Multinational Operations', *The Washington Quarterly*, vol. 15, no. 3, Summer 1992, pp. 113–131. This was affirmed by the Secretary-General's references to a second generation of UN operations: 'Secretary-General Says "Political Resilience" of Organization has Helped it Respond to New Demands in Peace-Keeping', Press Release SG/SM/4920 of 2 February 1993; 'Secretary-General, in Address to Grandes Conferences Catholiques, Stresses Belgium's Exemplary Contribution to Work of Blue Helmets', Press Release SG/SM/4985 of 28 April 1993.

3 'Note by the President of the Security Council', UN Doc. S/23500 of 31 January 1992.

4 On the interpretation of the breadth of this provision, see Bruno Simma, ed., *The Charter of the United Nations: A Commentary* (Oxford: Oxford University Press, 1994), pp. 50–52.

5 Townsend Hoopes and Douglas Brinkley, *FDR and the Creation of the U.N.* (New Haven, CT: Yale University Press, 1997), p. 73. Also see Ruth B. Russell, *A History of The United Nations Charter: The Role of the United States 1940–1945* (Washington, DC: The Brookings Institution, 1958), ch. V and generally.

6 Cf. Paul F. Diehl, *International Peacekeeping* (Baltimore, MD: The Johns Hopkins University Press, 1993); William J. Durch, ed., *The Evolution of UN Peacekeeping: Case Studies and Comparative Analysis* (New York: St Martin's Press, 1993); Thomas G. Weiss and Jarat Chopra, *United Nations Peacekeeping: An ACUNS Teaching Text* (Hanover, NH: Academic Council on the United Nations System, 1992); Alan James, *Peacekeeping in International Politics* (London: Macmillan and the International Institute for Strategic Studies, 1990); and United Nations, *The Blue Helmets: A Review of United Nations Peacekeeping*, 2nd edition (New York: United Nations Department of Public Information (UNDPI), 1990).

7 These were enunciated in the instructions for the establishment of the Second United Nations Emergency Force (UNEF II): 'Report of the Secretary-General on the Implementation of Security Council Resolution 340 (1973)', UN Doc. S/11052/Rev. 1 of 27 October 1973. For a personal account of their drafting, see Sir Brian Urquhart, *A Life in Peace and War* (New York: Harper & Row, Publishers, 1987), pp. 241–242.

8 On perceptions at the time of this critical mass point, see the special issue on 'United Nations Peace-Keeping', Jarat Chopra, ed., *Survival*, vol. XXXII, no. 3, May/June 1990.

9 Cf. Stephen John Stedman, 'Spoiler Problems in Peace Processes', *International Security*, vol. 22, no. 2, Fall 1997, pp. 5–53.

10 Cf. Richard K. Betts, 'The Delusion of Impartial Intervention', *Foreign Affairs*, vol. 73, no. 6, November/December 1994, pp. 20–33.

11 Cf. William J. Durch, ed., *UN Peacekeeping, American Politics, and the Uncivil Wars of the 1990s* (New York: St Martin's Press, 1996); and Rosemary Righter, *Utopia Lost: The United Nations and World Order* (New York: Twentieth Century Fund, 1995).

12 See further John Mackinlay and Jarat Chopra, *A Draft Concept of Second Generation Multinational Operations, 1993* (Providence, RI: Thomas J. Watson Jr Institute for International Studies, 1993), and compare: British Army Field Manual, United Kingdom Ministry of Defence, 'Wider Peacekeeping', Third Draft, January 1994; US Army Field Manual [unpublished draft, cited to reflect thinking at that time] 100–123, 'Peace Operations', Version 6, January 1994; North Atlantic Treaty Organization, 'NATO Doctrine for Peace Support Operations', 28 February 1994; as well as SHAPE (June 1993), US Center for Naval Analysis (CRM 93–140, July 1993), and Australian Defence Forces draft documents. Also see Richard Smith, *The Requirement for the United Nations to Develop an Internationally Recognized Doctrine for the Use of Force in Intra-State Conflict* (Camberley: Strategic and Combat Studies Institute, 1994).

13 Mackinlay and Chopra, 'Second Generation Multinational Operations'; Brian Urquhart interviewed by Helga Graham, 'UN Can Be Real Peacemaker in the Brave New World', *Observer* (London), 26 January 1992; Brian Urquhart, 'A Way to Stop Civil Wars', *Providence Journal*, 2 January 1992, p. A10; and cf. his development of this in 'For a UN Volunteer Military Force', *New York Review of Books*, 10 June 1993, pp. 3–4, as well as the commentary on the idea in the 24 June and 15 July editions of the *Review*, pp. 58–60 and 52–55 respectively. Also see the later article by John Gerard Ruggie, 'Wandering in the Void: Charting the U.N.'s New Strategic Role', *Foreign Affairs*, vol. 72, no. 5, November/December 1993, pp. 26–31.

14 'Supplement to an Agenda for Peace: Position Paper of the Secretary-General on the Occasion of the Fiftieth Anniversary of the United Nations', UN Doc. A/50/60 and S/1995/1 of 3 January 1995, para. 36 and 77–80.

15 UN Press Release SG/SM/5518 of 5 January 1995, pp. 5–6.

16 Cf. United Kingdom Ministry of Defence, *Wider Peacekeeping* (London: Headquarters, Doctrine and Training, November 1994); Charles Dobbie, 'A Concept for Post-Cold War Peacekeeping', *Survival*, vol. 36, no. 3, Autumn 1994, pp. 121–148; and Richard P. Cousens, 'Providing Military Security in Peace-Maintenance', *Global Governance*, vol. 4, no. 1, January–March 1998, pp. 97–105.

17 Cf. Alan James, 'Is There a Second Generation of Peacekeeping?', *International Peacekeeping*, vol. 1, no. 4, September–November 1994, pp. 110–113; the panel on 'UN Peacekeeping: An Early Reckoning of the Second Generation', *Proceedings of the American Society of International Law, 1995*, pp. 275–291; Boutros Boutros-Ghali, 'Introduction' to United Nations, *The Blue Helmets*, 3rd edition (New York: UNDPI, 1996), p. 5; and Commission of Inquiry into the Deployment of Canadian Forces to Somalia, *Dishonoured Legacy: The Lessons of the Somalia Affair* (Ottawa: Public Works and Government Services Canada, 1997), vol. 1, pp. 184–185. For a non-chronological definition, see Steven R. Ratner, *The New UN Peacekeeping: Building Peace in Lands of Conflict After the Cold War* (New York: St Martin's Press, 1995), p. 17.

18 Edmund T. Piasecki, 'Making and Keeping the Peace', in John Tessitore and Susan Woolfson, eds, *A Global Agenda: Issues Before the 48th General Assembly of the United Nations* (Lanham, MD: University Press of America, 1993), pp. 2 and 3.

19 Cf. Michael W. Doyle, 'Introduction: Discovering the Limits and Potential of Peacekeeping', in Olara A. Otunnu and Michael W. Doyle, eds, *Peacemaking and Peacekeeping for the New Century* (Lanham, MD: Rowman & Littlefield Publishers, 1998), pp. 5–7.
20 Cf. Roland Paris, 'Peacebuilding and the Limits of Liberal Internationalism', *International Security*, vol. 22, no. 2, Fall 1997, pp. 54–89.
21 Cf. the emerging literature on this, for instance: Jeffrey Herbst, 'Responding to State Failure in Africa', *International Security*, vol. 21, no. 3, Winter 1996/1997, pp. 120–144, and the correspondence in vol. 22, no. 2, Fall 1997, pp. 175–184; Chester A. Crocker, 'All Aid Is Political', *New York Times*, 21 November 1996, p. A29; Walter S. Clarke and Robert Gosende, 'The Political Component: The Missing Vital Element in US Intervention Planning', *Parameters*, vol. 26, no. 3, Autumn 1996, pp. 35–51; I. William Zartman, ed., *Collapsed States: The Disintegration and Restoration of Legitimate Authority* (Boulder, CO: Lynne Rienner Publishers, 1995), pp. 267–273; and Gerald B. Helman and Steven R. Ratner, 'Saving Failed States', *Foreign Policy*, no. 89, Winter 1992–93, pp. 3–20.
22 See, for example, Abba Eban, 'The U.N. Idea Revisited', *Foreign Affairs*, vol. 74, no. 5, September/October 1995, pp. 39–55; and Jesse Helms, 'Saving the U.N.: A Challenge to the Next Secretary-General', *Foreign Affairs*, vol. 75, no. 5, September/October 1996, pp. 2–7.
23 Cf. already the casual usage in discussions at the General Assembly, UN Press Releases GA/SPD/77 of 15 November 1995, p. 4; GA/PK/137 of 1 April 1996, p. 8; and PI/993 WOM/953 of 7 March 1997, p. 2. Also, compare the press usage in, for instance, Nirmal Mitra, 'India Criticizes Unwelcome U.N. Help', *India Abroad*, 15 December 1995, p. 12; 'WEU Approves Possible Operations in Albania', Agence France Press, 13 March 1997; 'chile not to request u.s. non-nato ally status', Xinhua News Agency, Item no. 1017107, 17 October 1997; as opposed to Gilonne d'Origny, 'Western Sahara's Difficult Path', *The Washington Times*, 3 July 1997, p. A17. Gareth Evans used the term only in its preventive sense in *Cooperating for Peace: The Global Agenda for the 1990s and Beyond* (St Leonard's, NSW: Allen & Unwin, 1993), p. 10 and part III.
24 James A. Baker, III, *The Politics of Diplomacy: Revolution, War and Peace, 1989–1992* (New York: G.P. Putnam's Sons, 1995), p. xv.
25 See further the review essay by W. Andy Knight, 'Beyond the UN System? Critical Perspectives on Global Governance and Multilateral Evolution', *Global Governance*, vol. 1, no. 2, May–August 1995, pp. 229–253.
26 F.H. Hinsley, *Power and the Pursuit of Peace* (Cambridge: Cambridge University Press, 1963).
27 Arnold J. Toynbee, *A Study of History* (Oxford: Oxford University Press, 1946).
28 See UN Secretary-General Kofi Annan's proposals for a 'quiet revolution' in 'Renewing the United Nations: Programme for Reform', UN Doc. A/51/1950 of 16 July 1997; and Barbara Crossette, 'U.N. Chief Promises to Overhaul Organization From the Top Down', *New York Times*, 17 July 1997, pp. A1 and A12.
29 Cf. Antonio Donini, Eric Dudley and Ron Ockwell, *Afghanistan: Coordinating in a Fragmented State* (New York: United Nations Department of Humanitarian Affairs, December 1996), pp. 42–50; and Amir Pasic and Thomas G. Weiss, 'The Politics of Rescue: Yugoslavia's Wars and the Humanitarian Impulse', *Ethics and International Affairs*, vol. 11, 1997, pp. 105–131.
30 Cf. Thomas G. Weiss, ed., *Beyond UN Subcontracting: Task-Sharing with Regional Security Arrangements and Service-Providing NGOs* (London: Macmillan Press, 1998).
31 See further Clement E. Adibe, 'Accepting External Authority in Peace-Maintenance', *Global Governance*, vol. 4, no. 1, January–March 1998, pp. 112–118.

32 Cf. the critical race theory approach of Ruth Gordon, 'Saving Failed States: Sometimes a Neocolonialist Notion', *American University Journal of International Law and Policy*, vol. 12, no. 6, 1997, pp. 903–974; and the material cited in Chapter 8 below.

33 John W. Halderman, 'Legal Basis for United Nations Armed Forces', *American Journal of International Law*, vol. 56, no. 4, October 1962, p. 972–974; *Certain Expenses of the United Nations* Case, *ICJ Reports* 1962, p. 165; Rahmatullah Khan, *Implied Powers of the United Nations* (New Delhi: Vikas Publications, 1970), ch. 2; and D.W. Bowett, *United Nations Forces* (London: Stevens & Sons, 1964), ch. 12.

34 Cf. Ramsay Clark, *The Fire This Time: U.S. War Crimes In the Gulf* (New York: Thunder's Mouth Press, 1992); and Kaiyan Homi Kaikobad, 'Self-Defence, Enforcement Action and the Gulf Wars, 1980–88 and 1990–91', *British Year Book of International Law 1992*, vol. 63, 1993), pp. 333–335.

35 On the principles of this kind of activity, see further Chester A. Crocker, *High Noon In Southern Africa: Making Peace in a Rough Neighborhood* (New York: W.W. Norton & Company, 1992), chs 19 and 20.

36 Cf. Jarat Chopra and Thomas G. Weiss, 'Prospects for Containing Conflict in the Former Second World', *Security Studies*, vol. 4, no. 3, Spring 1995, pp. 552–583; and Andrei Raevsky and I.N. Vorobev, *Russian Approaches to Peacekeeping Operations* (Geneva: UN Institute for Disarmament Research, 1994).

37 See, for instance, Richard N. Armstrong, *Red Army Legacies: Essays on Forces, Capabilities, and Personalities* (Atglen, PA: Schiffer Publishing, 1995), ch. 10.

38 Jarat Chopra and Thomas G. Weiss, 'Sovereignty is no Longer Sacrosanct: Codifying Humanitarian Intervention', *Ethics and International Affairs*, vol. 6, 1992, pp. 95–117.

2 INTERNATIONAL POLITICAL DEVELOPMENT

1 These include the United States, Japan, France, Germany, Italy, the United Kingdom, Canada, the Netherlands, Sweden, and Norway. Cf. John Tessitore and Susan Woolfson, eds, *A Global Agenda: Issues Before the 48th General Assembly of the United Nations* (Lanham, MD: University Press of America, 1993), pp. 163–164.

2 Boutros Boutros-Ghali, *An Agenda for Development 1995* (New York: United Nations Department of Public Information, 1995), p. 1.

3 'Note by the President of the Security Council', UN Doc. S/23500 of 31 January 1992, p. 3.

4 Elisabeth Uphoff Kato, 'Quick Impacts, Slow Rehabilitation in Cambodia', in Michael W. Doyle, Ian Johnstone and Robert C. Orr, eds, *Keeping the Peace: Multidimensional UN operations in Cambodia and El Salvador* (Cambridge: Cambridge University Press, 1997), pp. 186–205; William Shawcross, *Cambodia's New Deal* (Washington, DC: Carnegie Endowment for International Peace, 1994), pp. 75–88; and Jarat Chopra, *United Nations Authority in Cambodia* (Providence, RI: Thomas J. Watson Jr Institute for International Studies, 1994), pp. 55–75.

5 This is in reference to the Second United Nations Operation in Somalia (UNOSOM II). Cf. Terrence Lyons and Ahmed I. Samatar, *Somalia: State Collapse, Multilateral Intervention, and Strategies for Political Reconstruction* (Washington, DC: The Brookings Institution, 1995), particularly Appendix A, pp. 70–76; and Ken Menkhaus and John Prendergast, 'Governance and Economic Survival in Postintervention Somalia', *CSIS Africa Notes*, no. 172, May 1995, pp. 7–10.

6 Cf. Patricia Weiss-Fagen, *After the Conflict: A Review of Selected Sources on Rebuilding War-torn Societies* (Geneva: War-torn Societies Project, 1995), as well as the Project's website ⟨http://www.unrisd.org/wsp/⟩; and Jeremy Ginifer, ed., *Beyond the Emergency: Development within UN Peace Missions* (London: Frank Cass & Co., 1997).

7 'Supplement to an Agenda for Peace: Position Paper of the Secretary-General on the Occasion of the Fiftieth Anniversary of the United Nations', UN Doc. A/50/60 and S/1995/1 of 3 January 1995, cf. para. 33 and 53.

8 On the harmonization of national legislation concerning peace operations as a means to this, see Jarat Chopra, 'Commitment to Peace-Maintenance', in *Globalism and Regionalism: Options for the 21st Century* (Ottawa: Canadian Council on International Law, 1955), pp. 32–35.

9 Cf. Matthias Stiefel, 'UNDP in Conflicts and Disasters: An Overview Report of the "Continuum Project"' (Geneva: UNDP Project INT/93/709, August 1994); as well as Giles Carbonnier, *Conflict, Postwar Rebuilding and the Economy: A Critical Review of the Literature* (Geneva: War-torn Societies Project, 1998).

10 Cf. James P. Sewell and Mark B. Salter, 'Panarchy and Other Norms for Global Governance: Boutros-Ghali, Rosenau, and Beyond', *Global Governance*, vol. 1, no. 3, September–December 1995, pp. 373–382; and Anne-Marie Slaughter, 'The Real New World Order', *Foreign Affairs*, vol. 76, no. 5; September/October 1997, pp. 183–197.

11 Cf. the collection of essays in Ikuo Kabashima and Lynn T. White III, eds, *Political Systems and Change* (Princeton, NJ: Princeton University Press, 1986); and James N. Rosenau, *Turbulence in World Politics: A Theory of Change and Continuity* (Princeton, NJ: Princeton University Press, 1990).

12 Don Martindale, *Social Life and Cultural Change* (Princeton, NJ: Van Nostrand, 1962); and see his 'The Formation and Destruction of Communities', in George K. Zollschan and Walter Hirsch, eds, *Explorations in Social Change* (Boston: Houghton Mifflin Co., 1964), pp. 61–87.

13 Myron Weiner, 'Political Integration and Political Development', in Harvey G. Kebschull, ed., *Politics in Transitional Societies* (New York: Appleton-Century-Crofts, 1968), pp. 263–272.

14 Marshall D. Sahlins and Elman R. Service, eds, *Evolution and Culture* (Ann Arbor, MI: University of Michigan Press, 1970).

15 Samuel P. Huntington, 'Political Development and Political Decay', in Kabashima and White, *Political Systems and Change*, pp. 95–139.

16 S.N. Eisenstadt, 'Process of Change and Institutionalization of the Political Systems of Centralized Empires', in Zollschan and Hirsch, *Explorations in Social Change*, pp. 432–451.

17 Robert Axelrod, *The Evolution of Co-operation* (London: Penguin Books, 1984), pp. 21, 174 and generally.

18 Cf. Gregoire Nicolis, 'Physics of Far-from-Equilibrium Systems and Self-organisation', in Paul Davies, ed., *The New Physics* (Cambridge: Cambridge University Press, 1990), pp. 316–347.

19 Mircea Eliade, *The Sacred and the Profane* (New York: Harcourt Brace & Company, 1959), ch. II; and see further his *The Myth of the Eternal Return* (Princeton, NJ: Princeton University Press, 1954); Peter Osborne, *The Politics of Time* (London: Verso, 1995); and G.J. Whitrow, *Time in History* (Oxford: Oxford University Press, 1989), pp. 74–75.

20 George Steiner, *Nostalgia for the Absolute* (Toronto: Canadian Broadcasting Corporation, 1983).

21 Article 1, 'Montevideo Convention on the Rights and Duties of States' (1933). Cf. Jarat Chopra, 'The Obsolescence of Intervention under International Law', in Marianne Heiberg, ed., *Subduing Sovereignty: Sovereignty and the Right to Intervene* (London: Pinter Publishers, 1994), pp. 45–52.

22 Cf. Ernest Gellner, *Plough, Sword and Book* (Chicago: University of Chicago Press, 1988), ch. 1 and generally.

23 On the sociological dimensions of this process, see Anthony D. Smith, *The Ethnic Origins of Nations* (Oxford: Blackwell Publishers, 1993), part I.

24 Henri Frankfort, *Kingship and the Gods* (Chicago: University of Chicago Press, 1978), pp. 231–232.

25 F.H. Hinsley, *Sovereignty* (Cambridge: Cambridge University Press, 1986), p. 41.

26 Ernst H. Kantorowicz, *The King's Two Bodies: A Study in Medieval Political Theology* (Princeton: Princeton University Press, 1957), pp. 358–383.

27 Olga Tellegen-Couperus, *A Short History of Roman Law* (London: Routledge, 1993), pp. 73–77.

28 Cf. James Crawford, 'The Criteria for Statehood in International Law', *British Year Book of International Law*, vol. 48, 1976–77, pp. 93–182.

29 Cf. Nicholas Greenwood Onuf, '*Civitas Maxima*: Wolff, Vattel and the Fate of Republicanism', *American Journal of International Law*, vol. 88, no. 2, April 1994, pp. 280–303.

30 On some of the characteristics of this, see I. William Zartman, 'Introduction: Posing the Problem of State Collapse', in I. William Zartman, ed., *Collapsed States: The Disintegration and Restoration of Legitimate Authority* (Boulder, CO: Lynne Rienner Publishers, 1995), p. 10; and John Darnton, 'Zaire Drifting Into Anarchy As Authority Disintegrates', *New York Times*, 24 May 1994, p. A1.

31 Cf. Stuart J. Kaufman, 'The Fragmentation and Consolidation of International Systems', *International Organization*, vol. 51, no. 2, Spring 1997, pp. 173–208.

32 Cf. Adam Watson, *The Evolution of International Society* (London: Routledge, 1992), pp. 319–325. See further the discussion of the international constitutional process in: Anthony Carty, 'Myths of International Legal Order: Past and Present'; Jarat Chopra, 'Some Puzzles of International Society'; and Marc Weller, 'The Reality of the Emerging Universal Constitutional Order: Putting the Pieces of the Puzzle Together', all *Cambridge Review of International Affairs*, vol. X, no. 2, Winter/Spring 1997, pp. 1–63. Also cf. Peter Uvin and Isabelle Biagiotti, 'Global Governance and the "New" Political Conditionality', *Global Governance*, vol. 2, no. 3, September–December 1996, pp. 377–400.

33 Cf. Ram Charitra Prasad Singh, *Kingship in Northern India* (Delhi: Motilal Banarsidass, 1968), ch. II.

34 See, for example, the account of J. Royal Roseberry III, *Imperial Rule in Punjab: The Conquest and Administration of Multan, 1818–1881* (Riverdale, MD: The Riverdale Company, 1987).

35 Michael Barratt Brown, *Models in Political Economy* (London: Penguin Books, 1995), p. 311. On the de-industrialization of the Third World during colonialism, see further Paul Bairoch, *Economics and World History: Myths and Paradoxes* (Chicago: University of Chicago Press, 1995), ch. 8.

36 Cf. Frederick D. Lugard, *The Dual Mandate in British Tropical Africa* (Edinburgh: William Blackwood & Sons, 1922).

37 Basil Davidson, *The Black Man's Burden: Africa and the Curse of the Nation-State* (New York: Times Books, 1992), ch. 7.

38 Whitrow, *Time in History*, pp. 147 and 177–180.

39 W.W. Rostow, *The Stages of Economic Growth* (Cambridge: Cambridge University Press, 1960).

40 Cf. Talcott Parsons, *The Social System* (Glencoe, IL: Free Press, 1951); and Edward Shils, *Political Development in the New States* (The Hague: Mouton, 1966).

41 Cf. Gabriel A. Almond and James S. Coleman, eds, *The Politics of the Developing Areas* (Princeton, NJ: Princeton University Press, 1960); Gabriel A. Almond and G. Bingham Powell, Jr, *Comparative Politics: A Developmental Approach* (Boston: Little, Brown, 1966); and A.F. Organski, *The Stages of Political Development* (New York: Knopf, 1965).

42 Paul Baran, *The Political Economy of Growth* (New York: Monthly Review Press, 1957).

43 André Gunder Frank, *Capitalism and Underdevelopment in Latin America* (New York: Monthly Review Press, 1969).

44 Samir Amin, *Accumulation on a World Scale: A Critique of the Theory of Underdevelopment* (New York: Monthly Review Press, 1974); and Immanuel Wallerstein, *The Capitalist World-Economy* (Cambridge: Cambridge University Press, 1979).

45 Bill Warren, *Imperialism: Pioneer of Capitalism* (London: Verso, 1980).

46 Willy Brandt *et al.*, *North-South, A Programme for Survival: Report of the Independent Commission on International Development Issues* (Cambridge, MA: MIT Press, 1980).

47 Peter L. Berger, *The Capitalist Revolution* (New York: Basic Books, 1986).

48 Tessitore and Woolfson, *A Global Agenda: Issues Before the 48th General Assembly of the United Nations*, op. cit., p. 164.

49 Brown, *Models in Political Economy*, pp. 318–323.

50 Philip Allott, 'Philosophy and Global Social Development', unpublished paper presented to the United Nations Development Programme Roundtable on Global Change, Stockholm, July 1994; and cf. his *Eunomia: New Order for a New World* (Oxford: Oxford University Press, 1990), ch. 17.

51 *Reparation for Injuries Suffered in the Service of the United Nations* Case. Advisory Opinion, *ICJ Reports* 1949, p. 174.

52 Cf. Walter Clarke and Jeffrey Herbst, 'Somalia and the Future of Humanitarian Intervention', *Foreign Affairs*, vol. 75, no. 2, March/April 1996, pp. 70–85.

53 Jarat Chopra, 'A UN Emperor in Cambodia's Old Clothes', *Crosslines Global Report*, vol. 1, no. 1, April 1993, pp. 21–22; Karen Lee Ziner, 'Brown Observer Wary of Elections in Cambodia', *Providence Journal Bulletin*, 22 May 1993, p. A6; Jarat Chopra and Michael Doyle, 'U.N. Snatches Laurels From Defeat in Cambodia', *George Street Journal*, 27 August 1993, p. 8; Seth Mydans, 'Cambodia's Real Boss Rules From the No. 2 Post', *New York Times*, 25 March 1996, p. A3; Keith B. Richburg and R. Jeffrey Smith, 'What Went Wrong in Cambodia?' and Fred Hiatt, 'A Dying Peace in Cambodia', *The Washington Post National Weekly Edition*, 28 July 1997, pp. 14–15 and 29, respectively; and Nate Thayer, 'In Cambodia, A Truce That Almost Was', *The Washington Post National Weekly Edition*, 25 August 1997, pp. 15–16.

54 Alvaro de Soto and Graciana del Castillo, 'Obstacles to Peace-building', *Foreign Policy*, no. 94, Spring 1994, pp. 69–83.

55 Cf. Deborah L. Norden, 'Keeping the Peace, Outside and In: Argentina's UN Missions', *International Peacekeeping*, vol. 2, no. 3, Autumn 1995, pp. 334–339.

56 Anthony Parsons, *From Cold War to Hot Peace: UN Interventions 1947–1995* (London: Penguin Books, 1995), pp. 188–197.

57 Human Rights Watch/Asia, *Cambodia at War* (New York: Human Rights Watch, 1995).

58 Human Rights Watch/Africa, *Somalia Faces the Future* (New York: Human Rights Watch, 1995).

59 Cf. Heribert Weiland and Matthew Braham, Rapporteurs, *The Namibian Peace Process: Implications and Lessons for the Future* (Freiburg: Arnold Bergstraesser Institut/ International Peace Academy, 1994), pp. 163–178.

60 On this phenomenon in Rwanda, cf. Peter Uvin, *Aiding Violence: The Development Enterprise in Rwanda* (West Hartford, CT: Kumarian Press, 1998).

61 'Supplement to an Agenda for Peace: Position Paper of the Secretary-General on the Occasion of the Fiftieth Anniversary of the United Nations', UN Doc. A/50/60 and S/1995/1 of 3 January 1995, para. 31.

62 Cf. the concluding remarks on 'operationalizing panarchy' in W. Andy Knight, 'Towards a Subsidiarity Model for Peacemaking and Preventive Diplomacy: Making Chapter VIII of the UN Charter Operational', *Third World Quarterly*, vol. 17, no. 1, March 1996, pp. 47–49; as well as his 'Establishing Political Authority in Peace-Maintenance', *Global Governance*, vol. 4, no. 1, January–March 1998, pp. 19–40.

63 Cf. Philip Allott, *Eunomia*, ch. 18; and Thomas M. Franck, 'Tribe, Nation, World: Self-Identification in the Evolving International System', *Ethics and International Affairs*, vol. 11, 1997, pp. 151–169.
64 On the use of a committee structure in counter-insurgency, but which could be adapted for peace-maintenance, see Frank Kitson, *Low-Intensity Operations* (London: Faber & Faber, 1971), p. 54.
65 Brown, *Models in Political Economy*, pp. 362–363.
66 Primo Levi, *Survival In Auschwitz* (New York: Collier Books, 1993), p. 88.

3 INTERNATIONAL CIVIL ADMINISTRATION

1 Cf. Joseph Opala, 'Reflections on "The Coming Anarchy"', *Crosslines Global Report*, vol. 4, no. 3, issue 21, July 1996, pp. 13–15.
2 Cf. Dorothy V. Jones, 'The League of Nations Experiment in International Protection', *Ethics and International Affairs*, vol. 8, 1994, pp. 77–95.
3 See further, for instance, Norman L. Hill, *International Administration* (New York: McGraw Hill Book Co., 1931).
4 On the early experiments referred to in the remainder of this section, see further: D.W. Bowett, *United Nations Forces* (London: Stevens & Sons, 1964), ch. 1; David W. Wainhouse *et al.*, *International Peace Observation: A History and Forecast* (Baltimore, MD: The Johns Hopkins Press, 1966), part I, A; and Alan James, *Peacekeeping in International Politics* (London: Macmillan and the International Institute for Strategic Studies, 1990), parts I, II and III.
5 Bowett, *United Nations Forces*, pp. 4–5.
6 See further, Leland M. Goodrich and Edvard Hambro, *Charter of the United Nations: Commentary and Documents*, 2nd edition (Boston: World Peace Foundation, 1949), ch. XII.
7 See further: Paul W. van der Veur, 'The United Nations in West Irian: A Critique', *International Organization*, vol. XVIII, no. 1, Winter 1964, pp. 53–73; Rosalyn Higgins, *United Nations Peacekeeping 1946–1967, Documents and Commentary*, vol. 2, *Asia* (Oxford: Oxford University Press, 1970); Alan James, *Peacekeeping in International Politics*, pp. 190–196; and United Nations, *The Blue Helmets: A Review of United Nations Peacekeeping*, 2nd edition (New York: United Nations Department of Public Information, 1990), pp. 263–277.
8 See further: Georges Abi-Saab, *The United Nations Operation in the Congo, 1960–1964* (Oxford: Oxford University Press, 1978); Indar Jit Rikhye, *Military Adviser to the Secretary-General: U.N. Peacekeeping and the Congo Crisis* (London: Hurst & Co. and St Martin's Press, 1993); and Alan James, *Britain and the Congo Crisis, 1960–63* (New York: St Martin's Press, 1996).
9 See further: Chester A. Crocker, 'Southern African peace-making', *Survival*, vol. XXXII, no. 3, May/June 1990, pp. 221–232; Marrack Goulding and Ingrid Lehmann, 'Case Study: The United Nations Operation in Namibia', in United Nations, *The Singapore Symposium: The Changing Role of the United Nations in Conflict Resolution and Peace-Keeping, 13–15 March 1991* (New York: United Nations Department of Public Information, 1991), pp. 33–41; Heribert Weiland and Matthew Braham, Rapporteurs, *The Namibian Peace Process: Implications and Lessons for the Future* (Freiburg: Arnold Bergstraesser Institut/International Peace Academy, 1994); and the end-of-mission study by UNTAG's civilian Chief-of-Staff, Cedric Thornberry, 'UNTAG: Description and Analysis of the Mission's Operational Arrangements', September 1991, unpublished draft.

10 Interview with UNTAG's Civilian Police Commissioner, Stephen Fanning, Windhoek, November 1989. On the organization of CIVPOL, see Stephen Fanning, 'UN Peace Settlement Plan for Namibia (UNTAG)', in Nassrine Azimi, ed., *The Role and Functions of Civilian Police in United Nations Peace-Keeping Operations: Debriefing and Lessons* (The Hague: Kluwer Law International, 1996), pp. 113–118.

11 See further: Jarat Chopra, John Mackinlay and Larry Minear, *Report on the Cambodian Peace Process* (Oslo: Norwegian Institute of International Affairs, 1993); Hugh Smith, ed., *International Peacekeeping: Building on the Cambodian Experience* (Canberra: Australian Defence Studies Centre, 1994); Janet Heininger, *Peacekeeping in Transition: The United Nations in Cambodia* (New York: Twentieth Century Fund, 1994); Trevor Findlay, *Cambodia: The Legacy and Lessons of UNTAC* (Stockholm/Oxford: Stockholm International Peace Research Institute/Oxford University Press, 1995); Nassrine Azimi, ed., *The United Nations Transitional Authority in Cambodia (UNTAC): Debriefing and Lessons* (The Hague: Kluwer Law International, 1995); and Michael W. Doyle, *UN Peacekeeping in Cambodia: UNTAC's Civil Mandate* (Boulder, CO: Lynne Rienner Publishers and the International Peace Academy, 1995).

12 There is a paucity of literature on this topic, but see, for example, Cyrus R. Vance and David A. Hamburg, *Pathfinders for Peace: A Report to the UN Secretary-General on the Role of Special Representatives and Personal Envoys* (New York: Carnegie Corporation of New York, September 1997), pp. 6–8 and generally.

13 Interview with UNTAC's SRSG Yasushi Akashi, Phnom Penh, November 1992.

14 See further: David Holiday and William Stanley, 'Building the Peace: Preliminary Lessons from El Salvador', *Journal of International Affairs*, vol. 46, no. 2, Winter 1993, pp. 341–366; Alvaro de Soto and Graciana del Castillo, 'Implementation of Comprehensive Peace Agreements: Staying the Course in El Salvador', *Global Governance*, vol. 1, no. 2, May–August 1995, pp. 189–203; and Ian Johnstone, *Rights and Reconciliation: UN Strategies in El Salvador* (Boulder, CO: International Peace Academy and Lynne Rienner Publishers, 1995).

15 On the results of a forum on the definitions of 'success' and 'failure', see Daniel Druckman and Paul C. Stern, 'Evaluating Peacekeeping Missions', *Mershon International Studies Review*, vol. 41, supplement 1, May 1997, pp. 151–165.

16 Cf. the Report of the Government of Canada, *Towards a Rapid Reaction Capability for the United Nations* (Ottawa: The Government of Canada, September 1995).

17 See further Ruben P. Mendez, 'Financing the United Nations and the International Public Sector: Problems and Reform', *Global Governance*, vol. 3, no. 3, September–December 1997, pp. 295–304; and Anthony McDermott, *United Nations Financing Problems and the New Generation of Peacekeeping and Peace Enforcement* (Providence, RI: Thomas J. Watson Jr Institute for International Studies, 1994).

4 INTERNATIONAL RULES OF LAW

1 Malcolm N. Shaw, *International Law*, 4th edition (Cambridge: Cambridge University Press, 1997), p. 717.

2 (i) Standard Minimum Rules for the Treatment of Prisoners, and the Procedures for the Effective Implementation of the Standard Minimum Rules for the Treatment of Prisoners (adopted by the Economic and Social Council in Resolutions 663 (XXIV) and 1984/74, respectively); (ii) Body of Principles for the Protection of All Persons under Any Form of Detention or Imprisonment (adopted by the General Assembly in Resolution 43/173); (iii) Code of Conduct for Law Enforcement Officials, and the Guidelines for the Effective Implementation of the Code of Conduct for Law Enforcement Officials (adopted, respectively, by the General Assembly in Resolution

34/169 and the Economic and Social Council in Resolution 1989/61); (iv) Basic Principles on the Use of Force and Firearms by Law Enforcement Officials (adopted by the Eighth United Nations Congress on the Prevention of Crime and Treatment of Offenders, 1990); (v) Basic Principles on the Independence of the Judiciary and the Procedures for the Effective Implementation of the Basic Principles on the Independence of the Judiciary (adopted, respectively, by the Eighth United Nations Congress on the Prevention of Crime and Treatment of Offenders, 1990, and the Economic and Social Council in Resolution 1989/60); (vi) Basic Principles on the Role of Lawyers (adopted by the Eighth United Nations Congress on the Prevention of Crime and Treatment of Offenders, 1990); (vii) Guidelines on the Role of Prosecutors (adopted by the Eighth United Nations Congress on the Prevention of Crime and the Treatment of Offenders, 1990); (viii) Principles for the Effective Prevention and Investigation of Extra-Legal, Arbitrary and Summary Executions (adopted by the Economic and Social Council in Resolution 1989/65) and the UN's Manual on these Principles; (ix) Declaration on the Rights of Persons Belonging to National or Ethnic, Religious and Linguistic Minorities (adopted by the General Assembly in 1992 as resolution 47/135); (x) Declaration on the Protection of All Persons from Enforced Disappearances (adopted by the General Assembly in 1992 as resolution 47/133); and (xi) Declaration on the Elimination of Violence against Women (adopted by the General Assembly in 1993 as resolution 48/104). Cited in Amnesty International, *Peace-keeping and human rights* (London: AI Index: IOR 40/01/94, January 1994), pp. 44–45.

3 Crime Prevention and Criminal Justice Branch, *United Nations Criminal Justice Standards for Peace-Keeping Police* (Vienna: United Nations, February 1994). Also see 'Notes for the Guidance of United Nations Civilian Police', UN Doc. TU-104/97.

4 Karen Kenny, *Towards Effective Training for Field Human Rights Tasks* (Dublin: International Human Rights Trust, 1996); and K. English and A. Stapleton, *The Human Rights Handbook: A Practical Guide to Monitoring Human Rights* (Essex: Human Rights Centre, October 1995).

5 Mark Plunkett, 'Reestablishing Law and Order in Peace-Maintenance', *Global Governance*, vol. 4, no. 1, January–March 1998, pp. 61–79; and cf. Thomas Carothers, 'The Rule of Law Revival', *Foreign Affairs*, vol. 77, no. 2, March/April 1998, pp. 95–106.

6 Lyal S. Sunga, *Individual Responsibility in International Law for Serious Human Rights Violations* (Dordrecht: Martinus Nijhoff Publishers, 1992), p. 128. Although note the strong criticism of this distinction in 'Draft Articles on State Responsibility: Comments of the Government of the United States of America', *International Legal Materials*, vol. XXXVII, no. 2, March 1998, pp. 474–478.

7 *Barcelona Traction, Light and Power Co. Ltd.* Case. *ICJ Reports* 1970, para. 33.

8 Cf. Timothy L.H. McCormack and Gerry J. Simpson, 'The International Law Commission's Draft Code of Crimes against the Peace and Security of Mankind: An Appraisal of the Substantive Provisions', *Criminal Law Forum*, vol. 5, no. 1, 1994, pp. 1–55.

9 UNGA Res. 177 (II) of 21 November 1947.

10 'Definition of Aggression', UNGA Res. 3314 (XXIX) of 14 December 1974.

11 UN Doc. A/51/10 and Corr. 1, 1996.

12 UNGA Res. A/RES/51/160 of 30 January 1997, para. 2 and 3. Also, see further W. Andy Knight, 'Legal Issues', in John Tessitore and Susan Woolfson, eds, *A Global Agenda: Issues Before the 51st General Assembly* (Lanham, MD: University Press of America, 1996), pp. 265–268.

13 Mr Doudou Thiam, Special Rapporteur for the Draft Code, cited in Sunga, p. 137.

14 Telford Taylor, *The Anatomy of the Nuremberg Trials* (New York: Alfred A. Knopf, 1992), p. 90.

15 Note the distinction made between 'command' and 'staff' in the German Army. *Ibid.*, pp. 105–107.

16 Cf. 'Draft Report of the International Law Commission on the work of its forty-third session', UN Doc. A/CN.4/L.464/Add.4 (1991), paragraph (4) of Commentary on Article 3.

17 On the persisting problems associated with 'command responsibility', such as in the Celebici case, see the *Bulletin of the International Criminal Tribunal for the Former Yugoslavia*, no. 15/16, 10–III–1997, pp. 2–3.

18 Cf. 'International Law Commission Report on the Formulation of Nürnberg Principles', UN Doc. A/CN.4/22 of 12 April 1950.

19 Cf. the list of twenty-two international crimes identified by M. Cherif Bassiouni: aggression; war crimes; unlawful use of weapons/unlawful emplacement of weapons; crimes against humanity; genocide; racial discrimination and apartheid; slavery and related crimes; torture; unlawful human experimentation; piracy; aircraft hijacking; threat and use of force against internationally protected persons; taking of civilian hostages; drug offences; international traffic in obscene publications; destruction and/or theft of national treasures; environmental protection; unlawful use of the mails; interference with submarine cables; falsification and counterfeiting; bribery of foreign public officials; and theft of nuclear materials. *A Draft International Criminal Code and Draft Statute for an International Criminal Tribunal* (Boston: Martinus Nijhoff, 1987), pp. 28–29.

20 Sunga, p. 37.

21 *Ibid.*, pp. 37–38; Cf. Taylor, ch. 2.

22 UNGA Res. 95(1) of 11 December 1946.

23 D.W. Bowett, 'Reprisals Involving Recourse to Armed Force', *American Journal of International Law*, vol. 66, no. 1, January 1972, p. 1.

24 Note that this semicolon was changed to a comma, which was in the original Russian text, to render the 'jurisdiction of the Tribunal' applicable to the first part of the paragraph. Taylor, p. 648.

25 Adopted 9 December 1948; entered into force 12 January 1951.

26 Cf. the problem of defining 'peoples' and the 'self' with the right of self-determination: James Crawford, ed., *The Rights of Peoples* (Oxford: Clarendon Press, 1988).

27 *Reservations to the Convention on the Prevention and Punishment of the Crime of Genocide* Case, Advisory Opinion, *ICJ Reports* 1951, p. 23.

28 *Barcelona Traction* Case, para. 34.

29 Cf. Payam Akhavan, 'Enforcement of the Genocide Convention Through the Advisory Opinion Jurisdiction of the International Court of Justice', *Human Rights Law Journal*, vol. 12, no. 8–9, 30 September 1991, pp. 285–299.

30 Cf. Hurst Hannum, 'International Law and Cambodian Genocide: The Sounds of Silence', *Human Rights Quarterly*, vol. 11, no. 1, February 1989, pp. 82–138; and Ben Kiernan, *The Cambodian Genocide Program, 1994–1997* (New Haven, CT: Yale Center for International and Area Studies, February 1998), as well as its website (www.yale.edu/cgp).

31 Cf. Peter H.F. Bekker and Paul C. Szasz, 'Application of the Convention on the Prevention and Punishment of the Crime of Genocide', *American Journal of International Law*, vol. 91, no. 1, January 1997, pp. 121–126.

32 Adopted 30 November 1973; entered into force 18 July 1976.

33 'Statute for the Creation of an International Criminal Jurisdiction to Implement the International Convention on the Suppression and Punishment of the Crime of Apartheid', UN Doc. E/CN.4/1426.

34 UNGA Res. 46/84 of 16 December 1991.

35　This was composed of nineteen parties, including: the South African government, the African National Congress (ANC), the Inkatha Freedom Party, and the Bophuthatswana government.

36　Cf. The Most Reverend Desmond M. Tutu, 'The Search for Truth and Reconciliation in Post-Apartheid South Africa', *International Peace Academy Roundtable Report*, 11 November 1996, pp. 1–4; and Lyn S. Graybill, 'South Africa's Truth and Reconciliation Commission: Ethical and Theological Perspectives', *Ethics and International Affairs*, vol. 12, 1998, pp. 43–62.

37　Universal Declaration of Human Rights (1948), Article 5; International Covenant on Civil and Political Rights (1966), Articles 7 and 10(1); Geneva Conventions (1949), common Article 3; American Declaration of the Rights and Duties of Man, Article XXV; American Convention on Human Rights (1969), Article 5(2); African Charter on Human and Peoples' Rights (1981), Article 5; European Convention on Human Rights (1950), Article 3; European Convention for the Prevention of Torture and Inhuman or Degrading Treatment or Punishment (1987); UN Declaration on the Protection of All Persons from Being Subjected to Torture, Cruel, Inhuman or Degrading Treatment or Punishment (1975).

38　Adopted 10 December 1984; entered into force 26 June 1987.

39　Note for instance annual reports by Amnesty International. Also, see Edward Peters' excellent history of the subject, *Torture* (Philadelphia: University of Pennsylvania Press, 1996).

40　*Barcelona Traction* Case, para. 34.

41　International Covenant on Civil and Political Rights, Article 4; European Convention on Human Rights, Article 15(1); American Convention on Human Rights, Article 27.

42　International Covenant on Civil and Political Rights: Human Rights Committee (eighteen members); International Covenant on Economic, Social and Cultural Rights: Committee on Economic, Social and Cultural Rights (eighteen members); International Convention on the Elimination of All Forms of Racial Discrimination: Committee on the Elimination of All Forms of Racial Discrimination (CERD – eighteen members; see below); Convention on the Rights of the Child: Committee on the Rights of the Child (CRC – ten members); Convention on the Elimination of All Forms of Discrimination against Women: Committee on the Elimination of All Forms of Discrimination against Women (CEDAW – twenty-three members; see below).

43　Established 26 June 1987; Committee assumed functions as of 1 January 1988.

44　Cited in John Tessitore and Susan Woolfson, eds, *A Global Agenda: Issues Before the 47th General Assembly of the United Nations* (Lanham, MD: University Press of America, 1992), p. 237.

45　Cf. Declaration of Verona (1822); Treaty of London (1841); Treaty of Washington (1862); General Act of the Berlin Conference (1885); General Act of the Brussels Conference (1890).

46　Adopted 25 September 1926; entered into force 9 March 1927. Amended by a Protocol of 7 December 1953; amended Convention entered into force 7 July 1955.

47　Adopted 30 April 1956; entered into force 30 April 1957.

48　*Barcelona Traction* Case, para. 33.

49　Universal Declaration of Human Rights, Article 5; American Declaration of the Rights and Duties of Man, Article XXXIV; European Convention on Human Rights, Article 4; American Convention on Human Rights, Article 6; and African Charter on Human and Peoples' Rights, Article 5.

50　Cf. Preamble and Articles 13(1)(b), 55(c), 76(c), 62(2) and 68.

51　Cf. ILO Convention No. 111 Concerning Discrimination in Respect of Employment and Occupation (1958); ILO Convention No. 100 Concerning Equal Remuneration for Men and Women Workers for Work of Equal Value (1951); UNESCO

Convention against Discrimination in Education (1960) and Protocol (1962); Declaration on the Elimination of Discrimination against Women, UNGA Res. 2263 (XXII) of 7 November 1967; Convention on the Elimination of All Forms of Discrimination against Women, UNGA Res. 34/180 of 18 December 1979; Declaration on the Elimination of All Forms of Intolerance and of Discrimination Based on Religion or Belief, UNGA Res. 36/55 of 25 November 1981; UNESCO Declaration on Fundamental Principles concerning the Contribution of the Mass Media to Strengthening Peace and International Understanding to the Promotion of Human Rights and to Countering Racialism, *Apartheid* and Incitement to War (1978); and UNESCO Declaration on Race and Racial Prejudice (1978).

52 UNGA Res. 1904 (XVIII) of 20 November 1963.

53 Entered into force 4 January 1969.

54 *Barcelona Traction* Case, para. 32.

55 Cf. Theodor Meron, 'Rape as a Crime Under International Humanitarian Law', *American Journal of International Law*, vol. 87, no. 3, July, 1993, pp. 424–426; Beverly Allen, *Rape Warfare: The Hidden Genocide in Bosnia-Herzegovina and Croatia* (Minneapolis: University of Minnesota Press, 1996); and Mary Ann Tétreault, 'Justice for All: Wartime Rape and Women's Human Rights', *Global Governance*, vol. 3, no. 2, May–August 1997, pp. 197–212.

56 Sun Tzu, *The Art of War* (ca. 500 BC); *Code of Manu* (ca. 200 BC) and cf. Greek, Roman and Islamic Sharia law; the First and Second Lateran Councils of the Catholic Church (1122 and 1139); Natural Law as expounded by de Vitoria, Suarez and particularly Hugo Grotius, *De Jure Belli ac Pacis*, book II, ch. II (1625); the United States Lieber Code (1863); the St Petersburg Declaration (1868); the Hague Conventions and Regulations (1899 and 1907); the Geneva Protocol (1925); and the Geneva Conventions (1864 and 1929).

57 Note the comparison of African, Asian, Socialist, Islamic, Latin American and Western concepts of humanitarian law in Henri Dunant Institute/UNESCO, *International Dimensions of Humanitarian Law* (Dordrecht: Martinus Nijhoff Publishers, 1988), ch. I–VI.

58 Hague Convention concerning the Laws and Customs of War on Land (1899); Hague Convention on the Laws and Customs of War on Land (1907).

59 Geneva Convention for the Relief of the Wounded and Sick in Armies in the Field.

60 Ist Geneva Convention for the Amelioration of the Condition of the Wounded and Sick in Armed Forces in the Field; IInd Geneva Convention for the Amelioration of the Condition of the Wounded and Sick in Armed Forces in the Field; IIIrd Geneva Convention Relative to the Treatment of Prisoners of War; IVth Geneva Convention Relative to the Protection of Civilian Persons in Time of War.

61 Cf. Hague Convention for the Protection of Cultural Property in the Event of Armed Conflict (1954); Hague Protocol for the Protection of Cultural Property in the Event of Armed Conflict (1954); Zagreb Resolution of the Institute of International Law on Conditions of Application of Humanitarian Rules of Armed Conflict to Hostilities in which United Nations Forces May Be Engaged (1971); UN Convention of the Prohibition of Military or Any Other Hostile Use of Environmental Modification Techniques (1977); Red Cross Fundamental Rules of International Humanitarian Law Applicable in Armed Conflicts (1978); and UN Convention on Prohibitions or Restrictions on the Use of Certain Conventional Weapons Which May be Deemed to be Excessively Injurious or to Have Indiscriminate Effects (1981).

62 Geneva Convention I, Article 50; Geneva Convention II, Article 51; Geneva Convention III, Article 130; Geneva Convention IV, Article 147; Additional Protocol I, Article 85.

63 See the detailed analysis by Yves Sandoz, 'Implementing International Humanitarian Law', in Henri Dunant Institute/UNESCO, *International Dimensions*, pp. 259–282.

64 Geneva Conventions: French, English, Russian, Spanish; Protocols: Arabic, Chinese, English, French, Russian and Spanish.

65 Jean Pictet cited in Sandoz, p. 266.

66 *Ibid.*, p. 277.

67 UNGA Res. A/RES/49/59 of 9 December 1994. The Convention will enter into force upon twenty-two ratifications. See full text in *International Peacekeeping*, vol. 2, no. 5, August–September 1995, pp. 123–125; as well as *International Legal Materials*, vol. 34, no. 2, March 1995, pp. 482–488. Also see the recent literature on the subject: Evan T. Bloom, 'Protecting Peacekeepers: The Convention on the Safety of United Nations and Associated Personnel', *American Journal of International Law*, vol. 89, no. 3, July 1995, pp. 621–631; M.-Christiane Bourloyannis-Vrailas, 'The Convention on the Safety of United Nations and Associated Personnel', *International and Comparative Law Quarterly*, vol. 44, Pt. III, July 1995, pp. 560–590; Philippe Kirsch, 'The Convention on the Safety of United Nations and Associated Personnel', *International Peacekeeping*, vol. 2, no. 5, August–September 1995, pp. 102–106; and Robert C.R. Siekmann, 'The Convention on the Safety of United Nations and Associated Personnel: Its Scope of Application', in Nassrine Azimi, ed., *Humanitarian Action and Peace-keeping Operations: Debriefing and Lessons* (The Hague: Kluwer Law International, 1997), pp. 281–289.

68 Philippe Kirsch, 'The Convention', p. 105.

69 *Ibid.*, p. 104.

70 Amnesty International, *Peace-Keeping and Human Rights*, pp. 31–34.

71 Cf. the New Zealand draft in UN Doc. A/C.6/48/L.2 of 6 October 1993 and the following: Montreal Convention for the Suppression of Unlawful Acts against the Safety of Civil Aviation (1971); Convention on the Prevention and Punishment of Crimes against Internationally Protected Persons, including Diplomatic Agents (1973); International Convention against the Taking of Hostages (1979); and Convention for the Suppression of Unlawful Acts against the Safety of Maritime Navigation (1988).

72 Cf. InterPress Service, 'U.N. Seeks Code of Conduct for Peacekeepers', 3 February 1997. Also see Asbjørn Eide, Allan Rosas and Theodor Meron, 'Combating Lawlessness in Gray Zone Conflicts Through Minimum Humanitarian Standards', *American Journal of International Law*, vol. 89, no. 1, January 1995, pp. 215–223; and the 1971 Zagreb Resolution of the Institute of International Law on Conditions of Application of Humanitarian Rules of Armed Conflict to Hostilities in which United Nations Forces May Be Engaged, in Adam Roberts and Richard Guelff, eds, *Documents on the Laws of War* (Oxford: Clarendon Press, 1982), pp. 371–375.

73 Taylor, pp. 76 and 639–640.

74 Cf. Hans Kelsen, 'Will the Judgement in the Nuremberg Trial Constitute a Precedent in International Law?' *International Law Quarterly*, vol. 1, 1947, pp. 153–171; Richard H. Minear, *Victor's Justice: The Tokyo War Crimes Trials* (Princeton, NJ: Princeton University Press, 1972).

75 Note the efforts by Israel to try former Nazi war criminals such as Adolf Eichmann (*Attorney-General of the Government of Israel* v. *Eichmann* Case, *International Law Reports*, vol. 36, 1961, p. 5) and its reluctance to condemn Serbian atrocities. Cf. the advertisement in *New York Times* of 29 April 1993, p. A14, entitled, 'Mr. President, Do Not Bomb the Victims of Nazi/Croatian Genocide', placed by John Ranz, Chairman, Survivors of the Buchenwald Concentration Camp, USA.

76 Cf. the conviction, on the basis of a fraudulent British passport held for a short period, of 'Lord Haw-Haw' for high treason by United Kingdom courts and his appeal: *Joyce* v. *Director of Public Prosecutions* Case, *International Law Reports*, vol. 15, 1946, p. 91. Note also the 'gunboat extradition' of General Manuel Noriega by the United

States, in Barbara M. Yarnold, *International Fugitives: A New Role for the International Court of Justice* (New York: Praeger Publishers, 1991), pp. 59–66.

77 Note, for instance, the assistance afforded Pol Pot and the Khmer Rouge by Thailand to counter Vietnamese influence in Cambodia in the 1980s.

78 Although not an international criminal, but a murderer, note the refusal by the European Court of Human Rights to allow the United Kingdom to extradite a German national to the United States on the grounds that he would be exposed to the 'death row phenomenon', contrary to Article 3 of the European Convention for the Protection of Human Rights and Fundamental Freedoms (1950) concerning freedom from torture or inhuman or degrading treatment or punishment: *Soering v. United Kingdom* Case, *European Court of Human Rights*, Series A, vol. 161, 1989, para. 101–111.

79 Even within the United States, see the shifts in the scope of jurisdiction of the Alien Tort Claims Act (1789): *Filartiga v. Pena Irala* Case, 630 *Federal Reporter (Second Series)*, vol. 630 (Second Circuit 1980), p. 876; *Tel-Oren v. Libyan Arab Republic* Case, 726 *Federal Reporter (Second Series)*, vol. 726 (1984), p. 774; and *Kadic v. Karadzic*, *International Legal Materials*, vol. XXXIV, no. 6, November 1995, pp. 1592–1614.

80 Such as the kidnapping in Argentina of Eichmann by Israeli agents and the US invasion of Panama to obtain custody of Noriega.

81 At the instigation of the UK, US and France, Security Council Resolution 748 of 31 March 1992 imposed sanctions on Libya for its non-surrender of the two men suspected of bombing Pan Am Flight 103 over Lockerbie, Scotland.

82 Cf. 'Harvard Research Draft Convention on Jurisdiction With Respect to Crime, 1935', *American Journal of International Law*, vol. 29, nos. 1 and 2, January and April 1935, supplement, p. 443.

83 Preamble to the Nuremberg Charter.

84 See further Sunga, pp. 102–107.

5 INTERNATIONAL MEANS OF ORDER

1 Cf. 'Report of the Sixth Committee', UN Doc. A/47/584 of 19 November 1992, para. 6.

2 GA Official Records 47th Session, supplement no. 10, (A/47/10) of 1 September 1992.

3 UNGA Res. 44/39 of 4 December 1989, para. 1; and UNGA Res. 46/54 of 9 December 1991, para. 3.

4 James Crawford, 'The ILC Adopts a Statute for an International Criminal Court', *American Journal of International Law*, vol. 89, no. 2, April 1995, pp. 404–416.

5 UN Doc. A/51/22 (1996) and UNGA Res. A/RES/51/207 of 16 January 1997, para. 5. See further W. Andy Knight, 'Legal Issues', in John Tessitore and Susan Woolfson, eds, *A Global Agenda: Issues Before the 52nd General Assembly of the United Nations* (Lanham, MD: Rowman & Littlefield Publishers, 1997), pp. 283–287; and Christopher Keith Hall, 'The Fifth Session of the UN Preparatory Committee on the Establishment of an International Criminal Court', *American Journal of International Law*, vol. 92, no. 2, April 1998, pp. 331–339.

6 Although cf. General Dwight D. Eisenhower's proposals to liquidate 3,500 members of the German General Staff as well as 'leaders of the Nazi Party from mayors on up and all members of the Gestapo'. Cited in Telford Taylor, *The Anatomy of the Nuremberg Trials* (New York: Alfred A. Knopf, 1992), p. 108.

7 UN Doc. A/332 of 21 July 1947, para. 3.

8 UN Doc. A/362 of 25 August 1947, Appendix I and II.

9   UNGA Res. 260 B (III) of 9 December 1948.
10 'Report of the ILC, 2nd Session', *GAOR*, 5th Session, supplement no. 12 (A/1316), paras. 128–145.
11 'Report of the Committee on International Criminal Jurisdiction on its Session held from 1 to 31 August 1951', *GAOR*, 7th Session, supplement no. 11 (A/2136); and 'Report of the 1953 Committee on International Criminal Jurisdiction, 27 July–20 August 1953', *GAOR*, 9th Session, supplement no. 12 (A/2645).
12 UN Doc. A/362 of 25 August 1947: Appendix I, Articles 2(1), 28 and 37(1); Appendix II, Articles 2(1), 22 and 31(1).
13 UN Doc. A/CN.4/25 of 26 April 1950, para. 159.
14 UN Doc. A/CN.4/20 of 30 March 1950, para. 30–33.
15 UN Doc. A/1316, para. 138.
16 Commentary, UN Doc. A/2136, para. 104–109.
17 A/47/10, para. 518–527.
18 *Ibid.*, para. 528–545.
19 A/47/10, para. 546–549.
20 See further, W. Andy Knight, 'Legal Issues', in John Tessitore and Susan Woolfson, eds, *A Global Agenda: Issues Before the 51st General Assembly of the United Nations* (Lanham, MD: Rowman & Littlefield Publishers, 1996), pp. 262–265 and 268–282; and The Stanley Foundation, *The UN Security Council and the International Criminal Court: How Should They Relate?* (Muscatine, IA: The Stanley Foundation, 1998).
21 UN Doc. S/25274 of 10 February 1993, para. 74.
22 See John F. Burns, 'Balkan War Trial in Serious Doubt', *New York Times*, 26 April 1993, p. A9. See also the critical view by Herman Schwartz, 'What Can We Do About Balkan Atrocities?' *New York Times*, 9 April 1993, p. A27; and Bruce W. Nelan, 'Crimes Without Punishment', *Time*, 11 January 1993, p. A21.
23 UN Doc. S/25704 of 3 May 1993. Cf. the analysis of this in the American Bar Association Special Task Force on War Crimes in Former Yugoslavia of the Section of International Law and Practice, *Report on the International Tribunal to Adjudicate War Crimes Committed in the Former Yugoslavia* (Chicago, IL: American Bar Association, 1993).
24 Theodor Meron, 'International Criminalization of Internal Atrocities', *American Journal of International Law*, vol. 89, no. 3, July 1995, pp. 554–577.
25 On a procedural and substantive comparison of the Nuremberg and Yugoslav Tribunals, see ICTY *Bulletin*, no. 5/6, 24–IV–1996, p. 4.
26 UN Doc. S/25704, para. 28.
27 Personal interviews with ICTY staff, The Hague, June 1994.
28 UN Doc. IT/32 of 14 March 1994. By the end of 1996, these had been amended eleven times.
29 Security Council Resolution 936.
30 He was later replaced by Canadian Louise Arbour, who was appointed by Security Council Resolution 1047 of 29 February 1996 and took office on 1 October 1996. On the Office of the Prosecutor, see ICTY *Bulletin*, no. 4, 15–III–1996, pp. 2–3.
31 Cf. Luisa Vierucci, 'The First Steps of the International Criminal Tribunal for the Former Yugoslavia', *European Journal of International Law*, vol. 6, no. 1, 1995, pp. 134–143; and José E. Alvarez, 'Nuremberg Revisited: The *Tadic* Case', *European Journal of International Law*, vol. 7, no. 2, 1996, pp. 245–264.
32 On the jurisprudence of the case, see ICTY *Bulletin*, no. 17, 22–IV–1997, pp. 3–9; and Theodor Meron, 'Classification of Armed Conflict in the Former Yugoslavia: *Nicaragua*'s Fallout', *American Journal of International Law*, vol. 92, no. 2, April 1998, pp. 236–242. The judgement was released on-line at the inauguration of the Tribunal website (http://www.un.org/icty) and appears in *International Legal Materials*, vol. XXXVI, no. 4, July 1997, pp. 908–979.
33 ICTY *Bulletin*, no. 19, 04–VIII–1997, p. 3.

34 Cf. a report of the Committee of French Jurists submitted by France (UN Doc. S/25266 of 10 February 1993); a report by a Commission of Italian jurists submitted by Italy (UN Doc. S/25300 of 17 February 1993); the Report of the International Meeting of Experts on the Establishment of an International Criminal Tribunal submitted by Canada (UN Doc. S/25504 of 1 April 1993); and proposals submitted by the United States (UN Doc. S/25575 of 12 April 1993).

35 'Proposal for an International War Crimes Tribunal for the Former Yugoslavia' by Rapporteurs (Corell–Türk–Thune) under the CSCE Moscow Human Dimension Mechanism to Bosnia-Herzegovina and Croatia, 9 February 1993 (UN Doc. S/25307 of 18 February 1993). For a more detailed, insider's analysis of the background to these events, see Payam Akhavan, 'Punishing war crimes in the former Yugoslavia: a critical juncture for the New World Order', *Human Rights Quarterly*, vol. 15, no. 2, May 1993, pp. 262–289.

36 Although the UN Assistance Mission for Rwanda (UNAMIR) was authorized to conduct some policing tasks for the Rwandan Tribunal. On a comparison of the ICTY and the International Criminal Tribunal for Rwanda (ICTR), see further ICTY *Bulletin*, no. 9/10, 14–VIII–1996, pp. 1–2, and 5.

37 It drew on: the 1945 London Charter; the 1954 ILC Draft Statute; the Draft Statute for an International Criminal Court prepared by the International Law Association in 1981 (Report of the Sixtieth Conference of the ILA, Montreal 1982); and a Draft Statute for an International Criminal Tribunal presented by the *Association Internationale des Droits Pénale* (AIDP). Cited in UN Doc. S/25307, Annex 8, p. 141.

38 The Procuracy is provided for in Ch. III of the Draft Convention, Articles 22 and 23. UN Doc. S/25307.

39 *Ibid.*, p. 62.

40 Personal interviews with ICTY staff, The Hague, June 1994.

41 Personal interviews with ICTY staff, The Hague, July 1995.

42 Cf. ICTY *Bulletin*, no. 11, 17–X–1996, p. 1.

43 Cf. the guidelines established for remote testimony, ICTY *Bulletin*, no. 17, 22–IV–1997, p. 7.

44 *Ibid.*, pp. 6–7.

45 ICTY *Bulletin*, no. 8, 19–VII–1996, pp. 1–2 and 5–6.

46 ICTY *Bulletin*, no. 17, 22–IV–1997, pp. 1–2.

47 ICTY *Bulletin*, no. 20, 20–III–1998, p. 9.

48 Cf. UN Doc. S/25307, Ch. XV: 'International Judicial Assistance and other Forms of Co-operation'.

49 A/47/10, para. 518–526.

50 Akhavan, 'Punishing war crimes in the former Yugoslavia', p. 282.

51 John F. Burns, 'His Bosnia Trial Ending, Serb asks Death Penalty', *New York Times*, 28 March 1993, p. A8.

52 See the previous 'CSCE Report of the Rapporteurs (Corell–Türk–Thune) under the Moscow Human Dimension Mechanism to Croatia, 30 September–5 October 1992', Section 9.3, and reiterated in this Report, UN Doc. S/25307, Section 8.6.

53 A/47/10, para. 504.

54 Only the French proposal (UN Doc. S/25266) foresaw the possibility of trials *in absentia*. Cf. Paul Szasz, 'The Proposed War Crimes Tribunal for Ex-Yugoslavia', unpublished speech before New York University *Journal of International Law and Politics* Annual Banquet, 19 April 1993, p. 12; and Theodor Meron, 'International Responses to Alleged War Crimes in Former Yugoslavia', personal summary of views expressed at the Council on Foreign Relations on the subject, 24 March 1993, pp. 3–4.

55 UN Doc. S/25704, para. 101.

56　Although cf. US legislation passed, Robert Kushen and Kenneth J. Harris, 'Surrender of Fugitives by the United States to the War Crimes Tribunals for Yugoslavia and Rwanda', *American Journal of International Law*, vol. 90, no. 3, July 1996, pp. 510–518.

57　ICTY *Bulletin*, no. 3, 22–II–1996, p. 3.

58　*Ibid.*

59　See further for full text, *International Legal Materials*, vol. 36, no. 1, January 1997, pp. 92–99.

60　UN Doc. S/1996/556 of 16 July 1996.

61　UN Doc. S/PRST/1996/34 of 8 August 1996.

62　Personal interviews with ICTY staff, July 1995, The Hague.

63　Cf. ICTY *Bulletin*, no. 3, 22–II–1996, p. 2.

64　See further, ICTY *Bulletin*, no. 1, 15–XII–1995, p. 5.

65　ICTY *Bulletin*, no. 2, 22–I–1996, p. 1.

66　Judge Richard J. Goldstone, 'The Role and the Work of the International War Crimes Tribunals for the Former Yugoslavia and Rwanda', *International Peace Academy Roundtable Report*, 2 October 1996, p. 2.

67　ICTY Bulletin, no. 13, 18–XII–1996, p. 3. By March 1998, the number in custody had risen to twenty-four, including three indictees arrested by SFOR.

68　See further W. Andy Knight, 'Legal Issues', in Tessitore and Woolfson (1997), pp. 279–283; and Payam Akhavan, 'The International Criminal Tribunal for Rwanda: The Politics and Pragmatics of Punishment', *American Journal of International Law*, vol. 90, no. 3, July 1996, pp. 501–510.

69　UN Doc. S/25307, Section 8.5.

70　See further, ICTY *Bulletin*, no. 7, 21–VI–1996, p. 2.

71　UN Doc. S/25307, p. 70.

72　*Ibid.*

73　*Ibid.*, p. 200.

74　*Ibid.*, p. 202.

75　UN Doc. S/25704, para. 112.

76　See further, ICTY *Bulletin*, no. 12, 15–XI–1996, supplement no. 1.

77　UN Doc. S/25704, para. 121.

78　ICTY *Bulletin*, no. 17, 22–IV–1997, p. 2.

79　ICTY *Bulletin*, no. 12, 15–XI–1996, supplement no. 1.

80　Quoted in *ibid.*, p. 2.

81　ICTY *Bulletin*, no. 14, 27–I–1997, p. 4. On consideration of the guilty plea as a defence strategy, see p. 5. On Erdemovic's appeal, see ICTY *Bulletin*, no. 20, 20–III–1998, pp. 2 and 10.

82　ICTY *Bulletin*, no. 14, 27–I–1997, p. 4.

83　*Ibid.*

84　*Ibid.*, p. 5.

85　*Ibid.*

86　UNSC Res. 717 of 16 October 1991 established UNTAC. UNSC Res. 718 of 31 October 1991 fully supported the Paris Agreements and requested the UN Secretary-General to submit a report on their implementation. UNSC Res. 745 of 28 February 1992 approved the UN Secretariat's blueprint in S/23613. The four factions were: State of Cambodia (SOC); Democratic Kampuchea (DK) or the Khmer Rouge; Armeé Nationale Sihanoukiste (ANS); and Khmer People's National Liberation Front (KPNLF).

87　'Report of the Secretary-General on Cambodia', UN Doc. S/23613 of 19 February 1992.

88　Alan Riding, '4 Parties in Cambodian War Sign U.N.-backed Pact; Khmer Rouge Shares Rule', *New York Times*, 24 October 1991, p. A1.

89 Personal interviews with UNTAC Civil Administration and Human Rights officials, Phnom Penh, November 1992.

90 This material is drawn from Ben Kiernan, 'The Cambodian Crisis, 1990–1992: The UN Plan, the Khmer Rouge, and the State of Cambodia', *Bulletin of Concerned Asian Scholars*, vol 24, no. 2, April–June 1992, p. 19.

91 'Agreement on A Comprehensive Political Settlement of the Cambodian Conflict', Article 15; 'Annex 1: UNTAC Mandate', Section E.

92 S/23613, para. 8–22.

93 'Activities of UNTAC Human Rights Component', Human Rights Component brief, Phnom Penh, July 1992.

94 S/23613, para. 19.

95 'Agreement on A Comprehensive Political Settlement of the Cambodian Conflict', Article 6; 'Annex 1: UNTAC Mandate', Section B.

96 'Civil Administration's Five Areas of Control', UNTAC Spokesman's Office, Phnom Penh, 18 September 1992.

97 S/23613, para. 95.

98 Cf. Nassrine Azimi, ed., *The Role and Functions of Civilian Police in United Nations Peace-Keeping Operations: Debriefing and Lessons* (The Hague: Kluwer Law International, 1996); and International Peace Academy, *Peacekeeper's Handbook* (New York: Pergamon Press, 1984), pp. 309–322.

99 'Annex 1: UNTAC Mandate', Article 5; S/23613, para. 112–127.

100 Cf. S/23613, para. 126; in particular, 'Provisions Relating to the Judiciary and Criminal Law and Procedure Applicable in Cambodia During the Transitional Period', 10 September 1992.

101 'Civilian Police Component', UNTAC Spokesman's Office, 13 November 1992.

102 Nate Thayer, 'Legal Weapon: Untac Gains Powers to Stem Violence', *Far Eastern Economic Review*, 21 January 1993, p. 12.

103 *Ibid.*

104 *Ibid.*

105 *Indochina Digest*, 22 January 1993, p. 1.

106 *Ibid.*

107 *Indochina Digest*, 5 February 1993, p. 1.

108 *Ibid.*

109 *Indochina Digest*, 12 March 1993, p. 1.

110 *Indochina Digest*, 19 March 1993, p. 1.

111 *Indochina Digest*, 12 March 1993, p. 1.

112 *Indochina Digest*, 2 April 1993, p. 2.

113 Cf. J. Basil Fernando, *The Inability to Prosecute: Courts and Human Rights in Cambodia and Sri Lanka* (Hong Kong: Future Asia Link, 1993).

114 UNSC Res. 693 of 20 May 1991 approved the 'Report of the Secretary-General', UN Doc. S/22494 of 16 April 1991.

115 UN Doc. A/44/971, S/21541 of 16 August 1990, Annex.

116 'First Report of the Director of the Human Rights Division', Annex to 'Note by the Secretary-General', UN Doc. S/23037 of 16 September 1991, pp. 11–12.

117 Interview, San Salvador, 28 May 1992 cited in Cynthia Arnson and David Holiday, 'El Salvador–Peace and Human Rights: Successes and Shortcomings of the United Nations Observer Mission in El Salvador (ONUSAL)', *News From Americas Watch*, vol. IV, no. 8, 2 September 1992, p. 19.

118 *Ibid.*

119 UNSC Res. 729 of 14 January 1992.

120 Stephen Baranyi and Liisa North, *Stretching the Limits of the Possible: United Nations Peacekeeping in Central America* (Ottawa: Canadian Centre for Global Security, 1992), p. 30.

121 *News from Americas Watch*, p. 20. Cf. David H. McCormick, 'From Peacekeeping to Peacebuilding: Restructuring Military and Police Institutions in El Salvador', in Michael W. Doyle, Ian Johnstone and Robert C. Orr, eds, *Keeping the Peace: Multidimensional UN Operations in Cambodia and El Salvador* (Cambridge: Cambridge University Press, 1997), pp. 282–311.

122 *Ibid.*, p. 11.

123 'Fourth Report of the Director of the Human Rights Division', UN Doc. A/46/935, S/24006 of 5 June 1992, pp. 14–15.

124 'Truth Will Out', *The Economist*, 20 March 1993, pp. 47–48; Todd Howland and Libby Cooper, 'El Salvador Amnesty is a Travesty – Violates Peace Accords', *The Christian Science Monitor*, 25 March 1993, p. 18; and José María Tojeira, 'The Road to Reconciliation in El Salvador', 13 April 1993, p. 19.

125 Cf. The Washington Office on Latin America, *Demilitarizing Public Order: The International Community, Police Reform and Human Rights in Central America and Haiti* (Washington, DC: The Washington Office on Latin America, November 1995), pp. 34–37; and Gino Costa, The United Nations and Reform of the Police in El Salvador', *International Peacekeeping*, vol. 2, no. 3, Autumn 1995, pp. 365–390.

126 John Mackinlay and Jarat Chopra, *A Draft Concept of Second Generation Multinational Operations, 1993* (Providence, RI: Thomas J. Watson Jr Institute for International Studies, 1993), para. 23.

127 *Ibid.*, para. 24.

128 See further *ibid.*, pt III.

129 See further the cooperative developments between national police services described by Ethan A. Nadelman, such as in *Cops Across Borders: The Internationalization of U.S. Criminal Law Enforcement* (University Park, PA: Pennsylvania State University Press, 1993).

6 PEACE-MAINTENANCE IN ANARCHICAL SOMALIA

1 Donatella Lorch, 'As U.N. Girds to Leave Somalia, Renewed Fighting', *New York Times*, 27 February 1995, p. A3.

2 Donatella Lorch, 'Marines Cover U.N.'s Pullout From Somalia', *New York Times*, 28 February 1995, p. A1; Sam Kiley, 'Americans buy off Somalis for quiet exit', *The Times* (London), 28 February 1995, p. 12; and cf. UN Doc. S/1995/231 of 28 March 1995, paras. 52–61.

3 'Farewell to Africa', *Financial Times*, 28 February 1995, p.19.

4 Human Rights Watch/Africa, 'Somalia Faces the Future: Human Rights in a Fragmented Society', *Human Rights Watch/Africa*, vol. 7, no. 2, April 1995, p. 7–9. Cf. William Finnegan, 'Letter From Mogadishu: A World of Dust', *The New Yorker*, 20 March 1995, pp. 64–77.

5 Cf. Walter S. Clarke, *Humanitarian Intervention in Somalia Bibliography* (Carlisle, PA: Center of Strategic Leadership, US Army War College, 1995). An updated bibliography appears on-line (http://ralph.gmu.edu/cfpa/peace/clarke/).

6 See further Jarat Chopra, 'Fighting for Truth at the UN', *Crosslines Global Report*, vol. 4, no. 8, issue 26, November 1996, pp. 7–9.

7 On the renewed interest in the MSC at the end of the Cold War, see, for instance: Benjamin Rivlin, 'The Rediscovery of the UN Military Staff Committee', *Occasional Papers Series*, no. IV, Ralph Bunch Institute on the United Nations, May 1991; and Jane Boulden, 'Prometheus Unborn: The History of the Military Staff Committee', *Aurora Papers*, no. 19, Canadian Centre for Global Security, August 1993.

8 Cf. Inis Claude, *Swords Into Plowshares* (New York: Random House, 1964), pp. 223–260.

9 Cf. Hedley Bull, *The Anarchical Society: A Study of Order in World Politics* (London: Macmillan Press, 1977), ch. 6 and 7.

10 See for instance, John Keegan, *A History of Warfare* (New York: Vintage Books, 1993), pp. 3–60.

11 Cf. Judith Gail Gardam, 'Proportionality and Force in International Law', *American Journal of International Law*, vol. 87, no. 3, July 1993, pp. 391–413.

12 See for instance, Escott Reid, *On Duty: A Canadian at the Making of the United Nations, 1945–1946* (Toronto: McClelland and Stewart, 1983), pp. 12–13, and generally.

13 See further, D.W. Bowett, *United Nations Forces* (London: Stevens & Sons, 1964), pp. 15–18.

14 D.J. Harris, *Cases and Materials on International Law*, 4th edition (London: Sweet & Maxwell, 1991), p. 882. See also: Ian Brownlie, *International Law and the Use of Force by States* (Oxford: The Clarendon Press, 1963), p. 335; and Leland M. Goodrich and Edvard Hambro, *Charter of the United Nations: Commentary and Documents*, 2nd edition (Boston: World Peace Foundation, 1949), p. 281.

15 Cf. Hans Kelsen, *The Law of the United Nations: A Critical Analysis of its Fundamental Problems* (London: Stevens & Sons, 1950), p. 756.

16 Cf. *Reparation for Injuries Suffered in the Service of the United Nations* Case, *ICJ Reports* 1949, p. 174; and *Certain Expenses of the United Nations* Case, *ICJ Reports* 1962, p. 151.

17 On the definition of 'subsidiary organ', see Hans Kelsen, *The Law of the United Nations*, pp. 138 *et seq.* and 149 *et seq.*

18 Respectively, Security Council Resolutions: 1511 of 27 June 1950; 221 of 9 April 1966; and 678 of 29 November 1990.

19 Cf. Harris regarding Rhodesia, p. 882.

20 L.M. Goodrich, 'Korea: Collective Measures Against Aggression', *International Conciliation*, no. 494, October 1953, p. 169.

21 Burns H. Weston, 'Security Council Resolution 678 and Persian Gulf Decision Making: Precarious Legitimacy', *American Journal of International Law*, vol. 85, no. 3, July 1991, pp. 516–535. Also cf. José E. Alvarez, 'The Once and Future Security Council', *The Washington Quarterly*, vol. 18, no. 2, Spring 1995, pp. 5–20.

22 Caspar Weinberger, 'The uses of military power', speech to the National Press Club, Washington, DC, 28 November 1984.

23 Cf. Sterling D. Sessions and Carl R. Jones, *Interoperability: A Desert Storm Case Study* (Washington, DC: Institute for National Strategic Studies, National Defense University, 1993).

24 The French 'Opération Turquoise' in Rwanda was authorized by Security Council Resolution 929 of 22 June 1994; and the US invasion of Haiti was deployed pursuant to Resolution 940 of 31 July 1994, passed in exchange for acceptance of Russian-led Commonwealth of Independent States (CIS) operations in Abkhazia by Resolution 937 of 21 July 1994.

25 See for instance, United Kingdom Staff College, Camberley, *Quadripartite Study on Peace Support Operations in Situations of Chaos* (Camberley: UK Staff College, April 1993), p. 35 and figures 2 and 3.

26 'Supplement to an Agenda for Peace: Position Paper of the Secretary-General on the Occasion of the Fiftieth Anniversary of the United Nations', UN Doc. A/50/60 and S/1995/1 of 3 January 1995, para. 1.

27 Cf. Giandomenico Picco, 'The U.N. and the Use of Force: Leave the Secretary-General Out of It', *Foreign Affairs*, vol. 73, no. 5, September/October 1994, pp. 14–18.

28 Cf. S.L. Arnold and David T. Stahl, 'A Power Projection Army in Operations Other Than War', *Parameters*, vol. XXIII, no. 4, Winter 1993–1994, pp. 4–26.

29 'Supplement', para. 36.

30 *Ibid.*, para. 8–22 and 33–36.

31 *Ibid.*, para. 35.

32 On the PDD process, see Colonel James P. Terry, 'The Evolving U.S. Policy For Peace Operations', *Southern Illinois University Law Journal*, vol. 19, Fall 1994, pp. 119–129; and Donald C.F. Daniel, 'The United States', in Trevor Findlay, ed., *Challenges for the New Peacekeepers* (Stockholm/Oxford: Stockholm International Peace Research Institute/Oxford University Press, 1996), pp. 85–98.

33 On the relationship of Powell to the development of the Weinberger principles, see James Kitfield, *Prodigal Soldiers* (New York: Simon & Schuster, 1995), pp. 268–270.

34 John F. Hillen III, 'Peacekeeping Is Hell: America Unlearns the Lessons of Vietnam', *Policy Review*, no. 66, Fall 1993, pp. 36–39.

35 On the limits of military force, see Robert S. McNamara, *In Retrospect: The Tragedy and Lessons of Vietnam* (New York: Times Books, 1995), pp. 330–332.

36 Quoted in *Financial Times*, 28 February 1995.

37 Cf. the views in: Bob Dole, 'Peacekeepers and Politics', *New York Times*, 24 January 1994, p. A15, and Warren Christopher and William J. Perry, 'Foreign Policy, Hamstrung', *New York Times*, 13 February 1995, p. A19. See also, David Scheffer, 'Problems and Prospects for UN Peacekeeping', *Proceedings of the American Society of International Law 1995*, pp. 286–288.

38 See further his *Croire et Oser: Chronique de Sarajevo* (Paris: Grasset, 1993).

39 Cf. the work of Ken Menkhaus, including for instance, 'International Peacebuilding and the Dynamics of Local and National Reconciliation in Somalia', in Walter Clarke and Jeffrey Herbst, eds, *Learning from Somalia: The Lessons of Armed Humanitarian Intervention* (Boulder, CO: Westview Press, 1997), pp. 42–63.

40 I.M. Lewis, 'Misunderstanding the Somali Crisis', *Anthropology Today*, vol. 9, no. 4, August 1993, p. 1. Cf. his classic works on Somali social organization: *A Pastoral Democracy* (New York: Holmes and Meier, 1982) and *A Modern History of Somalia* (Boulder, CO: Westview Press, 1988). Also see his recent affirmation of this view in *Blood and Bone: The Call of Kinship in Somali Society* (Lawrenceville, NJ: The Red Sea Press, 1994), pp. 233–234 and generally.

41 Abdi Ismail Samatar, 'Destruction of State and Society in Somalia: Beyond the Tribal Convention', *The Journal of Modern African Studies*, vol. 30, no. 4, December 1992, p. 625. For a recent 'deconstruction' of Somali history along similar lines, see Ali Jimale Ahmed, ed., *The Invention of Somalia* (Lawrenceville, NJ: The Red Sea Press, 1995).

42 Captain Sir Richard F. Burton, *First Footsteps in East Africa* (New York: Dover Publications, 1987; first edition: London, 1856), vol. I, p. 88.

43 Quoted in Andrew S. Natsios, 'Food Through Force: Humanitarian Intervention and U.S. Policy', *The Washington Quarterly*, vol. 17, no. 1, Winter 1994, p. 136.

44 This and the following quotes are from Samatar, p. 630 *et seq.*

45 On the role of international law in this process, see Siba N'Zatioula Grovogui, *Sovereigns, Quasi Sovereigns, and Africans* (Minneapolis, MN: University of Minnesota Press, 1996).

46 Samatar, pp. 632–633.

47 See further, Anna Simons, *Networks of Dissolution: Somalia Undone* (Boulder, CO: Westview Press, 1995), pt 3.

48 Samatar, p. 633; and see further pp. 634–638.

49 *Ibid.*, p. 635.

50 For a literary but particularly illustrative account of this process, see Nuruddin Farah's trilogy, *Variations on the Theme of an African Dictatorship*: Bk 1, *Sweet and Sour Milk*, St Paul, MN: Graywolf Press, 1992 (first published: London; Exeter, NH: Heinemann Educational Books, African Writers Series 226, 1979); Bk 2, *Sardines*, (London; Exeter,

NH: Heinemann, 1981, AWS 252; Bk 3, *Close Sesame: A Novel* (London; New York: Allison & Busby, 1983).

51 See further, Samuel M. Makinda, *Security in the Horn of Africa*, Adelphi Paper No. 269 (London: International Institute for Strategic Studies and Brassey's, 1992), particularly pp. 24–37; and *Seeking Peace from Chaos: Humanitarian Intervention in Somalia* (Boulder, CO: International Peace Academy and Lynne Rienner Publishers, 1993). The six clan families of Somalia are the Dir, Issaq, Darod, Hawiye, Digil and Rahanwein.

52 See further on UNOSOM I, Mohamed Sahnoun, *Somalia: The Missed Opportunities* (Washington, DC: United States Institute of Peace, 1994).

53 See further on UNITAF, John L. Hirsch and Robert B. Oakley, *Somalia and Operation Restore Hope: Reflections on Peacemaking and Peacekeeping* (Washington, DC: United States Institute of Peace Press, 1995).

54 Cf. Louise Doswald-Beck, 'The Legal Validity of Military Intervention by Invitation of the Government', *British Year Book of International Law*, vol. 56, 1985, p. 189.

55 Now see Kofi Annan's refreshingly heretical treatment of 'inducing consent' in his 'Challenges of the New Peacekeeping', in Olara A. Otunnu and Michael W. Doyle, eds, *Peacemaking and Peacekeeping for the New Century* (Lanham, MD: Rowman & Littlefield Publishers, 1998), pp. 172–177.

56 See further, N.D. White, *Keeping the Peace: The United Nations and the Maintenance of International Peace and Security* (Manchester: Manchester University Press, 1993), pp. 38–49.

57 Africa Watch, 'Somalia Beyond the Warlords: The Need for a Verdict on Human Rights Abuses', *News From Africa Watch*, vol. V, no. 2, 7 March 1993, pp. 13–20; Amnesty International, 'Somalia: Update on a Disaster – Proposals for Human Rights', AI Doc. AFR 52/01/93 of 30 April 1993; and Amnesty International, 'Peace-Keeping and Human Rights', AI Doc. IOR 40/01/94 of January 1994, pp. 18–21.

58 AI Doc. IOR 40/01/94, pp. 29–34.

59 UNOSOM II Office of the Spokesman, *UNOSOM II Weekly Review*, Issue 2, 30 September 1993, p. 5.

60 The Hon. Enoch Dumbutshena, 'Report on Eight (8) Somali Detainees', January 1994 (unpublished internal report). The report recommended the release of SNA members or those suspected of supporting SNA activities held in detention for several months: Osman Hassan Ali (Atto); Omar Salad; Mohamed Hassan Awale; Abdikarim Duale Gelle; Mohamud Salad Farah; Ali Abdualla Abdi; Ali Hussein Mohamoud Isse; and Mohamed Mohamoud Afrah Awale.

61 Security Council Resolution 425 of 19 March 1978.

62 UN Doc. S/25354 of 3 March 1993.

63 Cf. *Somalia (A Republic)* v. *Woodhouse Drake and Carey (Suisse) SA, All England Law Reports*, no. 1, 1993, p. 371. While this case concerned the definition of the 'Government of Somalia', it was not disputed that Somalia continued to exist as a recognized state.

64 Brigadier-General Mohammed Farah Aidid, 'Democracy in Somalia – Its Roots and its Future Scenario', in Mohammed Farah Aidid and Satya Pal Ruhela, eds, *The Preferred Future Development in Somalia* (New Delhi: Vikas Publishing House Pvt, 1993), pp. 12–25. The following quotes are from pp. 24 and 20, respectively.

65 Joshua Hammer; *Newsweek*, 13 March 1995, p. 31.

66 Burton, *First Footsteps in East Africa*, pp. 77–78.

67 S/25354, para. 56–69.

68 Keith B. Richburg, 'U.N. Takes Command of Troops in Somalia' and 'Somali Police Force Back on the Beat', *Washington Post*, 5 and 17 May 1993, pp. A23 and A15, respectively.

69 Cf. Major Michael J. Kelly, *Peace Operations: Tackling the Military Legal and Policy Challenges* (Canberra: Australian Government Publishing Service, 1997), ch. 9.

70 The list of troop-contributors for UNOSOM II recommended by the Secretary-General and approved by the Security Council included: Argentina, Australia, Bangladesh, Belgium, Botswana, Egypt, France, Germany, Greece, Hungary, India, Indonesia, Ireland, Italy, Jordan, Malaysia, Morocco, Namibia, New Zealand, Nigeria, Norway, Pakistan, Republic of Korea, Romania, Saudi Arabia, Sweden, Tunisia, Turkey, Uganda, United Arab Emirates, United States, Zambia and Zimbabwe.

71 UN Doc. S/25354, para. 92.

72 See further, UN Doc. S/25168 of 26 January 1993, Annex III.

73 *Ibid.*, Annex II.

74 Cf. UN Doc. S/26317 of 17 August 1993, para. 23–42.

75 Interview with UNOSOM II Office of Political Affairs, Mogadishu, February 1994.

76 Cf. Mohamed Sahnoun, *The Missed Opportunities*, pp. 25–27.

77 Interview with UNOSOM II Office of Political Affairs, Mogadishu, February 1994.

78 Interview with General Mohammed Farah Aidid by Åge Eknes, Serena Hotel, Nairobi, 20 February 1994.

7 PEACE-MAINTENANCE IN DIVIDED WESTERN SAHARA

1 See further generally: Robert Taber, *The War of the Flea* (London: Paladin, 1970); T.E. Lawrence, *Seven Pillars of Wisdom* (New York: Doubleday & Co., 1935); V.I. Lenin, *What is to be Done?* (London: Penguin Classics, 1988), ch. IV; Mao Tse-Tung, *On Guerrilla Warfare* (New York: Praeger Publishers, 1961); Vo Nguyen Giap, *People's War, People's Army*, 2nd edition (Hanoi: Foreign Languages Publishing House, 1974); and Ernesto Che Guevara, *Guerrilla Warfare* (London: University of Nebraska Press, 1985).

2 Cf. United Kingdom Ministry of Defence, *Land Operations*, vol. 3, *Counter-Revolutionary Operations* (London: Ministry of Defence, 1977).

3 Cf. Anthony G. Pazzanita, 'Morocco versus Polisario: A Political Interpretation', *The Journal of Modern African Studies*, vol. 32, no. 2, 1994, pp. 265–278.

4 For MINURSO's timetable and results compared, see William J. Durch, 'Building on Sand: UN Peacekeeping in the Western Sahara', *International Security*, vol. 17, no. 4, Spring 1993, pp. 162–163.

5 UN Doc. S/23662 of 28 February 1992. Strength figures declined after this date.

6 George A. Pickart, *The Western Sahara: The Referendum Process in Danger*, A Staff Report to the Committee on Foreign Relations of the United States Senate, January 1992 (Washington: U.S. Government Printing Office, 1992); and Jarat Chopra, 'The Absence of War and Peace in the Western Sahara', Testimony before the Committee on Foreign Relations of the United States Senate, Subcommittee on African Affairs, Hearing on 'UN Peacekeeping in Africa: The Western Sahara and Somalia, 1 October 1992.'

7 The overall implementation plan for MINURSO appears in UN Docs. S/21360 of 18 June 1990 and S/22464 of 19 April 1991.

8 See further the Senate debate on Amendment no. 3334 in *Congressional Record*, 30 September 1992, pp. S15807–S15811.

9 Cf. M.N. Shaw, *Title to Territory in Africa* (Oxford: Clarendon Press, 1986), ch. 3; Heather A. Wilson, *International Law and the Use of Force by National Liberation Movements* (Oxford: Clarendon Press, 1988), pp. 79–88; and Steven R. Ratner, 'Drawing a Better Line: *Uti Possidetis* and the Borders of New States', *American Journal of International Law*, vol. 90, no. 4, October 1996, pp. 622–623.

10 *Western Sahara* Case, Advisory Opinion, *ICJ Reports* 1975, para. 165. For a view critical of the Court's decision, see George Joffé, 'The Conflict in the Western Sahara', in Oliver Furley, ed., *Conflict in Africa* (London: Tauris Publishers, 1995), pp. 110–133.

11 See further. Thomas M. Franck, 'The Stealing of the Sahara', *American Journal of International Law*, vol. 70, no. 4, October 1976, pp. 694–721; and 'The Theory and Practice of Decolonization: the Western Sahara Case', in Richard Lawless and Laila Monahan, eds, *War and Refugees: The Western Sahara Conflict* (London: Pinter Publishers, 1987), pp. 9–15.

12 On opposing views of the war, see Tony Hodges, *Western Sahara: The Roots of a Desert War* (Westport, CT: Lawrence Hill Publishers, 1983), and John Damis, *Conflict in Northwest Africa: The Western Sahara Dispute* (Stanford, CA: Hoover Institution Press, 1983).

13 David Seddon, 'Morocco at War', in Lawless and Monahan, *War and Refugees*, pp. 98–136.

14 OAU Doc. AHG/IMP.C/WS/RPT (I) Rev. 1 of 24–26 August 1981, p. 10.

15 UN Doc. S/21360 of 18 June 1990, para. 61.

16 UN Doc. S/22464 of 19 April 1991, para. 20.

17 UN Doc. S/23299 of 19 December 1991, Annex.

18 For the details of this criticism, see Teresa K. Smith de Cherif, 'Western Sahara: A Moroccan-style Election?' *Review of African Political Economy*, no. 58, November 1993, p. 102.

19 Javier Pérez de Cuéllar, *Pilgrimage for Peace: A Secretary-General's Memoir* (New York: St Martin's Press, 1997), p. 352.

20 Cf. David Seddon, 'Western Sahara Referendum Sabotaged', *Review of African Political Economy*, no. 53, March 1992, pp. 101–104; and 'Western Sahara: Postponement of Referendum', *Keesing's Record of World Events*, December 1991, pp. 38692–38693.

21 Smith de Cherif, 'Western Sahara', pp. 99–105.

22 UN Doc. S/25170 of 26 January 1993.

23 UN Doc. S/26797 of 24 November 1993.

24 'Statement of Ambassador Frank Ruddy' before the US House of Representatives, Review of United Nations Operations and Peacekeeping, Committee on Appropriations, Subcommittee on the Departments of Commerce, Justice, State, and the Judiciary and Related Agencies, Washington, DC, 25 January 1995.

25 Editorial, 'Rough and Ruddy', *The Washington Times*, 13 March 1995, p. A14.

26 Chris Hedges, 'Morocco is Accused of Interfering in Affairs of a Smaller Desert Neighbor', *New York Times*, 5 March 1995, p. 8.

27 Cf. Jane Kokan, 'Road to Saharan Freedom Vote is Way Off Track', *Guardian*, 25 February 1995, p. 16.

28 UN Doc. A/49/884 of 5 April 1995, Annex.

29 Cf. Gary Abramson, 'New UN Office Investigates Charges of Peacemaking Gone Awry', *Associated Press*, 23 March 1995.

30 Cf. UN Doc. S/1995/404 of 19 May 1995.

31 UNSC Res. 1056 of 29 May 1996.

32 UN Doc. S/1996/43 of 19 January 1996, para. 16.

33 Yahia H. Zoubir, 'Origins and Development of the Conflict in the Western Sahara', in Yahia H. Zoubir and Daniel Volman, eds, *International Dimensions of the Western Sahara Conflict* (Westport, CT: Praeger Publishers, 1993), p. 9.

34 *Ibid.*

35 On the role of outside powers, see further Benjamin Rivlin, *The Western Sahara: Towards a Referendum? The UN Political Process at Work* (New York: Ralph Bunche Institute on the United Nations, 1994), pp. 7–11.

36 UN Doc. S/1996/43 of 19 January 1996, paras. 11 and 31.

37 UNSC Resolution 1042 of 31 January 1996, para. 6.

38 This was presented to the UN General Assembly on 14 October 1993 (cf. UN Press Release GA/SPD/4). It was subsequently published as 'a peace proposal' in Jarat Chopra, *United Nations Determination of the Western Saharan Self* (Oslo: Norwegian Institute of International Affairs, 1994), pp. 96–97.

39 See further UN Press Release GA/SPD/84.

40 The full text of this speech, as well as the presentations before the UN General Assembly cited above, appear on-line (http://heiwww.unige.ch/arso/).

41 For the *modus operandi* of the 'Commission of Inquiry established pursuant to resolution 885 (1993) to investigate armed attacks on UNOSOM II personnel', see UN Doc. S/1994/653 of 1 June 1994.

42 Steven R. Ratner, 'The Cambodian Settlement Agreements', *American Journal of International Law*, vol. 87, no. 1, January 1993, pp. 9–12; and Michael W. Doyle, *UN Peacekeeping in Cambodia: UNTAC's Civil Mandate* (Boulder, CO: Lynne Rienner Publishers, 1995), pp. 26–27.

43 Bertrand de Rossanet, *Peacemaking and Peacekeeping in Yugoslavia* (The Hague: Kluwer Law International, 1996), ch. 1 and generally.

44 Cf. Mark Levine, 'Peacemaking in El Salvador', in Michael W. Doyle, Ian Johnstone, and Robert C. Orr, eds, *Keeping the Peace: Multidimensional UN Operations in Cambodia and El Salvador* (Cambridge: Cambridge University Press, 1997), pp. 248–253; Robert Maguire *et al.*, *Haiti Held Hostage: International Responses to the Quest for Nationhood, 1986–1996* (Providence, RI: Thomas J. Watson Jr Institute for International Studies and the United Nations University, 1996), p. 40 and generally pp. 31–41; and Christopher Louise, 'MINUGUA's Peacebuilding Mandate in Western Guatemala', *International Peacekeeping*, vol. 4, no. 2, Summer 1997, pp. 50–73.

45 Cf. Pavel K. Baev, 'Russia's Peacekeeping in the Caucasus', in Espen Barth Eide, ed., *Peacekeeping in Europe* (Oslo: Norwegian Institute of International Affairs, 1995), pp. 95–110; and Dmitriy Trenin, 'Russia', in Trevor Findlay, ed., *Challenges for the New Peacekeepers* (Stockholm/Oxford: Stockholm International Peace Research Institute/Oxford University Press, 1996), pp. 77–82.

46 Cf. Bruce George *et al.*, 'Coalition Diplomacy', in Bruce W. Watson, Bruce George and Peter Tsouras, eds, *Military Lessons of the Gulf War* (London: Greenhill Books, 1993), pp. 19–30; and Gérard Prunier, 'The Experience of European Armies in Operation Restore Hope', in Walter Clarke and Jeffrey Herbst, *Learning From Somalia: The Lessons of Armed Humanitarian Intervention* (Boulder, CO: Westview Press, 1997), pp. 135–147.

47 See further Gilonne d'Origny, 'Western Sahara's Difficult Path', *The Washington Times*, 3 July 1997, p. A17.

48 Permanent Observer Mission of the Organization of African Unity to the United Nations, 'Western Sahara: The Way Forward', New York, January 1997.

49 Fatemeh Ziai, *Keeping it Secret: The United Nations Operation in the Western Sahara* (New York: Human Rights Watch, 1995), pp. 8–9.

50 CLAIHR, 'Western Sahara: A Crisis Unresolved', written submission to the Sub-Committee on Human Sustainable Development of the Standing Committee on Foreign Affairs and International Trade, Ottawa, March 1997; and 'Western Sahara Initiative: Phase I Report', June 1997.

51 See UN Press Release GA/SPD/84 of 7 October 1996; as well as 'UN Representative Rejects Charges of Colonialism in Western Sahara', BBC Summary of World Broadcasts, 22 October 1996 (source: *L'Opinion*, Rabat, 10 October).

52 UN Doc. A/C.4/51/L.4 of 18 October 1996.

53 UN Doc. S/1997/166 of 27 February 1997, para. 5 and 16, respectively.

54 UN Doc. S/1997/208 of 10 March 1997, p. 3.

55 See further, UN Doc. S/1997/358 of 5 May 1997.

56 Roula Khalaf, 'Baker Tries to Untie Western Sahara Knot', *Financial Times*, 23 April 1997, p. 4; Roula Khalaf, 'Deserted in the "Desert of Deserts",' *Financial Times*, 29 April 1997, p. 6; Adela Gooch, 'Baker Renews Hope of End to Bitter Exile',*Guardian*, 29 April 1997, p. 8; Robert Fisk, 'UN Dove Brings Hope to Desert's Lost Tribe',*The Independent*, 29 April 1997, p. 8, p. 16; Robert Fisk, 'Prisoners Trapped in the War that Time Forgot', *The Independent*, 30 April 1997, p. 17; Robert Fisk, 'Becalmed on the Sahara's Ocean of Heat', *The Independent*, 1 May 1997, p. 18; Michael Binyon, 'Baker Embarks on UN Tour to Prevent New Desert Conflict',*The Times*, 2 May 1997, p. 17; Lara Marlowe, UN Envoy Meets POLISARIO for Talks on Autonomy for Sahrawi People', *The Irish Times*, 29 April 1997, p. 12; Lara Marlowe, 'Our Team Can't Smell Sand Yet to Get Home', *The Irish Times*, 30 April 1997, p. 12; and Lara Marlowe, 'Where the Women Still Wait for the Chance to Go Home', *The Irish Times*, 1 May 1997, p. 10.
57 Roula Khalaf, 'Sahara Compromise Rejected by Morocco', *Financial Times*, 16 May 1997, p. 7.
58 James A. Baker, III, *The Politics of Diplomacy: Revolution War and Peace, 1989–1992* (New York: G.P. Putnam's Sons, 1995), p. 11.
59 See for instance, Roula Khalaf, 'Date for Talks on Western Sahara', *Financial Times*, 13 June 1997, p. 6; as opposed to Ian Black, 'Sands Shift in a Forgotten War', *Guardian*, 11 June 1997, p. 17.
60 See further, UN Doc. S/1997/742 of 24 September 1997, Annexes I, II and III.
61 UN Doc. S/1997/882 of 13 November 1997, para. 50.
62 See further UN Doc. S/1998/316 of 13 April 1998. Also cf. Gilonne d'Origny, 'The Western Sahara Peace Plan in the Balance', *Middle East International*, 13 February 1998, pp. 17–19; and Michael Bhatia, 'Western Sahara: Humanitarian Success, Political Failure?', *Crosslines Global Report*, vol. 6, no. 1, issue 33, May/June 1998, pp. 51–55.

8 PEACE-MAINTENANCE PUZZLES

1 Cf. Duane Bratt, 'Rebuilding Fractured Societies', *Security Dialogue*, vol. 28, no. 2, June 1997, pp. 173–176; and Riccardo Cappelli, 'Peace-Maintenance is Not the Response', *Security Dialogue*, vol. 28, no. 4, December 1997, pp. 509–510.
2 Cf. Gideon Rose, 'The Exit Strategy Delusion', *Foreign Affairs*, vol. 77, no. 1, January/February 1998, pp. 56–67.
3 See further Antonio Donini, 'Asserting Humanitarianism in Peace-Maintenance', *Global Governance*, vol. 4 no. 1, January–March 1998, pp. 87–91; and David Shearer, *Private Armies and Military Intervention*, Adelphi Paper no. 316 (London: International Institute for Strategic Studies, 1998).
4 See particularly Paul Johnson, 'Colonialism's Back – And Not a Moment Too Soon', *New York Times Magazine*, 18 April 1993, p. F22.
5 Arrayed on the one side are, for instance: Charles Krauthammer, 'Trusteeship for Somalia; An Old Colonial Idea Whose Time Has Come Again', *The Washington Post*, 9 October 1992, p. A27; Claudio G. Segre, 'Colonialism May Be Worth Bringing Back', *The Philadelphia Inquirer*, 3 August 1993, p. A7; Ali A. Mazrui, 'Decaying Parts of Africa Need Benign Colonization', *International Herald Tribune*, 4 August 1994, p. 6; and William Pfaff, 'A New Colonialism? Europe Must Go Back into Africa', *Foreign Affairs*, vol. 74, no. 1, January–February 1995, pp. 2–6. Arrayed on the other side are, for instance: Jon H. Sylvester, 'Sub-Saharan Africa: Economic Stagnation, Political Disintegration, and the Specter of Recolonization', *Loyola of Los Angeles Law Review*, vol. 27, 1994, pp. 1299–1326; Ruth E. Gordon, 'Some Legal Problems with

Trusteeship', *Cornell International Law Journal*, vol. 28, no. 2, Spring 1995, pp. 301–347; Timothy M. Shaw and Clement E. Adibe, 'Africa and Global Developments in the Twenty-first Century', *International Journal*, vol. 51, no. 1, Winter 1995–96, pp. 1–26; Neta C. Crawford, 'Imag(in)ing Africa', *Press/Politics*, vol. 1, no. 2, 1996, pp. 30–44; and Henry J. Richardson III, 'Failed States', Self Determination, and Preventative Diplomacy: Colonialist Nostalgia and Democratic Expectations', *Temple International and Comparative Law Journal*, vol. 10, spring 1996, pp. 1–78.

6 José Ramos-Horta, *Funu: The Unfinished Saga of East Timor* (Lawrenceville, NJ: The Red Sea Press, 1987, 1996 printing), p. 160.

7 Cf. James Mayall, 'Introduction', in James Mayall, ed., *The New Interventionism, 1991–1994: United Nations experience in Cambodia, former Yugoslavia and Somalia* (Cambridge: Cambridge University Press, 1996), pp. 23–24.

Select bibliography

Abi-Saab, Georges, *The United Nations Operation in the Congo, 1960–1964* (Oxford: Oxford University Press, 1978).

Adibe, Clement E., 'Accepting External Authority in Peace-Maintenance', *Global Governance*, vol. 4, no. 1, January–March 1998, pp. 112–118.

Africa Watch, 'Somalia Beyond the Warlords: The Need for a Verdict on Human Rights Abuses', *News From Africa Watch*, vol. V, no. 2, 7 March 1993, 28 pp.

Ahmed, Ali Jimale, ed., *The Invention of Somalia* (Lawrenceville, NJ: The Red Sea Press, 1995).

Aidid, Mohammed Farah, and Satya Pal Ruhela, eds, *The Preferred Future Development in Somalia* (New Delhi: Vikas Publishing House Pvt, 1993).

Akhavan, Payam, 'Enforcement of the Genocide Convention through the Advisory Opinion Jurisdiction of the International Court of Justice', *Human Rights Law Journal*, vol. 12, no. 8–9, 30 September 1991, pp. 285–299.

——'Punishing War Crimes in the Former Yugoslavia: A Critical Juncture for the New World Order', *Human Rights Quarterly*, vol. 15, no. 2, May 1993, pp. 262–289.

——'The International Criminal Tribunal for Rwanda: The Politics and Pragmatics of Punishment', *American Journal of International Law*, vol. 90, no. 3, July 1996, pp. 501–510.

Allen, Beverly, *Rape Warfare: The Hidden Genocide in Bosnia-Herzegovina and Croatia* (Minneapolis: University of Minnesota Press, 1996).

Allott, Philip, *Eunomia: New Order for a New World* (Oxford: Oxford University Press, 1990).

Almond, Gabriel A., and James S. Coleman, eds, *The Politics of the Developing Areas* (Princeton, NJ: Princeton University Press, 1960).

Almond, Gabriel A., and G. Bingham Powell, Jr, *Comparative Politics: A Developmental Approach* (Boston: Little, Brown, 1966).

Alvarez, José E., 'The Once and Future Security Council', *The Washington Quarterly*, vol. 18, no. 2, Spring 1995, pp. 5–20.

——'Nuremberg Revisited: The *Tadic* Case', *European Journal of International Law*, vol. 7, no. 2, 1996, pp. 245–264.

American Bar Association Special Task Force on War Crimes in the Former Yugoslavia, *Report on the International Tribunal to Adjudicate War Crimes Committed in the Former Yugoslavia* (Chicago, IL: American Bar Association, 1993).

Amin, Samir, *Accumulation on a World Scale: A Critique of the Theory of Underdevelopment* (New York: Monthly Review Press, 1974).

Amnesty International, 'Somalia: Update on a Disaster – Proposals for Human Rights', AI Doc. AFR 52/01/93 of 30 April 1993.

———*Peace-Keeping and Human Rights* (London: AI Index: IOR 40/01/94, January 1994).

Annan, Kofi, 'Renewing the United Nations: Programme for Reform', UN Doc. A/51/1950 of 16 July 1997.

Armstrong, Richard N., *Red Army Legacies: Essays on Forces, Capabilities, and Personalities* (Atglen, PA: Schiffer Publishing, 1995).

Arnold, S.L., and David T. Stahl, 'A Power Projection Army in Operations Other Than War', *Parameters*, vol. XXIII, no. 4, Winter 1993–94, pp. 4–26.

Arnson, Cynthia, and David Holiday, 'El Salvador – Peace and Human Rights: Successes and Shortcomings of the United Nations Observer Mission in El Salvador (ONUSAL)', *News From Americas Watch*, vol. IV, no. 8, 2 September 1992, 26pp.

Axelrod, Robert, *The Evolution of Co-operation* (London: Penguin Books, 1984).

Azimi, Nassrine, ed., *The United Nations Transitional Authority in Cambodia (UNTAC): Debriefing and Lessons* (The Hague: Kluwer Law International, 1995).

———ed., *The Role and Functions of Civilian Police in United Nations Peace-Keeping Operations: Debriefing and Lessons* (The Hague: Kluwer Law International, 1996).

———ed., *Humanitarian Action and Peace-Keeping Operations: Debriefing and Lessons* (The Hague: Kluwer Law International, 1997).

Bairoch, Paul, *Economics and World History: Myths and Paradoxes* (Chicago: University of Chicago Press, 1995).

Baker, James A., III, *The Politics of Diplomacy: Revolution, War and Peace, 1989–1992* (New York: G.P. Putnam's Sons, 1995).

Baran, Paul, *The Political Economy of Growth* (New York: Monthly Review Press, 1957).

Baranyi, Stephen, and Liisa North, *Stretching the Limits of the Possible: United Nations Peace-keeping in Central America* (Ottawa: Canadian Centre for Global Security, 1992).

Bassiouni, M. Cherif, *A Draft International Criminal Code and Draft Statute for an International Criminal Tribunal* (Boston: Martinus Nijhoff, 1987).

Bekker, Peter H.F., and Paul C. Szasz, 'Application of the Convention on the Prevention and Punishment of the Crime of Genocide', *American Journal of International Law*, vol. 91, no. 1, January 1997, pp. 121–126.

Berger, Peter L., *The Capitalist Revolution* (New York: Basic Books, 1986).

Betts, Richard K., 'The Delusion of Impartial Intervention', *Foreign Affairs*, vol. 73, no. 6, November/December 1994, pp. 20–33.

Bhatia, Michael, 'Western Sahara: Humanitarian Success, Political Failure?, *Crosslines Global Report*, vol. 6, no. 1, May/June 1998, pp. 51–55.

Bloom, Evan T., 'Protecting Peacekeepers: The Convention on the Safety of United Nations and Associated Personnel', *American Journal of International Law*, vol. 89, no. 3, July 1995, pp. 621–631.

Boulden, Jane, 'Prometheus Unborn: The History of the Military Staff Committee', *Aurora Papers*, no. 19, Canadian Centre for Global Security, August 1993.

Bourloyannis-Vrailas, M.-Christiane, 'The Convention on the Safety of United Nations and Associated Personnel', *International and Comparative Law Quarterly*, vol. 44, part III, July 1995, pp. 560–590.

Boutros-Ghali, Boutros, 'Supplement to an Agenda for Peace: Position Paper of the Secretary-General on the Occasion of the Fiftieth Anniversary of the United Nations', UN Doc. A/50/60 and S/1995/1 of 3 January 1995.

———*An Agenda for Development 1995* (New York: United Nations Department of Public Information, 1995).

Bowett, D.W., *United Nations Forces* (London: Stevens & Sons, 1964).

——'Reprisals Involving Recourse to Armed Force', *American Journal of International Law*, vol. 66, no. 1, January 1972, pp. 1–36.

Brandt, Willy, *et al.*, *North–South, A Programme for Survival: Report of the Independent Commission on International Development Issues* (Cambridge, MA: MIT Press, 1980).

Bratt, Duane, 'Rebuilding Fractured Societies', *Security Dialogue*, vol. 28, no. 2, June 1997, pp. 173–176.

Brown, Michael Barratt, *Models in Political Economy* (London: Penguin Books, 1995).

Brownlie, Ian, *International Law and the Use of Force by States* (Oxford: The Clarendon Press, 1963).

Bull, Hedley, *The Anarchical Society: A Study of Order in World Politics* (London: Macmillan Press, 1977).

Burton, Captain Sir Richard F., *First Footsteps in East Africa* (New York: Dover Publications, 1987; first edition: London, 1856).

Cambridge Review of International Affairs, vol. X, no. 2, Winter/Spring 1997.

Canada, Report of the Government of, *Towards a Rapid Reaction Capability for the United Nations* (Ottawa: The Government of Canada, 1995).

Canadian Lawyers Association for International Human Rights, 'Western Sahara: A Crisis Unresolved', written submission to the Sub-Committee on Human Sustainable Development of the Standing Committee on Foreign Affairs and International Trade, Ottawa, Canada, March 1997.

Cappelli, Riccardo, 'Peace-Maintenance is Not the Response', *Security Dialogue*, vol. 28, no. 4, December 1997, pp. 509–510.

Carbonnier, Giles, *Conflict, Postwar Rebuilding and the Economy: A Critical Review of the Literature* (Geneva: War-torn Societies Project, 1998).

Carothers, Thomas, 'The Rule of Law Revival', *Foreign Affairs*, vol. 77, no. 2, March/April 1998, pp. 95–106.

Chopra, Jarat, ed., 'United Nations Peace-Keeping', special issue *Survival*, vol. XXXII, no. 3, May/June 1990, pp. 195–288.

——'The Absence of War and Peace in the Western Sahara', Testimony before the Committee on Foreign Relations of the United States Senate, Subcommittee on African Affairs, Hearing on 'UN Peacekeeping in Africa: The Western Sahara and Somalia, 1 October 1992'.

——*United Nations Authority in Cambodia* (Providence, RI: Thomas J. Watson Jr Institute for International Studies, 1994).

——*United Nations Determination of the Western Saharan Self* (Oslo: Norwegian Institute of International Affairs, 1994).

——'Commitment to Peace-Maintenance', in *Globalism and Regionalism: Options for the 21st Century* (Ottawa: Canadian Council on International Law, 1995), pp. 28–35.

——'Fighting for Truth at the UN', *Crosslines Global Report*, vol. 4, no. 8, issue 26, November 1996, pp. 7–9.

Chopra, Jarat, John Mackinlay and Larry Minear, *Report on the Cambodian Peace Process* (Oslo: Norwegian Institute of International Affairs, 1993).

Chopra, Jarat, and Thomas G. Weiss, 'Sovereignty is No Longer Sacrosanct: Codifying Humanitarian Intervention', *Ethics and International Affairs*, vol. 6, 1992, pp. 95–117.

——'Prospects for Containing Conflict in the Former Second World', *Security Studies*, vol. 4, no. 3, Spring 1995, pp. 552–583.

Clark, Ramsay, *The Fire This Time: U.S. War Crimes In the Gulf* (New York: Thunder's Mouth Press, 1992).

Clarke, Walter S., *Humanitarian Intervention in Somalia Bibliography* (Carlisle, PA: Center of Strategic Leadership, US Army War College, 1995).

Clarke, Walter S., and Robert Gosende, 'The Political Component: The Missing Vital Element in US Intervention Planning', *Paramotors*, vol. 26, no. 3, Autumn 1996, pp. 35–51.

Clarke, Walter, and Jeffrey Herbst, 'Somalia and the Future of Humanitarian Intervention', *Foreign Affairs*, vol. 75, no. 2, March/April 1996, pp. 70–85.

——*Learning From Somalia: The Lessons of Armed Humanitarian Intervention* (Boulder, CO: Westview Press, 1997).

Claude, Inis, *Swords Into Plowshares* (New York: Random House, 1964).

Commission of Inquiry into the Deployment of Canadian Forces to Somalia, *Dishonoured Legacy: The Lessons of the Somalia Affair* (Ottawa: Public Works and Government Services Canada, 1997).

Costa, Gino, 'The United Nations and Reform of the Police in El Salvador', *International Peacekeeping*, vol. 2, no. 3, Autumn 1995, pp. 365–390.

Cousens, Richard P., 'Providing Military Security in Peace-Maintenance', *Global Governance*, vol. 4, no. 1, January–March 1998, pp. 97–105.

Crawford, James, 'The Criteria for Statehood in International Law', *British Year Book of International Law*, vol. 48, 1976–77, pp. 93–182.

——ed., *The Rights of Peoples* (Oxford: Clarendon Press, 1988).

——'The ILC Adopts a Statute for an International Criminal Court', *American Journal of International Law*, vol. 89, no. 2, April 1995, pp. 404–416.

Crawford, Neta C., 'Imag(in)ing Africa', *Press/Politics*, vol. 1, no. 2, 1996, pp. 30–44.

Crocker, Chester A., 'Southern African Peace-Making', *Survival*, vol. XXXII, no. 3, May/June 1990, pp. 221–232.

——*High Noon in Southern Africa: Making Peace in a Rough Neighborhood* (New York: W.W. Norton & Company, 1992).

——'All Aid Is Political', *The New York Times*, 21 November 1996, p. A29.

Damis, John, *Conflict in Northwest Africa: The Western Sahara Dispute* (Stanford, CA: Hoover Institution Press, 1983).

Davidson, Basil, *The Black Man's Burden: Africa and the Curse of the Nation-State* (New York: Times Books, 1992).

Davies, Paul, ed., *The New Physics* (Cambridge: Cambridge University Press, 1990).

de Cuéllar, Javier Pérez, *Pilgrimage for Peace: A Secretary-General's Memoir* (New York: St Martin's Press, 1997).

de Rossanet, Bertrand, *Peacemaking and Peacekeeping in Yugoslavia* (The Hague: Kluwer Law International, 1996).

de Soto, Alvaro, and Graciana del Castillo, 'Obstacles to Peace-Building', *Foreign Policy*, no. 94, Spring 1994, pp. 69–83.

——'Implementation of Comprehensive Peace Agreements: Staying the Course in El Salvador', *Global Governance*, vol. 1, no. 2, May–August 1995, pp. 189–203.

Diehl, Paul F., *International Peacekeeping* (Baltimore, MD: The Johns Hopkins University Press, 1993).

Dobbie, Charles, 'A Concept for Post-Cold War Peacekeeping', *Survival*, vol. 36, no. 3, Autumn 1994, pp. 121–148.

Donini, Antonio, 'Asserting Humanitarianism in Peace-Maintenance', *Global Governance*, vol. 4 no. 1, January–March 1998, pp. 81–96.

Donini, Antonio, Eric Dudley and Ron Ockwell, *Afghanistan: Coordinating in a Fragmented State* (New York: United Nations Department of Humanitarian Affairs, 1996).

d'Origny, Gilonne, 'Western Sahara's Difficult Path', *The Washington Times*, 3 July 1997, p. A17.

——'The Western Sahara Peace Plan in the Balance', *Middle East International*, 13 February 1998, pp. 17–19.

Doswald-Beck, Louise, 'The Legal Validity of Military Intervention by Invitation of the Government', *British Year Book of International Law*, vol. 56, 1985, pp. 189–252.

Doyle, Michael W., *UN Peacekeeping in Cambodia: UNTAC's Civil Mandate* (Boulder, CO: Lynne Rienner Publishers and the International Peace Academy, 1995).

Doyle, Michael W., Ian Johnstone and Robert C. Orr, eds, *Keeping the Peace: Multidimensional UN Operations in Cambodia and El Salvador* (Cambridge: Cambridge University Press, 1997).

Druckman, Daniel, and Paul C. Stern, 'Evaluating Peacekeeping Missions', *Mershon International Studies Review*, vol. 41, supplement 1, May 1997, pp. 151–165.

Durch, William J., 'Building on Sand: UN Peacekeeping in the Western Sahara', *International Security*, vol. 17, no. 4, Spring 1993, pp. 162–163.

——ed., *The Evolution of UN Peacekeeping: Case Studies and Comparative Analysis* (New York: St Martin's Press, 1993).

——ed., *UN Peacekeeping, American Politics, and the Uncivil Wars of the 1990s* (New York: St Martin's Press, 1996).

Eban, Abba, 'The U.N. Idea Revisited', *Foreign Affairs*, vol. 74, no. 5, September/October 1995, pp. 39–55.

Eide, Asbjørn, Allan Rosas and Theodor Meron, 'Combating Lawlessness in Gray Zone Conflicts Through Minimum Humanitarian Standards', *American Journal of International Law*, vol. 89, no. 1, January 1995, pp. 215–223.

Eide, Espen Barth, ed., *Peacekeeping in Europe* (Oslo: Norwegian Institute of International Affairs, 1995).

Eliade, Mircea, *The Myth of the Eternal Return* (Princeton, NJ: Princeton University Press, 1954).

——*The Sacred and the Profane* (New York: Harcourt Brace & Company, 1959).

English, K., and A. Stapleton, *The Human Rights Handbook: A Practical Guide to Monitoring Human Rights* (Essex: Human Rights Centre, October 1995).

Evans, Gareth, *Cooperating for Peace: The Global Agenda for the 1990s and Beyond* (St Leonard's, NSW: Allen & Unwin, 1993).

Fernando, J. Basil, *The Inability to Prosecute: Courts and Human Rights in Cambodia and Sri Lanka* (Hong Kong: Future Asia Link, 1993).

Findlay, Trevor, *Cambodia: The Legacy and Lessons of UNTAC* (Stockholm/Oxford: Stockholm International Peace Research Institute/Oxford University Press, 1995).

——ed., *Challenges for the New Peacekeepers* (Stockholm/Oxford: Stockholm International Peace Research Institute/Oxford University Press, 1996).

Franck, Thomas M., 'The Stealing of the Sahara', *American Journal of International Law*, vol. 70, no. 4, October 1976, pp. 649–741.

——'Tribe, Nation, World: Self-Identification in the Evolving International System', *Ethics and International Affairs*, vol. 11, 1997, pp. 151–169.

Frank, André Gunder, *Capitalism and Underdevelopment in Latin America* (New York: Monthly Review Press, 1969).

Frankfort, Henri, *Kingship and the Gods* (Chicago: University of Chicago Press, 1978).

Gardam, Judith Gail, 'Proportionality and Force in International Law', *American Journal of International Law*, vol. 87, no. 3, July 1993, pp. 391–413.

Gellner, Ernest, *Plough, Sword and Book* (Chicago: University of Chicago Press, 1988).

Giap, Vo Nguyen, *People's War, People's Army*, 2nd edition (Hanoi: Foreign Languages Publishing House, 1974).

Ginifer, Jeremy, ed., *Beyond the Emergency: Development within UN Peace Missions* (London: Frank Cass & Co., 1997).

Goldstone, Judge Richard J., 'The Role and the Work of the International War Crimes Tribunals for the Former Yugoslavia and Rwanda', *International Peace Academy Roundtable Report*, 2 October 1996, 4 pp.

Gomes, Solomon, 'Western Sahara: The Way Forward', Permanent Observer Mission of the Organization of African Unity to the United Nations, New York, January 1997.

Goodrich, Leland. M., 'Korea: Collective Measures Against Aggression', *International Conciliation*, no. 494, October 1953, pp. 131–192.

Goodrich, Leland M., and Edvard Hambro, *Charter of the United Nations: Commentary and Documents*, 2nd edition (Boston: World Peace Foundation, 1949).

Gordon, Ruth E., 'Some Legal Problems with Trusteeship', *Cornell International Law Journal*, vol. 28, no. 2, Spring 1995, pp. 301–347.

——'Saving Failed States: Sometimes a Neocolonialist Notion', *American University Journal of International Law and Policy*, vol. 12, no. 6, 1997, pp. 903–974.

Graybill, Lyn S., 'South Africa's Truth and Reconciliation Commission: Ethical and Theological Perspectives', *Ethics and International Affairs*, vol. 12, 1998, pp. 43–62.

Grovogui, Siba N'Zatioula, *Sovereigns, Quasi Sovereigns, and Africans* (Minneapolis, MN: University of Minnesota Press, 1996).

Guevara, Ernesto Che, *Guerrilla Warfare* (London: University of Nebraska Press, 1985).

Halderman, John W., 'Legal Basis for United Nations Armed Forces', *American Journal of International Law*, vol. 56, no. 4, October 1962, pp. 971–996.

Hall, Christopher Keith, 'The Fifth Session of the UN Preparatory Committee on the Establishment of an International Criminal Court', *American Journal of International Law*, vol. 92, no. 2, April 1998, pp. 331–339.

Hannum, Hurst, 'International Law and Cambodian Genocide: The Sounds of Silence', *Human Rights Quarterly*, vol. 11, no. 1, February 1989, pp. 82–138.

Harris, D.J., *Cases and Materials on International Law*, 4th edition (London: Sweet & Maxwell, 1991).

Heiberg, Marianne, ed., *Subduing Sovereignty: Sovereignty and the Right to Intervene* (London: Pinter Publishers, 1994).

Heininger, Janet, *Peacekeeping in Transition: The United Nations in Cambodia* (New York: Twentieth Century Fund, 1994).

Helman, Gerald B., and Steven R. Ratner, 'Saving Failed States', *Foreign Policy*, no. 89, Winter 1992–1993, pp. 3–20.

Helms, Jesse, 'Saving the U.N.: A Challenge to the Next Secretary-General', *Foreign Affairs*, vol. 75, no. 5, September/October 1996, pp. 2–7.

Henri Dunant Institute/UNESCO, *International Dimensions of Humanitarian Law* (Dordrecht: Martinus Nijhoff Publishers, 1988).

Herbst, Jeffrey, 'Responding to State Failure in Africa', *International Security*, vol. 21, no. 3, Winter 1996/1997, pp. 120–144.

Higgins, Rosalyn, *United Nations Peacekeeping 1946–1967, Documents and Commentary*, vol. 2, *Asia* (Oxford: Oxford University Press, 1970).

Hill, Norman L., *International Administration* (New York: McGraw Hill Book Co., 1931).

Hillen, John F., III, 'Peacekeeping Is Hell: America Unlearns the Lessons of Vietnam', *Policy Review*, no. 66, Fall 1993, pp. 36–39.

Hinsley, F.H., *Power and the Pursuit of Peace* (Cambridge: Cambridge University Press, 1963).

——*Sovereignty* (Cambridge: Cambridge University Press, 1986).

Hirsch, John L., and Robert B. Oakley, *Somalia and Operation Restore Hope: Reflections on Peacemaking and Peacekeeping* (Washington, DC: United States Institute of Peace Press, 1995).

Hodges, Tony, *Western Sahara: The Roots of a Desert War* (Westport, CT: Lawrence Hill Publishers, 1983).

Holiday, David, and William Stanley, 'Building the Peace: Preliminary Lessons from El Salvador', *Journal of International Affairs*, vol. 46, no. 2, Winter 1993, pp. 341–366.

Hoopes, Townsend, and Douglas Brinkley, *FDR and the Creation of the U.N.* (New Haven, CT: Yale University Press, 1997).

Human Rights Watch/Africa, *Somalia Faces the Future: Human Rights in a Fragmented Society* (New York: Human Rights Watch, 1995).

Human Rights Watch/Asia, *Cambodia at War* (New York: Human Rights Watch, 1995).

International Peace Academy, *Peacekeeper's Handbook* (New York: Pergamon Press, 1984).

James, Alan, *Peacekeeping in International Politics* (London: Macmillan and the International Institute for Strategic Studies, 1990).

——'Is There a Second Generation of Peacekeeping?', *International Peacekeeping*, vol. 1, no. 4, September–November 1994, pp. 110–113.

——*Britain and the Congo Crisis, 1960–63* (New York: St Martin's Press, 1996).

Joffé, George, 'The Conflict in the Western Sahara', in Oliver Furley, ed., *Conflict in Africa* (London: Tauris Publishers, 1995), pp. 110–133.

Johnson, Paul, 'Colonialism's Back – And Not a Moment Too Soon', *The New York Times Magazine*, 18 April 1993, p. F22.

Johnstone, Ian, *Rights and Reconciliation: UN Strategies in El Salvador* (Boulder, CO: International Peace Academy and Lynne Rienner Publishers, 1995).

Jones, Dorothy V., 'The League of Nations Experiment in International Protection', *Ethics and International Affairs*, vol. 8, 1994, pp. 77–95.

Kabashima, Ikuo, and Lynn T. White III, eds, *Political Systems and Change* (Princeton, NJ: Princeton University Press, 1986).

Kaikobad, Kaiyan Homi, 'Self-Defence, Enforcement Action and the Gulf Wars, 1980–88 and 1990–91', *British Year Book of International Law 1992*, vol. 63, 1993, pp. 299–366.

Kantorowicz, Ernst H., *The King's Two Bodies: A Study in Medieval Political Theology* (Princeton: Princeton University Press, 1957).

Kaufman, Stuart J., 'The Fragmentation and Consolidation of International Systems', *International Organization*, vol. 51, no. 2, Spring 1997, pp. 173–208.

Kebschull, Harvey G., ed., *Politics in Transitional Societies* (New York: Appleton-Century-Crofts, 1968).

Keegan, John, *A History of Warfare* (New York: Vintage Books, 1993).

Kelly, Major Michael J., *Peace Operations: Tackling the Military Legal and Policy Challenges* (Canberra: Australian Government Publishing Service, 1997).

Kelsen, Hans, 'Will the Judgement in the Nuremberg Trial Constitute a Precedent in International Law?' *International Law Quarterly*, vol. 1, 1947, pp. 153–171.

——*The Law of the United Nations: A Critical Analysis of its Fundamental Problems* (London: Stevens & Sons, 1950).

Kenny, Karen, *Towards Effective Training for Field Human Rights Tasks* (Dublin: International Human Rights Trust, 1996).

Khan, Rahmatullah, *Implied Powers of the United Nations* (New Delhi: Vikas Publications, 1970).

Kiernan, Ben, 'The Cambodian Crisis, 1990–1992: The UN Plan, the Khmer Rouge, and the State of Cambodia', *Bulletin of Concerned Asian Scholars*, vol. 24, no. 2, April–June 1992, pp. 3–23.

Kirsch, Philippe, 'The Convention on the Safety of United Nations and Associated Personnel', *International Peacekeeping*, vol. 2, no. 5, August–September 1995, pp. 102–106.

Kitfield, James, *Prodigal Soldiers* (New York: Simon & Schuster, 1995).

Kitson, Frank, *Low-Intensity Operations* (London: Faber & Faber, 1971).

Knight, W. Andy, 'Beyond the UN System? Critical Perspectives on Global Governance and Multilateral Evolution', *Global Governance*, vol. 1, no. 2, May–August 1995, pp. 229–253.

——'Towards a Subsidiarity Model for Peacemaking and Preventive Diplomacy: Making Chapter VIII of the UN Charter Operational', *Third World Quarterly*, vol. 17, no. 1, March 1996, pp. 31–52.

——'Establishing Political Authority in Peace-Maintenance', *Global Governance*, vol. 4, no. 1, January–March 1998, pp. 19–40.

Krauthammer, Charles, 'Trusteeship for Somalia; An Old Colonial Idea Whose Time Has Come Again', *The Washington Post*, 9 October 1992, p. A27.

Kushen, Robert, and Kenneth J. Harris, 'Surrender of Fugitives by the United States to the War Crimes Tribunals for Yugoslavia and Rwanda', *American Journal of International Law*, vol. 90, no. 3, July 1996, pp. 510–518.

Lawless, Richard, and Laila Monahan, eds, *War and Refugees: The Western Sahara Conflict* (London: Pinter Publishers, 1987).

Lawrence, T.E., *Seven Pillars of Wisdom* (New York: Doubleday & Co., 1935).

Lenin, V.I., *What is to be Done?* (London: Penguin Classics, 1988).

Levi, Primo, *Survival In Auschwitz* (New York: Collier Books, 1993).

Lewis, I.M., *A Pastoral Democracy* (New York: Holmes and Meier, 1982).

——*A Modern History of Somalia* (Boulder, CO: Westview Press, 1988).

——'Misunderstanding the Somali crisis', *Anthropology Today*, vol. 9, no. 4, August 1993, pp. 1–3.

——*Blood and Bone: The Call of Kinship in Somali Society* (Lawrenceville, NJ: The Red Sea Press, 1994).

Louise, Christopher, 'MINUGUA's Peacebuilding Mandate in Western Guatemala', *International Peacekeeping*, vol. 4, no. 2, Summer 1997, pp. 50–73.

Lugard, Frederick D., *The Dual Mandate in British Tropical Africa* (Edinburgh: William Blackwood & Sons, 1922).

Lyons, Terrence, and Ahmed I. Samatar, *Somalia: State Collapse, Multilateral Intervention, and Strategies for Political Reconstruction* (Washington, DC: The Brookings Institution, 1995).

McCormack, Timothy L.H., and Gerry J. Simpson, 'The International Law Commission's Draft Code of Crimes against the Peace and Security of Mankind: An Appraisal of the Substantive Provisions', *Criminal Law Forum*, vol. 5, no. 1, 1994, pp. 1–55.

McDermott, Anthony, *United Nations Financing Problems and the New Generation of Peacekeeping and Peace Enforcement* (Providence, RI: Thomas J. Watson Jr Institute for International Studies, 1994).

Mackinlay, John, and Jarat Chopra, 'Second Generation Multinational Operations', *The Washington Quarterly*, vol. 15, no. 3, Summer 1992, pp. 113–131.

——*A Draft Concept of Second Generation Multinational Operations, 1993* (Providence, RI: Thomas J. Watson Jr Institute for International Studies, 1993).

Maguire, Robert, Edwige Balutansky, Jacques Fomerand, Larry Minear, William G. O'Neill, Thomas G. Weiss, and Sarah Zaidi, *Haiti Held Hostage: International Responses to the Quest for Nationhood, 1986–1996* (Providence, RI: Thomas J. Watson Jr Institute for International Studies and the United Nations University, 1996).

Makinda, Samuel M., *Security in the Horn of Africa*, Adelphi Paper no. 269 (London: International Institute for Strategic Studies, 1992).

——*Seeking Peace from Chaos: Humanitarian Intervention in Somalia* (Boulder, CO: International Peace Academy and Lynne Rienner Publishers, 1993).

Mao Tse-Tung, *On Guerrilla Warfare* (New York: Praeger Publishers, 1961).

Martindale, Don, *Social Life and Cultural Change* (Princeton, NJ: Van Nostrand, 1962).

Mayall, James, ed., *The New Interventionism, 1991–1994: United Nations Experience in Cambodia, Former Yugoslavia and Somalia* (Cambridge: Cambridge University Press, 1996).

McNamara, Robert S., *In Retrospect: The Tragedy and Lessons of Vietnam* (New York: Times Books, 1995).

Mazrui, Ali A., 'Decaying Parts of Africa Need Benign Colonization', *International Herald Tribune*, 4 August 1994, p.6.

Mendez, Ruben P., 'Financing the United Nations and the International Public Sector: Problems and Reform', *Global Governance*, vol. 3, no. 3, September–December 1997, pp. 295–304.

Menkhaus, Ken, and John Prendergast, 'Governance and Economic Survival in Postintervention Somalia', *CSIS Africa Notes*, no. 172, May 1995, pp.1–10.

Meron, Theodor, 'Rape as a Crime Under International Humanitarian Law', *American Journal of International Law*, vol. 87, no. 3, July 1993, pp. 424–426.

——'International Criminalization of Internal Atrocities', *American Journal of International Law*, vol. 89, no. 3, July 1995. pp. 554–577.

——'Classification of Armed Conflict in the Former Yugoslavia: Nicaragua's Fallout', *American Journal of International Law*, vol. 92, no. 2, April 1998, pp. 236–242.

Minear, Richard H., *Victor's Justice: The Tokyo War Crimes Trials* (Princeton, NJ: Princeton University Press, 1972).

Morillon, Phillipe, *Croire et Oser: Chronique de Sarajevo* (Paris: Grasset, 1993).

Nadelman, Ethan A., *Cops Across Borders: The Internationalization of U.S. Criminal Law Enforcement* (University Park, PA: Pennsylvania State University Press, 1993).

Natsios, Andrew S., 'Food Through Force: Humanitarian Intervention and U.S. Policy', *The Washington Quarterly*, vol. 17, no. 1, Winter 1994, pp. 129–144.

Norden, Deborah L., 'Keeping the Peace, Outside and In: Argentina's UN Missions', *International Peacekeeping*, vol. 2, no. 3, Autumn 1995, pp. 334–339.

Onuf, Nicholas Greenwood, '*Civitas Maxima*: Wolff, Vattel and the Fate of Republicanism', *American Journal of International Law*, vol. 88, no. 2, April 1994, pp. 280–303.

Opala, Joseph, 'Reflections on "The Coming Anarchy"', *Crosslines Global Report*, vol. 4, no. 3, issue 21, July 1996, pp. 13–15.

Organski, A.F., *The Stages of Political Development* (New York: Knopf, 1965).

Osborne, Peter, *The Politics of Time* (London: Verso, 1995).

Otunnu, Olara A., and Michael W. Doyle, eds, *Peacemaking and Peacekeeping for the New Century* (Lanham, MD: Rowman & Littlefield Publishers, 1998).

Paris, Roland, 'Peacebuilding and the Limits of Liberal Internationalism', *International Security*, vol. 22, no. 2, Fall 1997, pp. 54–89.

Parsons, Anthony, *From Cold War to Hot Peace: UN Interventions 1947–1995* (London: Penguin Books, 1995).

Parsons, Talcott, *The Social System* (Glencoe, IL: Free Press, 1951).

Pasic, Amir, and Thomas G. Weiss, 'The Politics of Rescue: Yugoslavia's Wars and the Humanitarian Impulse', *Ethics and International Affairs*, vol. 11, 1997, pp. 125–131.

Pazzanita, Anthony G., 'Morocco versus Polisario: A Political Interpretation', *The Journal of Modern African Studies*, vol. 32, no. 2, 1994, pp. 265–278.

Peters, Edward, *Torture* (Philadelphia, PA: University of Pennsylvania Press, 1996).

Pfaff, William, 'A New Colonialism? Europe Must Go Back into Africa', *Foreign Affairs*, vol. 74, no. 1, January–February 1995, pp. 2–6.

Picco, Giandomenico, 'The U.N. and the Use of Force: Leave the Secretary-General Out of It', *Foreign Affairs*, vol. 73, no. 5, September/October 1994, pp. 14–18.

Pickart, George A., *The Western Sahara: The Referendum Process in Danger*, A Staff Report to the Committee on Foreign Relations of the United States Senate, January 1992 (Washington: U.S. Government Printing Office, 1992).

Plunkett, Mark, 'Reestablishing Law and Order in Peace-Maintenance', *Global Governance*, vol. 4, no. 1, January–March 1998, pp. 61–79.

Raevsky, Andrei, and I.N. Vorobev, *Russian Approaches to Peacekeeping Operations* (Geneva: UN Institute for Disarmament Research, 1994).

Ramos-Horta, José, *Funu: The Unfinished Saga of East Timor* (Lawrenceville, NJ: The Red Sea Press, 1987, 1996 printing).

Ratner, Steven R., 'The Cambodian Settlement Agreements', *American Journal of International Law*, vol. 87, no. 1, January 1993, pp. 1–41.

——*The New UN Peacekeeping: Building Peace in Lands of Conflict After the Cold War* (New York: St Martin's Press, 1995).

——'Drawing a Better Line: *Uti Possidetis* and the Borders of New States', *American Journal of International Law*, vol. 90, no. 4, October 1996, pp. 590–624.

Reid, Escott, *On Duty: A Canadian at the Making of the United Nations, 1945–1946* (Toronto: McClelland and Stewart, 1983).

Richardson, Henry J., III, '"Failed States," Self-Determination, and Preventative Diplomacy: Colonialist Nostalgia and Democratic Expectations', *Temple International and Comparative Law Journal*, vol. 10, spring 1996, pp. 1–78.

Righter, Rosemary, *Utopia Lost: The United Nations and World Order* (New York: Twentieth Century Fund, 1995).

Rikhye, Indar Jit, *Military Adviser to the Secretary-General: U.N. Peacekeeping and the Congo Crisis* (London: Hurst & Co. and St Martin's Press, 1993).

Rivlin, Benjamin, 'The Rediscovery of the UN Military Staff Committee', *Occasional Papers Series*, no. IV, Ralph Bunch Institute on the United Nations, May 1991.

——*The Western Sahara: Towards a Referendum? The UN Political Process at Work* (New York: Ralph Bunche Institute on the United Nations, 1994).

Rose, Gideon, 'The Exit Strategy Delusion', *Foreign Affairs*, vol. 77, no. 1, January/February 1998, pp. 56–67.

Roseberry, J. Royal, III, *Imperial Rule in Punjab: The Conquest and Administration of Multan, 1818–1881* (Riverdale, MD: The Riverdale Company, 1987).

Rosenau, James N., *Turbulence in World Politics: A Theory of Change and Continuity* (Princeton, NJ: Princeton University Press, 1990).

Rostow, W.W., *The Stages of Economic Growth* (Cambridge: Cambridge University Press, 1960).

Ruddy, Frank, 'Statement of Ambassador Frank Ruddy' before the US House of Representatives, Review of United Nations Operations and Peacekeeping, Committee on Appropriations, Subcommittee on the Departments of Commerce, Justice, State, and the Judiciary and Related Agencies, Washington, DC, 25 January 1995.

Ruggie, John Gerard, 'Wandering in the Void: Charting the U.N.'s New Strategic Role', *Foreign Affairs*, vol. 72, no. 5, November/December 1993, pp. 26–31.

Russell, Ruth B., *A History of The United Nations Charter: The Role of the United States 1940–1945* (Washington, DC: The Brookings Institution, 1958).

Sahlins, Marshall D., and Elman R. Service, eds, *Evolution and Culture* (Ann Arbor, MI: University of Michigan Press, 1970).

Sahnoun, Mohamed, *Somalia: The Missed Opportunities* (Washington, DC: United States Institute of Peace, 1994).

Samatar, Abdi Ismail, 'Destruction of State and Society in Somalia: Beyond the Tribal Convention', *The Journal of Modern African Studies*, vol. 30, no. 4, December 1992, pp. 625–641.

Seddon, David, 'Western Sahara Referendum Sabotaged', *Review of African Political Economy*, no. 53, March 1992, pp. 101–104.

Segre, Claudio G., 'Colonialism May Be Worth Bringing Back', *The Philadelphia Inquirer*, 3 August 1993, p. A7.

Sessions, Sterling D., and Carl R. Jones, *Interoperability: A Desert Storm Case Study* (Washington, DC: Institute for National Strategic Studies, National Defence University, 1993).

Sewell, James P., and Mark B. Salter, 'Panarchy and Other Norms for Global Governance: Boutros-Ghali, Rosenau, and Beyond', *Global Governance*, vol. 1, no. 3, September–December 1995, pp. 373–382.

Shaw, Malcolm N., *Title to Territory in Africa* (Oxford: Clarendon Press, 1986).

——*International Law*, 4th edition (Cambridge: Cambridge University Press, 1997).

Shaw, Timothy M., and Clement E. Adibe, 'Africa and Global Developments in the Twenty-First Century' *International Journal*, vol. 51, no. 1, Winter 1995–1996, pp. 1–26.

Shawcross, William, *Cambodia's New Deal* (Washington, DC: Carnegie Endowment for International Peace, 1994).

Shearer, David, *Private Armies and Military Intervention*, Adelphi Paper no. 316 (London: International Institute for Strategic Studies, 1998).

Shils, Edward, *Political Development in the New States* (The Hague: Mouton, 1966).

Simma, Bruno, ed., *The Charter of the United Nations: A Commentary* (Oxford: Oxford University Press, 1994).

Simons, Anna, *Networks of Dissolution: Somalia Undone* (Boulder, CO: Westview Press, 1995).

Singh, Ram Charitra Prasad, *Kingship in Northern India* (Delhi: Motilal Banarsidass, 1968).

Slaughter, Anne-Marie, 'The Real New World Order', *Foreign Affairs*, vol. 76, no. 5, September/October 1997, pp. 183–197.

Smith, Anthony D., *The Ethnic Origins of Nations* (Oxford: Blackwell Publishers, 1993).

Smith, Hugh, ed., *International Peacekeeping: Building on the Cambodian Experience* (Canberra: Australian Defence Studies Centre, 1994).

Smith, Richard, *The Requirement for the United Nations to Develop an Internationally Recognized Doctrine for the Use of Force in Intra-State Conflict* (Camberley: Strategic and Combat Studies Institute, 1994).

Smith de Cherif, Teresa K., 'Western Sahara: A Moroccan-Style Election?' *Review of African Political Economy*, no. 58, November 1993, pp. 99–105.

Stanley Foundation, *The UN Security Council and the International Criminal Court: How Should They Relate?* (Muscatine, IA: The Stanley Foundation, 1998).

Stedman, Stephen John, 'Spoiler Problems in Peace Processes', *International Security*, vol. 22, no. 2, Fall 1997, pp. 5–53.

Steiner, George, *Nostalgia for the Absolute* (Toronto: Canadian Broadcasting Corporation, 1983).

Stiefel, Matthias, 'UNDP in Conflicts and Disasters: An Overview Report of the "Continuum Project" ', (Geneva: UNDP Project INT/93/709, August 1994).

Sunga, Lyal S., *Individual Responsibility in International Law for Serious Human Rights Violations* (Dordrecht: Martinus Nijhoff Publishers, 1992).

Sylvester, Jon H., 'Sub-Saharan Africa: Economic Stagnation, Political Disintegration, and the Specter of Recolonization', *Loyola of Los Angeles Law Review*, vol. 27, 1994, pp. 1299–1326.

Taber, Robert, *The War of the Flea* (London: Paladin, 1970).

Taylor, Telford, *The Anatomy of the Nuremberg Trials* (New York: Alfred A. Knopf, 1992).

Tellegen-Couperus, Olga, *A Short History of Roman Law* (London: Routledge, 1993).

Terry, Colonel James P., 'The Evolving U.S. Policy For Peace Operations', *Southern Illinois University Law Journal*, vol. 19, Fall 1994, pp. 119–129.

Tessitore, John, and Susan Woolfson, eds, *A Global Agenda: Issues Before the 47th General Assembly of the United Nations* (Lanham, MD: University Press of America, 1992).

——eds, *A Global Agenda: Issues Before the 48th General Assembly of the United Nations* (Lanham, MD: University Press of America, 1993).

——eds, *A Global Agenda: Issues Before the 51st General Assembly of the United Nations* (Lanham, MD: Rowman & Littlefield Publishers, 1996).

——eds, *A Global Agenda: Issues Before the 52nd General Assembly of the United Nations* (Lanham, MD: Rowman & Littlefield Publishers, 1997).

Tétreault, Mary Ann, 'Justice for All: Wartime Rape and Women's Human Rights', *Global Governance*, vol. 3, no. 2, May–August 1997, pp. 197–212.

Thornberry, Cedric, 'UNTAG: Description and Analysis of the Mission's Operational Arrangements', September 1991, unpublished draft.

Toynbee, Arnold J., *A Study of History* (Oxford: Oxford University Press, 1946).

Tutu, The Most Reverend Desmond M., 'The Search for Truth and Reconciliation in Post-Apartheid South Africa', *International Peace Academy Roundtable Report*, 11 November 1996, 4 pp.

United Kingdom Ministry of Defence, *Land Operations*, vol. 3, *Counter-Revolutionary Operations* (London: Ministry of Defence, 1977).

——*Wider Peacekeeping* (London: Headquarters, Doctrine and Training, November 1994).

United Kingdom Staff College, Camberley, *Quadripartite Study on Peace Support Operations in Situations of Chaos* (Camberley: UK Staff College, April 1993).

United Nations, *The Blue Helmets: A Review of United Nations Peacekeeping* (New York: United Nations Department of Public Information, 1990, 1996).

——*The Singapore Symposium: The Changing Role of the United Nations in Conflict Resolution and Peace-Keeping, 13–15 March 1991* (New York: United Nations Department of Public Information, 1991).

United Nations, Crime Prevention and Criminal Justice Branch, *United Nations Criminal Justice Standards for Peace-Keeping Police* (Vienna: United Nations, February 1994).

Urquhart, Brian, *A Life in Peace and War* (New York: Harper & Row Publishers, 1987).

Uvin, Peter, *Aiding Violence: The Development Enterprise in Rwanda* (West Hartford, CT: Kumarian Press, 1998).

Uvin, Peter, and Isabelle Biagiotti, 'Global Governance and the "New" Political Conditionality', *Global Governance*, vol. 2, no. 3, September–December 1996, pp. 377–400.

Vance, Cyrus R., and David A. Hamburg, *Pathfinders for Peace: A Report to the UN Secretary-General on the Role of Special Representatives and Personal Envoys* (New York: Carnegie Corporation of New York, 1997).

van der Veur, Paul W., 'The United Nations in West New Irian: a Critique', *International Organization*, vol. XVIII, no. 1, Winter 1964.

Vierucci, Luisa, 'The First Steps of the International Criminal Tribunal for the Former Yugoslavia', *European Journal of International Law*, vol. 6, no. 1, 1995, pp. 134–143.

Volden, Ketil, and Dan Smith, eds, *Causes of Conflict in the Third World* (Oslo: North/South Coalition & International Peace Research Institute, Oslo, 1997).

Wainhouse, David W., *et al.*, *International Peace Observation: A History and Forecast* (Baltimore, MD: The Johns Hopkins Press, 1966).

Wallerstein, Immanuel, *The Capitalist World-Economy* (Cambridge: Cambridge University Press, 1979).

Warren, Bill, *Imperialism: Pioneer of Capitalism* (London: Verso, 1980).

Washington Office on Latin America, *Demilitarizing Public Order: The International Community, Police Reform and Human Rights in Central America and Haiti* (Washington, DC: The Washington Office on Latin America, November 1995).

Watson, Adam, *The Evolution of International Society* (London: Routledge, 1992).

Watson, Bruce W., Bruce George and Peter Tsouras, eds, *Military Lessons of the Gulf War* (London: Greenhill Books, 1993).

Weiland, Heribert, and Matthew Braham, Rapporteurs, *The Namibian Peace Process: Implications and Lessons for the Future* (Freiburg: Arnold Bergstraesser Institut/International Peace Academy, 1994).

Weiss, Thomas G., ed., *Beyond UN Subcontracting: Task-Sharing with Regional Security Arrangements and Service-Providing NGOs* (London: Macmillan Press, 1998).

Weiss, Thomas G., and Jarat Chopra, *United Nations Peacekeeping: An ACUNS Teaching Text* (Hanover, NH: Academic Council on the United Nations System, 1992).

Weiss-Fagen, Patricia, *After the Conflict: A Review of Selected Sources on Rebuilding War-Torn Societies* (Geneva: War-Torn Societies Project, 1995).

Weston, Burns H., 'Security Council Resolution 678 and Persian Gulf Decision Making: Precarious Legitimacy', *American Journal of International Law*, vol. 85, no. 3, July 1991, pp. 516–535.

White, N.D., *Keeping the Peace: The United Nations and the maintenance of international peace and security* (Manchester: Manchester University Press, 1993).

Whitrow, G.J., *Time in History* (Oxford: Oxford University Press, 1989).

Wilson, Heather A., *International Law and the Use of Force by National Liberation Movements* (Oxford: Clarendon Press, 1988).

Yarnold, Barbara M., *International Fugitives: A New Role for the International Court of Justice* (New York: Praeger Publishers, 1991).

Zartman, I. William, ed., *Collapsed States: The Disintegration and Restoration of Legitimate Authority* (Boulder, CO: Lynne Rienner Publishers, 1995).

Ziai, Fatemeh, *Keeping it Secret: The United Nations Operation in the Western Sahara* (New York: Human Rights Watch, 1995).

Zollschan, George K., and Walter Hirsch, eds, *Explorations in Social Change* (Boston: Houghton Mifflin Co., 1964).

Zoubir, Yahia H., and Daniel Volman, eds, *International Dimensions of the Western Sahara Conflict* (Westport, CT: Praeger Publishers, 1993).

Index

General Framework Agreement for Peace in Bosnia and Herzegovina 98
Geneva: UN negotiations on Abkhazia 15; Western Sahara peace talks 176, 177
Geneva Convention (1929): regulations on war crimes 74
Geneva Conventions for the Protection of War Victims (1949) 74–5, 76–8, 92, 98, 143
genocide 58, 60, 64–5, 83, 196, 209n; attempts to establish tribunal court 88–9; Bosnia 56, 92; Cambodia 59, 106–7, 110; cultural 64; discriminatory basis 71; indictment of Karadzic and Mladic 98; Rwanda 56; UN Convention 58, 64–5, 67, 69, 88, 106; use of by warlords 187
geographical issues: conflict areas 52; limited deployments 190; peace-maintenance 196; Somalis 133, 136; Western Sahara people 166, 169–70
German Penal Code 92
German troops: in Somalia 153
Germans: prosecutions of at Nuremberg Trials 83
Germany: Allied bombing of 83; and disputed territories 40–1; and enforcement of ICTY sentences 103; mission on MINURSO's progress 173; Nazis 41, 126, 213n; participation of population in crimes against peace 61; postwar treaty implementation 39; and transference of Tadic to ICTY 92; war crimes against its own population 63–4
Gestapo 59, 213n
Golan Heights: conflict between Israel and Syria 5
Goldstone, Richard J. 91, 92, 99
Gomes, Solomon 180–1
government: absence of 80, 132, 144, 153, 159–60; as element of social organization 21, 23, 25, 35; institutions 49, 107; and international laws 56; restoration and assistance 114, 141–2, 144; *see also* civil administration
governorship 107, 124, 142; and constitutive and chaotic stages of peace-maintenance 34, 36, 54; UN mandate of 16, 23, 54, 149, 164, 188, 191, 193
Great Britain *see* Britain
Greece: and European invasion of Crete 39; truce with Bulgaria 32
Greek empire 26

Grenada: US rapid intervention 164, 190
Guatemala: Friends of 179
Guedira, Ahmed Reda 175
guerrilla warfare 74, 163, 164
Guizot, F.P.G. 29
Gulf War: as aberration 127; coalition forces 191; enforcement 6, 80, 127; precipitation of 56; theatre of war 188; and UN definition of security 143; US experience 127, 128, 129, 179; US rapid intervention 164

The Hague: prison for detainees of former Yugoslavia 55, 99, 103
Hague Conventions (1899 and 1907) 63, 74; regulations on war crimes 74
Haiti: fragility of civil society 192; Friends of 179; US invasion 219n
Hakim, Brahim 177
handicapped: care of 22
Hargeysa 138
Hassan II, King of Morocco 167, 168, 169, 173, 175–6, 176, 182, 184
Hersi, Gen. Mohamed Said ('Morgan') 156–7, 160
Hinduism: *Laws of Manu* 24
historical issues: conflict areas 52
Hitler, Adolf: as super-warlord 18
Honduras: mission on MINURSO's progress 172
hostages: taking of UN troops 57
Hou Leang Bann 110
Houston: Western Sahara Peace Accords 184
Howe, Adm. Jonathan 154
human rights: abuses in El Salvador 111–13, 178; component of Paris Agreement on Cambodia 106, 107, 108, 111; conventions 143; education 48, 107; inability of UN to investigate 49, 112; international laws and codes 22, 52, 56, 71, 81, 143; organizations 48, 55–6; protection 8, 11, 22, 33, 37, 52, 54, 72, 106; standards in Somalia 154, 155; UN Commission 67, 68, 69, 73; UN operation in El Salvador 48–9, 112–14; UNTAC officers 110, 111; violations and abuses 55, 60, 73, 109, 110, 111–13, 142–3, 178, 196
Human Rights Watch 181
humanitarian law: international codes 80, 81; violations 75, 76, 90, 91; on war 74, 126, 143